Regulating Labor

Regulating Labor

THE STATE AND
INDUSTRIAL RELATIONS REFORM
IN POSTWAR FRANCE

Chris Howell

PRINCETON UNIVERSITY PRESS

PRINCETON, NEW JERSEY

Library of Congress Cataloging-in-Publication Data

Howell, Chris, 1962–
Regulating labor : the state and industrial relations reform
in postwar France / Chris Howell.
p. cm.
Based on the author's thesis (PhD.—Yale University).
Includes bibliographical references and index.
ISBN 0-691-07898-X (acid-free paper)
1. Trade-unions—Government policy—France. 2. Trade-unions—
France. 3. Industrial relations—Government policy—France.
4. Industrial relations—France. 5. France—Politics and
government—1958–   I. Title.
HD6684.H68 1992   92-904
331′.0944--dc20

To my parents, Mike and Joan Howell

Contents

Tables

Acknowledgments

THIS BOOK AROSE out of the research for my doctoral dissertation at Yale University. In writing it I received encouragement and support from many quarters. My field research would not have been possible without financial support from the Yale Center for International and Area Studies and the Mellon-West European Studies program. I was also lucky to be able to spend time at the Harvard Center for European Studies and MIT Center for International Studies in 1988 and 1989. These institutions and their ever-friendly staffs gave me both an ideal environment in which to write and also provided a much-needed escape from New Haven.

In France I received the invaluable support of the late Georges Lavau and of Denis Segrestin, both of whom generously provided me with facilities and prodded me in the right direction when I arrived. I also received tremendous help in obtaining and understanding government data from Daniel Furjot of the Service des études et de la statistique of the Ministry of Social Affairs and Employment. I would like to give special thanks to Rand Smith, who was unceasingly helpful during the time I was in Paris but also maintained a close interest in my research after I returned to the United States, by reading and commenting on the entire manuscript.

My greatest debt is to my dissertation committee at Yale of David Cameron, Miriam Golden, and Vicky Hattam. They provided just the right mix of encouragement and exhortation, and I find it hard to imagine a more helpful, supportive, dependable, and approachable committee. David Cameron deserves special thanks. It was David who persuaded me to study French labor in the first place, and he has always known just when to object to my enthusiasm for the latest intellectual import from Paris and when to let me be.

Numerous people have read all or part of the manuscript and given up valuable time to talk to me about the project. My thanks go to Marc Blecher, Robert Boyer, Barbara Jenkins, Margaret Keck, Sylvia Maxfield, David Plotke, George Ross, Miriam Smith, Harlan Wilson, Jeff Winters, and Susan Woodward. It is also to Susan Woodward's teaching and enthusiasm from my first days in graduate school that I owe my enduring interest in political economy. In addition, I owe a special debt to Peter Hall whose close reading of the manuscript and copious comments guided me through the final draft. Peter often had a clearer sense of where I wanted to go than I did, and the final structure of this book owes a great deal to his clear-sightedness.

In particular I want to thank Paul Pierson. Paul not only read the entire manuscript and spent long hours discussing it, but he also demonstrated, by example, the importance of maintaining a balance between the exciting and giddy world of theory-building and the more mundane task of solid empirical research. Over the years Paul has done his best to keep me honest, and I hope he is satisfied with the result.

On a more personal note, I would like to thank Susan Clayton for friendship, encouragement, understanding, and diversions. Finally, this book is dedicated to my parents, Michael and Joan Howell, who have always supported me, and always been proud of me, even when it became clear that I was not going to be the kind of doctor they had hoped.

A version of chapter 7 has previously appeared in *Comparative Politics*. Permission to reprint is gratefully acknowledged.

Acronyms

AFCERQ	L'Association Française pour les Cercles de Qualité
CERES	Centre d'Études, de Recherches et d'Éducation Socialiste
CFDT	Confédération Française et Démocratique du Travail
CFTC	Confédération Française des Travailleurs Chrétiens
CGC	Confédération Générale des Cadres
CGPME	Confédération Générale des Petites et Moyennes Entreprises
CGT	Confédération Générale du Travail
CGT-FO	Confédération Générale du Travail–Force Ouvrière
CGTU	Confédération Générale du Travail Unitaire
CNPF	Conseil National du Patronat Français
EGF	Électricté et Gaz de France
EMS	European Monetary System
FEN	Fédération d'Éducation Nationale
PCF	Parti Communiste Française
PS	Parti Socialiste
RATP	Régie Autonome des Transports Parisiens
SEM	Single European Market
SFIO	Section Française de l'Internationale Ouvrière
SMIC	Salaire Minimum Interprofessionnel de Croissance
SMIG	Salaire Minimum Interprofessionnel Garanti
SNCF	Société Nationale des Chemins de Fer Française

PART ONE

Introduction

CHAPTER ONE

A Theory of Labor Regulation

COMPARING 1968 AND 1986

I arrived in Paris to start the field research for this project in January 1987. My arrival coincided with both a wave of industrial unrest, unlike anything seen in recent years, and the coldest winter in living memory. As I tramped around Paris in the bitter cold searching for an apartment, on foot because the metro was not running, my normal sympathy for the French working class reached its nadir! It was, nonetheless, an exciting time for a student of the French labor movement. I had come to Paris to find out what had happened to the labor movement since its high point of militancy during the massive strike wave of May and June 1968.[1] Had there been a "normalization" of the French labor movement in the two decades that had intervened? Were there signs of convergence with other West European labor movements, or had France followed a different path altogether, and if so, what was it? For someone of my generation, who had unavoidably missed 1968, a comparison between May 1968 and December 1986–January 1987 was inevitable.

At first glance the similarities were remarkable. As in May 1968, the signal for the wave of strikes in December 1986 was widespread student unrest, this time against the proposed Devaquet reform of the universities. As in 1968, it was public-sector workers who dominated the strikes, primarily railroad and metro workers with some minor support from the postal and electricity workers. The immediate causes were also similar. In 1986 public-sector workers were reacting angrily to the previous four years when first Socialist and then conservative governments had made the public sector bear the brunt of a rigid policy of wage restraint. The more amorphous costs of economic modernization were also important. Skilled workers were experiencing a deterioration of their previously privileged position. Faced with a declining position, these workers were engaging in what one commentator referred to as "existential strikes."[2]

The most striking similarity between 1968 and 1986–87 was the degree to which the strikes were spontaneous, taking place without union instigation or control. The trade unions were taken by surprise in December 1986, and despite efforts to put themselves at the head of the movement, the most notable feature of the strikes was the cross-union coordination and unity of action among rank-and-file workers as "comités de coordination" sprang up to organize the industrial action. The strikes of 1968 and those of 1986–87 thus shared an important structural characteristic.

However, there are important limits to the comparison. Something had changed between 1968 and 1986. The scale of the unrest in 1968 was vastly greater than that in 1986–87. There was no private-sector participation in the latter period, and the main victims were the consumers of public services rather than businesses. The 1986–87 strikes occurred at a time of historically low levels of industrial unrest, and indeed the December and January strikes did not even reverse the steady annual decline in days lost to industrial action which had begun in 1983.[3] Unlike 1968, the strike wave of 1986–87 was never a serious political threat to the hapless government of Jacques Chirac. The only attempt to politicize the conflict came from the government itself when Chirac attempted to blame communists in the Confédération Générale du Travail (CGT) and Parti Communiste Français (PCF) for the unrest.

Above all, it was in the conclusions drawn from the unrest that the two periods differed. The structural weakness of French trade unionism was a dominant, and much-remarked-upon, feature of both strike waves, yet while in 1968 stronger unions were seen as a potential solution, in 1986–87 they were seen as fundamentally unimportant. To be sure, Chirac finally agreed to hold meetings with individual union leaders a full year after taking office (itself an indication of the slide in the trade unions' fortunes), and Philippe Séguin, the minister of social affairs and employment, called for a "relaunching of collective bargaining" in *Le Monde*,[4] but there was no grand Grenelle-style conference as there had been in 1968, and no concrete measures favoring trade unions. As *Le Monde*'s Michel Noblecourt put it, the "outpouring of social spontaneity is first of all a defeat for a unionism that has not succeeded in overcoming its decline."[5]

In the twenty years following May 1968 the proportion of the work force who were trade unionists dropped from about 25 percent to (in one estimate) 9 percent.[6] While it is true that union membership is only one measure of a labor movement's influence, it is certainly a measure of one *type* of influence, and a country in which trade union members constitute about one-tenth of the labor force is almost unique in the advanced capitalist world. In 1968 French trade unionism appeared to be at the dawn of a golden age of growth and importance. In 1986 its irrelevance was unmistakable. This study seeks to explain that evolution in the French labor movement through the lens of state policy.

THE STATE AND SOCIAL ACTORS

The central focus of this study is the impact that successive packages of state policy have had upon the French labor movement. Its concern is less the day-to-day dealings of French governments with the labor movement, and more the ways in which state policies, intentionally or unintentionally, structured and restructured the French labor movement. The time period treated here allows not only a comparison of Gaullist, neo-Gaullist, liberal, and socialist strategies for dealing with labor but also a sufficiently long period for observing the (inherently slow and gradual) manner in which the labor movement evolved. An extended period of time is required if the complex relationship between political initiatives and broader economic and social changes is to become clear.

A focus upon the state as an actor begs a number of crucial theoretical questions concerning the relative explanatory importance of states, social classes, and the economy. At this point it is worth laying out some of the theoretical assumptions that underlie this study. The state is an important, and at times central, actor in the sphere of industrial relations. As Jonathan Zeitlin puts it, "at certain moments the state has played a key role not only in overcoming employer opposition to trade unionism, but also in eroding managerial prerogatives at the workplace."[7] And it should be added that historically states have been at least as active in curtailing union rights as in promoting them.

That said, it is important to avoid the position—at least theoretically—that the state is *always* the dominant actor. The recent resurgence of interest in the state as actor rather than arena still has some way to go before it can demonstrate convincingly that states are relatively unconstrained by civil society.[8] Within the time period covered in this study, it is clear that as the French economy went into deep recession in the 1970s, and then emerged in the 1980s—with greater emphasis placed upon the market, decentralized decision-making, and flexibility (the ability of firms to respond rapidly to market stimuli)—the French state's room for maneuvering has narrowed, and it has become increasingly impotent. So this study is not arguing that the French state was at all times the dominant actor. It takes the state as its object, without making any a priori assumptions about the extent to which the state is simultaneously a subject. That question can only be answered empirically.

It is true, I think, that most scholars working in the area of French industrial relations have concentrated upon actors within "civil society"—employers' and workers' organizations—to the exclusion of a systematic study of state actions in the field of industrial relations.[9] In part, the distinction between state and societal actors is misleading because so much of what governments do in the field of industrial relations is a response to the concerns of the "social partners,"[10] and indeed specific policy initiatives are often taken in concert with employers and/or workers. The origins of state policies can be exceedingly murky, and the policies may not in fact have been initially formulated within the state itself. Nonetheless, in practice this distinction seems a reasonable one.

At certain critical moments trade unions and employers' organizations played very important roles in the evolution of the industrial relations system. The changing attitude of employers and trade unions toward collective bargaining and flexibility, for example, is an important subtext of the story being told here and will be discussed at some length. Nevertheless, the focus will remain the state and the actions of the state because not only has the state been relatively neglected in research on industrial relations, but also because a strong case can be made that in modern democratic capitalist societies, the state is the terrain par excellence where a myriad of competing social and economic pressures become focused and crystallize into specific policies and discourses. Emphasis on the state is justified because it provides an unparalleled window into civil society.

There are important reasons for taking the ideologies and strategies of trade unions and employers' organizations seriously. An important strand of scholarship emphasizes that "unions ought to be considered as strategic actors."[11] This position has been put most eloquently and forcefully by Lange, Ross, and Vannicelli:

> It is likely to be more fruitful to understand change or continuity in union behavior by starting with unions, rather than by assuming that unions are historical objects created and battered about by exogenous forces. Thus at any given point in time, unions can be seen as agents with their own ideas, needs, and purposes, and not just as passive institutional entities responding to contextual forces which, in combination, determine how the unions will (and must) behave.[12]

As an antidote to the fairly crude economism and determinism of approaches to industrial relations in the 1950s and 1960s, this is a necessary correction, and hard to deny. But it is possible to be skeptical as to how far this case can be pushed. Viewed cross-nationally, some union movements seem more successful than others (and there is a tendency to measure all union movements against the apparent success of the Swedish Landsorganisationen). But *within* countries, over time, the possibility of significantly changing the political economy, or improving the terms under which unions are able to act, seems much weaker. Perhaps this pessimism stems from the French case where the two largest unions have gone through many strategic and ideological somersaults, some of them quite sophisticated, with no discernible improvement of a more than conjunctural nature.

Unions are actors, and union strategy is important, but in a very real sense labor, however organized and with whatever ideological and strategic map, remains ultimately reactive, and thus an object in a capitalist economy. Under different conditions trade unions can be weaker or stronger, more or less able to bargain successfully with employers, but a basic asymmetry of power is embedded within any economy based upon wage labor, and that sets very concrete limits to what trade unions can achieve.[13] The quasi manifesto contained within the introduction for a conference on "Union Politics, Labor Militancy, and Capital Accumulation" is a useful corrective in this regard:

> The changing conditions of capital accumulation can be seen as a determinant—arguably, the primary determinant—of the overall balance of power between labor and capital. They also determine the bargaining agenda between labor and capital, and shape union politics by virtue of their impact on the interests of different union constituencies and the distribution of power among such constituencies.[14]

Underlying the approach used in this study is the notion of a *structural relationship* in which a certain type of economy and form of class organization is seen as setting structural limits to what is possible and making certain outcomes more probable, while excluding others.[15] This is not to say that structures *determine* what the state does, or the fate of state initiatives, in some complete and mechanistic way. On the contrary, I will be at pains to argue that the state is an important actor possessing the capacity to intervene successfully in the sphere of industrial relations. My concern is precisely with those institutions that intervene between structure and outcome, and hence are the target of state policy. Insofar as these institutional forms can be altered, outcomes too can be changed. That is why, as we shall see in the French case, successive French governments have devoted so much time and energy to industrial relations policy. But that said, structures have effects. Social institutions (such as those in the sphere of industrial relations) are not infinitely plastic, and states cannot pick and choose among such institutions at will. Given particular economic and social conditions, certain institutions will work and others will not. Recognizing the structural factors that are beyond the control of states is thus a crucial part of understanding why states act in the ways they do, and where and when they succeed and fail.

It follows that my concern is with the structural implications of policies rather than their rhetorical or ideological impact, or even their short-term behavioral impact. The problematic history of incomes policies, and wage-restraint policies more generally, testifies to the structural barriers that exist regardless of the intentions of important social actors. Such a perspective may lead me at times to imply that there was greater coherence to a set of policies than actually existed. The policies of governments are usually the result of competing, short-term factors. But that does not prevent the policies or their effects from having a wider coherence than was intended.

Unintended consequences are important. The same piece of legislation, or the same institution, can have very different effects at different times. Corporatist bargaining between the peak organizations of capital and labor, for instance, might have been effective and economically efficient during the long postwar boom, but unworkable and economically disastrous in the 1980s. To take another example, the Auroux industrial relations reforms of 1982–83 in France affected the strength and role of trade unions very differently because they were put in place during a period of historic union weakness than had they been introduced ten years earlier. As a result, the actual results have differed from the expectations of the Socialist government that put them in place.

All in all, my interest is as much the *space* for choice as the choices made within that space. The pressures of economies and the class structure set boundaries (which can be wider or narrower at different times and in different places) and delimit the options available to states. The choices themselves are often the result of a wide variety of largely conjunctural factors, and they are important. But whether explicitly or not, it is the *space* that both sets the menu of choices and helps determine the fate of particular choices.

APPROACHES TO COMPARATIVE POLITICAL ECONOMY

Comparative political economy lacks a systematic theoretical approach to labor. The relationship between the state and the working class in advanced capitalism has rarely been the object of systematic study. The particular dilemmas of left-wing parties that operate in capitalist democracies have received attention, and there is now a considerable literature on the pitfalls of incomes policies since the onset of economic crisis in the mid-1970s. However, an approach is needed that can be applied both to periods of economic crisis *and* prosperity, to Left *and* Right governments.

The insertion of labor into a capitalist economy is problematic in practice because an antagonistic relationship exists between capital and labor. This means simply that given the nature of the wage relationship and work process, workers and employers will, in the normal course of events, see their interests as opposed. Since the processes of production and accumulation are central to the functioning of a capitalist economy, it follows that *how* that relationship is mediated and organized is a central and critical problem for all governments that operate in capitalist economies. It is also true that the relationship between capital and labor can be a problem not only where a labor movement is strong, but also where it is weak. France is an excellent example of a country where a relatively weak labor movement could not simply be ignored or treated as unproblematic by the state.[16]

Comparative political economy needs a way of relating global changes in patterns of economic activity, and economic imperatives that are common to all capitalist economies, to the particular conditions and circumstances of class organization in each country. This linkage is all too often missing, or not made explicit. The result is either overabstraction and a lack of national specificity, or "political" explanations that minimize the extent to which states operate under economic constraints beyond their control.

This section discusses the theoretical contribution of three bodies of literature in political economy—the French "Regulation School," and corporatist and power resources theories—in the development of the notion of a "mode of labor regulation." The term "mode of labor regulation" used here corresponds closely to Davis's formulation of "the specific institutional forms in which the wage relation has been reproduced"[17] over time and across countries.

The Regulation School of political economy and the corporatist/power resources approaches are rarely treated as complementary[18] and are rooted in very different social scientific traditions. Nevertheless, once integrated, they form the point of departure for the theoretical task of developing the notion of labor regulation while simultaneously offering a way to avoid the twin dangers outlined above.

The label "Regulation School" refers to a disparate collection of studies[19] by French political economists which are tied together by the recognition that accumulation is a social process, rather than a purely economic or technical one. What this means is that the process by which the wage relation between capital and labor produces profits for capital is neither "natural" nor automatic. Rather, an infrastructure of social institutions is required in order for accumulation to take place (what Bowles, Gordon, and Weisskopf call a "social structure of accumulation").[20] This insight shifts the focus of inquiry to the specific structural conditions necessary for capital accumulation: what they are; how they vary over time; and how they differ from one country to another. The main concern of the Regulation School has been to delineate the variety of institutional frameworks that are conducive to the smooth functioning of a capitalist economy. Richard Edwards captures this perspective particularly well:

> Economic activity occurs within a wider social and institutional framework, or what has been termed a social structure of accumulation. This institutional framework may be more or less favorable to capitalist production and investment, and economic activity may be more or less reproducing of this framework. As the constellation of pressures, constraints and inducements emanating from the framework changes, so will the activity of economic actors change, and therefore so will the pattern and level of economic activity also be altered (and conversely, economic performance may shape the dynamics of institutional development).[21]

Broadly speaking, a particular pattern of accumulation may be said to correspond to a set of institutions that are necessary for that accumulation to take place. In the language of the Regulation School: for a "regime of accumulation" to reproduce itself, it requires a corresponding "mode of regulation." As Alain Lipietz put it:

> We will therefore call a "mode of regulation" the ensemble of institutional forms, the networks, the explicit or implicit norms, which assure the compatibility of behaviors in the framework of a regime of accumulation, in conformity with the state of the social relations, and thereby through the contradictions and the conflictual character of the relations between agents and social groups.[22]

It is important to stress that the term "regulation" is not used here in the American sense of the word, implying *active*, purposeful regulation by the state. As understood by Regulationists, regulation can occur independently of the actions of one actor (as, for instance, when regulation takes place impersonally through the labor market). It may also take place without the participation of the state, as in decentralized collective bargaining. Thus regulation is going on all the time, whether the state plays an active role or not.

Two regimes of accumulation and modes of regulation are usually cited. The first is a regime of extensive accumulation which was dominant in the nineteenth and early twentieth centuries, during which "capital grew by successive waves, with only moderate growth of productivity and stable consumption patterns. For the most part, accumulation meant the addition of productive factors to the capitalist circuit. Growth was possible because capitalism was expanding into new areas and new countries."[23] In this phase demand is external to the wage relation in that wages are viewed by each individual capitalist simply as costs, not components of demand. Thus high wages are unnecessary and the mode of regulation is "competitive," with market regulation of wages, wage-cutting, and a large reserve army of the unemployed.

The Depression marked the exhaustion of the extensive regime of accumulation.[24] With noncapitalist sources of demand used up, accumulation became intensive. Now wages paid to workers became the main source of demand. Competitive regulation—appropriate to a low-wage economy— had to be replaced by a new form of regulation, usually called "monopolistic" by the Regulationists.[25] This term refers to the wide variety of means used to maintain high effective demand: tying wages to productivity, insulating wages from cyclical downturns in the economy, the new task of demand-management assigned to the state, and so on.

There are also suggestions that the intensive regime of accumulation— often called "Fordism"—is itself nearing exhaustion and is giving way to a new regime elusively called "post-Fordism." So far there is little consensus as to what constitutes this new regime of accumulation. The line between evolution within a regime of accumulation and change to another one altogether is blurred. Surprisingly, there is rather more agreement as to what kind of regulation might be appropriate to such a new, as yet undefined, regime of accumulation. The danger here is that of uncritically incorporating the latest demands of employers—principally flexibility in wages and work practices—into the conditions for a new regime of accumulation.[26] Insofar as a consensus exists, it is around the notion that national solutions—particularly the socialization of wages and full employment of the postwar boom—are no longer possible. The future for advanced capitalist economies is said to lie in international competitiveness, rapid innovation, decentralized production, and, above all, flexibility.[27]

The advantage of the Regulation School approach is obvious. With a periodization of capitalism and an understanding of accumulation as a social process corresponding to a particular set of social institutions, we have a link between global economic change and the specific conditions of their reproduction. The importance of the Regulation approach is that it directs attention not simply to the strategies of actors, and their capacities for achieving goals—though these are important parts of the story—but also to how successfully these strategies correspond to the pressures and constraints imposed on them from a constantly evolving capitalist economy.

Within the Regulation School approach, my theoretical concern is with the manner in which labor is integrated into the political economies of capitalist societies. By integrated I mean simply the variety of practices and institutional forms that mediate the relationship between the working class, the state, and business. Examples of such forms and practices include the labor market, decentralized collective bargaining, and corporatist bargaining. Thus, my interest is in what types of mediation exist, why they appear where and when they do, and what implications each specific form has for union strategy, state policy, and capital accumulation.

To emphasize my focus on the relationship between capital and labor, I will use the term "mode of labor regulation" instead of the much broader "mode of regulation." The obvious alternative would be to talk about systems or modes of "industrial relations." But the term "industrial relations," while a useful approximation, is too narrow in that while it adequately covers collective bargaining and corporatism, it fails to capture such mechanisms as labor market regulation and state intervention, both of which are tremendously important factors mediating the relationship between workers and employers. So I have chosen to use the term "labor regulation," which has the additional advantage of expressing my intellectual debt to the Regulation School approach.

Despite the enormous potential of this approach, only limited work has been done on the elaboration of the social institutions that constitute a mode of regulation, and the reasons for the wide divergence between national types of regulation. Much work has skimmed over these divergences, implying that all advanced capitalist economies adopted the same mode of regulation in the postwar period: regularized collective bargaining, productivity agreements, indexed wages, and so on.[28] This is in fact not the case. There are clear national differences, as later sections will show. Part of the problem is conceptual fuzziness. The term "mode of regulation" can be used so broadly as to mean almost any aspect of contemporary capitalist society that serves to assure accumulation. Defined this broadly it is impossible to use the concept of a mode of regulation to provide national specificity. If any and all mechanisms that serve to maintain high and regular wage progression can be considered part of monopolistic regulation, then it is possible to distinguish between broad historical epochs (extensive and intensive accumulation), but not between countries that share the same regime of accumulation.[29]

Recently this weakness has been addressed, particularly in the work of Boyer and his collaborators.[30] He has argued that there are significant national differences in the institutional forms of regulation that have been adopted in the postwar period. Boyer focuses upon the wage relationship and enumerates a list of mechanisms which enable high real wages to be maintained in a Fordist regime of accumulation. However, while Boyer has addressed the issue and provided some much-needed specificity, the problem of how to *explain* national variations remains. The mechanisms of wage regulation are descriptions only, and too often reference is made to national "types," or "traditions," without explaining how and why national patterns emerge and persist.

There is an additional danger that, while a variety of mechanisms have now been specified (collective bargaining and indexation, for example), the institutional relationships between capital and labor which make them possible are still obscure. A good example is provided by the current interest in flexibility. There are many ways in which flexibility can be introduced into wage determination and the work process. But what specific institutional relationships between capital and labor facilitate this development? Why are certain countries more able to introduce flexibility, and how can states that see flexibility as a necessary goal encourage its adoption?

This study attempts to take the Regulation approach a step further along the path indicated by Boyer. More than one form of labor regulation is compatible with a given regime of accumulation. The original relationship between regime of accumulation and mode of labor regulation—that a mode of labor regulation is required for a regime of accumulation to reproduce itself—remains, and some modes of labor regulation are clearly still ruled out (for instance, competitive regulation of wages is inappropriate for intensive accumulation). We are, however, left with a number of different kinds of regulation, all of which are compatible with a particular regime of accumulation. It is possible, for instance, for one mode of labor regulation to substitute for another. The task still remains to explain why one mode of labor regulation is more likely to arise in a particular country, and at a particular time, than another. For this I turn to the corporatist and power resources literatures.

In the almost two decades since Philippe Schmitter initiated the corporatist debate[31] and spawned what one scholar has called a "growth industry,"[32] the corporatist paradigm has been taken in many directions and Schmitter's original formulation has been changed a great deal.[33] The power resources literature is included at this point because, it will be argued, a certain configuration of power resources is the precondition for corporatism.

The corporatist paradigm grew out of an attempt to explain both the markedly different ways in which advanced capitalist economies responded to the first oil shock and subsequent ending of the long postwar boom, and the surprisingly ambiguous relationship that was shown to exist between left-wing political power and the pursuit of policies that might be considered in some sense left-wing.[34] The implications of this work were paradoxical: on the one hand, politics did seem to affect the response (and resulting macroeconomic performance) of capitalist economies to economic crisis; on the other hand, state economic management seemed subject to societal constraints more fundamental than the political stripe of the government. Moreover, the practical experiences of left-wing governments in Britain (1974–79) and France (1981–86) made the assertion that differing political control of the polity could be translated into significantly different policy outcomes more difficult to sustain. The reaction of scholars was to shift the focus of inquiry below the level of policy to the structural conditions that make policy possible. By structural conditions most scholars meant the organization and articulation of interest groups. Thus, Korpi identified those structural characteristics of a labor movement—high union density, high levels of union organization, a lack of craft or other divisions, and collective bargaining at the highest possible level—which make possible the participation of labor in national-level institutions, a participation that is called corporatist.[35]

However, soon after the initial formulation of corporatism, two shifts in focus occurred that changed the paradigm—for some scholars at least—from a "group-theoretic" to a "class-theoretic" one.[36] First, despite lip service to the study of all interest groups, research almost immediately concentrated on only capital and labor, and increasingly, in practice, only on labor. It became clear that for most governments the often-stated general goals of a corporatist organization of interest groups—reducing and channeling demands upon the state, combating "overload" and "ungovernability"—in practice came to mean one thing: obtaining wage restraint and labor peace from powerful labor movements.

Second, research generally centered upon the structural characteristics of labor and capital rather than the practices of tripartism and bipartism. This shift found its most complete form in a paper by Cameron in 1984.[37] Cameron used a set of measures of the "organizational power of labor" in order to generate the results that were supposed to flow from corporatist practices without any reference to those practices themselves. Thus he focuses our attention on the structure and organization of labor rather than on the corporatist institutions themselves. This work provided the link between the corporatist and power resources literatures.

Now, there are clearly problems with the corporatist paradigm.[38] As critics have repeatedly pointed out, its advocates are often overly optimistic about both the possibility of social democracy transcending a capitalist organization of the economy,[39] and the ultimate stability of corporatist patterns of bargaining.[40] From the perspective of the early 1990s, corporatism—the product of a relatively brief period of postwar economic expansion—seems restricted in geographical scope and timebound, even in its homeland of Sweden.

An additional failing of these bodies of literature is the narrow and mechanistic manner in which they conceptualize class power. Working-class power is understood as essentially being exercised by top union officials, who barter their control over a disciplined labor movement for power via a social democratic party. These theorists do not offer an alternative way of organizing working-class power, and indeed explicitly reject one. Other forms of working-class strength, organization, and militancy are viewed as signs of weakness. The result is that countries tend to be ranked by the degree of their deviation from the model, usually taken to be Sweden. It is unclear whether the social conditions necessary for corporatism are historically determined—for instance by the mode of industrialization—or can be gradually created by far-sighted labor leaders. If the former, then such theorists can say little about noncorporatist countries; if the latter, they can do little but search for embryonic forms of corporatism elsewhere.

Nevertheless, the approach used by the corporatist and power resource theorists remains tremendously fruitful. If the struggle over the distribution of the social product is central to the accumulation process, a crucial determinant of the outcome will be the collective power of labor. As Therborn has pointed out: "The fundamental power resource available to the working class, therefore, is its collectivity: especially its capacity for unity through interlocking, mutually supportive and concerted practices. The rise of the labor movement was above all a process of enlarging, deepening and structuring this collectivity."[41] The working class cannot act against capital unless it can act collectively. In most advanced capitalist countries the collective power of the working class is expressed through trade unions, though other forms of organization can be imagined.

The corporatist and power resources approach shows a causal chain in which a given structure and organization of the working class implies a particular way of regulating labor, which in turn makes certain economic policy outcomes likely and closes off others. This approach provides a means of generating a wider typology, going beyond a simple corporatist/noncorporatist dichotomy, applicable to the whole gamut of capitalist democracies, which would be both a description and an explanation of the national specificity of modes of labor regulation.

It is worth making one final comment at this point concerning the choice this study makes in focusing upon the organization and strength of labor rather than capital. That choice is only partly explained by the need to delimit the task at hand. It is remarkable that, almost without exception, capitalist states have sought to restructure labor organizations rather than those of capital in response to threats to accumulation. There has been a marked contrast between the great interest states have shown in attempts to modify the organization of the labor movement and the almost total disinterest they have shown in the reform of employers' organizations. This is very clear in the French case. Where states have shown an interest in capital it has tended to be with the purpose of industrial restructuring to improve economic efficiency. It is significant that when states attack labor they limit its organizational capacities, its collectivity; on the rare occasions that they attack capital, it has to be by measures of partial or full expropriation.

The main explanation for this, I think, is Offe and Wiesenthal's insight into the differential role played by the class organizations of capital and labor.[42] The structure of capital—in the sense of the balance between traditional and advanced, domestic and international, and industrial and financial capital—is important for the degree to which the state finds it necessary to manage conflict and to substitute for, or override, capital. Nevertheless, the "insuperable individuality" of the working class means that the way in which workers are aggregated is important, both to the manner in which they perceive their own interests, and to their ability to act in those interests, in a way that is not as true for capital. The organization of capital is important for its political power—its ability to influence the state, and vice versa. But its economic power is exercised by individual capitalists, irrespective of organization. As Lindblom puts it: "Business people do not have to debate whether or not to impose the penalty. They need do no more . . . than tend to their own businesses, which means that, without thought of effecting a punishment on us, they restrict investment and jobs simply in the course of being prudent managers of their enterprises."[43] The working class, on the other hand, cannot exercise either political or economic power without organization to enhance its collectivity.

MODES OF LABOR REGULATION

The task of labor regulation is an important one for any state, regardless of political stripe. The institutions that regulate the relationship between employers and workers are at the core of the accumulation process and the capacity of firms, sectors, and economies to respond to market changes. They influence the level of industrial conflict, and they play a role in the ideological construction, and hence political action, of the working class. This gives all states an interest in labor regulation.

The job of outlining the range of different modes of labor regulation remains. The modes of labor regulation discussed in this section are best understood as *ideal types*, or pure forms, in that they are considered at a fairly high level of abstraction. Nonetheless, past and present forms of labor regulation in France and elsewhere in the advanced capitalist world will be clearly recognizable.

The five modes of labor regulation discussed here do not exhaust the universe of forms of labor regulation. No consideration is given here to a situation in which labor is regulated at the supranational level (for example, by European political institutions). The reason for the omission is partly that no such form of regulation exists (though some indicators, such as the discussion of a "Social Charter," point to this development),[44] and partly that, in the discussion of state regulation of labor below, a supranational state could be substituted for a nation-state without significant changes in the form of labor regulation. In addition, various intermediate forms of labor regulation are not discussed. This is not because they are unimportant in practice, but because their features are captured by "purer" forms of labor regulation. A good example here is sectoral or industry-level bargaining, which is widespread. However, at the level of ideal types, this level of bargaining is understood as a hybrid, encompassing features of corporatist bargaining and decentralized collective bargaining.

The construction of these ideal types of labor regulation is motivated by two considerations. The first is a concern with the *level* at which labor regulation takes place because this is an indicator of the degree of influence that the state can wield over labor regulation. For example, the state is only able to exercise a minor regulatory role when labor regulation takes place at the level of the firm, either through unilateral management dictate or some form of bargaining between management and workers in the firm. Where labor regulation takes place at the national/confederal level, the potential exists for the state to play a decisive role in labor regulation.[45] An intermediate degree of influence would be where bargaining is at the industry or sectoral level.

The second consideration is the form of labor collectivity. As discussed above, the extent of the collective organization of labor when it confronts capital is the crucial measure of the class capacity of workers. The extent of labor collectivity indicates the collective resources of labor—its capacity to inflict damage on capital by a withdrawal of labor—and hence the extent to which labor can insulate itself from the labor market. As they constitute themselves into wider forms of collectivity, workers are able to impose greater damage upon capital and thus improve their bargaining position. The form of labor collectivity also indicates where the primary identification of the worker might be expected to lie: to a firm, to a trade or craft, or to a class. Three forms of labor collectivity are considered here: the individual worker confronting an employer alone; an enterprise union or works council bargaining with an employer; and a labor union representing, and bargaining on behalf of, workers from many firms or sectors. Hence there are two key transitions from one form of labor collectivity to another: (1) the distinction between some collective power and none, and (2) collective power that is exercised within, and restricted to, the firm as opposed to collective power that spills outside the boundaries of the firm to encompass a particular category of worker or an entire class.

Table 1.1 represents these two dimensions schematically and produces five modes of labor regulation (national/confederal bargaining with a firm-specific organization of workers is a logical impossibility so that space has been left empty). It is important to stress that I am not arguing that only one form of labor regulation will exist in a given time and place. On the

TABLE 1.1
Modes of Labor Regulation

	Forms of Labor Collectivity:		
	Individual	*Firm-specific*	*Labor Union*
Level of Labor Regulation:			
Firm	Labor market regulation	Micro-corporatist regulation	Collective-bargaining regulation
Industry/Sectoral			
National/Confederal	State regulation		Corporatist regulation

contrary, in practice various modes of labor regulation can coexist. These forms are closely interconnected. For instance, in all market economies the labor market will be the ultimate determinant of wages, while the other forms of labor regulation can be understood as acting as degrees of insulation from the market.

Furthermore, in a given economy it is possible, indeed likely, that some sectors will exhibit one form of labor regulation, while others have different forms. This is most obviously important when distinguishing between the public and private sectors, but it is also true within the private sector. The important question is whether one particular type of labor regulation is dominant, in the sense that it imparts a dynamic to the process of labor regulation in the economy as a whole. For instance, as the French case will demonstrate, it is entirely possible that a relatively small unionized sector can be highly influential in the rest of the economy through a variety of mechanisms to spread the results of collective bargaining to the nonunionized sector.

One final example: countries and historical periods that are characterized as having labor market or microcorporatist forms of regulation may also have labor unions. However, those unions are likely to be weak and present only in certain sectors of the economy. Labor unions and collective bargaining may exist without constituting the driving force behind labor regulation. Thus in real social formations two or more forms of labor regulation can coexist and indeed complement each other.

Before discussing each mode of labor regulation in more detail, the causal argument should be made clear. A mode of labor regulation mediates the structural resources of labor and the outcomes of wage bargaining. A given strength and organization of labor delimits the range of possible mechanisms of labor regulation. A mode of labor regulation in turn has consequences for the kinds of economic policy available to state managers. It can constrain policy options, but it can also enlarge them. For instance, certain types of labor regulation provide the state with an element of control over wages. Keynesian, protectionist, and industrial policy strategies are all heavily influenced by whether the wage bill is a macroeconomic policy variable available to state managers.

Labor Market Regulation

Labor market regulation is the equivalent of the term "competitive regulation," used by Regulationists to describe the dominant form of regulation in the nineteenth and early twentieth centuries. And it will be argued in the next chapter that the labor market was the dominant form of regulation in postwar France, at least until the mid-1960s. For reasons to be described below, it no longer exists as the sole means of regulation. At the same time, this form of regulation is always present, underlying other forms that seek to partially decommodify wages. A complete de-coupling of wages from the labor market is impossible, by definition, in capitalist economies.

Labor market regulation means that labor finds itself unable to use industrial or political means to insulate itself from the labor market. Workers face employers as individuals in the marketplace and under such circumstances labor is likely to be disadvantaged. This was true in the nineteenth century when the shrinking agricultural sector simultaneously created a large pool of unemployed farm laborers and an almost inexhaustible supply of industrial workers. There are also examples—France, Italy, Japan—of late industrializers where this transition from an agrarian to an industrial economy was not completed until the period following the Second World War.

However, this situation is not a complete blessing for capital and the state, even one controlled by the Right. There will be periods—of increasing frequency as surplus labor dries up—of tighter labor markets in which even an unorganized working class can make important gains. Flanagan, Soskice, and Ulman point to cyclical patterns of increasing labor militancy in tightening labor markets, followed by recession, looser labor markets, and decreasing militancy.[46] At the peaks of these cycles accumulation and production can be disrupted by strike action and employers bidding against each other to attract labor. The danger in this situation is that, with labor unorganized, these periods of militancy are unpredictable and uncontrollable. The point is that while labor is structurally weak it can be conjuncturally strong where the labor market is the dominant form of regulation. Without a union movement, neither state nor capital has anyone to deal with. The dangers of labor market regulation are aggravated further when the transition to intensive production is made and higher, more stable wage levels become necessary. Even if individual employers or state managers recognize the need for wages to bolster internal demand, there is a collective-action problem. This situation poses problems for states of whatever political stripe, and they are likely to attempt to reform the industrial relations system in one of the following directions.

State Regulation

State regulation of labor means simply that the state is deeply involved in wage determination and in setting the rules and conditions within which wage bargaining takes place. Thus the state can set minimum wages for certain industries or categories of labor, it can legislate rules for hiring and firing, and it can legislate an incomes policy of some kind. These interventions either influence wages directly or do so indirectly by changing the bargaining environment. The period between 1969 and 1978 in France provides a good example of a high degree of state intervention in industrial relations.

In practice state regulation is closely associated with labor market regulation. Where the working class is very poorly organized and the labor market is the dominant form of wage regulation, one might expect the state to step in—setting minimum wages, regulating basic conditions of work, and so on—to substitute for workers' organizations. This would be unnecessary, and probably unwelcome, where collective bargaining is highly developed.[47]

Thus the working class remains weak and poorly organized, but the state no longer feels able to leave labor regulation to the market. In countries where labor is weak, one can expect political control by right-wing parties,[48] but even here there are very good reasons why such governments might seek to influence wage determination and even provide a measure of protection for labor. There are the periodic threats to accumulation and production when labor markets are tight. Also, with the shift to intensive accumulation, some means have to be found to maintain aggregate demand. The state can achieve this by indexing wages, setting minimum wages, maintaining full employment, and even using its own expenditures to expand aggregate demand. Where labor is too weak to have developed regularized collective-bargaining structures that assure steady increases in wages, the state can, in effect, substitute for labor organizations in order to ensure wage increases. Earlier it was suggested that the Regulationists saw all countries as adopting the collective bargaining mechanisms of "monopolistic regulation" appropriate to intensive accumulation. Here, by contrast, it is argued that where the structural conditions for such a form of regulation are lacking, the state can step in with an alternative regulatory mechanism that achieves the same end.

Along with fulfilling a necessary economic role, a state, despite, or indeed because, it is controlled by the Right, might want to provide some insulation from the labor market for workers on strictly political grounds (to win an upcoming, close election or to deprive a left-wing party of support), to prevent social disruption, and to defend the legitimacy and apparent impartiality of the state.[49]

The danger with this strategy is clearly that of politicization. Not only wage demands but the whole constellation of social relations and of class struggle between capital and labor are displaced upward and become focused on the state. The incentives to bargain are removed or weakened as whichever partner—labor or capital—feels weakest in the market will attempt to force the state to intervene on its behalf. One can hypothesize that where labor is too weak to bargain for itself there will be a constant dialectic between two tendencies: on the one hand, the state will seek to disengage itself from labor regulation and encourage concertation between labor and capital each time politicization becomes so great as to threaten the stability of the political regime; on the other hand, there will be a constant tendency for the state to be forced back into labor regulation in order to safeguard accumulation and to protect its political legitimacy. Labor is simply too weak to take on the task of collective bargaining for itself.

Decentralized Collective Bargaining

Characterizing this mode of labor regulation is difficult because it is situated in the middle ground between a poorly unionized work force able to engage in collective bargaining only sporadically and a highly unionized work force able to engage in corporatist-style bargaining at the national level. Nevertheless, despite this being in many ways an ill-defined form, it is the form that most closely approximates a large number of advanced capitalist societies. An alternative label might be the "British model."

A decentralized collective-bargaining model is premised on a labor movement that is well unionized but divided into multiple unions, which fractures the work force and with it the possibilities for interunion cooperation. Craft unions of the British kind, or ideologically divided unions of the Italian kind, most closely conform to this model. Workers are organized into collectivities that stretch beyond the walls of the firm, often including all workers of a particular trade in a country, or sector. Thus workers are powerful enough to be able to force employers to bargain thanks to the threat of withdrawal of labor. However, this form of union organization makes unified confederal-level negotiations very difficult. There are too many actors involved, and too many opportunities for deals outside national guidelines. Thus bargaining tends to be decentralized to the firm or sectoral level.

The collective-bargaining model involves the creation of regularized practices and institutions for bargaining between the recognized representatives of labor and employers. Both the bargaining process and the bargaining partners must be accepted as legitimate by both sides. This implies a recognition of the legitimacy of labor unions on the part of employers, and a recognition of the legitimacy of private ownership and control on the part of labor. It also implies that unions accept that capital has legitimate needs which must be considered in the wage-bargaining process.

This model was formalized in the 1950s and 1960s by the "Industrial Relations School" of industrial sociologists.[50] The model has been justly criticized for its normative overtones and overly sanguine view of the untroubled future of class relations. Theories concerning the institutionalization of class conflict had difficulty dealing with the upsurge of worker militancy between 1968 and the early 1970s. Nevertheless, there is much that remains relevant for any discussion of the implications of mechanisms of labor regulation for accumulation and state economic management. The purpose behind creating regular collective-bargaining practices is the creation of an "autonomous sphere of industrial relations" which channels class struggle away from both the streets and the state. It is a solution—albeit a temporary and partial one—to the critical problem of politicization. Collective-bargaining mechanisms form a buffer that helps to prevent a spillover from industrial militancy to political radicalism. At the same time, the state is able to stand above class conflict and leave the management of social relations to the social partners themselves.

Collective bargaining provides a partial insulation from the labor market, which affords some protection to workers, provides a mechanism for regular wage increases in line with productivity and growth, and gives a degree of predictability to wage demands, making planning decisions by the managers of firms easier.

However, for the state this ability to stand above class relations is double-edged. While the threat of politicization is lessened, the state also finds itself with a much-reduced capacity to influence wages. Wage bargaining is decentralized, with the result that state-initiated wage restraint is almost impossible to achieve. The miserable experience of incomes policies in Britain testifies to this problem.[51] The state is forced to rely on indirect, macroeconomic forms of wage control, such as the "stop-go" deflationary strategy of successive British governments, Labour and Conservative alike. These global macroeconomic solutions have serious negative effects on economic performance.[52] Faced with this situation, governments (particularly of the left) have frequently sought to encourage corporatist labor regulation.

Corporatist Labor Regulation

The label "corporatist" is used here to describe a mechanism of labor regulation. But that mechanism is only part of a wider structure which we can call the "Social Democratic Model." The power resources and, to a lesser extent, the corporatist literatures are essentially a theorization of social democracy in its Swedish and Austrian forms, in the sense that social democracy is premised upon a strong, highly organized, disciplined working class, and corporatist labor regulation.[53]

Corporatist regulation is best understood as operating under the dual constraints of a capitalist economy and a powerful labor movement that can no longer be regulated solely by the labor market. Thus exclusion of labor is not a possible solution. The model is premised both upon the *need* to integrate the working class (because it has become sufficiently powerful to disrupt capital accumulation) and the *ability* to integrate it (because it is organized and disciplined enough for union leaders to be able to impose wage restraint). Above all, corporatist regulation requires that union leaders be able to gain autonomy from their members. Failure to do so makes them ineffective corporatist partners because they will not be able to deliver their side of the bargain.

For this reason corporatist regulation depends on a particular structure of the working class, rather than the *institutions* of bipartism or tripartism. It is important to recognize this structural precondition because otherwise corporatism will be measured by counting institutions and meetings that bring the representatives of capital and labor together. France, for instance, has had formal tripartite institutions (planning commissions, the Social and Economic Council) since 1945, but never corporatism.

The upshot is that the very strength and organization of the working class both permits, and makes necessary, a form of wage restraint that enhances macroeconomic performance. Wages become a macroeconomic policy variable through the mechanism of "political exchange,"[54] or the translation of industrial strength into political power. Political exchange is used to barter working-class industrial quiescence (and hence favorable conditions for capital accumulation) for social democratic goals. The mechanism by which corporatism operates is an exchange of wage restraint in return for a high social wage and full employment, along with the more intangible gain of periodic access to political power via "its" social democratic party.[55]

In short, corporatist regulation provides a way of universalizing the interests of workers. The ability to achieve wage restraint gives added room for maneuver to social democratic parties. They are able to maintain full employment without paying for it in higher inflation.[56] However, a word of caution is in order. Both corporatism and social democracy have come under attack recently in Sweden and Austria. The impressive economic performances of the 1960s and early 1970s gave way to lackluster and fragile growth in the 1980s. It seems likely that corporatism is unable to sustain its partial decommodification of wages from the labor market through prolonged periods of recession, or if it does, the price will be diminished economic performance.

Microcorporatist Labor Regulation

Microcorporatist labor regulation has been left until last because it is the least theorized in the existing literature. Microcorporatism is a partial form in that it can very easily coexist with both labor market and collective-bargaining types of labor regulation. Microcorporatism tends to be associated with a dual labor market, so one would in fact expect it to coexist with other regulatory forms.

The term microcorporatism comes from Wolfgang Streeck[57] and refers to corporatist-style bargaining between labor and capital at the firm, rather than the confederal or industry level. Hence bargaining is between an employer and either an enterprise union or a works council.[58] Workers are organized in a firmwide collectivity, and significant incentives exist for these workers to identify primarily with the needs of the firm. Streeck has examined microcorporatism in West Germany. In later chapters it will be argued that the label of microcorporatism also fits the French case in the 1980s.

Microcorporatism is premised upon a decentralized industrial relations system centered upon the firm, in which there is "a decapitation of the workplace-based structures of interest accommodation whose functioning ceases to be controlled by, and conditioned upon, bargaining agreements at the central level."[59] What follows is "the integration of workers at the level of individual enterprises in cooperative alliances with their employers."[60] The terms of microcorporatist bargains center around employment. Existing workers receive employment security, and perhaps other forms of protection,[61] from the firm in return for flexibility and an acceptance of the legitimacy of the economic goals of the firm. Thus wages, bonuses, the organization and control of work, new technologies, and so on are all centered around the needs of the firm.

This is the reason for the use of the term "corporatism," suitably modified to refer to the firm. Under corporatist labor regulation, it is the disruptive potential of a centralized trade union that leads it to incorporate economic considerations into its demands and to ultimately trade restraint for jobs, a social wage, and some degree of political influence. This is essentially what happens under microcorporatist labor regulation, though here the bargain is restraint and flexibility in return for job security, firm-related benefits, and perhaps some form of worker participation in the running of the firm.

Now, clearly employers are only likely to propose this form of bargain in situations where they need the active cooperation of workers. Scholars such as Piore and Sabel argue that this is precisely the situation that is becoming generalized in a post-Fordist economy.[62]

Streeck understands microcorporatism as resulting from the degeneration of corporatist regulation. Such a degeneration could result from increased levels of unemployment and/or a conscious employer strategy of undermining the collective power of the working class. But microcorporatism might also be a more general response to the exhaustion of the intensive regime of accumulation, and hence appear where bargaining was never very centralized. Fordism was conditioned upon a full employment and high-wage economy. But the rigid, centralized bargains of corporatist regulation are inappropriate for the rapid change, flexibility, and decentralization that are often considered necessary for any post-Fordist regime of accumulation. Microcorporatism may be more appropriate for such a new regime of accumulation. If so, it is possible that there will be a general shift toward microcorporatism in the advanced capitalist world. This possibility, and the likelihood of microcorporatist bargains emerging (as opposed to a simple return to unilateral managerial control), will be discussed in chapters 8 and 9.

One final rather speculative point: it may be that microcorporatism has both a "Right" and a "Left" version. Microcorporatism is not incompatible with certain conceptions of self-management, or what the French call *autogestion*. (My concern here is with notions of self-management that operate within a market, not a planned economy.) Thus part of the bargain struck might provide workers with places on the board of directors, veto power over certain kinds of production decisions, and even worker stock ownership. The works council could wield very real powers. This would not, however, change the central feature of microcorporatism: that workers will tend to identify with the economic needs of the firm.[63] Workers will identify with their firms in a self-managed system, in a similar way to the microcorporatism described by Streeck. Microcorporatism and self-management have similar economic outcomes: low labor absorption, self-restraint in wage demands, and only limited state capacity to influence wages.[64]

The point of this speculation is not that microcorporatism contains within it the seeds of a progressive form of workers' control; in light of the conditions under which microcorporatism has been imposed upon workers' movements, such a claim would be rash indeed. On the contrary, this might serve as a warning to the often inflated claims made for self-management. The point is to show the structural similarities and, perhaps unsurprisingly, the similarity of outcomes, of both the "Left" and "Right" versions of microcorporatism. These similarities imply that the differences may be more rhetorical than real.

Bringing the State Back In

If modes of labor regulation are as important as has been argued here, and if states have a correspondingly important interest in labor regulation, the fundamental question must be: can a mode of labor regulation be changed? The question is particularly important since a constant refrain in this chapter has been the structural nature of labor regulation. In the discussion of the Regulation School it was argued that more than one regulatory mechanism can be compatible with a given regime of accumulation. It is this that provides the space for effective state policies to change the form of labor regulation. Influencing the regime of accumulation is by and large beyond the control of states, but while the structure of a labor movement is difficult to change, it is not impossible.

Thus the concern of later chapters will be state policies that, for instance, encourage a widening of labor collectivity by providing new legal rights and protection to unions, or encourage collective bargaining by giving labor and capital an incentive and a legal base for bargaining. Inevitably these kinds of policies are long-term ones. One cannot "create" the preconditions for regularized collective bargaining overnight. Often the results of a government policy will only be seen long after that government has left office. This means judging success and failure by different standards from those often used by political commentators. The highly visible initiatives of governments in the industrial relations field are often not those that bear fruit in the long term. In the study of industrial relations it is easy to pay too much attention to government attempts to bring the social partners together, and to utterances of good faith from union leaders and employers. A more important task is to understand the structural implications of policy, even when the results diverge significantly from the intentions of policymakers.

The table of modes of labor regulation, discussed earlier, provides a sense of the possible strategies available to states that wish to change an existing mode of labor regulation. For instance, a state concerned by the cyclical strike waves associated with labor market regulation can follow two paths. It can seek to increase the involvement of the state in labor regulation by legislating parts of the wage-determination process so that the operation of the labor market is constrained. Schematically this would be represented by moving down the vertical axis, changing the level at which labor regulation takes place. Alternatively, or at the same time, the state can seek to encourage the expansion of labor collectivity (favoring unionization, for example) so that workers are able to insulate themselves, to some degree, from the labor market. Schematically, this would involve moving along the horizontal axis. Similarly, a state concerned with the economic rigidities and politicization of industrial relations associated with corporatism is likely to attempt some combination of weakening labor collectivity, decentralizing collective bargaining, and withdrawing itself from a role in labor regulation. Thus table 1.1 shows the lines of possible development from one mode of labor regulation to another.

THE STATE AND LABOR REGULATION IN POSTWAR FRANCE

The empirical sections of this study tell a particular story of the evolution of labor regulation in France. In brief, its focal point is the crisis posed by May 1968, though it is necessary to go back somewhat further in time to explain the origins of that crisis. This date is of pivotal importance for the political economy of postwar France. The events of May and June 1968 marked the peak of working-class militancy since 1936 and as such provide the necessary point of comparison with the present period of passivity and industrial quiescence. The year 1968 also marked the collapse of the form of social relations and industrial conflict that had dominated the postwar era. While the postwar model of "labor exclusion,"[65] in which trade unions were excluded from the shopfloor and a role in economic decision-making at the national level, had been breaking down and becoming increasingly unsustainable well before 1968, the events of May and June of that year made that fact obvious to politicians, business people, and trade unionists alike. Insofar as broad economic and social shifts ever become visible to contemporaries, the industrial strife of 1968 marked both a real as well as a symbolic exhaustion of the postwar model. The year 1968 also put the issue of labor's deradicalization and integration (in both an institutional and an ideological sense) on the agenda of every post-1968 government. The labor movement could no longer be ignored and left to regulation by the labor market alone. A variety of solutions to the "problem" of labor have been on offer since 1968, but all of them have taken the events of May and June of that year as their central political fact, and the labor movement as a key social actor.

It is also true that, in a very basic sense, 1968 was a failure. There was, in Capdevielle and Mouriaux's words, a remarkable "discrepancy between the strength of the movement and the meagerness of the results."[66] No political transformation followed, and even if the arrival of the Left in power thirteen years later can somehow be attributed to the events of 1968, its services to the labor movement between 1981 and 1986 were at best ambiguous and contradictory. The strike wave of 1968 was not even translated into sustainable material gains for workers. The wage increases granted in the heat of the conflict were eroded, first by inflation and devaluation, and then more dramatically by the onset of economic crisis after 1973. The failure of the greatest challenge to the French state from workers in the postwar period needs explaining, particularly if, as seems likely, 1968 represented the *last* great challenge to the state that the French labor movement was able to mount.

The story told in the empirical chapters of this book takes place at a number of levels. The state policy that is its focus was the result of a complex interrelationship between economic pressures, institutional change, and the actions and interests of major social actors and of particular governments. The specific state-reform projects, Jacques Chaban-Delmas's "New Society" program, or the Socialists' Auroux Laws, for example, all took place against the backdrop of a profound and gradual economic transformation of France, and the evolution in the interests and organization of capital and labor.

It is important not to lose sight of this wider context. In the time period covered by this study, two broad economic transformations took place in

France, each of which had profound implications for employers, trade unions, and the state. The first was the slow and hesitant development of Fordism: an advanced industrial economy based on the constant expansion of domestic demand and a virtuous circle of mass consumption and mass production, each feeding upon the other. As Fordism became better implanted in France, it set up intolerable strains on the dominant model of labor market regulation and ultimately resulted in the events of May 1968. This first transformation created a potential role for organized labor in economic management, a role that had been lacking in the immediate postwar period, and it also created a constituency within French business for a less conflictual industrial relations system.

Yet within a very short time, Fordism in France, as elsewhere, began to show signs of exhaustion. The fragility of mass production based upon ever-increasing living standards and ever-expanding domestic markets became clear. Thus there are now indications that the Fordist economies are giving way to ones which are being forced to compete more ferociously for saturated markets, and in so doing emphasize flexibility and reduced wage levels above the rigid work rules and steadily increasing wages of the past. The result has been new employer strategies for dealing with workers, the unraveling of class compromises where they existed, and an entirely new, as yet unclear, role for organized labor in the political economy.

It is within this wider context that French governments have pursued strategies of labor regulation since 1968. Broadly speaking, two strategies have been followed, each with a particular form of labor regulation as its goal. While these strategies have received different emphases at different times within this twenty-year period, there has been a basic continuity in the sense that each strategy has appeared and reappeared throughout the period. There has been no linear succession in which one strategy has been superseded by another, or one strategy associated exclusively with one political party. The first strategy was to incorporate unions, strengthen them insofar as they pursued "responsible" goals, and foster decentralized collective bargaining with trade unions as the privileged negotiating partners. This strategy largely failed, though it was seriously pursued for important parts of the period under study. Unions proved too weak, especially after the onset of economic crisis. By the time the Socialists came to power it was too late, and in any case they had an economic crisis of their own. By the time France emerged from economic crisis in the mid-1980s, trade unionism's conjunctural weakness had been turned into a structural weakness.

The second strategy, which was the direct competitor of the first, appeared sporadically after 1968 and with a vengeance from 1983 onward (albeit often unintentionally during the Socialist period). It was to weaken and exclude unions, and instead incorporate workers at their place of work either in firm-specific organizations cut off from wider labor collectivities, or as individual workers via individualized payment schemes. This was a modified version of the old Gaullist goal of *"participation"* which had seemingly been discredited in 1968. It is no small irony that twenty years later the general can be said to have had some measure of revenge as this mode of labor regulation has become widespread in France.

Both strategies envisaged the withdrawal of the state from labor regulation and throwing responsibility for labor regulation onto the social partners and civil society more generally. While this goal was largely achieved in the decade following 1978, there was in fact an *increase* in state intervention and involvement in labor regulation at certain critical moments, and particularly in the first half of the 1970s, for reasons detailed in chapter 4.

The plan for this book is as follows: The four chapters that comprise part two deal with the period in which a Fordist economy first took root in France and then faltered. They provide a broadly chronological account of the evolution of labor regulation from 1945 to 1981. Thus chapters 2 and 3 discuss the labor exclusionary/labor market–based mode of labor regulation which existed until 1968, and its collapse under the weight of economic modernization, resulting in May 1968. Chapters 4 and 5 examine in some detail the responses of the immediate post-1968 governments to the crisis in the mode of labor regulation. The industrial relations reform projects of Jacques Chaban-Delmas, Valéry Giscard d'Estaing, and Raymond Barre are emphasized.

Part two also sets the scene for part three of the book, which examines the Socialist approach to labor regulation in the period 1981–86. It is argued in part two that the neo-Gaullist and liberal reform projects ultimately failed, leaving a system of labor regulation that was in crisis in 1981. It was within the context of this crisis that the French Socialists attempted their own project of labor regulation.

The three chapters that make up part three, therefore, are organized less chronologically than topically. They examine the relationship between the Parti Socialiste (PS; the French Socialist party) and the labor movement (chapter 6), the Auroux industrial relations reforms (chapter 7), and the introduction of flexibility in France (chapter 8). It is argued that the Socialist reform project, partly intentionally, partly unintentionally, created a new, and probably durable, mode of labor regulation in France. The defining feature of this mode of labor regulation, termed microcorporatism, is its reversal of the historic process of the expansion of the collective power of labor, expressed in most capitalist societies through the growth of national trade union movements, and the construction in its place of microlevel collectivities of workers, centered on, and limited to, the firm.

The concluding chapter attempts to place the French experience into a broader comparative context. It is common to view France as something of an anomaly in Western Europe. The weakness of labor, the exclusion of the

Left from political power until 1981, the bitterly conflictual nature of industrial relations—in short, the absence of a postwar settlement, in the sense of a broad class compromise between capital and labor—set France apart from its largely social democratic neighbors.

Yet, for all the truth of this observation in the 1950s and 1960s, from the perspective of the 1990s France is far less of an outlier than it once was. To a remarkable extent the transformation in the political economy of France in the past decade, and the developments in labor regulation described in part three of this study, mirror those occurring throughout the advanced capitalist world. The process of economic change, dramatically accelerated by the current preparations for the construction of a single European market (SEM) by the end of 1992, and the concomitant withdrawal of the state from the management of national economies, raises the possibility of a convergence in national forms of labor regulation. If so, the "exceptionalism" of the French labor movement, which was so apparent for forty years after the Second World War, is a thing of the past.

The Rise and Decline
of Fordist Labor Regulation

PART TWO OF THIS STUDY examines the evolution of labor regulation in France up to 1981 when the Socialists arrived in power. In the first chapter the notion of labor regulation was introduced and a series of ideal-type models of labor regulation were constructed. It was argued that each form of labor regulation results from the combination of a specific stage of capitalist growth and a particular structure and organization of the working class. It is this dual determination that gives states the capacity to influence labor regulation because, while the pattern of economic growth is usually outside the control of particular governments and individual states, at least in the short to medium term, states are able to alter the way in which workers are organized and the institutional forms that mediate the relationship between capital and labor. It is these latter factors that the French state, in its Gaullist, neo-Gaullist, liberal, and Socialist guises sought to change after 1968.

This part of the study is divided into four broadly chronological chapters. The period covered, from 1945 to 1981, saw a dual movement in the evolution of the French economy. There was first, in the period between the mid-1950s and the early 1970s, the slow transformation of the French economy from extensive accumulation, with a reliance upon the transfer of resources from agriculture to industry and upon protected colonial markets, to a modern industrial economy in which mass-production techniques are linked, through mechanisms that ensure regular increases in domestic demand (collective bargaining, transfer payments), to mass consumption, thus completing the virtuous circle of growth, which is associated with the term "Fordism." Then, after the first oil shock, and almost as soon as it had appeared in France, the Fordist regime of accumulation appeared to go into crisis all over the advanced capitalist world. France was no exception.

Against this backdrop of tremendous change in the very nature of the French economy, the chapters covering the period 1945–81 trace the construction and then collapse of a mode of labor regulation appropriate to the transformations taking place in the economy. Thus within the context of structural change in the economy, these chapters are concerned with the ways in which different governments responded to those pressures emanating from economic change. State policy is important precisely because those pressures transmitted no clear message, nor did they offer clear solutions. Rather governments had choices, and how they formulated those choices, how they implemented them, and what fate befell them is the main subject matter of these chapters.

It is this that explains the pivotal significance accorded the events of May–June 1968 in this study. The year 1968 was important for two reasons. First, it was one of those very rare occurrences in which the incongruence between deep structural change in the economy and the societal institutions that regulate such change become clearly visible to contemporaries, visible in such a way as to *demand* action of some kind. Second, the scale of the events of 1968, and their interpretation by government officials and major social actors, set the agenda of industrial relations reform for the next twenty years. Thus 1968 gave the French state a stake in the evolution of labor regulation.

Chapter 2 examines the period up to 1958, with the emphasis on the period after the Liberation. The chapter first describes what was peculiar, in comparative perspective, about labor organization and labor regulation in France. Thus the chapter discusses the historical frailty of the French labor movement, the weakness of trade unions, the poor institutionalization of collective-bargaining mechanisms, the high level of industrial conflict, and the reliance upon the labor market as the main instrument of labor regulation.

These characteristics of the labor movement and labor regulation in France were able to survive well into the postwar period, in marked contrast to much of the rest of Western Europe. This was possible because the French economy was not yet fully Fordist in this period. The main engine of growth remained the addition of new productive factors through the gradual shift of resources out of agriculture and colonial trade. Domestic mass consumption was not yet a major component of growth. The result was that there was no incompatibility between regulation by the labor market and continued economic growth, and thus only limited pressure for a change in the mode of labor regulation.

Chapter 3 documents the way in which this situation changed, under the impetus of the program of rapid economic modernization launched by Charles de Gaulle after 1958. This program had as its goal precisely the creation of a modern Fordist economy, able to compete with the advanced capitalist economies in the newly created European Economic Community (EEC). The very success of this program, however, set up severe strains in the industrial relations system. The trade unions, and labor more generally, were excluded from the Gaullist coalition and bore the heavy costs of modernization and restructuring in terms of unemployment and wage restraint in both the public and private sectors. The mode of labor regulation, relying as it did upon the labor market, lacked the mechanisms for dealing with industrial conflict in the workplace, particularly collective-bargaining mechanisms. That absence became increasingly dangerous as the decade of the 1960s wore on, and was severely felt by the large, modern technologically advanced firms being created by economic restructuring that had the most to lose from labor market regulation.

The result, in the context of a student revolt, was May 1968—the largest strike wave in postwar French history. Various interpretations of May

1968 were proffered in the weeks and months that followed, but the most influential were those that stressed the need to "modernize" French industrial relations in such a way as to make industrial relations more capable of defusing social conflict in the workplace before it snowballed into the political arena. The appeal of this interpretation was that it did not challenge the goal of continued economic modernization, but rather sought to better adapt the structures of French society to that modernization. Thus both the importance of industrial relations reform, and the agenda for that reform, were set by 1968. That agenda, with small exceptions, was followed up to the first years of the Socialist experiment in power after 1981.

Chapter 3 ends with a brief discussion of the abortive reform effort undertaken by de Gaulle after 1968. This effort sought to bypass trade unions, and through *participation*, create an embryonic microcorporatist mode of labor regulation. The project ran into the renewed strength of French trade unions, and the incompatibility between microcorporatist labor regulation and Fordist accumulation. In short, neither trade unions nor employers saw *participation* as a solution. De Gaulle left office within a year of May 1968.

Chapter 4 is a detailed examination of the "New Society" industrial relations reform of George Pompidou's first prime minister, Jacques Chaban-Delmas. This reform project very deliberately set out to replace the labor market, as the main instrument of labor regulation, with collective bargaining. Thus a coherent set of measures sought simultaneously to strengthen trade unions and encourage collective bargaining in both the private and public sectors. The reform effort was undertaken in a privileged economic and political conjuncture and at a time when important segments of the business class supported reform.

Nevertheless, the reforms were only partly successful. Collective bargaining did take hold in the public sector, where the government had the most influence, and there was an increase in bargaining at the industry (or branch) level in the Fordist sector of the private economy. But elsewhere, and particularly at the firm level, unions remained largely excluded and collective bargaining was very limited. Here the early 1970s saw an expansion of state intervention in labor regulation to, as it were, *substitute* for the weakness of trade unions and collective bargaining. Thus the French state, despite being controlled by a conservative, neo-Gaullist government, in fact stepped in to take a more active role in labor regulation in a way that benefited workers.

By the time of the first oil shock it was the case that, even where collective bargaining did exist, it remained contingent upon the favor of employers and the state, and on a strong economy. Chapter 5 traces the collapse of both these conditions. The oil shock soon revealed the weakness of Fordism in all advanced capitalist economies. In the face of a profits squeeze, ballooning budget deficit, and economic uncertainty, the pillars of the New Society began to erode. Lucrative public-sector wage contracts could no longer be afforded, extensive state intervention now appeared to obstruct the ability of firms to adapt to economic uncertainty, and even large firms, which had spearheaded the drive for collective bargaining after 1968, began to question its utility in the new economic context. Thus the highly contingent nature of the New Society's success was revealed.

In this context Giscard d'Estaing and his prime ministers Jacques Chirac and Raymond Barre attempted a series of industrial relations reforms, including a reform of the firm in 1975–76 and an effort to reinvigorate collective bargaining after 1978. But these reform efforts largely failed because they ran into a stalemate. Trade unions were still too strong, and workers too important in political terms, to be ignored, and yet the material base for collective bargaining had collapsed. The result was that the old mode of labor regulation was in crisis, but no alternative had appeared.

This was the situation facing the French Socialist party when it came to power in 1981. Part III will examine the attempt by the French Socialists to deal with this stalemate, and with the construction, under their aegis, of a new mode of labor regulation.

CHAPTER TWO

Exclusionary Labor Regulation, 1945–58

DEBATES CONCERNING France have often used the notion of exceptionalism to describe the peculiarity of French political and social life. The term has enjoyed a renaissance in the late 1980s as commentators argue about the facts and merits of "normalization." Many see the enduring achievement of François Mitterrand's first decade in the Élysée Palace as bringing about a fundamental modernization, deradicalization, and general "catching up" with the rest of the advanced capitalist world. Whatever the merits of this case (and I will have more to say about it in later chapters), it assumes postwar exceptionalism. This judgment is essentially accurate. The specificity of France lies in its lack of an historical compromise between capital and labor, either in the 1930s or 1940s. While the terms of the historical compromise varied in West Germany, Austria, Britain, and the Scandinavian countries, that some form of class compromise was reached is not in doubt. In contrast, France did not develop an institutionalized collective-bargaining system, its trade unions were weak and legally insecure in the workplace, wage determination occurred primarily through the labor market, and leftist parties played little or no role in the political life of the country. In short, the political and industrial representatives of the working class were essentially excluded from the political and economic structures that emerged from World War II. This situation did not begin to change until 1968.

This chapter describes and explains that exclusionary settlement. It has two main purposes. The first is largely descriptive: to describe the system of French industrial relations and the structural and organizational weakness of the French working class, both in an effort to understand why France did not develop the corporatist or collective-bargaining mechanisms that were common elsewhere, and because it was this system of industrial relations that became the object of the state's attention after 1968. The chapters that follow tell the detailed story of attempts to intervene and change the industrial relations system. This chapter, therefore, sets the scene for the rest of the study.

Second, this chapter argues that at least until 1968 France had a mode of labor regulation that accorded primacy to labor market wage determination. Labor market regulation was possible because of the structural and organizational weakness of the French working class, but it was also a *necessary* component of the model of economic growth adopted after World

War II. France did not develop a Fordist or intensive form of accumulation until the second burst of modernization initiated by de Gaulle after 1958. In the postwar model of development, growth depended more on low wages and work intensification than the consumer demand–led growth characteristic of Fordism.

INDUSTRIALIZATION, WORKING CLASS FORMATION, AND LABOR REGULATION

The physiognomy of the French working class diverges from that of its European counterparts in significant ways. Understanding the characteristics of this workers' movement is a necessary precondition for discussion of the possibilities and limitations of labor regulation in France.[1] The previous chapter argued that a mode of labor regulation is a product of a dual determination—the organization and structure of labor, and the stage of capitalist growth. The next four sections will discuss the organizational and structural characteristics of the French labor movement, and the sixth section will discuss the evolution of the French economy up to 1958.

The relationship between a mode of industrialization and the process of working-class formation is complex and the subject of contentious debate. The debate centers on the relative importance of economic and political determinants of class formation. It is probably true that the traditional picture of economic backwardness and slow industrialization in France, leading in turn to the creation of a backward working class—both more militant and less strong organizationally—is a caricature. The mode of industrialization was a different (not simply more backward) version of the British industrial revolution.[2] This difference did influence the particular development of the French working class. At the same time, however, Judt and Gallie have strongly argued that the political development and social organization of the working class cannot be simply read off from the type of economic development.[3] Let us look first at the early stages of French industrialization in the nineteenth century.

The process of industrialization in France was marked by a strong rural bias. Not only did the agricultural sector remain strong well into the twentieth century, but even industry itself was often located in rural areas and tended to employ workers who kept one foot in agriculture and the other in industry.[4] The implications for working-class formation and organization were threefold. First, the process of proletarianization—both structural separation from the means of production, and the ideological construction of proletarian identity—was limited because industrial workers in rural areas often retained property, a means of subsistence, and a rural identity. Second, this rural bias ensured that an individual "escape hatch" always existed as an alternative to industrial organization and militancy. Cottereau has pointed out that no equivalent to England's New Poor Law existed to cut off alternatives to wage labor.[5] The persistence of a large rural sector acted as a kind of equivalent to the American frontier. Third, the industrial structure that emerged in the middle of the nineteenth century, based on an economy in which luxury goods remained the leading sector until well into the 1870s, was equally unconducive to working-class organization. Firms were tiny and dispersed. Noiriel points out that at the end of the century there was one worker for every two employers.[6] This was, then, overwhelmingly an economy based on small commodity production with limited wage labor.

The structural factors were exacerbated by political ones, primarily repression during the Second Empire. Repression against worker organizations by the police was accompanied by a withdrawal of the state from labor regulation. For instance, the *livret*, used to control the behavior and movement of workers, was abolished in 1854. One outcome of the Paris Commune was the decapitation of the nascent workers' movement, with the result (as both Judt and Sewell confirm) both that the degree of worker organization was weakened, and its ideology shifted from a socialist orientation toward less statist, more industrial forms.[7] Thus, revolutionary syndicalism was the ideological and organizational response and the manner in which the French working class entered the twentieth century.

While French economic growth accelerated in the twentieth century, especially from 1920–29, it did so in ways that did not encourage working-class organization. Again, the size of industrial establishments was a constraint. There was a remarkable stability in the industrial structure throughout the twentieth century. While there was a steady decline in the proportion of firms employing less than eleven employees,[8] the proportion of those employed in firms with eleven or more employees remained almost static. Even as late as 1962, 88.2 percent of all firms employed less than ten people.[9]

Ingham has argued that a relationship exists between the size and concentration of business, and the organizational capacity of labor.[10] This relationship clearly made labor organization very difficult in France. With many firms being family owned and managed, the familiar pattern of paternalistic management, and a virulent antiunionism (with unions characterized as "outsiders"), combined with a precarious economic existence at the margins of profitability to make social relations in the firm deeply conflictual.

The actual size of the working class is only a rough indication of the potential for organization, but it nevertheless remains an outer limit for a certain kind of traditional blue-collar trade union organization. So it is significant that the size of the working class stagnated throughout the twentieth century, until the late 1960s.[11] Wage earners (the working class broadly defined) remained at a constant 40 to 42 percent of the adult population from 1901 to 1968. Using a narrower definition, the industrial, manual working class peaked at 18 percent of the adult population in 1931 and thereafter declined. This is in contrast with Sweden (in many ways the polar opposite of France in terms of worker organization) where not only was the working class larger, but it increased steadily in size until 1950, twenty years after the French working class had begun to decrease in size relative to other social groups.[12] Also of tremendous importance was the massive wave of immigration in the 1920s, which was on a larger scale than immigration into the United States at the same time, and which destroyed the areas of working-class combativity, except for the public sector where jobs were reserved for French citizens.[13]

Once again, the importance of structural economic factors for working-class formation was compounded by politics. Gallie has discussed the repressive state response to worker militancy during and after the First World War.[14] Then there was the split on the Left into Communists and Socialists—mirrored briefly in the union movement by the split into the Confédération Générale du Travail (CGT) and the Confédération Générale du Travail Unitaire (CGTU)—which was both cause and consequence of the chronic weakness of labor in France. Finally, the interwar period saw a series of unfriendly or incompetent governments, sometimes both at the same time, which denied legislative protection or encouragement to an already crippled workers' movement. Despite the rapid growth of collective bargaining at the time of the Popular Front, gains were never institutionalized as the coalition of the Left showed a marked reluctance to antagonize employers.

This, then, was the situation in 1945: a small, poorly organized working class; social and political repression; and very limited collective bargaining. The question that must still be posed is why this initial weakness was not overcome in the postwar period. Up until 1945, the story of French working-class formation was not markedly different from much of the rest of Western Europe. While differences certainly existed, low unionization and the exclusion of organized labor from both the political and the industrial spheres was not unusual in the interwar period in Europe. French exceptionalism appears in the divergence of the French experience in the postwar period. Three key features of postwar French industrial relations will now be examined: the absence of collective bargaining, the weakness and division of the trade union movement, and the peculiar dual form of worker representation in the firm.

COLLECTIVE BARGAINING AND THE STATE

It is important to note that 1945 marked a break in the role of the state in industrial relations, as well as more broadly in the area of economic intervention. France is often assumed to have had an unbroken tradition from

1789 to the present, by way of Bonapartism, of a strong, dominant state. In fact, the interventionist state in France dates from 1945. Kuisel has done an excellent job of showing the persistence of laissez-faire, market-conforming tendencies on the part of the French state, and the repeated failure of planning and interventionist initiatives.[15] By and large, governments acknowledged the necessity of leaving economic growth to the market and business. Thus, when the state emerged in its more familiar interventionist guise after 1945, it was not because of a Jacobin tradition stretching back a hundred and fifty years, but rather because of the new demands of the French economy and a new balance of social forces. This new situation was marked by the weakness of business leaders who stood accused of both collaboration during Vichy and responsibility for the economic backwardness that had ensured swift military defeat in 1940.[16]

Before World War II the state had kept out of industrial relations, leaving the regulation of industrial conflict to workers and employers. Under the circumstances, this meant that industrial relations were regulated on the employers' terms. What collective bargaining did exist was usually a response to an outburst of militancy. Thus collective bargaining correlated strongly with high strike levels (in 1919 and 1936 for instance, when employers had their backs to the wall and had to negotiate to end strikes).[17]

In 1945 the French state attempted to make a radical break with its past noninterventionist role in industrial relations. The law of December 23, 1946, was an attempt to reconcile collective bargaining with *dirigiste* economic planning (this was the phase of reconstruction) that completely failed. National bargaining agreements were required as a precursor to regional or local agreements. Only one agreement was permitted in each branch, and it was fully inclusive; in other words, it would include all workers and employers in that branch of economic activity. Finally, every agreement required government approval. It is hardly surprising that these restrictions ensured that collective bargaining would not occur, and only twelve agreements were signed between 1946 and 1950.

This failure led to a major revision of the law on collective bargaining in the law of February 11, 1950, which remains the basis for French industrial relations today, albeit in much amended form. This framework was more realistic, not least because the economic situation was less urgent. While it placed fewer restrictions on free collective bargaining, it nevertheless remained, as Durand stresses, a clear break with the prewar situation, in that a wider role was accorded the state and significant legislative restrictions were placed on the bargaining process.[18] The branch level was privileged with the intention that firm-level accords *follow* and *modify* agreements reached at a higher level. The 1950 legislation retained the 1946 innovation which only allowed "representative" trade unions to sign agreements. Representativeness was decided by the state on the basis of certain criteria relating to membership and independence from employers. In addition, while government approval was no longer required for collective agreements, an agreement could be "extended" so that it applied more widely than the signatories intended. Thus a partial agreement might be extended to an entire industry or a whole region.

The 1950 legislation, therefore, left the social partners free to bargain on wages. But with the introduction of the *Salaire Minimum Interprofessionnel Garanti* (SMIG), or minimum wage, in 1947, the state developed the capacity to influence wage levels. The SMIG was the floor from which collective bargains departed, and for large sectors of industry and commerce where collective bargaining was absent the SMIG was the wage level.

The only major development in the realm of collective bargaining between 1950 and 1968 was the "Renault-style" works agreement.[19] A firm-level agreement was signed at Renault in 1955, following widespread industrial disruption. Its new elements made it an important departure from the norm of collective-bargaining agreements. First, it was an accord initiated at the firm level and not simply a modification or adaptation of a branch-level agreement. Second, the Renault agreement was a two-year contract rather than the usual practice of agreements which lasted indefinitely until supplanted by a new agreement or revoked by the employer. Third, the agreement had an impressive package of benefits, particularly the introduction of three weeks' paid vacation. Fourth, the signatories agreed to exhaust all the bargaining and mediation possibilities before resorting to industrial action. This kind of commitment from trade unions had been completely absent from industrial relations in France (for reasons that will be discussed in the next section). Fifth, and most important, wage levels were explicitly tied to the cost of living and anticipated productivity gains (4 percent a year in the case of the Renault agreement).

The Renault works agreement was deeply Fordist in inspiration in that it provided high wages, pegged to prices and productivity, in order to encourage industrial peace, limit work-force turnover, allow long-term planning on the part of the firm, and ensure a regular, steady rise in demand. At the microlevel the Renault agreement was tying consumer demand to productivity. As a modern advanced firm, Renault on the one hand could afford to pay high wages, while on the other hand it needed cooperation from its work force to avoid turnover and disruption.

However, it would be wrong to see the works agreements as a harbinger of the future, initiating a development of decentralized collective bargaining. While it is true that a Gaullist incomes policy after 1963 was responsible for the collapse of bargaining in the 1960s, the works agreements had exhausted their potential well before then. This form of agreement was not widely copied. About fifty such accords were signed, all in very large and modern metalworking, electrical, and chemical firms. The popularity of these accords was very brief, and only a few were signed after mid-1956. The potential of Fordist wage agreements was quickly exhausted in the French economy of the mid-1950s. The French economy was in fact remarkably homogeneous in the sense of not being divided into advanced and traditional sectors.[20] The firms that made this kind of agreement were few and unlike the bulk of French industry. The CNPF was deeply suspicious of the works agreements, and smaller firms were outraged by the high level of wages being offered. Most firms could not afford this level of wages.

The potential for replicating these agreements was also limited by the trade unions. The labor peace clause was only possible where unions were strong and had a fairly stable membership. Nowhere outside these few firms was this true. Even at Renault the CGT was deeply suspicious of the agreement, and when it expired in 1957 negotiations to extend or replace it repeatedly broke down, until a new agreement was finally signed in 1959. Thus, while the Renault-style works agreements were a significant development, their importance lay more in demonstrating just how limited the applicability of Fordist productivity and industrial peace agreements was in France in the 1950s.

Collective bargaining grew in the postwar period, but it did so fitfully, with wild swings that corresponded closely to the state of the economy, government economic policy, and the strike level. Rather than varying inversely with the strike level, collective bargaining occurred in conjunction with strikes. This is particularly clear in the period after 1954 as table 2.1 demonstrates. Thus bargaining was not an *alternative* to industrial conflict so much as a *response* to it. This underscores the fragility of collective bargaining and its lack of an existence independent of the business cycle.

It is hard to evaluate the importance of the state in explaining the weakness of collective bargaining. It can be argued that the state smothered autonomous bargaining with its direct intervention in industrial relations via the procedure of extension and the national minimum wage. This seems implausible. The extension procedure was used when it became clear that important gains from a contract were not going to be replicated *unless* the state intervened. The generalization of the three-week paid vacation is a case in point. Certainly the state often pursued economic policies that made collective bargaining more difficult (for instance after 1963), but it is precisely the point of regularized bargaining that it can operate both in good and poor economic conditions. The outcomes may be different due to the different economic context, but the process should remain. This was not the case in France.

Numerous commentators have stressed that strike action and negotiation in France exist in an unarticulated relationship. As Adam and Reynaud put it, in France, "There has never been an institutional and almost automatic articulation between strikes and negotiations, between negotiations

44 · Chapter Two

TABLE 2.1
Strikes and Collective-Bargaining Agreements, 1950–67

	Work Days Lost in Strikes (in millions)	Collective-Bargaining Agreements
1950	11.71	47
1951	3.29	156
1952	1.75	104
1953	9.72	91
1954	1.44	184
1955	3.08	578
1956	1.42	538
1957	4.12	835
1958	1.32	1,023
1959	1.94	624
1960	1.07	529
1961	2.60	940
1962	1.90	1,020
1963	5.99	1,197
1964	2.50	814
1965	0.98	906
1966	2.52	1,054
1967	4.20	1,162

Source: Adapted from figures provided in René Mouriaux and Françoise Subileau, "Données statistiques concernant le syndicalisme des salariés en France (1945–1986)," Document du Travail (Paris: CEVIPOF, 1986), 24, 37–38.

and agreements, between agreements and industrial peace, of the type common to the Anglo-Saxon countries."[21] French industrial relations are a constant conflict in which neither side recognizes gains as legitimate or durable. Negotiations occur when unions are strong enough to impose them on management (and then they often follow industrial action), or when management needs the cooperation of workers. In the first twenty years after World War II neither of these conditions occurred with any regularity, with the result that collective bargaining was unable to develop a regular and stable existence independent of economic conditions and cyclical waves of industrial militancy. The key to understanding this weakness lies in the nature of French trade unionism.

FRENCH TRADE UNIONS

The French trade union movement fragmented in the postwar period for largely political reasons. The public-sector federations of the CGT split to form the CGT–Force Ouvrière (CGT-FO, or FO for short), and the large education federation formed an independent union as the Fédération d'Education Nationale (FEN), in protest against communist domination of the CGT. In 1964 the growing ideological division within the Confédération Française des Travailleurs Chrétiens (CFTC) concerning deconfessionalization became an organizational division, and the Confédération Française Démocratique du Travail (CFDT) was formed.[22]

French trade unions have, historically, faced tremendous disadvantages. The predominance, and persistence, of small firms has meant that the environment has been deeply hostile to trade unions, and indeed to any form of workers' organization. In 1967, half of those firms that by law should have created works councils (*comités d'entreprises*) had not, and since such councils were obligatory only in firms employing over fifty employees or more, the overwhelming majority of firms had no works council.[23] Unions had no legally secure place in the firm until 1968, and even after 1968 small firms (employing less than fifty people) were not obligated to allow union sections. Aujard and Volkoff have shown that where professional elections are held for works councils the proportion of votes cast for the nationally representative unions decreases rapidly as firms get smaller.[24] Repression in the firm—the intimidation of union activists—has not been something limited to only a few rare cases, nor is it a thing of the past. Certain forms of legal protection exist, particularly since 1968, but there are too many gray areas for real safeguards.

In addition, French unions have very limited funds and tiny organizational apparatuses. No "dues checkoff" exists and the closed shop has arisen only in a very few unusual cases. The result is a low and strongly fluctuating level of unionization. The average for the postwar period is close to 25 percent, which compares unfavorably with most West European countries.[25] Sellier has estimated the rate of unionization as ranging wildly, from 9.5 percent in 1930–31, to 45 percent in 1936, back down to 23 percent in 1954 and 17.3 percent in 1962, and up to 25 percent in 1972.[26] There appears to be no "ratchet effect," in that sudden gains in membership due to particular political and economic conditions—the Popular Front, for instance—are lost in their entirety once the conditions pass. French trade unions have been unable to institutionalize their periodic gains and create a high and stable level of membership.

It is also important to note that this low level of unionization is fairly constant from one industry to another in the private sector. According to Reynaud, even the metalworking sector had only about a 20 percent level of unionization in 1962.[27] Thus there is no real *motor*, or leading sector, in the area of unionization. This accords well with Piore's assertion that the French economy, until the late 1960s, did not exhibit marked segmentation into sectors that were covered by collective agreements and those that were not, or between those that were organized and those that were not.[28]

The big exception to this picture is the public sector. Greater job security and less repression have been more conducive to unionization. All unions are overrepresented in the public sector. In 1975 the public sector accounted for 27.3 percent of all employees, but it made up 42.6 percent of CGT membership, over 50 percent of the membership of FO, and 32 percent of the CFDT's membership.[29]

This study limits itself to discussion of the CGT, CFDT, and FO. The CFTC is now a withered rump of its former self, and the Confédération Générale des Cadres (CGC) and FEN, while interesting, are limited to managerial staff and the educational field respectively. The issues of labor regulation are different in those areas. Of the three largest unions, there is one crucial difference that sets FO apart from the other two and no doubt largely explains its more reformist and contractualist ideology, and cooperative strategy.[30] That difference lies in the fact that while the CGT and CFDT compete for the same constituency of workers, FO does not. Despite recent advances in the private sector, FO is still overwhelmingly a public-sector union. Clearly the CFDT has areas of strength and weakness that differ from those of the CGT, but the two unions nevertheless compete in many sectors and are deeply aware of being competitors. As Adam puts it, a "relationship of exclusion exists between the CGT and the CFDT: their competitive relationship means that the progress of one almost always comes at the expense of the other."[31] This competition has crucial implications for the ideologies and behavior of the CGT and CFDT. Knowing that they compete for the same membership, there is a disincentive for one to call for sacrifice from rank-and-file members because of the expectation that the other union will be able to pose as defender of workers and make inroads into their membership.[32] This is exacerbated by the system of professional elections, a problem that will be discussed in the next section.

The relationship between the weakness of collective bargaining and the major trade unions' undeniable ambivalence toward negotiation is complicated. Two kinds of argument are usually made to explain the reluctance of the CGT and CFDT to engage in collective bargaining. The first is structural, relating to the costs and dangers of collective bargaining for unions, and argues that unions are organizationally unable to enter into agreements that limit their freedom to take industrial action. This is the argument that will be advanced here (and elaborated below). The second argument is a political one, and it is sufficiently widespread to make consideration of it necessary. It is incumbent on me to offer at least a tentative model of union action, especially because how and why unions reacted to reform initiatives after 1968 was a function of the degree to which their motivations are structural and organizational rather than political.

The political argument has essentially two strands. The first stresses the strong links that exist between French unions (the political argument concerns the CFDT and CGT, the most combative, militant unions) and the sphere of politics, particularly political parties. Thus the CGT has close ties to the PCF, and it has been argued that CGT industrial action has often been subordinated to the electoral needs of the PCF.[33] Politics is of less clear importance to the CFDT, but it is true that after 1970 the CFDT became explicitly committed to socialist transformation and the success of the Socialist-Communist political alliance. The second strand of the political argument focuses on the radical, oppositional ideologies that bias the CGT and CFDT against any "normalization" of industrial relations, and integration into bargaining structures.

The charge that French unions are overly politicized, in some comparative sense, is difficult to sustain. French trade unions are actually less politicized, in terms of their links to political parties and their agendas, than many more successful national union movements (such as their British, Swedish, and West German counterparts). All these union movements have repeatedly called upon their members to make material sacrifices for the electoral needs of social democratic and labor parties. The politicization charge, in fact, slides into the more general argument about radical ideologies. The CGT's problem is not that it subordinates its activity to *a* political party, but rather that it does so to a *communist* party.

Now clearly the ideological radicalism of the CGT and CFDT is important. Until recent strategic changes in the CFDT, neither union has placed much emphasis on stable industrial relations and both have been deeply hostile to wage restraint. Employers' hostility to trade unions is no doubt related to the antisystem, anticapitalist rhetoric of the CGT and CFDT. Valenzuela has described French trade unionism as a "contestatory" unionism, a notion that parallels Sartori's notion of "polarized pluralism" in the realm of political parties.[34] For Valenzuela, the characteristics of a polarized and divided union movement, a union leadership highly responsive to the rank and file, and the politicization of industrial conflict leads to "demand maximalization," similar again to Sartori's description of centrifugal pressures acting on political parties in a situation of polarized pluralism.

However, the question that must be posed is whether these undeniably radical ideologies are the cause of union action, or whether union action results from other factors. The answer is important because any attempts to "modernize" industrial relations—of which there were many after 1968—must decide whether the problem lay in the structures of industrial relations or the ideologies of the players.[35] The position taken here is that ideology is considerably more *plastic* and justificatory than the political explanation admits. Unions in France seek to "valorize their exclusion" from the industrial and political sphere. An oppositional ideology is more a response to, than a cause of, the exclusion of French unions.

Gallie has characterized French workers as having "political class consciousness," in the sense of correctly identifying themselves as workers, of being resentful toward employers, and of seeing a link between exploitation in the firm and the potential for wider political change. But Gallie discovered that the source of this greater radicalism lay not in exposure to radical union or party ideologies, but rather in the industrial relations system. As he put it: "It was above all the experience of work and the way in which it was mediated by the institutional system of industrial relations that appeared to account for the much more intense resentment."[36] Thus Gallie's study echoes the arguments of the British School of Industrial Relations in its focus on the role that institutionalized structures and procedures of collective bargaining have in creating a buffer to prevent industrial conflict from spilling over into political conflict. This emphasis on the structures of industrial relations is shared in French industrial sociology and is well demonstrated in Adam and Reynaud's *Conflits du Travail et Changement Social*.

From the corporatist perspective, Schain has made a similar point.[37] He sees the problem of French trade unions as being organizational. In contrast to, say, Sweden, union elites are unable to control their members. Union competition, the lack of stable membership, and so on means that unions are unable to enter into long-term contracts that limit their ability to resort to industrial action without risking organizational fragmentation. In France unions are rarely able to call up strikes; rather they adopt strikes that arise spontaneously (hence the relatively low level of unofficial, or wildcat strikes in France; most strikes originate unofficially, but they are soon supported by unions). If unions limited their own ability to follow strikes they would risk being viewed as irrelevant by their members. When unions do call strikes they are likely to be short "political" strikes, not because the unions are deeply politicized but because such strikes have a low organizational cost.

Thus the primary reason why French trade unions are reluctant to enter into regularized collective bargaining lies in the structural weakness and underinstitutionalization of the industrial relations system. This sets up incentives for "irresponsible" actions on the part of unions and employers. Unions excluded from the workplace until 1968 were unable to build up a stable membership or control their members. The result was that they could not sign agreements that committed them to maintaining industrial peace. French unionism is a "mobilizational" unionism so that unions give up their ability to mobilize workers at the cost of organizational extinction. Trade unions in France "canalize and amplify" spontaneous action,[38] they do not call it up or control it.

On the employers' side there is a deep-seated hostility to trade unions that is no doubt exacerbated by union rhetoric and the particular form of authoritarian paternalism associated with small firms operating at the margins of profitability. But, more important, even if employers were more progressively minded, they would have no incentive to deal with unions because the latter are unable to deliver industrial peace. For both unions and employers, there was little likelihood of a modernization of attitudes until a modernization of the structures of industrial relations occurred.

WORKER REPRESENTATION IN THE FIRM

The third major feature of postwar French industrial relations, after the weakness of collective bargaining and the peculiarity of trade union action, is the system of worker representation in the workplace. Until 1968 unions did not have a legally secure place in the workplace and existed largely *outside* the walls of the firm. France thus had a dual form of worker representation and the potential for competition and conflict between trade unions and firm-specific forms of worker representation.

In February 1945 legislation was enacted that made it obligatory to set up a works council in all firms in the private sector employing fifty people or more.[39] The potential range of functions of the works council was very wide, but the only subject on which the employer was obligated to negotiate with it was use of the funds earmarked for social works in the firm.[40] On other collective issues, like working conditions and the introduction of new technology, the works councils were advisory only. The function of the works councils was explicitly integrative—that is to say, their purpose was to eliminate conflict between workers and management inside the firm. Elections for works councils are held every two years and operate in two rounds. In the first round there is a so-called union monopoly, which means that only "representative" unions can present candidates. In the second round nonunion and "house unions" can present candidates. Thus trade unions gained access to the firm (before 1968) not directly, via union sections, but indirectly as candidates competing for votes in elections for the works council.

In April 1946 another piece of legislation created the *délégués de personnel* in all firms with eleven or more employees. They were designed to present individual claims to management, though in places where no works council existed they also performed the functions of the works council.

There are two important implications of this form of worker representation. First, trade unions in France view workers in a variety of different roles: as members, as clients, and as electors. With union membership so low and subject to rapid fluctuation, the strength and influence of trade unions tends to be judged by their capacity to win votes in professional elections. Thus unions relate to workers as candidates for election, and there is a strong disincentive for unions to call for sacrifice. Professional elections are popularity contests that privilege short-term horizons. When a union does badly in elections the reaction is typically to become *more* militant and defensive of workers' material interests. The result is to set up a dynamic that is the opposite to that of corporatism. Corporatist trade union movements use their control over the rank and file to call for sacrifice in the industrial sphere in return for political and social gains, what Pizzorno termed "political exchange."[41] French trade union leaders are controlled by their rank-and-file members *and* all other workers who are potential voters. This makes them highly responsive to the immediate concerns of workers and unwilling to attempt political exchange.

The second implication of the firm-specific form of worker representation in France is the potential danger it posed for the period after 1968. Employers did not like the institution of the works council. They suspected any form of worker organization or counterweight in the firm, and they rarely shared the left-wing Gaullists faith in the potential for labor-management harmony in the firm.[42] As mentioned above, by 1967 fully half of those firms subject to the 1945 legislation had not created works councils. However, these firm-based worker collectivities contained within them the seeds of an alternative to union penetration of the firm. They provided the *structural potential* of a "microcorporatist" form of labor regulation. It was a potential that assumed increasing importance after 1968.

The nature of French industrial relations and the weakness of the trade union movement made the establishment of regularized collective bargaining very difficult. The preconditions for bargaining simply did not exist. The critique of collective bargaining in France made by Lyon-Caen is useful here.[43] Lyon-Caen argues that regularized collective bargaining in the sense of negotiating *real* wages, and involving commitments on both sides—for instance, industrial peace for the life of the contract—has typically not occurred. Rather agreements are reached to end industrial disputes or do not involve real wages or reciprocal commitments. There has not been, in other words, any need for trade unions in these agreements. Collective bargaining does not regulate wage levels; the labor market and employers do: "Negotiation is only a pretence. The employers make suggestions; one either subscribes to them or one doesn't. Is that negotiating?"[44] Real collective bargaining can only occur with stronger unions. A relative balance between unions and management is the precondition for collective bargaining that is anything more than disguised management dictate: "If there is no balance of power one cannot speak of collective bargaining. . . . One cannot develop negotiation without developing trade unionism, and without limiting, in compensation, certain of the employers' prerogatives."[45]

Corporatist labor regulation was equally impossible. A series of corporatist *institutions* were created after World War II—planning commissions and the Conseil Économique et Social—but they were empty institutions with purely advisory functions. Successive French governments showed no willingness to modify the direction or pace of economic modernization in the 1950s and 1960s in response to the concerns of the trade unions. The CGT boycotted the planning commissions; the CFDT stayed until the Sixth Plan, but without enthusiasm.

However, regardless of the intentions of policymakers, it was structurally impossible to turn these institutions into meaningful tools of corporatist regulation. The national union confederations could not make the necessary commitment to wage restraint, which would be needed to make them reliable corporatist partners. Following the description above, French industrial relations encourages a *reversal* of the corporatist model in the sense that union elites are incapable of gaining autonomy from their members. Keeler, by demonstrating that corporatism did develop in the agricultural sector, has shown that the lack of corporatism in industry was due to the characteristics of the groups involved, not some innate predisposition of the French state against corporatism.[46] The result was what Ross has called a "labor exclusionary postwar settlement."[47] Labor was excluded both from the workplace and national economic policy-making by virtue of organizational weakness and the lack of a labor-based political party capable of winning power.

Both collective-bargaining and corporatist mechanisms of labor regulation require a widening of labor collectivity and, ultimately, a strengthening of trade unions. The French state did not contemplate moving in this direction until the crisis of May 1968.

The Historical Frailty of Fordism in France

One part of French exceptionalism lies in the absence of an "historical compromise" in the 1930s or in the immediate postwar period. Such a compromise would have rested on the mutual recognition by business and labor of each other's right to exist. Business would accept the legitimacy of unions, their right to operate within the firm, and their role as the natural interlocutor of the working class. Unions, in turn, would acknowledge the legitimacy of private property, and the right of employers to appropriate surplus value and control the work process. Wherever historical compromises have occurred they have generally been characterized by Keynesian policies to maintain full employment, welfare programs, and the acceptance of labor-based political parties as legitimate parties of government. This picture contrasts with postwar France in almost every respect. The labor exclusionary settlement ensured weak, divided trade unions, limited collective bargaining, and no solid Socialist majority until 1981.

This situation raises two important questions. One concerns the relationship of this postwar settlement to the development of French capitalism. The pattern of historical compromise in much of Western Europe was not *only* a response to stronger labor movements (a threat that was lacking in France) but was also a response to the new patterns of growth in the advanced capitalist economies that emerged from World War II. Thus collective bargaining (including its high-level corporatist form) and stronger trade unions served to redistribute income toward workers who formed a mass consumer market for intensive growth. This was one manner of avoiding a repetition of the chronic lack of demand that had plagued economies in the late 1920s, and that ultimately led to the Depression. There has already been discussion of why France lacked a strong labor movement, but if there was no push by labor for integration, why was there no pull from business or the state toward integration? Why did the French state apparently not need a form of regulation that permitted the translation of productivity gains into wage gains, and hence consumer demand? In short, why did the state not try more actively to strengthen labor?

The second question is more straightforward. If the mode of labor regulation in postwar France was not based upon collective bargaining or corporatism, as was the norm elsewhere in Western Europe, how was the working class regulated? A weak working class does not inevitably mean that labor regulation is unproblematic, particularly when industrial relations are underinstitutionalized. Problems of politicization and cyclically tight labor markets may make labor market regulation dangerous for both regime stability and profitability.

The argument that will be made here is that the French economy was not Fordist in 1945 and cannot be said to have been Fordist until the mid-1960s, following the acceleration of economic modernization under de Gaulle. Fordism, it will be recalled, refers to an intensive regime of accumulation in which "production and consumption [are] constantly transformed through high productivity growth and rapidly rising wages"[48] into a dynamic virtuous circle in which higher productivity is translated into higher wages, greater consumer demand, investment, and, ultimately, further increases in productivity. As Bertrand succinctly puts it, the "combination of Taylorist methods and access to mass consumption for workers defines a new form of integration of wage earners into capitalism: Fordism."[49]

The point is that if France did not in fact have a recognizably Fordist form of accumulation there was no need for a mode of labor regulation that was in some sense "monopolistic" or "administered," because a mechanism for translating productivity gains into wage gains (a means of closing the circuit between mass consumption and mass production, as it were) was unnecessary. Rather French economic growth rested upon a combination of *extensive* growth (the addition of productive factors and transfer of re-sources from noncapitalist to capitalist sectors) and an intensification of labor exploitation.

Boyer provides a strong indication of this possibility in his seminal 1978 article,[50] and additional evidence comes from a later study in *Travail et Emploi*.[51] Purchasing power fluctuated wildly between 1952 and 1962, ranging between an annual rise of 11 percent and an annual fall of 4.6 percent. In addition the 1947–59 period saw remarkable instability, remi-niscent of the interwar period. The range between maximum and mini-mum money wages, cost of living, and real wages were 50.9 percent, 60.4 percent, and 20.1 percent respectively. The contrast with the post-1960 period is dramatic. Between 1960 and 1973 there was great regularity and stability in the rise of real wages. The ranges for money wages, cost of living, and real wages in this period were 8.2 percent, 6.6 percent, and 7.4 percent respectively.[52] These stark figures indicate that the classic Fordist situation of regular, stable rises in real wages, necessary for those wages to become the central component of demand in the economy, did not appear until the 1960s.

Boyer also lists a series of characteristics of a new mode of regulation in the postwar period: (1) workers and unions assent to reconstruction and modernization; (2) labor contracts embody a link between wages, prices, and productivity; (3) there are steady increases in the indirect, or social wage; (4) wage labor becomes the dominant form of productive activity; and (5) there is a rise in mass consumption.[53] These characteristics were largely absent in France before the 1960s.

It is ironic that France, where the "Regulation School" approach to po-litical economy was developed, and whose theorists elaborated the concept of "Fordism," in fact only developed Fordism at a very late date, well after much of the rest of Western Europe and North America. Unfortunately, this has led some French commentators to predate the actual development of Fordism, and consequently to exaggerate the degree to which an "ad-ministered" form of labor regulation, and especially collective bargaining, appeared in France. For instance, Boyer, one of the most sensitive Regula-tion scholars, argues that all (except the last) of the characteristics listed above appeared before the 1960s, and hence were part of a dominant post-war " 'New Deal' in labor-management relations."[54] This "new deal" would have been news to most trade unionists and employers in the 1950s. Aglietta and Brender, in their study of the evolution of the "salaried soci-ety" in France, also give too much weight to the role of collective bargain-ing in France in arguing that: "Collective bargaining is a structuring ele-ment of wage conflicts. It has played a decisive role in the regulation of capitalism for almost half a century."[55] I hope the early sections of this chapter have demonstrated that this is to greatly exaggerate the role of collective bargaining in France before 1968. The cause of this tendency to predate the development of widespread collective bargaining lies in the predating of the arrival of Fordism in France. If France did not have a Fordist regime of accumulation, the problem disappears.

So what were the key features, or components, of postwar economic growth in France? If France was not yet Fordist, it is necessary to explain what accounts for the rapid economic growth of the 1950s, and how labor exclusion *aided* that pattern of growth.

The first feature of postwar growth was a new role for the state in the economy, and more specifically, the rise of planning. The story of French planning is well known and can be briefly told.[56] Kuisel has emphasized the degree to which this planning represented a break with the laissez-faire state of the nineteenth century and the interwar period.[57] He has also described the defeat of socialist aspirations for planning and nationalization, with the result that the newly created nationalized sector was run along commercial lines, and the planning mechanism was deeply technocratic and growth-oriented. In essence the "window of opportunity" for the Left in 1945–47 was too small, the influence of the United States (and aid from the Marshall Plan) too great, and the Left too weak to capitalize on the post-Liberation hopes for fundamental change. The next thirty-five years demonstrated that centrist or right-wing governments had no qualms about using a strong state for interventionist purposes. Successive French governments pursued aggressive policies, first of reconstruction and then modernization, using the "credit-based, price-administered" financial system described by Zysman.[58]

The interest here, however, is less with the technical aspects of planning than the social preconditions of planning and its implications for labor regulation. Many scholars have exaggerated the importance of institutional tools and skills of French planners and have implied that the French state was largely autonomous from civil society.[59] But a strong or activist state is not the same thing as an autonomous state (in Nordlinger's sense of a "type I" state able to consistently act against the interests of dominant groups in society).[60] In fact, the French model was distinctive not because of highly developed tools for economic intervention but rather because of the close links between the advanced sectors of French industry and the bureaucracy, and the exclusion of labor from a voice in economic decision-making. What distinguished France from Britain—a frequently made comparison—were not the instruments of planning (instruments the British periodically created only to leave unused), but the existence of a de facto labor veto in Britain as a result of the more powerful labor movement; such a labor veto did not exist in France. State activism in France was designed to enhance private-capital accumulation. It was made possible by the exclusion or im-mobilization (in the case of small business and agricultural producers) of potential losers from the process of capitalist modernization.

The initial corporatist hopes for planning disappeared almost immedi-ately. As Kuisel dryly puts it: "The 'économie concertée' seemed better suited for administrators and businessmen than for labor."[61] Zysman has described very well the manner in which, while labor was simply ignored, the traditional sector in industry, commerce, and agriculture (which formed a large part of the electoral base of Gaullism) was subsidized and protected.[62] This protection came partly from inflated food prices, which meant that industrial workers bore the cost.

The political significance of planning was that it allowed a transfer of resources from the industrial working class, and the traditional sectors of the economy, in order to pay for capitalist modernization. As Herberg put it:

> The French system of organized industrial growth succeeded not because of agreement on the necessary strategy between labor and capital, but on the ability of those at the center of the process to subordinate the interests of labor and other groups in their plans. It was predicated on and required the tradi-tional political weakness of wage-earning groups in French politics. It would otherwise never have succeeded.[63]

The primary focus of postwar planning (up until 1960) was the expan-sion of productive capacity and resources for investment, rather than an expansion or regularization of demand. This was clearly true of 1945 to 1953 when reconstruction was the first order of the day, and the shortages recognized by planners were physical ones—plant, labor—not consumer demand. But this emphasis remained throughout the 1950s with the Sec-ond and Third Plans (1953–57 and 1957–61, respectively).

An indication of this is provided by fiscal policy. Boyer has made the useful distinction between two kinds of Keynesian economic policy: "fun-damentalist Keynesian reformism," which focuses upon direct public con-trol over investment, and "effective-demand Keynesianism," which empha-sizes fine-tuning the level of aggregate demand.[64] It was the first kind of Keynesianism that was dominant in France in the period 1945–60; the second only appeared in the course of the 1960s, precisely because the problem was not lack of demand in the first period but rather lack of pro-ductive capacity. Industry could not produce enough to keep up with de-mand. The French economy suffered from an inflationary gap rather than an unemployment gap. Thus whether we agree with Boyer's broad defini-tion of what comes under the umbrella of Keynesianism or not, France did not share the emphasis on demand that was the central feature of Anglo-American postwar Keynesianism.[65]

It is perhaps not surprising that the tools available for demand management were poorly developed in France until the end of the 1960s. French social spending was in fact high relative to other OECD (Organization for Economic Cooperation and Development) countries and grew fairly steadily in the postwar period. Growth in social expenditure experienced spurts in the early 1960s and mid-1970s.[66] However, the problem with spending on social welfare in France was less its overall level than its components. Expenditure did not tend to be countercyclical in nature; instead most spending went toward pensions and child allowances, neither of which could compensate for downswings in demand during recessions. Unemployment compensation was well below the OECD average in 1960.[67] Finally, taxes were fairly low, only weakly progressive, and of limited countercyclical use because of the lag between economic change and the ability to change tax levels.[68]

The French economy grew, in the twenty years following the Liberation, not because of a virtuous circle of demand feeding investment, but because of a transfer of resources toward industrial profits and investment. This transfer took three main forms. The first involved a transfer from the agricultural sector. The decline in the agricultural sector accelerated rapidly in the period after World War II, after a long period of very slow decline. The share of agricultural actives among adults decreased at an annual rate of 1.65 percent between 1921 and 1936, 1.68 percent between 1936 and 1954, before accelerating to an annual decrease of 4.97 percent until 1968.[69] The stubborn resistance of the agricultural sector was broken in this latter period, freeing up people and capital for more productive activity.

The second form of transfer resulted from the intensification of work for the manual, industrial working class, whose members worked both longer and harder. Dubois, Durand, and Erbès-Seguin point out that working hours in France were among the highest in the industrialized world, even after the statutory extension of an annual three-week paid vacation, and only began to decline after 1963.[70] France also had a higher level of productivity per worker than the United States, Britain, and West Germany in the period 1959–68. The important thing to note about these productivity gains, however, is that until the 1960s productivity was higher in small firms in the less concentrated sectors of industry than in the large, modern, technologically advanced firms. This strongly suggests that productivity gains were a result of authoritarian management and work intensification rather than increased technical efficiency.[71]

The third form of transfer was relative, and the result of a welfare state that was regressive both in its financing and the direction of transfer payments. Thus the poorest segments of the French population paid a higher proportion of the cost of social programs and benefited less from them than elsewhere in Western Europe. In 1971 in France, direct taxes generated 30.3 percent of total tax revenues (only 10.8 percent came from income taxes) while 35.8 percent of total revenues came from excise and sale taxes. This was a much lower proportion of total revenue from direct taxes than in the United States, Britain, or Sweden.[72] Transfers were also remarkably regressive. Sawyer noted that the bottom two income deciles in France (the poorest 20 percent of the population) received *less* than 20 percent of transfers (in fact only 17.7 percent). This contrasts with Britain where the bottom two income deciles took over 42 percent of transfers. All this contributed to Sawyer's 1975 finding that France had the most unequal pre- and post-tax income distribution in the OECD.[73] The implication of this manner of financing social expenditure is that taxes can be kept low and resources (both public and private) directed into economic modernization rather than social infrastructure. The direction of transfer payments also ensured that spending was of limited use in stimulating consumer demand among the least well-off segments of the population.

The role of wage growth in the French economy was complicated. While productivity outstripped wage gains, living standards in France did increase significantly. The problem from the point of view of Fordist growth is that wage growth was highly unstable and unpredictable. Boyer's figures, noted earlier, point to that instability and the degree of fluctuation from year to year. Industrial workers, by and large, were able to make gains, but not as a result of regularized collective bargaining, perhaps on an annual or multiyear basis. Instead wage growth came in spurts after cyclical outbursts of militancy. For instance, real wage growth went from 9.9 percent in 1957 to *minus* 1.8 percent in 1958, and then from 2.7 percent in 1960 to 6.8 percent in 1961, and back down to 4.7 percent in 1962.[74] In addition, much of the gain in money wages made by workers was offset by government willingness (at least until the 1960s, when international competitiveness became an issue) to tolerate high levels of inflation. Thus while wage gains were made, they were both too low and too unpredictable to form the basis for a mass consumer market.

The final feature of the French economy in the immediate postwar period worth mentioning here is industrial structure. The Fordist wage relation, based upon trade union recognition, collective bargaining, and the linkage of productivity gains to wage gains, has always been more appropriate to large, modern firms where labor is stronger, wage drift (from bargaining at a higher level) is a problem, and predictability of labor costs for planning purposes is important. Under these circumstances a variety of agreements between management and labor are possible. Clearly such agreements *did* exist in France, as the 1955 Renault works agreement demonstrates, but their scope was very limited. The modern corporation was very slow in developing in France. Lévy-Leboyer has argued that the modern corporation emerged twenty years later in France than in the United States and West Germany.[75] Industrial structure remained essentially unchanged until 1960. As Carré, Dubois, and Malinvaud put it, "Postwar French growth took place without substantial change in the degree of concentration of industrial production in effect at the beginning of the century or earlier."[76] The rate of mergers did not begin to accelerate until 1959, and only peaked in 1969. So throughout this period the cutting edge of the economy were medium-sized firms, often producing for regional markets or protected colonial markets.[77] These firms were less likely to be able to sustain high wages or vigorous unions. Thus for the first fifteen to twenty years of the *trente glorieuses*, French economic growth was not recognizably Fordist. It was not primarily based upon a motor driven by consumer demand, but upon extensive growth and work intensification. In short, economic growth did not require the integration of labor, but rather its exclusion.

The French economy did not need a mode of labor regulation compatible with Fordist accumulation, nor was the structure and organization of the French working class susceptible to regulation by collective bargaining or corporatism. But it is still necessary to specify what the dominant mode of labor regulation in postwar France was.

Labor regulation in France was a hybrid of mechanisms with three main components. First, there was the slow development of firm-level decentralized collective bargaining in the leading sectors of the economy after 1955. In a few limited sectors a combination of stronger labor and the need on the part of the firm for steady, predictable wage rises and industrial peace made collective bargaining both possible and necessary. But these sectors were very limited in the French economy of the 1950s and remained so until the rapid modernization and restructuring of the French economy that began in the 1960s. For the most part collective bargaining was of the kind described by Lyon-Caen: taking place at the branch level, and involving the setting of minimum wages rather than real wages. Real wages were determined at the firm level where unions were weak or absent.

The second component of labor regulation involved state intervention. The state was involved in labor regulation, though to a lesser degree than was to be the case in the 1970s. The minimum wage was scarcely used as an economic or social tool. It was indexed to a basket of prices, but not to changes in the average hourly wage. The result was that the minimum wage increasingly lagged behind real wages.[78] Only in 1953 and 1955 did French governments consciously try to raise the SMIG beyond what was indicated by the price level. From 1956 to 1967 the SMIG stagnated and the gap between it and hourly wages widened. Thus it had a limited impact on wages. It provided a safety net for sectors completely uncovered by collective agreements, and hence without branch-negotiated wage minimums. The process of "extension" of collective-bargaining agreements had some impact, particularly for the generalization of social benefits, like the three-week paid vacation.

The third and most important component of labor regulation was provided by the labor market. France had a very weakly institutionalized labor market in the sense that the role of supply and demand in wage determination was very important. There were low levels of unemployment throughout this period. The needs of reconstruction ensured that the French economy could absorb most of the available labor. However, the French labor market closely resembled the "restricted, compartmentalized market" described by Dubois, Durand, and Erbès-Seguin with low labor mobility.[79] Thus small increases in unemployment could have an effect on wage demands. The statistical evidence is unclear but Boyer argues that from 1947–1954 fluctuations in money wages were broadly related to the unemployment level. The influence of unemployment declined in 1954–66, with the exception of 1958–59 when wages fell dramatically in response to a government-induced rise in the unemployment level.[80]

Perhaps more important than the size of the unemployed pool was the quality of the labor force. While unemployment remained low because of the absorptive ability of the economy and the growth of the tertiary sector, many new workers entered the labor force either as a result of rural migration or immigration (particularly following decolonization). By 1970 there were two million immigrants in France, comprising 10 percent of the employed labor force.[81] These workers were, at least initially, less susceptible to organization and militancy. The "revolt of the marginals" did not come until 1968 and beyond. Hence low unemployment did not automatically translate into worker militancy.

For the fifteen to twenty years following World War II, the labor market worked to diffuse strong working-class pressure on wages. Real wages were rarely collectively negotiated, either being set unilaterally by the employer or following the branch minimums closely. In this period employers were largely content for the state to remain aloof from labor regulation so that wages could be set at the firm level where workers were weak, unions nonexistent, and the overall balance of power lay firmly on the side of employers. Wage rises tended to be the result of cyclical explosions of militancy, largely unmediated and underinstitutionalized. In addition, state economic policies regulated the level of wages and responded to strike waves, using *labor market tools*. For instance, the wage explosion of 1955–57 was dealt with by a stabilization plan involving deflation to generate unemployment and sap the militancy of workers. When the state did choose to intervene in wage determination it did so through the labor market rather than statutory controls or encouragement of a voluntary incomes policy.

Until the early 1960s this form of labor regulation functioned reasonably well from the perspective of the French state and capital. Low wages and high productivity fueled French reconstruction and growth, while the occasional outburst of militancy could be handled with a dose of deflation. However, in the course of the 1960s the conditions underlying this reliance upon the labor market regulation disintegrated and new economic pressures appeared. The next chapter describes these developments and their implications for labor regulation in France.

CHAPTER THREE

Labor Regulation in Crisis, 1958–69

THE LAST CHAPTER argued that labor market regulation made sense given the structure of the French labor movement and the form of economic growth adopted after 1945. But as the French economy developed over the first twenty years of the postwar period, it changed, and so did the labor movement. Once the tasks of reconstruction and industrialization were completed, the model of growth began to change. The return to power of de Gaulle in 1958 marked a new phase of economic development—one in which labor market regulation was less appropriate. De Gaulle chose to ignore the problem of labor regulation and to attempt to continue economic modernization without any modernization of social relations. The result was May 1968. While the events of May–June 1968 had many specific and conjunctural causes, it was fundamentally a response to the prolonged exclusion of workers from the benefits of growth and the disproportionate share of the costs of growth that they had to bear. In any case, after the events of May 1968 few politicians or business people were in any doubt that the old form of labor regulation was in need of replacement.

This chapter examines the transformation that took place in the French economy in the ten years following de Gaulle's reassumption of power in 1958 and his initiation of a program of rapid economic modernization. Economic transformation brought with it stresses and strains for the existing mode of labor regulation. This chapter then discusses the impact of the events of May–June 1968 on contemporary thinking about French labor regulation, and concludes with a brief examination of the abortive and short-lived response of de Gaulle to 1968, the failure of which set the scene for the ambitious "New Society" industrial relations reforms that are the subject of chapter 4.

ECONOMIC MODERNIZATION

By the mid-1960s the French state had used up many of the advantages of backwardness. French leaders then had to deal with the realities of industrial society, and one of these realities was organized labor. The early stages of modernization could take place without the incorporation of unions, and indeed took place largely at the expense of workers. But the thrust toward modernization that occurred after de Gaulle took power in 1958 was of a different kind. The paradox lies in de Gaulle's attempt to use the traditional mode of labor regulation—the labor market—to accompany that modernization.

De Gaulle launched a modernizing drive that went well beyond reconstruction and the simple expansion of productive capacity. His goal was a modern, diversified industrial structure capable of competing with the rest of the industrialized world. This goal of competitiveness was of crucial importance in this period. With decolonization France lost the bulk of her protected colonial markets, and with the signing of the Treaty of Rome in 1957 it was imperative for France to be able to compete internationally. Import controls were no longer acceptable tools of economic management, and high levels of inflation could not be tolerated. Hall has described the transition from one form of economic growth to another very well.[1] The Fourth and Fifth Plans (1962–65 and 1966–70, respectively) were different from their predecessors in two important respects.

First, these plans envisaged a shift in the direction of investment from a small number of heavy, basic industrial sectors to the most advanced and modern sectors of the economy. The Fourth Plan, for instance, targeted telecommunications, chemicals, construction, and consumer electronics. The direction was consumer-oriented. Paralleling this shift was a micro-interventionist approach; individual firms were targeted rather than entire sectors.

Second, the importance of international competitiveness implied firm competitiveness. For the first time, the Fifth Plan contained detailed income targets. For the life of the Fifth Plan real wages were to rise 2.8 percent per annum, with 0.5 percent for wage drift and 1.5 percent anticipated price-level changes. Hence nominal wage rises were to be held to 4.8 percent per annum. At the same time, it was hoped that profits would increase by 8.6 percent per annum. Containment of wage costs was to be accompanied by industrial restructuring to create large competitive firms, the so-called national champions. In 1965 a series of legal and tax changes were enacted to promote mergers. The result (as table 3.1 shows) was a rapid acceleration in the number of mergers, which peaked in 1969 when there were 263 mergers (139 in industry).

The basic thrust of these changes was toward a qualitatively different kind of economy. From 1960 onward, France saw the first significant shifts in industrial structure for a century or more. This was accompanied by a change in the work force. After being stagnant since 1936, the working population began to grow between 1962 and 1968. This work force was increasingly finding itself in large firms where opportunities for solidarity were wider and easier. This made collective organization less difficult than it had been when the bulk of the working class labored in small, paternalistic firms.

TABLE 3.1
Number of Mergers, 1950–77

	Total Mergers	Mergers in Industry
1950–58	61	32
1959–65	166	74
1966–77	213	109

Source: François Caron, An Economic History of Modern France (New York: Columbia University Press, 1979), 302–3.

Above all, the firms and sectors targeted by de Gaulle were not the same ones that had been on the cutting edge of the earlier modernization drive. Rather, they more closely resembled Fordist firms. That is to say, they were demand-driven—that demand being both domestic and international. For these firms, wages were clearly important, but they were often not the most important component of costs. Research and development, marketing, a technologically advanced plant, and so on were also very costly. What was perhaps more important than low wages was "to achieve a predictable, controllable movement of income which will be closely related to changes in productivity,"[2] and hence permit planning. In this environment trade unions might be acceptable precisely because, by operating beyond the boundaries of the firm, they take labor costs out of competition. The reliance on branch-level agreements was inappropriate for this kind of firm because increased labor strength in such firms made wage drift a real danger. Firm-level agreements, requiring the cooperation of workers, were more appropriate to controlling wage costs. Finally, these firms were deeply vulnerable to industrial disruption as a result of being highly capitalized and interdependent.

All these features put a premium on cooperation with the work force and decentralized collective bargaining. They also provided an important role for trade unions as recognizable representatives of the work force. Thus the conditions that had allowed the 1955–56 wave of Renault-style agreements were now being widened and generalized. The dominant postwar mode of labor regulation was increasingly ill-suited to the economy it was supposed to regulate.

However, de Gaulle chose to pursue modernization using the existing manner of labor regulation. He chose, as Flanagan, Soskice, and Ulman put it, the "labour market option."[3] That implied no cooperation with the trade unions unless they accepted the plan targets for wages. Since trade unions were presented with the choice of taking it or leaving it, they decided to leave it. Hence wages could be controlled either by traditional deflationary measures to increase unemployment and moderate wage demands, or by an incomes policy that operated through the actions of employers and the public sector, without union involvement. De Gaulle's government pursued both strategies simultaneously.

In March 1961 Prime Minister Debré wrote to employers suggesting a limit of 4 percent per annum in wage increases. In early 1963 a Conférence des Revenus (conference on incomes) was held, at which unions and employer representatives were present. The conference failed. The potential perhaps existed for union cooperation in the incomes policy in return for recognition of union rights in the workplace. However, even had the CFDT been willing to cooperate, the CGT was deeply hostile to any cooperation with the government, and it was far and away the biggest player on the union side. In any case, while it is perhaps possible that the government could have offered more to the unions to sweeten the pill of wage restraint, it had no intention of relaxing its targets for wage rises. It is unlikely that union agreement would have made any difference to the reaction of workers; it would simply have sealed their irrelevance. It was, after all, largely spontaneous industrial action that launched the strikes of May 1968.

Instead the government imposed an incomes policy via the use of price controls. Price controls provided a direct incentive for employers to limit wages. The government also signed *contrats de programme* with certain firms, which provided exemption from price controls in return for agreement to keep wages within the targets. The undeniable result of the incomes policy was to bring an almost complete halt to collective bargaining. The decline in collective bargaining was a clear result of the political decisions of French policymakers, but it underlines the fragility of collective bargaining in France. The system of collective bargaining had such shallow roots that it was unable to ride out the deflationary effects of government policy.

A footnote to the wage policy of the government in the private sector in this period concerns the 1967 ordinance on *participation*. This will be discussed in much greater detail at the end of this chapter where it forms the centerpiece of de Gaulle's attempt to reform industrial relations. But one aspect of it was that it served as a forced savings scheme in that some part of any potential wage increase would go into a fund to be used for investment in the firm, and from which nothing could be withdrawn by workers for five years.

While the government used indirect controls to limit wage increases in the private sector, it had direct control over wage levels in the public sector, and hence it was the public sector that bore the brunt of wage control. In 1963 two commissions presented their findings on wage negotiations in the public sector. The result was the Toutée-Grégoire procedure. This operated in such a way that the government would unilaterally decide on the total wage bill—the *masse salariale*—which it could afford, and which fitted in with plan objectives. Only then were trade unions invited to discuss how that sum would be divided up among categories of workers.

The results of the government's wage policy were a success in the narrow sense that wages were kept low. Table 3.2 presents figures from Mitchell for what he calls the "administrative" and "commercial" sectors (which roughly correspond to the public and private sectors). In 1962 and 1963 wage rises were much higher in the administrative sector than in the commercial sector. This was reversed from 1964 to 1967 when the wage control policy was in effect. Clearly the public sector suffered most from the wage policy. But it was fairly effective in the private sector as well. In 1963 and 1964 real wages increased faster than productivity, whereas from 1965 to 1967 this was reversed.[4] Thus, on the face of it de Gaulle's gamble had worked. He had successfully continued the French tradition of economic modernization at the expense of labor.

However, in retrospect, the events of May–June 1968 were a direct consequence of this attempt to modernize the economy while maintaining a labor exclusionary form of labor regulation.[5] The wage compression in the public sector accounts for the disproportionate influence of public-sector workers in the industrial disruption of 1968. The strikes in the power and transport sectors were a direct outcome of a perceived falling behind the private sector. Unemployment steadily climbed in the course of the 1960s, both from deflationary policies and as a result of industrial restructuring. May 1968 coincided with a relatively *slack* labor market. Unemployment had risen steadily in the course of the 1960s, reaching 1.7 percent of the active labor force in 1968.[6]

While the events of 1968 came as a surprise, the potential for some social reaction was recognized. The thaw in collective bargaining—blocked since the failure of the Conférence des Revenus in 1963—is usually dated from 1967. An important agreement was signed in the iron and steel industries

TABLE 3.2
Nominal Wage Increases, 1962–67

	Administrative Sector (in percent)	Commercial Sector (in percent)
1962	17.0	10.8
1963	14.6	11.1
1964	4.5	9.2
1965	3.8	6.4
1966	4.8	6.6
1967	4.9	6.1

Source: Daniel Mitchell, "Incomes Policy and the Labor Market in France," *Industrial and Labor Relations Review* 25, no. 3 (April 1972): 321.

that summer which had the deliberate aim of obtaining union agreement on the procedures to be used for dealing with lost employment due to restructuring and the benefits to be made available to those concerned.

In August 1967 Prime Minister Georges Pompidou sent a letter to all the unions and employers' organizations which called for bilateral talks on the same issues of finding mutually acceptable procedures for layoffs and compensation. Pompidou's aim was to encourage the social partners to reach agreement on how to deal with the consequences of restructuring in order to avoid industrial upheaval and a politicization of the policy and process of modernization itself. His letter called for negotiations on five specific issues: the creation of joint committees on industrial change; providing advance notice of layoffs; job reclassification resulting from restructuring; a rise in the level of unemployment compensation; and some form of compensation for short-time working.

However, it would be misleading to allow this modest relaunching of *la politique contractuelle* to diminish the importance of the events of May 1968 in providing a stimulus to industrial relations reform. Pompidou's initiative was too little too late. The response of the employers to the Pompidou letter was at best cautious. They consistently refused national-level talks with the union confederations, and by May 1968 agreement had been reached on only one of the five points raised by Pompidou back in August 1967: that of compensation for short-time working. May 1968 was a clear demonstration of the failure of an exclusionary form of labor regulation, and it provided the urgency necessary for a change in that form of regulation.

Along with the economic ills of wage control and industrial dislocation went a particularly French problem: politicization. Tilly and Shorter have argued that after 1936 strikes in France have been less concerned with concrete economic demands and more with political symbolism. Thus political strikes were the only way workers could respond to the blocked system of industrial relations at the firm level and the exclusion of the Left at the political level.[7] This analysis was particularly appropriate to the public sector where unions were relatively strong but negotiations were blocked administratively. The problem with an industrial relations system that is weak at the firm level and unable to respond to workers' concerns where they originate is that those demands become politicized and directed up toward the state. As Adam and Reynaud put it, "In a system continually threatened with anomie, appeal to the state appeared to be the most natural solution for the settlement of conflicts."[8]

Thus May 1968 demonstrated that not only was the economic policy a failure—there was widespread industrial disruption, with nine million workers on strike at one point, and very large wage increases were conceded—but that the industrial relations system proved to be a threat to the regime itself. The decision of de Gaulle to couple economic modernization with labor market regulation was therefore not simply a policy failure, it was a political disaster.

THE IMPORTANCE OF MAY 1968

The student and worker upheavals of May 1968 were almost entirely unexpected. Both state officials and the *patronat* were caught largely by surprise and were badly shaken. They negotiated with the unions at the Ministry of Labor, rue de Grenelle, but without a strong sense of what was actually going on in the factories and workplaces of France. It soon became clear that this incomprehension was shared by the largest labor unions, particularly the CGT. When the unions refused to sign the Grenelle Accords because of widespread rank-and-file opposition to their moderation, the weakness of the supposedly natural representatives of the working class appeared in sharp relief.

Furthermore, while the growing contradiction between the pattern of economic growth and the highly conflictual and uninstitutionalized system of industrial relations is apparent in hindsight, its resolution was not inevitable in the immediate future. De Gaulle, for instance, was firm in his refusal to deal with the trade unions. The crucial importance of the upsurge of worker militancy in May and June of 1968 was that it brought that contradiction to the surface and forced it onto the political agenda. It is comparatively rare that economic and social tensions crystallize so visibly into political crisis. May 1968 was such an occasion.

The scale of French industrial unrest during May and June 1968 was unprecedented in the advanced industrial world. At its peak nine million workers were on strike. Disruption was widespread across both the public and private sectors, particularly the former.[9] Along with halting production and preventing the transport and distribution of goods, the events of May and June 1968 cost the employers dearly in wage gains. At the height of the unrest the major trade union confederations, employers' organizations, and the government met at the Ministry of Labor and hammered out a series of agreements that became known as the Grenelle Accords. In fact the unions never signed the accords because of widespread dissatisfaction with the terms of the agreement on the part of striking workers, but the employers and government honored them all the same.

The Grenelle Accords are important for their concessions to workers, though it should be stressed that they formed a base from which negotiations going on in each firm to end strikes could begin. According to the accords, wages were to rise by 7 percent on June 1 with a further 3 percent increase on October 1. In practice nominal wages increased by a lot more.[10] The minimum wage was raised by 35 percent to three francs an hour. Between December 1967 and December 1968 nominal wages rose by 15.5 percent in the private sector, the civil service, and at Électricité et Gaz de France (EGF), and by 13.5 percent at the Société Nationale des Chemins de Fer Français (SNCF). With an inflation rate of 5.25 percent in the same period this represented an increase in purchasing power of close to 10 percent in the private sector and much of the public sector.[11] In addition workers in the public and nationalized sector, and many in the private sector, received the income they had lost while on strike as back pay.[12]

The Grenelle Accords covered many areas including a progressive shortening of the working day, but for the purposes of this chapter the most important gain for workers came under the heading of "Droit syndical dans l'entreprise." Until 1968 trade unions did not receive legal protection when their representatives attempted to set up union "sections" inside the firm. The term union "section" refers simply to firm-level organizations of the nationally representative trade union confederations. Without legal protection union delegates were vulnerable to employer hostility, harassment, and discrimination. Prior to the Grenelle Accords about one hundred and fifty firm-level agreements had allowed for union representation inside the firm (the 1955 Renault works agreement being perhaps the most well known).[13] The Grenelle Accords granted the right to union sections, in principle, and left it up to legislation to fill in the details. The legislation was passed in December 1968. It allowed for union sections in any private-sector firm that employed fifty people or more. This meant, in practice, that it applied to about half the workers (around five and a half million) in the private and nationalized sectors. The legislation also laid out the rights and protections available to union delegates. It is important to stress that the legislation did not make union sections *mandatory*; it only granted protection to unions that sought to establish sections, and it exempted firms of less than fifty employees, precisely the firms where workers tended to be most vulnerable.

The upsurge of worker militancy in 1968 was interpreted by politicians, government officials, and employers alike as a response to dislocation caused by the modernization process, which had been accelerating throughout the 1960s. But if the ultimate cause was modernization the real culprit was widely perceived to be the dominant form of postwar labor regulation that had proved itself unable to absorb and channel the social shocks created by modernization. Thus the reaction of state officials in the immediate aftermath of May 1968 was not to slow down or temper the process of economic modernization, but rather to "modernize" the form of regulation and the system of French industrial relations so as to allow continued economic growth without its concomitant political and social shocks.

If 1968 created and mobilized a constituency for change, it did not create a consensus on the form that change should take. The period immediately following 1968 saw two very different attempts to remold the mode of labor regulation. The first, and most short-lived, was the Gaullist solution of bypassing labor unions and decentralizing conflict by integrating workers at the firm level. This solution represented a move away from the mixture of labor market and state regulation that had gone on before, but it clearly hoped to avoid giving any larger role to the unions, which (despite having had to run to catch up with the workers) had emerged strengthened from the events of May 1968. (The last section of this chapter examines this experiment.) The second approach came from the attempt by Jacques Chaban-Delmas to create a "New Society" around strengthened unions and regularized bargaining practices (this is the subject of the next chapter). Both projects were concerned with creating the structures that would depoliticize wage bargaining and decentralize it. However, they differed in the crucial area of whether to work with or without trade unions.

May 1968 inspired a wide range of interpretations, from the broadly psychosocial to the narrowly political.[14] The focus here is on sociological explanations for the wave of worker militancy, which had policy implications for government. I am not concerned with explaining the student revolt here. Rather, the student revolt will be seen, whatever its own dynamics, as essentially a "detonator" for the industrial unrest.[15] What is interesting about the various interpretations of May 1968 is the weight that many of them assign to the maladaptation of the French system of industrial relations for a modern industrial society. At its broadest, such an interpretation followed from a general critique of the relationship between civil society and the state in France. Michel Crozier's description of a "blocked society" painted a stark picture of the underdeveloped nature of France's intermediary institutions (political parties, trade unions) and the suffocating weight of the state in many areas of social life.[16]

In the area of industrial relations this interpretation was given precision and specificity by the influential team of industrial sociologists centered around the "Groupe Sociologie du Travail."[17] They blamed the crisis on the failure of the existing system of industrial relations. In their analysis, the social discontent resulted from a series of economic adjustments which had built up and was then unable to find expression. The role of an industrial relations system was seen, from this perspective, as providing a safety valve, or a buffer, for grievances that result from the labor process and the wage relationship. The organizations of capital and labor in France were too weak to handle the demands coming from workers. So the demands flowed over and around the existing labor unions and institutions of collective bargaining leading to a loss of control by the unions and rapid politicization. The area of greatest weakness in the existing system was the workplace. It was there that discontent arose and struggle took place; it was also where labor unions and collective bargaining were most weakly developed.

This interpretation was largely shared by an OECD analysis that made explicit the connection between economic modernization and the need for a structure of conflict resolution in the workplace.[18] The OECD report stressed the extent to which the modernization program led to "layoffs and redundancy on a scale unheard of in France" and to a de facto incomes policy. The problem according to the report, however, lay not with these *results* of economic restructuring so much as a failure of the mode of labor regulation. Thus "too much reliance [was] placed on the automatic adjustments, the mobility, of the market mechanism." There was, therefore, a "disparity between ends and means." The report concluded that the implications of 1968 were "not simply the underlying need for consultation and co-operation of the government and the social partners. What the events demonstrated was that a modern industrial state could be driven to the edge of disaster by a piecemeal labor market policy. . . . In short the events burst the framework of traditional labor market or manpower policy."[19]

This analysis—that May 1968 was above all a crisis of the *institutions professionelles*—was highly influential both inside and outside the academic community. Its themes appeared again and again in newspapers and the speeches of prominent politicians in the months following May 1968. Its importance—and a large part of the reason for its widespread acceptance—was that it implied that a solution could be found in industrial relations reform, so there was no inherent need for a halt in economic modernization. The goal of economic modernization could, and did, remain the top priority, and the Sixth Plan (1970–75) both continued and accelerated modernization.[20] Thus, in one sense, post-1968 governments were spared the need to question their economic goals and instead were able to see the solution as lying in a modernization of *social structures* so as to make them compatible with economic modernization, and not vice versa.

I am most concerned with the implications of these interpretations for state policy, but it is worth briefly looking at the responses of French employers and trade unions because much of the disagreement concerning the reasons for the ambiguous results of reform efforts pivots on the reactions of the social partners to May 1968. The degree to which attitudes and strategies really shifted is therefore important for understanding what happened after 1968.[21]

The transformation of the French economy in the ten years after 1958 had two important implications for the interests of French capital and the organization and representation of those interests. First, it strengthened those large modern firms, which tend to have different concerns (beyond basic profitability), from those of small backward firms. The interdependence and heavy capitalization of such firms puts a premium upon continued production and predictability. Industrial conflict and unpredictable labor costs were tremendously damaging to these modern firms. In addition, many of them relied on a large domestic market for their products and hence emphasized a steady increase in consumer purchasing power rather than a low-wage economy. Finally, the larger firms, often the product of mergers, tended not to operate at the margins of profitability, as did the smaller, more traditional firms. This made possible, and indeed gave such firms an interest in, an industrial relations system that traded steady, predictable increases in real wages (ideally in line with productivity gains) for labor peace. This was not the industrial relations system that France possessed, and in the course of the 1960s the contradiction between this new "regime of accumulation" and the old "mode of labor regulation" had grown more apparent.

The second major implication of the broad shift in the economy was felt at the political level. The influence of small producers, in industry, commerce, and agriculture, had been predominant in the 1950s. Economic policy emphasized stability. All this changed with the arrival of de Gaulle in 1958. De Gaulle's geopolitical vision of French greatness was premised upon a strong, modern economy. As the economy changed, so the influence of large industrialists, representing the new modernized sectors of the economy, was bound to grow, both within government[22] and within employers' organizations—particularly the main such organization in France, the CNPF.

Thus, the important change that occurred within the *patronat* after 1968 was a shift in the balance of power within the CNPF from the smaller, more traditional firms, to the larger, more modern ones. These latter firms consolidated their grip on the organizational structure of the CNPF. The new employer think tanks and pressure groups formed after May 1968— Centre national des dirigeants d'entreprise (CNDE), Groupement d'études et de réformes de l'organisation patronale (GEROP), L'Association des grandes entreprises françaises faisant appel à l'épargne (AGREF)—were formed at the initiative of the owners of very large firms. They brought together the industrialists that represented the largest and most modern firms in French industry: Roger Martin of Saint-Gobain-pont-à-Mousson, Amboise Roux of Companie Générale d'Électricité, Renaud Gillet of Rhône-Poulenc, Maurice Boyra of Usinor, François Gautier of Peugeot, and so on. As Weber points out, AGREF in fact represented twenty-two of the twenty-five firms that the PCF considered monopolies worthy of nationalization by a future leftist government.[23] Parallel to the rise of the large firms was the decline in influence of the smaller, more traditional firms. Their political influence went into eclipse until Jacques Chirac became prime minister in 1974.

This shift in power within the CNPF was important. First, because such firms had less to fear from labor unions. The costs involved in the creation of union sections were more easily borne by large firms, and their primary concern tended to be less that of controlling wage costs than assuring continuous production in capital-intensive, highly interdependent industries. For this task unions could conceivably be of help. They provide identifiable work-force representatives and regularized, predictable bargaining practices. It might be worthwhile for large firms to give higher wages in return for some kind of union control over rank-and-file members. Smaller firms would be less likely to be able to sustain the increased labor costs. For individual firms to encourage unions might put them at a competitive disadvantage, but if legislation was used for the same purpose this particular collective-action problem could be solved. This provided a useful role for government in the eyes of large employers.

Second, it was these groups of employers that were most committed and had most to gain from continued economic modernization. It was these industrialists who became actively involved, in cooperation with government officials, in formulating and implementing the Sixth Plan. The CNPF was now dominated by employers that shared a similar perspective to that of the governments of the immediate post-1968 period. For them the aim of social reform was to allow, and indeed encourage, economic modernization, not to slow it down. As Yvon Chotard of the CNPF put it, social policy should not be conceived of "as a set of measures designed to compensate for the injustices created by progress [but] as a key element of an economic policy assuring prosperity."[24]

Thus key elements within the *patronat* developed an interpretation of May 1968 and a response to it that was remarkably similar to that outlined above. The problem was seen as weak union organizations that were unable to contain and control workers. At the July 1968 General Assembly of the CNPF, its president regretted "the weakening of the authority of trade union organizations in the face of these new circumstances."[25]

As far as the unions were concerned, however, remarkably little changed. May 1968 accelerated the process of radicalization inside the CFDT. In May 1970 the 35th Congress made socialism one of the goals of the CFDT. This was important in that it both ensured the failure of any plans that post-1968 governments had to create a privileged relationship between the CFDT and the government, and it encouraged joint action between the CGT and the CFDT. However, the unions remained fundamentally *reactive*. The two largest unions, the CGT and CFDT, felt there was no need for a fundamental reassessment of their strategies. Since both were now committed to socialist transformation, their strategies were designed to further that end. For the CGT this meant large-scale "political" strikes that, it was hoped, would bring a leftist government to power, while for the CFDT it meant encouraging and supporting local actions. These strategies corresponded to the structural weakness of the unions. For the CGT, large brief political demonstrations were much easier to organize than prolonged strikes, while the CFDT was committing itself only to support conflict wherever it appeared spontaneously. So long as unions remained structurally weak and unable to control their members, an *attentiste* strategy was hardly surprising. Neither union drew the lesson from 1968 that a strengthening of the negotiating process with employers and the state was the way forward.

The events of May and June 1968 brought the economic dilemmas of the Gaullist government into sharp focus. In the short term, May 1968 had led to a rapid rise in wages and an erosion of profit levels. Hence the immediate priority was to restore profitability. The first post-1968 government, led by Maurice Couve de Murville, stimulated investment via expanded credit and tax incentives, reduced government spending on social infrastructure in order to balance the budget, and resisted further wage increases while allowing inflation to rise. The next government (after de Gaulle's resignation), with Georges Pompidou as president and Jacques Chaban-Delmas as prime minister, further eroded living standards by devaluing the franc in August 1969. This short-run stabilization plan put severe limits on the initiatives that post-1968 governments could take in the area of social relations, and were hardly designed to encourage union cooperation.

Nevertheless, the long-term goal of economic modernization remained and indeed was accelerated. The events of May 1968 demonstrated beyond reasonable doubt that the mode of labor regulation had become an obstacle to the goal of economic modernization. Continued economic restructuring risked another explosion. Since post-1968 governments were unwilling to subordinate economic modernization to social peace they chose instead to modernize social relations, or in regulation terms, to change the mode of labor regulation. Two very different ways of regulating labor were attempted between 1968 and 1974. But while the means differed, the central dilemma remained that of trying to find a way of regulating labor that was both appropriate to economic modernization and also possible in the French context.

AN EXPERIMENT IN *PARTICIPATION*

The period between May 1968 and the resignation of de Gaulle a year later was more than simply a transitional one. An attempt was made to breath new life into the old Gaullist notion of *l'association capital-travail* or, more simply, *participation*. The experiment was short-lived and collapsed with the defeat of de Gaulle's proposals in the April 1969 referendum, but it is worth fairly close attention—both in its ideological justification and its execution—because as a model of labor regulation it has resurfaced, in a variety of guises, again and again over the last twenty years, and with particular force since 1983. If such a mode of labor regulation was inappropriate in the immediate post-1968 situation, it became less so as the French economy underwent profound changes from the mid-1970s onward.

The notion of *participation* is associated with the left wing of the broad Gaullist coalition (which spanned the political spectrum from the reactionary to Catholic socialism), and with such left-wing Gaullists as René Capitant and Louis Vallon. At its most grandiose, *participation* was an attempt to find a third way between capitalism and socialism. One of de Gaulle's reactions to the events of May 1968 was to admit that "from the human point of view capitalism does not offer a satisfactory solution."[26] The idea was to associate labor and capital in such a way as to make any difference of interests disappear. Thus class struggle would wither away; in de Gaulle's view:

> Each worker will become, and will feel himself to be, more than simply an instrument in the activity to which he contributes. It is difficult to see why, and in what spirit of the firm, productivity, good order, and the exercise of responsibilities in the factory will suffer from this. On the contrary, what economic and social progress will be accomplished when the spirit and the fact of partnership replaces, little by little, the spirit and the fact of class struggle.[27]

In the Gaullist schema there were three forms, or perhaps three stages, on the road to full *participation*: a share in the profits generated by a firm; a share in the capital of that firm; and finally, a share in the management of the firm.

It is important to note that *participation*, in its Gaullist form, did not entail a withering away of the state or a withdrawal of the state from an active coordinating role in society. On the contrary, the decentralization of labor regulation to the level of the firm would require a wider role for the state as the guardian of the general interest. Thus *participation* went hand in hand with an expanded role for the plan.[28]

This vision of a third way capable of superseding class struggle was never dominant within the Gaullist coalition, but in a less ambitious form it nevertheless strongly influenced de Gaulle's policies. Its importance lies in the fact that it implies a particular model of labor regulation, one that is close to that identified in chapter 1 as microcorporatism. Once the ideological trappings are laid aside, the structural implications of this model become clear. Workers would be cut off from labor organizations outside the firm and, increasingly, income would be tied directly (and automatically) to firm performance. Thus *participation* meant a structural integration of workers into the firms where they worked, independent of any labor collectivity extending beyond the boundaries of the firm.

One implication of *participation* was a profound hostility to trade unions. Trade unions aim to enhance the bargaining power of workers by expanding collective action beyond the firm to an entire industry, or category of worker, or even the working class as a whole. Expanded collectivity has the effect of both increasing the potential damage from industrial action and allowing workers to partially divorce their interests from those of their specific place of work. The Gaullist notion of *participation* aimed to bypass trade unions so as to cut workers off from any wider collectivity beyond the firm in order for them to identify with the economic needs of the firm. There was, therefore, no role for trade unions in *participation*, or more accurately, no role for trade unions in the normal sense of their purpose. Unions that were limited to the members of a particular firm (enterprise unions), or trade unions that operate outside the firm only, could coexist with *participation*. But trade unions that sought to link workers inside the firm with workers in other firms would lead to conflict between two models of labor regulation. This is indeed what happened after unions received legal protection in the workplace in 1968.

There had been a number of measures promoting *participation* in the postwar period. The creation of the works council in 1945 was explicitly designed to promote cooperation between workers and management rather than conflict. The preamble to the 1945 legislation creating the works council made this clear: "The motivating idea behind [this legislation] has been the necessity of involving workers in the running of firms and in the management of the economy."[29] The works council was a structure that had a built-in proclivity for promoting cooperation because, being firm-based and cut off from any wider form of labor collectivity, it was more likely to derive its interests from those of the firm than those of a trade or class. In addition it had the potential for rivalry with union sections once the latter became legally protected within the firm.

A 1959 ordinance was designed to encourage profit-sharing in firms by providing tax advantages for such schemes.[30] The ordinance was facultative only. It received only very limited interest from employers. The main reason for this was that profit-sharing agreements had to be negotiated with, and signed by, *union* delegates in the firm. This meant allowing unions a foothold in firms that did not already have them and giving a wider role and legitimacy to unions in firms where they already existed. A 1967 ordinance made financial *participation* much more attractive to employers. It was not limited to profit-sharing but could include any one of a variety of schemes that would allow workers to share directly in the benefits of growth in the firm. Compliance in firms with over one hundred employees was mandatory. A part of the profits (after various deductions) would be distributed to workers but could not be claimed for five years so that in the meantime it could be used for investment in the firm. Thus the employer received not only tax advantages from these schemes but also a form of forced savings plan. Employers could attempt to offer a higher proportion of profits to workers in lieu of regular wages. But what made the schemes most attractive was that accords could now be signed with the works council rather than union delegates. Between December 1967 and May 1974, as many as 8,819 accords were signed, overwhelmingly with works councils.[31] However, until May 1968 *participation* had been pursued only half-heartedly. It inspired little interest outside a small circle of Gaullist intellectuals and was regarded more as a gimmick than a serious reform project.

After the events of May 1968, however, the reaction of de Gaulle was to extend and accelerate the process of *participation*. For de Gaulle, 1968 was an expression of rebellion against powerlessness, a powerlessness that *participation* could mitigate. With the tools for financial *participation* already in place, de Gaulle planned to concentrate on *participation* via greater consultation.[32]

At the height of the unrest in France's universities and factories, on May 24, de Gaulle addressed the nation.[33] He announced that legislative elections were to be held at the end of June 1968, and that these would be followed by a referendum (sometime in 1969) whose purpose would be to provide a mandate for reform and a reinvigoration of *participation*. The legislative elections and the referendum were not intended to serve the same function. The legislative elections were designed to rally the population behind order and stability after the events of May 1968. They succeeded in that Gaullists won a large majority in the new National Assembly—358 out of 485 seats. But that victory was not a mandate for fundamental reform. It was the purpose of the referendum to provide that mandate.

De Gaulle's plans required an extension of *participation* at three levels. The first involved the transformation of the Senate into a new upper chamber composed of representatives of the economic and social interests in society. The new chamber would have the right to debate government proposals and make recommendations. But its powers were consultative only. The proposal for a new senate was an explicit attempt to create a corporatist-style institution that would, it was hoped, make government legislation on social and economic matters more palatable to the rank-and-file members of the organizations represented in the Senate. Government proposals would then emerge from the Senate with enhanced legitimacy. The second prong of the proposed package entailed a decentralization of this corporatist-style consultation to the regional level via the creation of regional social and economic councils modeled on the new national Senate.

Finally, *participation* at the firm level was to be extended by a law that would make it obligatory for firms to make information about their financial and economic health available to the work force. But, crucially, de Gaulle envisaged that information being made available to representatives of each category of employee "chosen by all their members, in a secret ballot, from candidates *put forward freely*."[34] This phrase was a coded challenge to the so-called union monopoly, which allowed only representatives of nationally recognized union confederations to stand in the first round of professional elections.

A number of features of de Gaulle's plans to extend *participation* are worth noting. First, this was corporatism without the structural preconditions for corporatism. In other words, the plan called for the creation of institutions that would allow national-level bargaining while doing nothing to help the representatives of capital and labor control their members. Even if the social partners, as represented in the new Senate, could be induced to endorse government legislation, they had no way of disciplining their members. The central problem of French unionism was ignored. This alone doomed the scheme. Second, the overall plan was incoherent because it attempted to decentralize and centralize labor regulation at the same time. The goal of depoliticizing labor regulation by shifting its focus to the regional level and the firm was intelligible in light of the events of May 1968, but the proposal for a new national Senate would have created a national forum in which the state's role in labor regulation would have been highlighted rather than mystified. Intelligent labor unions could have used such a forum to further politicize labor regulation.

Third, de Gaulle's plan was explicitly antiunion. Even after May 1968 and the creation of a legally secure position for union sections on the shopfloor, it was clear that de Gaulle did not acknowledge a role for labor unions in labor regulation. He regarded them as alien influences in the firm, detrimental to the notion of a classless capital-labor association. Finally, de Gaulle was actually giving away very little. The new law providing for information exchange in the firm would be consultative only and was not intended to institutionalize a new role for worker representatives in the firm.

There were economic as well as ideological considerations involved in limiting this extension of *participation* to the more intangible realm of consultative issues. The wage increases won by workers in the course of May–June 1968 made the first priority of the government that of rebuilding profitability. The aim of de Gaulle in the immediate post-May 1968 period was to allow firms to restore profit margins by holding down wage increases while allowing prices to rise, thus eroding the real value of the wage increases. This strategy made any notion of relaunching collective bargaining inappropriate because the unions were determined above all else to protect their wage gains against inflation. It also meant that the government had nothing to give away that might win some union support.

This led to the disaster of the "Tilsitt Conference." The Grenelle Accords had specified that another tripartite (employers, unions, and government) national-level meeting would take place in March 1969 in order to check on the progress made in the intervening period, particularly with regard to the impact of inflation on real wages. From December 1968 onward government and employer declarations concerning the need to limit wage increases in the battle against inflation multiplied. In order to remain internationally competitive, it was argued, workers should exercise self-restraint and there should be a "pause" in the rate of social reform. Hence, from this perspective, Tilsitt should be consultative only and avoid Grenelle-style across-the-board wage increases. The unions had other ideas, particularly since inflation was accelerating, and the result was deadlock and bitter recriminations.

A social strategy that involved encouraging *la politique contractuelle* was simply impossible when the government and employers felt they had nothing to give away. Hence *participation* with its deliberate goal of bypassing unions and integrating the incomes of workers into the accumulation needs of the firm was not only more palatable to the ideological proclivities of de Gaulle, it also conformed to the economic strategy followed in the first few months after May 1968.

The reaction of the social partners to the Gaullist strategy was predictable: there was almost unanimous hostility. All the unions pointed out the corporatist implications of the plan. As the CGT put it, the plan "tends, in reality, to make workers collaborate in their own exploitation under the misleading cover of *participation*, which is a new label stuck onto the old theory of a partnership of capital and labor. The core of this project is a new attempt to integrate trade unions into the state."[35] The CFDT remarked that the failure of the Tilsitt conference was a clear indication of the government's unwillingness to make material concessions to workers.

The *patronat* was also wary. On the one hand, many large employers recognized that after May 1968 no scheme that ignored or bypassed unions was viable. On the other hand, for small employers there was a fear that the reality of *participation* might catch up with its rhetoric. An infringement of managerial prerogative might be expected to alarm employers under any circumstances, but particularly those of France. *Le Nouvel Observateur* (September 3, 1973) quoted one employer as saying: "If we were in West Germany, with reformist trade unions, we would be in favor of *participation*. But in France we have to deal with the CGT and the CFDT. . . . We do not wish to set the fox to mind the geese." In addition many employers hoped to claw back some of the wage increases that had been conceded in May and June 1968 with increased productivity and a restructuring of the work process. Increased *participation* of the kind suggested by de Gaulle could only act as an obstacle to this.

The referendum took place on April 27, 1969, and the reform proposals were defeated by 52.4 percent to 47.6 percent. The defeat was significant because de Gaulle had made it quite clear that he intended to resign if defeated. Much of the "yes" vote can probably be attributed to support for de Gaulle himself rather than his proposed reforms.[36] The truth was that de Gaulle's reforms had no real constituency, and this was particularly true of the firm-level elements. The trade unions saw it as an attack on their very existence and function. Workers saw nothing in the reforms or the government's behavior in the previous nine months to indicate that they would make any material gain. The "modernist" employers recognized that unions could not be simply bypassed, while the "traditional" employers feared any diminution of managerial prerogative. As Capdevielle and Mouriaux put it: "Imposing *participation* in the firm is like playing with fire, because it risks re-creating a united trade union front against the project. It means fighting on two fronts at the same time: against the employers and against the trade unions."[37]

Thus de Gaulle's proposals for giving a legislative impetus to *participation* were never implemented. Ultimately the reforms failed because de Gaulle was completely out of touch with how much May 1968 had changed the social landscape. It was generally recognized that one had to deal with the unions. French unions remained weak in a structural sense, even after May 1968, but they had proved themselves to be the natural channel for industrial conflict. Labor regulation that bypassed trade unions might have been possible at a time of union weakness and decline, but French trade unions were probably stronger in the immediate post-1968 period than at any other time in their history. So long as conflict remained, and particularly when it was at the heightened levels of the period after May 1968, labor unions would have a fundamental role to play in labor regulation. They could not be bypassed, nor could conflict be contained at the firm level.

De Gaulle also missed the importance of the relationship between a mode of regulation and a regime of accumulation. The basic task that French governments set themselves in the 1960s and right up to the onset of economic crisis in 1973 was the modernization of the French economy, and with it the consolidation of Fordism in France. The role of labor regulation was to ease this process, a task that required modernizing social relations. The social costs of restructuring had to be "managed," predictability enhanced, and industrial disruption minimized. The *participation* schemes of 1968–69 could not achieve these goals. Conflict existed; it could not be made to disappear, nor could it be contained at the firm level. So the task of labor regulation was to channel that conflict. This was not, in short, the time to further fragment the labor movement, even had that been possible. Economic modernization required the cooperation of labor, not its emasculation.

However, there is a wider importance to this failed historical episode. The theme of *participation*—what I have identified analytically as microcorporatist labor regulation—outlived de Gaulle. *Participation* has reappeared repeatedly. Indeed its popularity appears to enjoy a kind of inverse relationship with that of collective bargaining. Whenever the latter is in difficulty, the old Gaullist notion of bypassing unions and economically incorporating workers into their place of work resurfaces.

Thus, from 1972 onward the language of *participation* reappeared. In May 1972, in front of the National Assembly, and only weeks before his replacement as prime minister by Pierre Messmer, Chaban-Delmas called for a new impetus to be given to profit-sharing and *participation*. His proposal was to make profit-sharing more appealing to workers by allowing them to choose between schemes that allowed them immediate access to a proportion of profits and schemes that blocked access for a number of years. Politically, this was a deliberate attempt to woo the left-wing Gaullists, but it also marked Chaban-Delmas's recognition that his strategy of working with unions to develop collective bargaining had proved disappointing.

Once Messmer became prime minister the measures to encourage *participation* multiplied. Most importantly, in 1973 a series of laws were passed that provided a stimulus to the existing 1959 and 1967 legislation on *participation*. First, a new form of *participation*—worker shareholding—was introduced. Workers would now be able to own shares in their firms and ultimately to have their own representatives on the board of directors. Second, the 1959 and 1967 legislation on profit-sharing was "harmonized." All profit-sharing accords could now be signed by the works council, whereas previously the 1967 legislation had allowed this procedure while the 1959 legislation had maintained a privileged role for labor unions. Hence, the hostility of employers to signing such accords, because they involved dealing with union delegates, could be overcome.

As *participation* schemes resurfaced so did hostility to the "union monopoly." In 1972 a group of forty-six deputies sponsored a legislative proposal that aimed to end the privileged role of unions in the first round of professional elections, and that also sought the right for employers to negotiate salary accords with the works council as well as union delegates.[38]

These are indications of the continued hostility of important sections of French business and government to the role of unions in French industrial relations, and the wish to privilege firm-based labor collectivities (primarily the works council) at the expense of organizations that linked workers across firms into wider collectivities on the basis of trade or class. But, paradoxically, it was the arrival of the union section in the workplace with legal protection that provided the biggest impetus to expanding the role of the works council and hence the goal of *participation* in France (as chapter 4 will demonstrate).

Nevertheless, whatever the long-term viability of a nonunion form of labor regulation, in the short term the Gaullist social project failed. Workers saw the plan as a weak attempt to co-opt them without giving either real influence or material gain. Trade unions saw it as an attempt to reduce them to irrelevance. Employers either feared that *participation* was really some form of comanagement or recognized that unions were too strong to be ignored in the heady aftermath of May 1968. Thus *participation* lacked a constituency among the very social groups—workers and employers—to which it was directed.

The failure of the Gaullist project, and the resignation of its architect after the April 1969 referendum, cleared the way for a radically different response to the crisis of labor regulation posed by May 1968. The New Society program of Georges Pompidou's first prime minister, Jacques Chaban-Delmas, was a deliberate, very ambitious effort to remold labor regulation in France. The goal was a system of regularized collective bargaining between trade unions and employers. The fate of this project is the subject of the next chapter.

CHAPTER FOUR

The New Society and Its Enemies, 1969–74

> "The transformation of social relations in France [is my main goal]. It is not reasonable that in 1969 the relationship between employers and employees be perpetually those of conflict. We must establish new practices founded upon the idea and respect of contracts. We must make employers understand that the trade unions are their natural interlocutors and that they must take the trade unions' opinions into account before acting."
>
> —Georges Pompidou[1]

> "It's a good speech," said one. "But it's only a speech," replied the other.
>
> —Two parliamentarians after Jacques Chaban-Delmas's "New Society" speech.[2]

THE CONJUNCTURE AND GOALS OF THE NEW SOCIETY

The period of the New Society corresponds very closely to the premiership of Jacques Chaban-Delmas, who became prime minister in July 1969 and remained in that post until June 1972. The speech that launched the New Society came on September 16, 1969, in front of the National Assembly. That speech ranged widely over the areas of French backwardness and the modernization necessary for France to take its place among the other advanced capitalist democracies. I will be concerned, in this chapter, only with those reforms that relate to industrial relations and labor regulation. However, the package of reforms taken together made a coherent whole. Its goal was *social* modernization, in the hope that such modernization would reduce ideological extremism and permit economic modernization.

When Georges Pompidou was elected president in the wake of de Gaulle's resignation, he had two somewhat contradictory electoral objectives. The first was to consolidate Gaullist support for himself, thus cementing his legitimacy as de Gaulle's successor, and the second was to reach out to new social groups, mostly white-collar and middle-class groups. But whereas de Gaulle had been able to hold together a broad cross-class coalition with charismatic nationalism and anticommunism, Pompidou would have to find material incentives for keeping such groups out of the socialist and communist camps.

Pompidou's solution was to choose Chaban-Delmas as prime minister. He was a popular choice among Gaullists. But Chaban-Delmas in turn chose a number of most un-Gaullist advisers, capable, he hoped, of formulating an appeal to the center. The most important of these was Jacques Delors (indeed one commentator has referred to the reforms of this period as "social-delorisme").[3] Delors had been a CFTC activist and then worked in the plan bureaucracy. He typified the modernist, techno-cratic current that was becoming increasingly fashionable, particularly among Catholic groups, in the 1960s. The period in which Delors was adviser to Chaban-Delmas for social issues, and chief architect of the New Society, has had a long-term importance. After the fall of Chaban-Delmas, Delors joined the Socialist party and many of the same ideas that shaped the New Society were uncritically adopted by the PS, and later came to dominate its thinking on industrial relations when the PS came to power in 1981. The similarities in the diagnosis and prescription for the problems of labor regulation in France between the neo-Gaullist and the socialist approaches is striking, and in Delors we have an individual intel-lectual link between the two periods of reform which, if it cannot explain the similarity of approach, does at least help to explain the similarity of language.[4]

Chaban-Delmas became prime minister at a key conjuncture. In 1969 there were no national elections scheduled for three years, providing a breathing space in which *immediate* electoral needs would not impinge on the reform effort. And by mid-1969 it had become clear that there had been a successful restoration of profitability after May 1968. As rapid growth once again became the norm the government was no longer in the position of having to constantly respond to short-term economic pressures and, above all, had the room to give something away in order to entice the social partners to the negotiating table. Thus Chaban-Delmas was in the unusual position of being able to formulate and carry through a medium-to long-term project of reform with a coherence normally denied elected governments.

Chaban-Delmas was further aided by the shift in power within the CNPF, described in the last chapter, in favor of modern, Fordist firms which largely shared his goals. Certainly business did not present a united front of support, but its division into two distinct blocs—the most visible and vocal being supportive of the government—prevented a business veto of the New Society and provided the social space in which to implement it.

The New Society carried with it an impressive array of theoretical jus-tifications which were often sophisticated and borrowed directly from in-dustrial sociology, in its *Sociologie du Travail* form. It is worth spending a little time elaborating this theoretical armory both because it helps to ex-plain what the architects of the New Society hoped to achieve and because it is the same set of theoretical propositions that lay beneath the industrial relations reform efforts of the next fifteen years.

Just as in the Gaullist approach, the driving force behind the New Soci-ety was the notion that economic modernization required a modern set of social relations and social structures, and hence that the continued archaic nature of industrial relations was a brake on France's greatness. As Delors put it: "The point of departure is clear. An industrial society can only function well if its industrial relations are strong and properly adapted to the diverse issues that face them."[5]

However, in a way that was fundamentally different from the Gaullist position, this view argued that industrial conflict was inevitable. It could not be superseded or eliminated in industrial society. The point, therefore, was to channel conflict in ways that minimized the negative consequences for the French state and economy. The development of regularized forms of bargaining between social groups, *without* the constant mediation of the state, would reduce the politicization of social relations and avoid the situation in which all conflict, of whatever form, ended up directing itself against the state. For Delors, "Only a society that is decentralized can find the mechanisms to deal with tension at the correct level and avoid the least little issue becoming a national drama."[6] In addition, since, according to Chaban-Delmas, "this conservatism of the social structures fosters ideological extremism,"[7] then modernizing social relations would, it was hoped, also reduce the ideological polarization that marked French society and discourse. There are interesting echoes here of the reasoning of the "end of ideology" theorists—interesting not least because one might have assumed that the events of 1967–69 throughout the advanced capitalist world had crippled that thesis.

The main problems of the existing system of labor regulation, as identified by theorists of the New Society, were threefold. First, the organizations representing workers and employers were very weak. The French system of industrial relations encouraged irresponsibility. Unions would not sign contracts that committed them to refrain from industrial action because of their inability to control their members and the competitive rivalry between unions. Employers had equally little incentive to bargain and sign contracts with unions since the unions could not ensure industrial peace for the life of the contract. The problem, therefore, lay primarily with the organizations representing workers. Second, the role of the state in labor regulation was too great. This was both a cause and a consequence of the weakness of existing collective-bargaining practices. An enlarged role for state regulation had the obvious consequence of politicizing industrial conflict, but it also diminished the ability of the state to act in other areas. As Delors put it:

> I decry the powerlessness of the state, in its present form, to reach a new decisive stage of French progress. This omnipresent state lacks muscle because it is stuck with the useless fat of tasks that would be better performed by decentralized collectivities; it discourages the taking of responsibility, the creativity, and the involvement of groups of citizens.[8]

Third, the locus of labor regulation in the past had been misdirected. It took place at the branch level, or by state intervention, whereas the firm should be the locus of labor regulation because that was where conflicts originated and hence where they should be dealt with.

These arguments shared some features with the Gaullist critique, in particular the focus on the firm as the locus of conflict regulation. But while de Gaulle might have recognized the weakness of trade unions, he had no wish to strengthen them. Rather he sought to bypass unions and resolve conflict in the firm by measures that would tie workers' interests more closely to those of their firm. In addition, de Gaulle did not blame excessive state intervention for problems of labor regulation. A strong state was a necessary part of de Gaulle's vision of France.

Given the diagnosis of Delors and Chaban-Delmas, the prescription for a new, modernized form of labor regulation was fairly clear. It would be necessary to develop the practice of collective bargaining between representatives of workers and employers at the firm level. A decentralized, firm-based form of labor regulation would in turn allow the state to withdraw from the regulatory role that it had previously played. This implied a new role for the state: "I must stress the new standpoint the state has adopted: that of a vigilant partner, inclined not so much to circumscribe its own sovereignty, as to shape its texts and financial interventions while taking the largest possible account of the aspirations of the social partners."[9]

The means for this change lay in a strengthening of trade unions. This was the defining feature of the New Society. While de Gaulle had been hostile to unions, Chaban-Delmas believed that any new form of regulation that hoped to avoid a repeat performance of May 1968 must include the unions. This was because of the curious juxtaposition of structural weakness and conjunctural strength endemic to French unionism. This dualism was well captured by Delors' characterization: "French trade unionism is strong in particular instances, but, before 1968, it was relatively weak in practical day-to-day life."[10] French unions were not strong enough to have developed the institutional forms for collective bargaining (either at the firm or the national level), but they were still the channel through which the exceptional militancy of French workers flowed. That is why, in marked contrast to the periods before and after the New Society, there was an almost complete absence of antiunion rhetoric emanating from the government, and time and time again government officials refused to question the "union monopoly."[11]

The discussion of the role of trade unions by Chaban-Delmas, Delors, and other proponents of the New Society shows an explicit understanding of the structural preconditions necessary for a form of labor regulation based on collective bargaining. The problem was to strengthen union organizations so that they would be able to discipline their members sufficiently to keep their side of a bargain. A contract that was liable to be disrupted by industrial action would hold no appeal for employers. As Capdevielle and Mouriaux point out, with the benefit of hindsight, the long hard industrial disputes of the period from 1969 to 1973 tended to be in firms where unions were weak or absent.[12]

Nevertheless, the problem of the ideological radicalism of the CGT and CFDT remained. Chaban-Delmas did appear to believe that the CFDT could be won over to the side of the New Society, and the choice of Delors as adviser on social issues was not based solely on his expertise. Delors was a representative of a particular current of Catholic unionism. There was much in the ideology of the CFDT in the 1960s that made it susceptible to an appeal from Chaban-Delmas. Democratic planning had been endorsed by the radical wing of the CFTC and carried over into the CFDT. The notion of a *salaire de progrès*, based on a link between wages, national growth, and firm productivity had been supported by the CFDT in the 1968 Électricité et Gaz de France (EGF) contract. But Chaban-Delmas, and Delors himself, miscalculated the impact of the events of May 1968 on CFDT thinking. In this respect the timing of the New Society reforms, coming at precisely the moment of the greatest radicalization of the CFDT, was unfortunate for the proponents of the reforms. As events in the public sector were soon to show, the CFDT had moved from cautious interest to outright opposition in the course of 1970.

The CGT was still far and away the largest union, and it remained closely aligned to the PCF. Strengthening the CGT was an unlikely goal for a Gaullist government. One part of Chaban-Delmas may have believed that the radicalism of the CGT was a consequence rather than a cause of the poor development of the system of industrial relations, and hence that the CGT could be drawn into collective bargaining, regardless of its "antisystem" rhetoric, provided that the incentives were sufficient. (This was the sense of the remark quoted earlier, that conservative social structures give rise to extreme ideologies.) But more generally, there was recognition on the part of the government that the existing system could only benefit the CGT and the PCF. This was the reasoning behind Pompidou's often-quoted remark to Eugene Descamps of the CFDT during the Grenelle talks of May 1968:

> You are demanding legal rights for unions in the firm. The communists have party cells in the factories, so it is not important for them that unions be recognized in the firm. FO does not exist in private-sector firms. You are the only [union] that is really interested. Well listen, so that we can have done with this and start work again tomorrow morning, I grant you the right to legal protection for unions in the firm.[13]

Thus the theorists of the New Society saw a clear link between the structures and institutions of industrial relations systems and the ideology and strategy adopted by trade unions. A deradicalization and "regularization" of social relations was believed possible if the form of labor regulation could be changed. But clearly, the highly abstract sociological argumentation had force because it responded to concrete problems faced by the post-1968 French state and economy. The nature of these problems is important because ultimately it would be upon its ability to deal with specific, concrete problems, rather than grand schemes of social engineering, that the New Society would be judged. Thus the wider issue of politicization (and the overflow from industrial to political radicalism), while very salient to those who had experienced the events of May 1968, became less immediate and took second place to the economic consequences of 1968.

The modernization of French industry required industrial peace and a measure of predictability. It was this that May 1968 had shown the old form of labor regulation to be unable to provide. The highly capitalized and interdependent modern industries needed to maintain constant production. The massive public-sector strikes of May 1968 posed a serious challenge to the ability of firms to achieve this. The goal of the New Society in the public sector was to create a stable system of collective bargaining which would minimize strike disruption.

In the private sector the aim of the New Society was to regulate the relationship between wages and accumulation. As the French economy became more Fordist, and wages became a component of demand for employers rather than simply a cost of production, various forms of linkage between wages, productivity, and inflation became important. Whether these mechanisms were indirect (regularized collective bargaining) or direct (indexation), their purpose was to allow real wages to rise steadily in line with productivity so as to assure a high level of demand. The dilemma was how to tie wages to productivity, in order that demand could grow steadily and inflation be minimized, while at the same time avoiding the rigidity that would result either from wage-setting by the state, or from high-level wage negotiation of the corporatist kind (which was in any case impossible in the French situation). The dilemma was nicely captured by Minister of Labor Joseph Fontanet's call for a manner of determining wages that avoided the extremes of either a "libéralisme sauvage" (unrestrained liberalism) or a "politique des revenus" (incomes policy). Neither would be an answer to the needs of the French economy at this time, nor were they possible under French conditions. Hence, with "the type of economy and social relations that we have [in France], wage negotiations must be decentralized."[14] The New Society was designed to encourage firm-level bargaining, which would allow the negotiation of *real* wages.

Thus the New Society came at a particular conjuncture. On the one hand it was needed to respond to the economic and social imperatives of modernization. On the other hand there was a brief political and economic "window of opportunity" which made the experiment possible. In this space the government of Chaban-Delmas sought to create the legal and political environment within which decentralized collective bargaining between strong, responsible trade unions, and employers that treated unions as legitimate negotiators, could take place.

New Society initiatives in the area of industrial relations can be usefully divided into those aimed at the public sector and those intended for the private sector. The two were connected, not least because the government hoped that the public sector could be used as an arena for experimentation which would in turn serve as a model for the private sector. However, the conditions in the public and private sectors were very different, and the impetus driving reform also differed between the two.

THE PUBLIC-SECTOR REFORMS

The attempt to rationalize industrial relations in the public sector made sense for two reasons.[15] First, the largest, most visible industrial disturbances of May 1968 had taken place in the public sector. These strikes had angered public opinion and also had had severe economic repercussions for businesses that relied upon rail transport or used electricity. These massive strikes were the most obvious sign of the failure of a particular mode of labor regulation in the public sector. The thrust of the New Society initiatives in the public sector was to minimize industrial disputes, and the government was prepared to sweeten the pot in order to achieve this end. Real wage rises in 1968 had been high (on average about 9 to 10 percent in nationalized firms),[16] and while the government wanted some control over the wage bill, that took second place to buying industrial peace.

The second reason for focusing reform efforts on the public sector was that unionization levels were much higher in the public sector than the national average. In the public sector union density approached the norm for Western Europe, and hence a strategy built around bringing unions into collective-bargaining practices would stand a better chance here than elsewhere; the structural preconditions for "responsible" unionism already existed.[17] The problem, in 1968, was that bargaining, when it did take place, was high-visibility, national-level bargaining. The goal of the Chaban-Delmas government was to decentralize and depoliticize this bargaining so that negotiations would occur between the unions and the managers of the firms themselves, not state officials.

The process of wage determination had long been a source of dispute. The Toutée Report of 1963, which led to the implementation of the Toutée-Grégoire procedure for wage bargaining, set up a three-stage process that effectively cut unions out of all but the last stage. In the first phase an independent body reported on the wage bill of the previous year. In the second phase the government decided how much it could afford in total wages for each firm in the coming year. Only then, in the third phase of deciding how to divide up that sum among different categories of workers, were the unions involved. Interestingly, one aspect of the original Toutée proposals, which the government chose not to adopt when it set up the wage-determination procedure in 1964, was the suggestion of *contrats de progrès* which would be multiyear, binding wage contracts (binding in the sense that strikes could not be called over clauses agreed upon in the contract). This notion of a *contrat de progrès* (a "progress contract") was a key element of the New Society reforms.[18] In fact in March 1968 a wage contract signed at EGF incorporated a *salaire de progrès* which tied a component of total wages to the evolution of firm productivity. This contract was signed by all the trade unions (the CFDT included) except the CGT, but it was soon overwhelmed by the events of May 1968. Nevertheless, this type of contract was another harbinger of the future.

In the wake of May 1968 the new government of Couve de Murville had asked a civil servant, René Martin, to look into new ways of determining wages in the public sector. However, the terms of the enquiry were strictly circumscribed. In February 1969, when Martin began work, the government priority was to limit wage increases, and above all to avoid high public-sector wages from being translated into high wages in the rest of the economy. This was the period of the disastrous tripartite Tilsitt conference. In any case, by the time Martin presented his report in August 1969, de Gaulle had gone and there was a new government headed by Chaban-Delmas. Thus the Martin Report was dead even before it was finished. It was inappropriate because its brief had not allowed it to offer anything by way of material gains to the unions. However, the Martin Report did give some partial indications of the approach that Chaban-Delmas would follow. Its goal was clearly to depoliticize the process of public-sector wage determination with the emphasis laid upon technocratic, "neutral" measures of income and inflation (in the hope that the unions would agree with them as a basis for discussion), and the report stressed the need to provide management with autonomy in dealing with unions so that wage bargaining would not turn into a confrontation with the state. A report that had appeared in 1967, conducted by Simon Nora, who was to become one of Chaban-Delmas's closest advisers, had focused upon the relationship between public-sector firms and the state. It had recommended that *contrats de programme* be signed between each public-sector firm and the state, laying out the financial relationship between them as well as the degree of autonomy of the firm. The Martin Report endorsed the idea of financial autonomy of public-sector firms from the state in order to depoliticize the process of wage determination and stimulate collective bargaining, because for this to happen it would be necessary for unions to seek wage increases that were consistent with the needs and performance of the firm itself, and not to expect the government to bail out any wage negotiations that were going badly.

The key to the new government approach in the public-sector were the progress contracts. The idea was that:

> They will allow workers in the public sector to share both in the fruits of national [economic] expansion and in the specific progress of each firm. Thus multiyear progress contracts, which deal notably with improving working conditions as well as ways of assuring the proper functioning and continuity of public service, can be discussed and concluded in each firm.[19]

In fact the first progress contract was signed in October 1969 in the civil service, but it dealt with grade classifications rather than wages. Thus the first real progress contract (and, in fact, the only pure one of its kind) was signed at Électicité et Gaz de France (EGF) in December 1969. It is worth looking at this contract closely because it incorporated much of the logic of the New Society. EGF was chosen both because of the disruptive impact of strikes in that industry (the *patronat* frequently mentioned the costs of power cuts on business) and because of the strength of unions at EGF. There was over 90 percent turnout at professional elections at EGF, and at the last elections in July 1969 the CGT had received over 55 percent of the votes cast.[20] Thus the choice of EGF illustrated the belief on the part of Chaban-Delmas and Delors that unions were necessary for achieving social peace.

The EGF contract was, in essence, a complex formula for arriving at the annual wage figure. The formula included an indexation to the gross domestic product (GDP), plus an indexation to firm productivity (which was measured in terms of sales and profits). In addition, the contract was a multiyear contract (management initially wanted three years, but the final agreement was for two years) during which time there could be no industrial dispute resulting in a withdrawal of labor. At any point in the life of the contract the unions could "denounce" the contract, which meant rejecting it in its entirety, and they would then have to wait three months before initiating any industrial action. When the contract was signed Chaban-Delmas triumphantly declared that there would be no power cuts for two years. A final feature of the EGF contract was that it was signed by the management of EGF and not, as was usual, the minister responsible for public services.[21]

The logic and purpose of the progress contract at EGF was threefold. First, wage bargaining would become technocratic and automatic, rather than open-ended. A proportion of the wage bill was calculated on the basis of set formulas that were tied to a set of measures beyond the control of workers. It was hoped this would depoliticize the process. Second, there was an *integrative logic*, in the sense that wage negotiations would now internalize the needs of both the firm and the economy. Wages would reflect productivity gains within the firm and growth in the economy as a whole. The point was made most clearly by Gilbert Declercq, who opposed the signing of the contract from inside the CFDT:

> The fundamental difference between a collective agreement that leaves the trade union free and independent, and the *"contrat de progrès et de paix sociale,"* is that the latter ties the fate of workers to the uncertainties of capitalist economic policy. So it is exactly what is termed "integration." When it is admitted, as in the EGF contract for example, that the greater part of the evolution of wages will depend on anticipated growth in GDP or productivity in the firm, without fixing precise figures, one is fully integrated into the system. There is not a difference of degree but one of kind, between the progress contracts and the traditional collective agreement.[22]

Thus both the automaticity and integrative logic of the progress contract made it a form of incomes policy. Third, the progress contract at EGF limited the right to strike. Thus it aimed to make the unions "responsible"; signing a contract would now involve reciprocal obligations and not an open-ended agreement that unions could denounce at will.

So what happened at EGF? The CFDT and the other unions signed the wage contract, with only the CGT refusing. The CGT called a referendum among employees of the firm on the contract in which a majority rejected the contract (the percentage for rejection was slightly higher than the percentage of people voting for the CGT in the last professional elections), though the contract continued to operate and the other unions denounced the practice of calling referendums on contracts. Whatever its official position, the referendum put tremendous pressure on the CFDT, particularly at a time when it was undergoing its post-1968 radicalization. On the defensive, the CFDT denied charges coming from within its own ranks that it had acceded to the abrogation of the right to strike and to integration into the logic of capitalism. Opposition within the CFDT grew. There was significant opposition within the Fédération Gaz-Électricité of the CFDT (FGE-CFDT), which had actually negotiated the December 1969 contract.[23] The opposition also manifested itself more widely within the CFDT at the confederal council meeting of the CFDT in March 1970[24] and at the 35th Congress of the CFDT in May 1970.[25] The attitude of the CFDT to the progress contracts hardened throughout the summer and autumn of 1970, and in 1971 it insisted that two codicils be added to the original December 1969 agreement that stripped it of its initial purpose. The three-month delay in calling for industrial action was eliminated, and it was agreed that there would be an automatic, minimum rise in wages (*above* inflation) of 2.5 percent in 1971 and 2 to 3 percent in 1972. Thus the original formula still existed, but a floor was created for a minimum increase. Thus both the incomes policy and the social peace elements of the contract were eliminated.

As Bunel and Meunier have pointed out, there were in fact three types of progress contract used in this period of the New Society.[26] The EGF contract was the only example of the no-strike, full indexation type. A contract signed at the SNCF in February 1970 was of a second type, providing a minimum increase (usually 2 to 3 percent per annum) in wages above inflation and lasting one year only. A third type was signed at RATP in March 1971 and Charbonnages de France in February 1971 (and the EGF contract resembled this kind after the amendments of 1971). This type was also a one-year contract, with a guaranteed minimum above inflation, but it also had a component that was indexed to gross domestic product. The second and third types were completely different in effect. Indeed, from 1971 onward, Chaban-Delmas stopped using the term *contrat de progrès*.[27]

The important question is why the original idea of the progress contracts failed.[28] The most frequent explanation, particularly from within the government, was that the fault lay primarily with the CGT, which used its industrial strength to destroy the progress contracts for the directly political aim of discrediting the project of the New Society because of its potential appeal to workers and rank-and-file unionists. This explanation can be at best only partial. After all, the CGT had refused to sign the March 1968 *salaire de progrès* contract at EGF well before Chaban-Delmas appeared on the scene, and the CGT did in fact sign a number of the other public-sector contracts of 1970 and 1971, including one in the civil service in April 1970 and one in the SNCF in January 1971. In fact, the CGT signed the amended version of the EGF contract in February 1971. It is unclear why the CGT would have chosen to oppose only the original EGF-style contract if its opposition was political.

The answer must lie in the nature of the original EGF contract itself, and in the fact that it struck at the heart of the dilemma of French unionism. The CGT, and soon the CFDT, recognized that French unions could not cope with the kind of industrial relations system being proposed by Chaban-Delmas. The no-strike clause confronted head-on the problem of labor discipline. Even where union density was fairly high, as in the public sector, unions could not control their members, particularly where rival unions fought with each other for members. While it was possible for the CGC and FO to sign these contracts because their memberships did not overlap, such was not the case for the CGT and CFDT. The shift in the position of the CFDT must be largely attributed to its fear that sticking to an unpopular contract would lead to a shift in support to the CGT. Above all, in a system in which unions are best described as "skilled surfboard riders"[29] it is tremendously difficult to make a commitment not to strike.

French unions, by and large, follow strikes, they do not lead them. In explaining his abandonment of the original intent of the progress contracts, Delors implicitly recognized this: "In each contract of a certain fixed duration it is necessary to reconcile two contradictory aspects of social policy: the necessity of allowing for the spontaneity of the rank and file and the positions of union representatives; and the necessity of a certain adaptation to the often uncertain variations in prices and production."[30]

The EGF contract was also dangerous for labor because its logic was a demobilizing one. Mobilizing union members for wage negotiations was difficult when the wage contract emerged in an automatic fashion from the application of a formula to economic variables outside the control of unions. French unionism is a mobilizational unionism; unions depend on periodic mobilization of their members in order to maintain organizational integrity.

Ultimately, then, the problem was not one of political hostility but rather of the structural weakness of French unionism, a weakness that the progress contracts did not address. The hope of the government was that if sufficient material incentives could be provided the unions would be drawn to the negotiating table, regardless of their misgivings, and eventually regularized bargaining would lead to a shift—essentially a moderation—in union attitudes. But the contracts, while materially attractive, did not change the *ability* of French unions to sign contracts which tied their hands. The obstacles were structural, not ideological.

Nevertheless, the progress contracts, in their revised, watered-down form, did have some important effects. Regularized negotiations, in which unions were genuinely involved, did take place and set a pattern for the future. The contracts were sufficiently generous that it was hard for any union to take a principled stand against them. This was clearly superior to the pre-1968 situation as far as the government was concerned. There were also some minor "copy-cat" effects in the private sector. The aspect of the progress contracts that was most copied was indexation of wages to the cost of living.[31] An agreement at Berliet was the only one to include a no-strike clause and this led to an interesting dispute between the local Union Metaux CFDT de Lyon, which signed the contract, and the Fédération Générale de la Métallurgie (CFDT), which condemned the no-strike pledge.[32]

However, it is hard to say just how much of this spate of indexation agreements would have occurred anyway in a period of accelerating inflation, when unions saw their main task as defending the purchasing power of their members. Perhaps the contracts in the public sector indirectly helped because indexation was technically illegal and so long as the state was doing it, it was unlikely to challenge the practice in the private sector.[33]

Nevertheless, the original objectives of the progress contracts went unfulfilled. In addition, the process initiated by the progress contracts had unintended consequences that served to store up problems for the future. First, the objective of reducing industrial disruption in the public sector was largely unsuccessful. The mean number of days lost to strike action did not decline significantly in public-sector firms (with the exception of EGF where Chaban-Delmas's triumphalism proved more merited).[34] Thus whatever the gains in terms of regularized bargaining, social peace was not among them.

Second, the focus of union negotiation remained the state, with the consequence that wage determination remained highly politicized. The *contrats de programme* between the state and public enterprises were a failure. This had been seen as the key to depoliticization. Only if the managers of these firms were seen as autonomous from the state would unions consider negotiations with the managers worthwhile. Most public firms never achieved the status of being self-financing, particularly with the onset of economic crisis. This was clearest at EGF, where the rise in oil prices from 1973 onward destroyed any hopes of financial independence and autonomy. Ultimately the unions ended up confronting the state and its policies, not the autonomous management of public firms. The unions were quick to demand meetings with the minister of labor or the prime minister whenever negotiations ran into difficulties. Throughout 1970, 1971, and 1972 a similar pattern repeated itself. Negotiations in the public sector would go badly in the spring, the unions would schedule protest demonstrations, commentators would announce the end of *la politique contractuelle*, and then the government would step in at year's end to ensure an agreement was reached.

This leads to the third and most important consequence of the 1969–72 period. The development of regularized annual negotiations did not just draw reluctant unions into the bargaining process. The Chaban-Delmas government, and even more so its successors, also had a stake in continued negotiations. The agreements were important enough to make successive governments willing to make significant concessions to keep them going. The agreements had an economic purpose, but even more, they had a political purpose, particularly as France entered a period of hard-fought elections. The public-sector agreements were the visible sign of the government's commitment to collective bargaining, and no government wanted to be held responsible for its collapse. However, the only way to keep the process running was to make the wage contracts attractive, which in turn meant a solid assurance that wages would keep pace with the cost of living and that guaranteed minimum annual real wage increases. While Chaban-Delmas and Delors had initially made increases contingent on national growth and gains in productivity, this became translated into guaranteed increases (usually at least 2 percent a year) regardless of how the economy was performing.

Both unions and the government had a stake in these agreements. However, as the state of the economy worsened from 1973 onward, and inflation became the primary fear of governments, these agreements became increasingly hard to sustain. Unions were determined to defend the purchasing power of their members. Thus from 1973 onward governments faced a stark choice. They could preserve regular bargaining by continuing to offer attractive wage contracts despite the impact on the economy, and the carryover effect on private-sector wages, or they could end the real wage increases and inflation-proofing, and in the process cripple collective bargaining in the public sector, perhaps abandoning the middle ground to the Left in the process. The problem came not only from the CGT and CFDT but also from the more moderate FO. FO made the defense of purchasing power its sine qua non for participation in public-sector negotiations.

The policy inheritance of the 1969–72 period was in fact an *increased* rigidity of wages, and the building-in of price indexation to the collective-bargaining system. The New Society came back to haunt succeeding governments as they faced the dilemma of whether to continue with the process or end it. One indication of this dilemma was the proliferation of calls for an incomes policy which emanated from the Ministry of Finance during this period.

THE PRIVATE-SECTOR REFORMS

The approach of the government of Chaban-Delmas to labor regulation in the private sector was different from that in the public sector for two reasons. First, the state was not a direct participant in collective bargaining in the private sector, and so had to incite private actors; it could not coerce them to act in a certain way. Second, the level of unionization was generally much lower in the private sector, meaning that unions had to be strengthened as a precondition to bargaining. While the hope in the public sector had been that the mere existence of regular negotiations (so long as the stakes were made attractive enough) would lead to an attitudinal shift on the part of the social partners, in the private sector a deliberate effort had to be made to alter the locus of bargaining and expand labor collectivity.

The traditional focus of collective bargaining had been the branch (or industry) level, and the government now attempted to encourage bargaining both at the national/confederal level and at the level of the firm. High-level bargaining between union confederations and employers' organizations would permit negotiation on a wide range of social issues that, up until then, had been absent from the bargaining table. Bargaining at the firm level would, it was hoped, both provide a role for unions on the shopfloor, thus making them more relevant to workers' needs, and allow the negotiation of *real* wages, rather than the traditional reliance on wage minimums negotiated at the branch level. The plans of the Chaban-Delmas government in the private sector were designed to build upon, and take advantage of, the December 1968 law protecting union sections in the workplace. Greater scope for bargaining could be expected to stimulate the newly created union sections, setting off a virtuous circle of expanding unionization and greater collective bargaining.

A marked feature of the period after 1968, which, importantly, continued beyond the resignation of Chaban-Delmas in 1972, was the negotiation and signing of a wide variety of accords between the CNPF and some or all of the unions at the national/confederal level.[35] These accords were applicable to all the member firms of the employers' organization, and not limited to a particular branch or industry as had the been the norm in the past. At first glance this flowering of national-level accords has an air of corporatism about it. The accords were overwhelmingly concerned with social welfare issues, such as: job security (February 10, 1969), maternal leave (July 2, 1970), industrial training (July 9, 1970), early retirement (March 27, 1972), unemployment benefits (October 31, 1974), and work conditions (March 17, 1975).[36] There was also a joint employer-union declaration on the need to speed up the transfer of workers from hourly pay to salaried status.[37]

However, the status and implications of these accords must be understood in order to be clear just what trend in labor regulation they represented. In the first place the accords required no commitment from the unions. To overstate the case slightly, the unions were present at the negotiations for consultation, and to legitimize the agreements rather than as serious bargaining partners. Unions were never asked to deliver some action, or promise inaction, on the part of their members. Thus the structural weakness of French unionism was sidestepped and neither addressed nor challenged. Wages were not discussed in the context of these negotiations so there was no question of a quid pro quo of wage restraint for social benefits (the heart of corporatist bargaining). Indeed the *patronat* was so adamant that it refused any repeat of the Grenelle talks, which ensured the failure of the "Tilsitt rendez-vous" and scotched the unions' hopes for any future "mini-Grenelle." Thus, while national/confederal talks were undergoing a renaissance, they were strictly limited to social-welfare issues, not economic ones. Lyon-Caen characterized this kind of negotiation nicely by saying that the negotiation of social protection was not real negotiation, in the sense of a reciprocal engagement, but rather the negotiation of consequences.[38]

Second, as all contemporary commentators noted, the role of the state was of crucial importance. The state incited the negotiations by pressuring the social partners: it threatened legislation if the talks failed, and it often provided a part of the funds necessary for the success of a particular scheme. This should come as no surprise since the agreements were often followed by legislation that made their applicability universal, rather than limited to member firms of the signatory organizations. The flowering of high-level bargaining was underwritten at every stage by the state. A good example of both these points is provided by the accord that was reached on industrial training. The government constantly threatened legislation should the talks fail, and the outcome of the agreement gave full power and responsibility for the implementation of industrial-training programs to managers, and none to union delegates in the firm.[39] Thus a curious relationship existed between the law and bargaining. Bargaining at the national/confederal level flourished, but it was always just one step ahead of legislation, and it was bargaining in which the unions' agreement was largely incidental to the implementation of any agreement.

The way to understand this paradox is by recognizing that these accords were not in fact really part of any strategy of "relaunching" collective bargaining, as the government claimed. Rather they were part of the wider project of the New Society: the social modernization of France. These accords were designed to enable France to catch up with the rest of the advanced industrialized world by providing the basic social infrastructure necessary for continued economic modernization: training, unemployment benefits, and so on. Hence it is no surprise that these kinds of accords continued to be signed well after 1972 and into a period in which the economic situation made *wage* negotiations much more difficult. Indeed, as the economy moved into crisis from 1973 onward, there was, initially at least, *more* need for agreements on unemployment benefits and redundancy procedures, not less. It was particularly important to the Chaban-Delmas government that the social partners negotiate and finance the bulk of these social benefits themselves, because it was anxious to focus its expenditure on economic modernization rather than social infrastructure. The Sixth Plan placed a low priority on social infrastructure. While the dramatic increase in the extent of this kind of high-level bargaining was a part of the wider goals of the New Society, it should not be considered an indication of an autonomous growth in bargaining that would indicate a change in the mode of labor regulation.

There was also an attempt to shift the locus of bargaining downward to the firm level. The government of Chaban-Delmas, as indicated earlier, was convinced of the need to work with trade unions. The goal was to take advantage of the situation created by the December 1968 law (following the unsigned Grenelle Accords), which provided a legal place on the shopfloor for unions. It was hoped that providing legal protection for union sections would strengthen unions which in turn was a precondition for decentralized collective bargaining, along the lines of the British model. The general goal was outlined by Delors: "In the private sector this would involve negotiations on real wages, taking into account general economic data and data particular to the firm, with undertakings on both sides for a fixed duration."[40]

Delors wrote those lines in mid-1970, and he was clearly modeling his hopes for the private sector on the ideas behind the progress contracts in the public sector. As the public-sector progress contracts became adapted to the realities of French unionism, this hope faded in the private sector. However, the goal of a structural change in the mode of labor regulation remained.

More concretely, a change in the locus of collective bargaining would have an effect on wage determination. Here the aim was not so much to limit wages as to provide predictability, wage increases in line with productivity, and negotiations over real wages. The year 1968 had demonstrated the danger of the existing system: it had led to a wage explosion and across-the-board increases. The decentralization of wage bargaining would allow the negotiation of real wages, in which unions would, it was hoped, see some link between the firm's prosperity and their wage claims, a link that was much more opaque when bargaining occurred at higher levels.

In July 1971 the government legislated a reform of the 1950 law on collective bargaining (the basic law governing collective bargaining in France). This reform was a natural complement to the December 1968 law legalizing union sections in firms with over fifty employees in the sense that its aim was to take advantage of the new union presence in the firm in order to encourage firm-level bargaining. The original law of 1950 had made the branch level the privileged, but not exclusive, locus of bargaining. The aim of the reform was to revitalize both national/confederal and firm-level bargaining. Previously, firms could only sign *accords* (which dealt exclusively with wages), while *conventions collectives* (which cover the whole range of working conditions and social guarantees) could be signed only at the branch level. This was considered a disincentive to bargaining in the firm. With the reform, firms could now sign full *conventions collectives* as well as *accords* which made firm-level bargaining more attractive to both unions and employers. In addition, the reform made the procedure whereby the minister of labor could "extend" an agreement (so that it covered industries or regions wider than simply the signatories of the agreement) easier by reducing the veto power of the nationally representative trade union confederations to such an extension of an agreement.[41]

The goal of the reform was to bring a wider area under the coverage of negotiated agreements rather than leaving whole sectors uncovered and subject only to state regulation on minimum wages and working conditions. It was paradoxical, though typical of France, that transferring firms or industries from the domain of state regulation to that of bargaining should be done by legislation and the decisions of the minister of labor.

An interesting footnote to this reform is that the government did not choose to make bargaining obligatory, despite the claims by the CFDT that, under French conditions, inciting bargaining was not enough. The CFDT was convinced that the *patronat* would not bargain at the firm level with the newly legalized union sections unless coerced. That argument continued to be made until the socialists came to power in 1981 and made such bargaining obligatory.

How successful was the attempt to encourage a form of labor regulation based upon decentralized collective bargaining? The answer is unclear, not least because data of this sort is hard to find. Unlike the public sector there are no clear measures of success or failure. Indications can be found by looking at levels of unionization, the formation of works councils, the number of agreements signed, and the incidence of work stoppages. Together these factors help build a picture of industrial relations in the immediate post-1968 period.

Overall figures for union density are notoriously unreliable in France, as mentioned above. The research bureau of the CFDT has used the declared membership numbers of the CGT and CFDT to argue that the spurt in unionization due to the events of May 1968 *alone* was fairly low in comparison to similar growth periods in 1936–37 and 1945–47. Between 1967 and 1969 the CGT increased its membership by 18 percent and the CFDT by 21.7 percent.[42] Mouriaux and Subileau provide figures for the period after 1968 (see table 4.1). These figures show large gains for FO but surprisingly small gains for the two "revolutionary" unions. But if the overall levels of unionization did not increase much, union implantation (in the

TABLE 4.1
Union Membership, 1969–74

	CGT	CFDT	CGT-FO
1969	2,301,543	—	636,392
1970	2,333,056	882,052	810,886
1971	2,327,637	917,955	826,112
1972	2,318,120	966,863	843,552
1973	2,339,857	1,010,084	861,512
1974	2,342,811	1,015,401	874,427
Percent increase	1.8	15.1	37.4

Source: René Mouriaux and Françoise Subileau, "Données statistiques concernant le syndicalisme des salariés en France (1945–1986)," Document de Travail (Paris: CEVIPOF, 1986), 2–4.

sense of the number of union sections operating inside the workplace) did, in response to the December 1968 law. The law applied to firms with fifty or more employees, and of those firms the percentage having one or more union section rose from 27.5 percent in 1970 to 43 percent in 1974.[43] These figures disguise the very wide variations between firms of different sizes, with union sections being much more likely to exist in larger firms. For example, while 31.6 percent of firms employing between 50 and 149 workers had one or more union sections in 1974, the figure for those employing more than one thousand workers was 95.7 percent.[44]

The works council is the representative of workers' collective interests inside the firm, and there was a large increase between 1966–67 and 1970–71 when the number of works councils more than doubled.[45] But the key feature in the evolution of the works councils in this period was the steady decrease in votes cast in works council elections for nationally representative unions, and especially the "revolutionary" ones. After winning 84.5 percent of the votes in 1966–67, the five national union organizations won only 78.8 percent in 1970–71.[46] The lost votes were now being cast for the two categories entitled "nonunion" and "other union" (which usually meant enterprise unions, created or sponsored by the employer in a firm). The "nonunion" and "other union" vote also varies inversely with firm size: the smaller the firm the higher the vote for the nonunion–other union categories. Thus this period saw an increasing vitality of works councils, and yet a declining influence of the major, nationally representative unions within these institutions.

Records of collective agreements, particularly those signed at the firm level, are particularly poor.[47] The figures of the Ministry of Labor show a gradual rise in the number of agreements at all bargaining levels, beginning in 1965. Firm-level agreements show relative stability between 1960 and 1967 and then a sharp rise after 1968. Thus the events of May 1968 do seem to have stimulated firm-level bargaining (see table 4.2).

As for strikes, before 1975 there was no separation of strikes into categories on the basis of whether the strike order originated outside or inside the firm, and no subdivision into public- and private-sector strikes. Although the number of days lost to strike action declined in 1969 and 1970, it rose sharply in 1971, 1972, and 1973, before falling off in 1974. The level of strikes in 1971 was the highest since 1963 with the obvious exception of 1968 (see table 4.3). The pattern of strikes exhibited suggests that strike levels were still closely related to the state of the business cycle. Clearly, if a new mode of labor regulation was in the process of emerging it was not bringing industrial peace in its wake.

The picture that emerges then is murky: more union sections, more works councils, but also weaker union presence in the works councils;

TABLE 4.2
Firm-Level Agreements (including codicils), 1960–70

	Firm Agreements	Codicils
1960	50	228
1961	51	261
1962	52	378
1963	47	336
1964	55	235
1965	48	347
1966	44	309
1967	56	352
1968	52	529
1969	91	493
1970	84	574

Source: Liaisons Sociales: Législation Sociale, no. 3785 (July 20, 1971): 8.

greater collective bargaining but also an expansion of strike activity. The problem of interpretation remains.

The first issue is the relationship between unions and works councils. An important study of the evolution of works councils in this period has suggested that the increase in their number is best understood as a managerial response to the law legalizing union sections.[48] The institution of the works council could be used to preempt the strong implantation of unions in the firm. The *patronat* had been largely hostile to works councils before 1967, but attitudes changed in response to three pieces of legislation. The December 1968 law that had provided legal protection for union sections may have encouraged employers to establish works councils, in the hope of forestalling the creation of union sections. The 1967 ordinance on *participa-*

TABLE 4.3
Strikes, 1969–74

	Work Days Lost to Strikes (in millions)
1969	2.21
1970	1.78
1971	4.39
1972	3.76
1973	3.91
1974	0.34

Source: Mouriaux and Subileau, "Données Statistiques concernant le syndicalisme," 24.

tion, and the 1971 *interprofessionnel* agreement on industrial training, made accords on these issues between management and workers obligatory but left open whether the workers should be represented by union delegates or a works council. Employers therefore scrambled to create works councils in order to avoid having to negotiate with unions. This interpretation is confirmed by the fact that the "nonunion" and "other union" vote was much higher in recently formed works councils (those created since 1967). This casts a shadow over the notion that a new system of collective bargaining between unions and employers was created in this period. The changes appear to have been the result of a search by employers for an alternative bargaining partner to the trade unions.

The long-term implications of these developments were ominous for trade unions in France. Extending the potential role of the works council in conjunction with the potential threat from union sections gave employers an incentive to create works councils where none existed before, and to break with their previous opposition to any form of worker representation in the firm. The multiplication of works councils in this period represented a real change from the situation before. Workers' demands and interests would no longer be unmediated, but the mediator would now be a firm-based labor collectivity and not a trade union. Hence the process of creating the preconditions for *participation,* or what I have called microcorporatism, received an important, though unintended, boost.

A second issue is that of the interpretation which should be given to the increase in the amount of collective bargaining, and especially firm-level bargaining. Here the most convincing analysis is that of Bachy, Dupuy, and Martin.[49] The central question is whether the undeniable rise in firm-level bargaining was due to developments within the firm—the effect of the laws creating union sections and making bargaining at this level easier—or to events outside the firm, particularly the "fermentation" of the events of May 1968. For if the latter was the case, then the impetus came not from a greater willingness to bargain on the part of employers and unions but from a "one-shot" stimulus provided by the events of 1968.

A detailed study of accords signed in this period shows that the content was largely determined by government legislation or *interprofessionnel* agreements made at the national/confederal level by employers and unions. For instance, the categories of agreements that saw the largest increases were those concerning the working out of the details of *mensuelisation,* union rights in the firm, and reduction of the workday. These were all cases in which a general framework was set by legislation, or a high-level agreement between the social partners, and the details were left to be hammered out in the firm. In other words, the impetus clearly came from outside the firm.

The implication is that France did not experience the transition to a mode of labor regulation based on regularized collective bargaining between unions and employers, each recognizing the other as a legitimate bargaining partner. In this respect, at least, Chaban-Delmas's vision of a New Society was unfulfilled. In explaining this failure it is important to stress structural rather than ideological or attitudinal factors. Blaming the highly charged and polarized nature of French industrial relations and ideological discourse raises more questions than it answers.

The explanation for failure given by Chaban-Delmas, and to a lesser extent by Delors, hinges on the attitude of those in power.[50] Chaban-Delmas blamed Pompidou for not being fully committed to the New Society program. While this was certainly true, there is no evidence that Pompidou hindered the implementation of the program, nor that the program itself would have been more radical, and by implication more effective, had Pompidou been more fully behind his prime minister. Thirteen months after Chaban-Delmas outlined his New Society program in front of the National Assembly, the prime minister's office published a long document comparing the promises made in September 1969 with the measures achieved thus far.[51] Even allowing for the self-serving purpose of the document, it is clear that Chaban-Delmas had been remarkably successful in translating the rhetoric of the New Society into legislation. Delors is closer to the mark when he points to the profound ambivalence on the part of the government to any strengthening of a union movement dominated by the CGT and CFDT. But again, certain policies *were* implemented. If they failed, the causes must be sought elsewhere.

The explanation most often used is that the social partners were ideologically opposed to the reforms and hence hindered their successful implementation. The CGT was close to the PCF, the CFDT was radicalized by 1968, and the *patronat* had a long history of rejecting any limitation on managerial prerogative and attempts to institutionalize union influence in the firm. The stereotypical management style was one of authoritarian paternalism. There is plenty of evidence to back up the claim that this attitude persisted well beyond 1968. The study of works councils cited above shows a very clear reluctance on the part of employers to recognizing union sections in the firm. The union press was full of examples of employer tactics for bypassing union sections: setting up rival enterprise unions, blacklists, challenging the qualifications of union candidates, even reorganizing the structure of the firm to avoid the obligation to recognize a union section.[52] These reactions were most marked in the smaller firms, and that posed a serious problem because of the weight of such firms in the French economy. In these firms the problem was not just a more paternalistic attitude on the part of employers. The greater hostility to unions had a material base. Union sections could impose costs on small firms operating at the margins of profitability, which could not be sustained. It was no coincidence that the "modernist" employers came from the larger firms.

However, attitudes are not independent of the structural contexts within which they operate. Given the structural weakness of French unionism there were very good reasons for even modernist employers to feel that they had everything to lose and nothing to gain from acquiescing in the implantation of union sections and from giving unions an equal and full role in collective bargaining. As mentioned above, the Chaban-Delmas government backed away from its initial support for progress contract–style agreements in the private sector, which would entail reciprocal commitments. As Fontanet put it, "One of the reasons why we have more difficulty in France than in other countries in making the notion of a reciprocal undertaking in collective bargaining appear is the weakness of our trade unions."[53] So long as unions were unable to exercise a minimum of control over their members, no change in attitudes, no deradicalization could have improved the chances of collective bargaining. The radical ideologies of the CGT and CFDT, with their stress on the need to avoid integration into bargaining structures with the state or capital, can be interpreted as justifications for what was in fact a structural inability to undertake the kinds of commitments that regularized bargaining entailed.

Insofar as the goal of Chaban-Delmas was to create the legal framework and political environment that would allow unionization to expand (and with it the conditions for collective bargaining), he had some success. Union membership did rise, bargaining did increase. But that goal was a long-term one and further success required that the experiment be continued. However, the period of 1969–72 occupied a privileged economic and political conjuncture, free of major national elections and economic difficulties. After 1972 there was a spate of important elections, and the alliance between socialists and communists made the threat to right-wing hegemony a real one. As *L'Express* said of the new prime minister, Pierre Messmer, in 1972: "The unblocking of relations between trade unions and management in the public sector was the great concern of M. Jacques Chaban-Delmas. That of M. Pierre Messmer is to win the elections. With or without collective bargaining."[54] In addition, 1973 saw the onset of a national obsession with inflation, and a prolonged and deep-rooted economic crisis. Ultimately, the New Society program had been contingent upon continued economic growth.

Too many of the gains of the period were dependent on having a sympathetic government in place. The government incited and underwrote the national/confederal agreements, and it offered attractive wage deals in the public sector. The New Society had some success, particularly in the modern sectors of the economy, but it was ultimately a failure both because it proved unable to spread collective bargaining to the large traditional sector and because it was highly contingent. The New Society was never *institu-*

tionalized, and as a result it evaporated when the government fell and the economy turned sour.

CONCLUSION

The events of May and June 1968 posed serious problems for the sweeping economic changes that de Gaulle and his immediate successor Pompidou wished to see effected. The problems were both short-term, conjunctural ones (resulting from a rapid rise in nominal wage levels and the subsequent erosion of profitability) and the much more fundamental issue of finding a way of regulating the French labor movement that did not jeopardize continued economic modernization. As the nature of French economic growth changed from an extensive to an intensive, or Fordist, pattern, regulation based solely on the labor market was not sufficient. Economic modernization created a sector of the economy whose interests lay in more consensual industrial relations which permitted industrial peace, and steady, predictable wage rises (to fuel internal demand and allow planning at the firm level). May 1968 was an unmistakable signal that the continued mismatch between the type of economic growth and manner of labor regulation could not go on.

The strategy of Chaban-Delmas was to strengthen unions in the firm, building on the major gain of the workers' movement in May 1968: the legal protection of union sections. It was hoped that this would stimulate regular collective bargaining, which in turn would reduce conflict and allow negotiation to become the dominant form of labor regulation. This strategy had some success in that collective bargaining did become more widespread and union sections were able to gain a foothold inside many firms. But the end result was far from the hopes of the architects of the New Society. The reforms were predicated on strong unions because only such unions could entice employers to the bargaining table. Employers had to believe that unions could deliver industrial peace. This was too heavy a burden for French trade unionism. Its strength in 1968 and 1969 was conjunctural; it remained structurally weak. It was a mobilizational unionism, dependent on the threat of strike action to maintain organizational control. Whatever gradual changes in the union movement that were occurring after 1968 were abruptly snuffed out when the economy turned sour and electoral concerns once again became uppermost in the minds of politicians.

However, if the Chaban-Delmas government was unable to institutionalize a collective-bargaining form of labor regulation, it is also true that the aspirations of those who directly participated in the events of May 1968 went unfulfilled. The failure of post-1968 governments was, in this sense, only partial. Those who saw the events of May 1968 as the harbinger of a new period in which the influence of workers and their industrial and political representatives would be much greater than before were cruelly disappointed. The great success of post-1968 governments was to protect accumulation in the context of heightened worker militancy. Wages did rise rapidly, both in the private and public sectors, but they were eroded by government macroeconomic policies (inflation and devaluation) and by productivity gains. Profits, after a brief dip, climbed to high levels and the period 1969–74 saw one of the "longest and most intense expansive periods"[55] in French economic history. Thus the most extensive episode of worker militancy in the advanced capitalist world was not translated into immediate political gains, nor were workers the beneficiaries of a significant redistribution of economic wealth.

Paradoxically, May 1968 was followed not by a revolution but by a period of unparalleled capitalist prosperity. No doubt some part of this success was due to the macroeconomic policies of post-1968 governments. Salvati has demonstrated the differences between the French and Italian experiences in this respect.[56] But something more fundamental had changed. French economic success after 1968 was in part a result of a change in the way labor was regulated. Labor regulation was not the same in 1974 as in 1968, and without this change French industry could not have reacted so well to the economic conditions of 1968–74.

In 1968 the labor market had been the primary determinant of wages. France had a very "underinstitutionalized" labor market, meaning that supply and demand in the labor market overwhelmingly determined wage levels. By 1974 the influence of the labor market was somewhat reduced. There was, in other words, a partial *decommodification* of the labor market. The landmark study by Boyer, cited in chapter 2, demonstrated that from "1969–1976, whereas wages are more sensitive to prices, unemployment, however measured, appears to have no systematic effects."[57] A Brookings Institution study also argues that the French labor market exhibited a reduced sensitivity of real wages to labor market tightness.[58]

This should come as no surprise in light of the greatly increased use of cost-of-living indexation in wage settlements in both the public and private sector. A study by Mery shows that from 1968 onward, and largely encouraged by the state, the practice of indexation became widespread. Whereas before 1968 it had been sporadic and informal, it now became increasingly explicit in wage contracts that contained automatic price-level adjustments. Mery estimates that in 1973 about six million workers benefited from cost-of-living safeguards.[59]

If the role of the labor market was reduced in this period, what replaced it? One candidate would be collective bargaining. While the more grandiose vision of the New Society went unfulfilled, collective bargaining did increase, as table 4.2 showed. A series of caveats concerning this increase are necessary. Collective bargaining was driven by developments outside the firm, it was dependent on a period of remarkable prosperity, and it lacked the no-strike commitment desired by the state and employers.

It is also important to stress that the developments with which this chapter has been concerned overwhelmingly affected larger firms, be they in the public or private sector. The crucial December 1968 law on union sections affected only about half of all workers, and those in the larger firms. The point is that insofar as a new form of decentralized collective bargaining appeared in France it was in the large, modern firms, in the leading sectors of the economy. It was in these firms that unions gained a foothold and bargaining became the norm. Again, this should come as no surprise because a new mode of labor regulation appropriate to a modern, Fordist economy was of interest to precisely these firms. The New Society was, in a very real sense, the product of the needs of those firms, and insofar as it succeeded it was in these same firms. The primary source of encouragement for the New Society and for collective bargaining, outside the government, was the CNPF and its recently formed research groups which were dominated by the directors of large, modern enterprises.

One consequence of the growth of collective bargaining in this sector of the economy was an exacerbation of the emerging dualism of French labor regulation. Increasingly, France saw the development of two parallel modes of labor regulation. Workers in the large, modern firms, protected by relatively strong unions and increasingly regular collective bargaining, were relatively privileged with employment security and wages protected against inflation. The firms in this sector benefited from more stable work forces, less industrial conflict, and predictable wage growth. These firms could also use the traditional sector, via subcontracting, in periods of surplus demand or labor militancy, in the ways detailed by Berger and Piore.[60]

That still leaves the traditional sector, with about half the labor force, in a large number of small firms employing less than fifty people and often less than ten, operating on the margins of profitability where labor was above all a cost of production, and low wages were more important than predictability or industrial peace. Here unions were very weak and traditional paternalistic managerial patterns persisted. In this sector the labor market remained very important as a form of labor regulation. But here too there was a change between 1968 and 1974. That change was a vastly expanded role for the state in labor regulation.

This was a paradoxical consequence of the New Society period. The rhetoric of its proponents was rich with calls for the withdrawal of the state from its regulatory role in society. A reduction in state regulation would, it was hoped, not only free the state from excessively politicizing tasks (thus allowing it to act more effectively in other areas) but also throw responsibility for regulating industrial relations onto the social partners, and impart a new flexibility and "normalcy" to labor regulation.

However, the period after 1968 actually saw an expansion in the role of state regulation. The state was active in setting the terms for wage bargaining in the public sector and used the minimum wage to influence the lower end of the income scale in the private sector. At the same time, the state took the initiative in the area of social modernization, using legislation or exhortation to create the basic social infrastructure appropriate for a modern economy.

The state's regulatory role was clearly dominant in the public sector, and it was also important in the Fordist sector of the economy where the state took a leading role in encouraging social modernization: the creation of an increasingly complicated web of benefits and safeguards for workers covered by the high-level agreements. Both of these aspects of labor regulation by the state have been discussed in this chapter. But it was in the traditional sector where the role of the state in labor regulation expanded most in this period.

Most importantly, the period after 1968 saw a much-increased role for the state in wage regulation via its use of the minimum wage. Prior to 1970 the minimum wage (SMIG) was indexed to the cost of living, but in January 1970 the SMIG became transformed into the *Salaire Minimum Interprofessionnel de Croissance* (SMIC). Now it could be increased in three ways. The minimum wage remained indexed to the price level. To that was added a partial indexation to the rise in the general wage level in the economy (in the form of an annual increase equivalent to at least half of the rise in the purchasing power of the average hourly wage), and an annual increase that was not indexed but was at the discretion of the government. These changes were designed to avoid the wide divergence between the level of the minimum wage and that of the average wage that had existed prior to 1968 and been corrected as a result of the one-shot increase of 35 percent in June 1968. The minimum wage was an economic as well as a social tool. It aided the modernization and restructuring process by driving marginal firms to the wall, and increased the purchasing power of low-paid workers.

From 1964 until 1967 about 2 to 3 percent of workers benefited directly from the SMIG (the indirect effects are difficult to calculate but would be significantly higher precisely because of the weakness of collective bargaining in France).[61] As a result of the 1968 increase this figure jumped to 14 percent and then dropped between 1969 and 1972 to 4 to 6 percent, before it began to climb again in 1973.[62] With the change to the SMIC in 1970 the level of the minimum wage became a more flexible policy tool. From 1970 to 1972 the government chose not to make much use of this new capability, preferring to rely on collective bargaining, but after 1973 the government gave large annual discretionary increments.[63] It appears that the limited success of contractual wage bargaining stimulated greater direct intervention by the state in wage regulation.

State intervention was also enlarged by the aforementioned 1971 reform of the 1950 basic law on collective bargaining which made the procedure of "extension" easier. The practice of allowing the state to widen the applicability of an agreement reached between employers and unions is particularly important in a dualistic economy with highly uneven union strength. It allows wage gains by powerful groups of workers to be generalized to other sectors of the economy and can be seen as connecting islands of Fordism to the rest of the French economy. After the easing of the extension procedure, more frequent use was made of it in the early and mid-1970s.[64]

The French state also acted (increasingly as the economy went into crisis) to curb the impact of the labor market thus enlarging the role of collective bargaining and legislation in labor regulation, either directly or through encouraging the social partners to act. Hence in October 1974, under heavy government pressure, the unions and employers' organizations signed an accord that created an additional unemployment benefit, to be worth 90 percent of the previous salary of a worker made redundant, for up to a year.[65] Then an agreement reached in November 1974 was generalized through legislation in January 1975 that extended the requirement that administrative authorization be sought before firing workers for economic reasons.[66] Together these measures served to limit the role played by labor market regulation.

A comparison with Sweden is instructive. State use of the "extension" procedure, and the minimum wage, acted as the functional equivalent of Sweden's "solidaristic wage policy" and powerful trade unions. Generalizing the wage gains of the most modern sectors of the economy and vigorous use of the minimum wage served the dual purpose of allowing mass consumption, and hence the internal market, to expand, and encouraging the restructuring of industry by eliminating marginal firms. In the absence of a strong labor movement and centralized wage bargaining, these tasks were undertaken by the state in France. The French state, in other words, *substituted* for strong trade unions and the existence of regularized collective bargaining.

The expansion of state regulation must be understood in the dual context of the failure to create a decentralized form of labor regulation and the priority given to economic modernization by all governments in this period. The social projects were designed to facilitate economic modernization, not vice versa, and this ensured that, ultimately, the social goals would be sacrificed to economic needs. The New Society was an attempt to create a new mode of labor regulation that would be appropriate to a Fordist economy. The project failed to change the structure of the labor movement, and this doomed the widespread adoption of a collective-bargaining–based mode of labor regulation. However, the French state was able to substitute for the lack of collective bargaining by expanding its own role in labor regulation. Insofar as contractual bargaining did take root, it was in the larger, modern, and advanced firms. This left a vacuum in the rest of the economy which the state filled.

It is interesting that the French state, which was at this time controlled by a conservative, neo-Gaullist government, chose to intervene in the process of labor regulation in a way that benefited labor. The gains for workers that are usually associated with the presence of trade unions were extended to a broad range of workers despite the weakness of unions in France. It was a case in which gains for labor were not automatically losses for capital, and this opened up space for state action.

By 1974 France could be said to have a dualistic form of labor regulation: collective bargaining was becoming implanted in the modern, Fordist parts of the private sector and in the public sector; and the traditional sector became ever more subject to intervention and regulation by the state. Thus France did experience a change in the mode of labor regulation after 1968, one that allowed the process of economic modernization to continue.

The French experience between 1968 and 1974 challenges the notion that there is only one mode of labor regulation appropriate to the Fordist regime of accumulation, and in particular, that there is a phase of advanced capitalism in which trade unions become acceptable and even necessary. The mode of labor regulation has to be consistent with the strength and organization of the working class in a particular historical time and place. In France, after 1968, it was possible to construct a viable mode of labor regulation based on extensive state intervention in social relations and wage determination.

However, such a form of labor regulation was not without its costs. It was dependent on both the willingness and the ability of the state to underwrite labor regulation. The result was a highly contingent and ultimately fragile mode of labor regulation, one whose weakness was soon exposed by the onset of economic crisis.

CHAPTER FIVE

Labor Regulation in Transition, 1974–81

THE PERIOD from 1968 to 1974 was dominated by the specter of May 1968 and by the attempt to reduce the conflictuality of French industrial relations by creating a form of labor regulation appropriate to the new, modern Fordist economy. The goal of a stable system of decentralized collective bargaining fell far short of the hopes of policymakers, and moreover the experiment took place in a privileged conjuncture of economic and political peace.

The events described in this chapter were also haunted by the memory of May 1968, but that memory was nonetheless less immediate and was filtered through the intervening experience of high growth, right-wing political domination, and, if not social peace, at least industrial unrest shorn of the direct political threat of May 1968. More importantly, 1974 marks the opening of a completely different political and economic conjuncture. In 1974 Valéry Giscard d'Estaing narrowly defeated François Mitterrand in the presidential election and opened four years of intense, and closely fought, electoral campaigns. In 1974, also, the oil shock broke into the consciousness of political and economic elites, and the ensuing economic crisis dominated the rest of the decade.

This chapter deals with three episodes in the period of Giscard d'Estaing's presidency. The first is the attempt to "reform the firm" following the Sudreau Report commissioned by Giscard d'Estaing in July 1974 and completed in February 1975. The report was important because it represented an attempt to modernize the French firm by changing social relations within the firm. This chapter will attempt to explain the motivation behind this experiment and the vision of labor regulation that it embodied. Since most contemporaries argued that this project was a failure, an assessment of that judgment, and an explanation of the reception accorded the Sudreau Report, will be made.

The second episode is that of the Barre Plan and its attempt to control inflation and restore profitability from September 1976 through the end of 1977. Raymond Barre inherited a form of labor regulation (described in the last chapter) in which a fragile form of collective bargaining in the public sector had been bought with highly lucrative and rigid wage contracts. Indexation of wages and an activist use of the minimum wage made wage control very difficult. Barre's response was an incomes policy. It is important to explain his choice of type of incomes policy—nonconsensual and dependent upon employer cooperation—and to assess its success.

The third episode discussed in this chapter begins in March 1978, with the unexpected victory of the Right in the legislative elections, and concerns the attempt to breath new life into collective bargaining, which had all but ground to a halt for the duration of the incomes policy. This attempt is interesting because it quite explicitly set out to withdraw the state from collective bargaining and wage determination more generally. However, this was attempted at a time of profound trade union weakness and resurgent employer activism. Those circumstances were responsible for the limited success of the attempt to reinvigorate collective bargaining.

These three episodes were separate initiatives, undertaken in response to different circumstances. Yet they share a certain coherence. All were responses to a crisis in the existing mode of labor regulation, and all either failed or were strictly circumscribed in their success. The explanation, I think, lies in the fact that the period 1974–81 was a transitional one. It was a period in which the Fordist dynamic of the French economy faltered but no new dynamic appeared, and also a period in which the long domination of politics by the Right began to break down.

Thus this chapter is transitional in the sense that it helps to set the scene for the period of Socialist rule from 1981 onward. It covers the breakdown of the hybrid model of labor regulation based upon collective bargaining and state intervention which had been created between 1969 and 1974. But no alternative model of labor regulation was created, nor was there a full return to regulation by the labor market. Collective bargaining broke down because it had not reduced conflictuality, as employers hoped it would, and the fragile consensus among employers disappeared. The attempt by the Barre government to stimulate more bargaining after 1978 came at a point when unions were too weak to take advantage of it and, as a result, what bargaining did occur was employer-dominated.

At the same time, in response to the experience of prolonged economic crisis the economic goals of the government changed, and after increasing state intervention in the process of labor regulation in the first half of the 1970s, there was an attempt made from 1978 onward to start the slow process of withdrawal of the state from labor regulation. This attempt was unsuccessful for the most part precisely because the precondition for its success was a system of collective bargaining that devolved labor regulation onto trade unions and employers. Without such a system in place the social costs of state withdrawal (in terms of unemployment, for instance) were too high. As it was, the costs were enough to tip the balance against the Right in the 1981 presidential elections.

Thus both legs of the post-1968 mode of labor regulation began to collapse. The result, by 1981, was a model of labor regulation that was itself in crisis, threadbare, and held together by the state, and that was increasingly perceived as an obstacle to much-needed structural changes in the French economy.

Conjunctures

The most striking feature of this period is the difference between this political and economic conjuncture and that of the preceding period. Starting in 1974 there were important elections almost every year until 1978. There was a presidential election in 1974, cantonal elections in 1976, municipal elections in 1977, and legislative elections in 1978. There was a widespread assumption that the Left would win in March 1978, and thus most of this period (with the exception of the third episode, beginning in 1978, which explicitly followed from the defeat of the Left) was played out to the constant drumbeat of electoral concerns. This was important for two reasons. First, it led to the short-term character of all the political projects of the period, in a way that the New Society, for example, had been able to avoid. This, in large part, accounts for the lack of a consistent strategy in this period. But second, and more profoundly, the reform of social relations came to be viewed directly through the prism of its consequences for the political orientation of critical social classes. More precisely, as Ross has pointed out,[1] that amorphous social grouping, the new middle classes, itself a creation of the modernization of the French economy, became the political battleground over which Left and Right fought. The allegiance of this group was seen, with good reason, as the key to victory in the closely fought elections of the 1970s. As this chapter will attempt to show, the battle for the allegiance of the new middle classes was also fought at the level of labor regulation. An important part of the purpose of much of the reform activity in the area of industrial relations in this period was to cement the identification of this group with capital rather than labor.[2]

Elections were not the only things on the minds of politicians in this period. The *trente glorieuses* came to an end in 1973. The next ten years were dominated by low growth, consistently high inflation, rapidly accelerating unemployment, and periodically high trade and budget deficits. The economic crisis was important in a conjunctural sense because it greatly narrowed the room for maneuver of French governments. After 1974 governments could no longer afford high wage contracts, and as profit margins were squeezed, neither could private-sector firms. Thus the material base of the collective-bargaining strategy of the New Society period evaporated. In addition, the financial costs of unemployment became increasingly heavy on both state and employers. This is not to say that the economic crisis made labor regulation irrelevant, or less important. On the contrary, just as in 1968–74, economic goals were seen as dependent on labor regulation. This was abundantly clear in the economic goals of firm reform and the attempt to stimulate collective bargaining after 1978. It was this economic situation that formed the backdrop to the attempts to reform labor regulation.

The economy was important in another, perhaps more indeterminate, way. It was argued in chapter 2 that France had made the shift to a Fordist economy—that is to say, one in which regular increases in mass domestic demand fuel growth—much later than most of the rest of Western Europe. It is somewhat ironic that Fordism triumphed in France precisely at a time when it began to falter in the rest of the advanced capitalist world. The economic crisis brought on by the oil shock exposed structural weaknesses in the economies of Western Europe, Japan, and the United States which did not appear remediable by the familiar Fordist recipe of a virtuous circle of mass consumption feeding mass production which in turn raised mass consumption via regular wage rises in line with productivity gains, and Keynesian deficit-spending. This was the period when Keynesian demand management was pronounced dead right across the political spectrum.[3] In short, Fordism was in crisis in France almost as soon as it appeared.

Regulation theorists, who have provided compelling explanations of the rise and global diffusion of Fordism, have found it far more difficult to explain the source of the crisis of Fordism and describe what, if anything, is taking its place. The issue, in a nutshell, is whether Fordism, as a regime of accumulation, has become exhausted and is being replaced by a new regime of accumulation (neo- or post-Fordism) or whether what is in crisis is not Fordism but the mode of regulation. The debate is important because the period from roughly 1977 onward saw a clear shift away from a mode of labor regulation based on collective bargaining with workers' interests mediated by trade unions. This shift, as future chapters will show, has been confirmed and accelerated in the 1980s. It is a shift that is also visible in changing employer strategies.

The debate is difficult to resolve precisely because (as discussed in chapter 1) Regulationists do not have a good means of analytically separating regimes of accumulation and modes of regulation. This issue will be treated in more detail in chapters 8 and 9, but in brief the position taken here is that the declaration of the death of Fordism may be premature, or at least only partially true. What was seen in the 1970s was not solely the economic exhaustion of Fordism but also the collapse of a mode of regulation which, by encouraging unions and collective bargaining, had strengthened the capacity of workers to maintain high wage demands despite high unemployment. The relative insulation of wages from the labor market—at least in certain sectors of the economy—prevented business from rebuilding profits. It was as much a *social* exhaustion of Fordism as an *economic* one. The solution thus lay in a change in the mode of labor regulation. It will be argued that from the mid-1970s onward, and particularly after 1983, attempts were made to overcome the rigidities of existing labor regulation by withdrawing the state, bypassing unions, and decentralizing labor regulation to the firm level. Much of this shift was carried out under the banner of bringing "flexibility" to the industrial relations system.

THE ACTORS

In the immediate post-1968 period the *patronat* was not an obstacle to the reform plans of the Chaban-Delmas government. The employers in small firms were politically immobilized and a sizable chunk of larger employers—the owners of modernized, Fordist firms—identified with the New Society project of institutionalizing class conflict by establishing regularized collective-bargaining practices and recognizing trade unions as the natural representatives of the working class. In the course of the 1970s, as electoral competition intensified, small employers became politically important once again,[4] and even the influential group of large employers came to reject a model of labor regulation centered on trade unions. The shift in patronal strategy is central to an understanding of labor regulation since the mid-1970s.[5]

A brief discussion of what it means to say that employers have a strategy is needed here. The exact role of the CNPF—the main peak organization of French business—is murky. It has operated as a lobbying organization, and as a kind of think tank for owners, in the sense that it organizes conferences and exhibitions of new management practices. Its autonomy vis-à-vis individual employers and branch federations has always been limited. The CNPF has not played a genuinely corporatist role except perhaps very briefly during the 1976–77 Barre Plan in which an incomes policy operated via price controls and was policed jointly by the CNPF and the government.

Thus, when patronal strategy is discussed in these pages that term is used as shorthand for the practices and decisions of individual French employers. The CNPF played a very active propagandizing role and from 1977 onward embraced a new model of labor regulation, one that I have identified analytically as microcorporatism, but it had no capacity to impose that model on its members, still less on employers who were not members of the CNPF. Its role, rather, was to diffuse new management techniques widely and to lobby government for legislation that, somewhat paradoxically, would allow greater flexibility in industrial relations.

The initial enthusiasm of large employers for collective bargaining and trade unions disappeared in the mid-1970s for two reasons. First, because it failed; unions proved poor bargaining partners and the level of industrial conflict rose rather than fell. As Dubois put it in 1980: "One can say that the gamble made that the trade unions would be the agency of institutionalizing conflict is recognized to have failed in France. . . . The consequence is that in the second half of the 1970s another policy was chosen, a more traditional gamble: union repression was attempted as a means of reducing industrial conflict."[6]

Second, as the Fordist regime of accumulation went into crisis, prompted by the oil shock, the collective-bargaining model of labor regulation was increasingly inappropriate. Its rigidities, which could be considered beneficial in a period of steady growth, prevented firms from responding to economic crisis in adaptive and flexible ways.

According to Weber, CNPF strategy underwent two shifts. From 1975–76 the post-1968 strategy of *"la grande politique contractuelle"* gave way to *"les négociations donnant-donnant"* (give and take). This was an immediate response to economic crisis, and while it involved demands for flexibility and restraint from workers it did not fundamentally challenge the role of collective bargaining and trade unions. However, from 1977 onward this strategy coexisted with a third one, *"la gestion concurrentielle du progrès social."* This meant nothing less than an effort to wrest control of the work force from trade unions and give it to management. This strategy was on display at the Fourth National Assizes of the Firm in October 1977. It had three main themes. First, the need to fit the organization of work to the particular situation in a firm and hence avoid uniform legislation. As the CNPF's main journal put it: "Experimentation must be the rule. It would be vain to wish to freeze in legislation a technique that is still evolving."[7]

Second, this strategy gave a central role to the *cadres* as an alternative channel for the control of workers. No longer could management leave it to trade unions to represent workers. The problem, as François Ceyrac of the CNPF put it, was that the "generalized practice of collective agreements had led to the virtual subcontracting of social questions to the unions."[8] This explained the CNPF's position on the right of workers to have an institutionalized forum for expression in the firm. It was crucial that workers express themselves *directly* (not via trade unions or union-dominated works councils) and with supervisory staff present. It also explained the mounting calls for an end to the union monopoly in the first round of elections to the works council, so as to separate the contestatory role of unions from the cooperative role of the works council.

Third, collective bargaining was not rejected, at least not formally, but the emphasis shifted away from the national/confederal level (which had been the focus of bargaining activity and the most visible successes of collective bargaining in the decade after 1968) to the branch level and even the firm level. This fitted well with the focus on flexibility and on solutions tailored to the situation and needs of the firm. It also decentralized bargaining to the level where unions were weakest.

It is important to note that it was now large employers, in modern, advanced firms (represented by the CNPF) that were decrying the rigidities imposed by collective bargaining with trade unions. Unions were only weakly implanted in small and medium-sized firms, and collective bargaining was poorly developed. In these firms it was the state that represented the main source of rigidity via its minimum wage and legislative restrictions on hiring and firing.

Weber has argued that, for all the changes in employer strategy, at no point did employers revert to the pre-1968 position of authoritarian management and unremitting hostility to trade unions and *all* forms of worker organization. For Weber the employer strategy described above was new and modernist. However, it is important, from the late 1970s, to distinguish *two* types of modernist strategy. One was the pro-union, pro-collective bargaining strategy which was most in evidence immediately after 1968. The other, bypassing trade unions and setting up new forms of firm-specific worker groups (quality circles, expression groups), was also much-touted as a modern strategy, one appropriate to the new emphasis on developing human creativity and allowing maximum ability of the firm to adapt to rapidly changing economic conditions. Nonetheless, the impact of these two strategies on the capacity of workers to organize, and the forms that organization would take, were very different. It is that structural impact which is of interest here.

The years of the New Society turned out to be the golden age of postwar trade unionism in France. The decline in union membership and influence began in the mid-1970s. The evolution in strategy of the CGT and CFDT during this period has been described by Ross.[9] Both revolutionary unions combined a broad transformative project—for both of them it was the transcendence of capitalism, though they differed in their vision of socialism— with a defensive bread-and-butter strategy which guided day-to-day action. For the CGT certainly, and for the CFDT more reluctantly, the link between daily struggle in the workplace and societal transformation was found in political action. Promoting the victory of the Union de la Gauche (Union of the Left) and hence the implementation of the Common Program in the 1978 legislative elections came to dominate union activity. The CFDT had deep misgivings about this politicization of union actions, and about the Common Program itself, which it felt was too focused upon centralized planning of a nationalized but otherwise unchanged core economy. However, particularly as recession hit and the labor market slackened, it was hard to envisage alternative strategies, and the CFDT came to follow (in practice at least) the path of the CGT.

The importance of this strategy, as Ross has demonstrated, was that it left the trade unions without a response when the Left failed to win in March 1978. The trade unions were also unprepared for the shift in employer strategy and unsure of how to respond. The CGT responded, after a brief flirtation with "industrial counterpropositions," with defensive resistance to change and an enhanced concern to protect its core blue-collar membership. The CFDT responded with a strategic shift to "*recentrage.*" In essence *recentrage* involved a focus upon negotiation as an end in itself. This strategy, as Moreau put it in the report that launched *recentrage*, had far-ranging consequences: "We say we are for negotiation. But have we adjusted our objectives, our demands, our modes of action, and our information on the basis of that requirement? [We must] obtain concrete results, give hope, [and] go through the necessary compromises with those who manage the economy and social life."[10]

Yet whatever the wisdom, or lack of it, of the strategies of the two revolutionary unions, it must be recognized that the space for union strategy to make a difference was heavily constrained. The two largest French trade unions began to lose members faster than they recruited new ones from about 1976 onward (see table 5.1). There is a large literature on "desyndicalization,"[11] and a multiplicity of factors are usually adduced for the decline of unions. It is certainly true, for instance that the messy divorce of the Union of the Left and its subsequent electoral defeat caused widespread disillusionment and hastened the decline in trade union membership. The politicization of trade union activity in the run up to the 1978 legislative elections made it even harder for the revolutionary trade unions to respond to defeat. New employers' strategies and hostility to unions also played their part in weakening unions.

That decline was overdetermined in the sense that the electoralism of the unions and the employers' new strategy pushed in the same direction, but that decline was initiated and took its character from the economic crisis and structural shifts in the French economy (and can be dated from the onset of economic recession). Economic forces damaged unions both

TABLE 5.1
Union Membership, (in millions), 1974–81

	CGT	*CFDT*
1974	2.34	1.02
1975	2.38	1.07
1976	2.35	1.08
1977	2.32	1.08
1978	2.19	1.05
1979	2.03	1.01
1980	1.92	0.96
1981	1.93	0.95

Source: René Mouriaux and Françoise Subileau, "Les Effectifs Syndicaux en France, 1895–1986," Document de Travail (Paris: CEVIPOF, 1987), 4, 9.

through the cyclical effect of high levels of unemployment and the structural effect of a recession that disproportionately hit the old core sectors of blue-collar strength, taking away jobs precisely where trade unions were strongest.[12] It is unclear whether a different choice of strategy could have significantly changed the outcome.

The French state intervened in labor regulation in a wide variety of ways, as described in chapter 4. Through its activist use of the minimum wage and role in the public and nationalized sector, it influenced wage levels directly. Through the procedure of "extension"—the use of which greatly increased in the early 1970s—it could apply collective agreements to sectors and regions where one or other of the social partners (usually the unions) were too weak to negotiate themselves. And through a dense network of unemployment compensation schemes and regulations limiting layoffs, the state was able to limit the role of the labor market, at least for the core, primary segment of the industrial working class. There is thus a great deal of accuracy in Boyer's comment that "it was as if a socio-political regulation in some degree replaced market forces."[13]

This form of state regulation of labor at first became *more* extensive in response to the onset of economic crisis and the highly competitive political situation. The initial response to economic crisis was to increase the protection for workers, from both unemployment (by legislative regulations and encouraging the greater use of short-time working) and loss of purchasing power from inflation (by maintaining the indexation of wages in the public and nationalized sector and using the minimum wage in an activist manner).

However, state regulation of labor had damaging consequences for French capital. The high wage settlements in the public and nationalized sector produced budget deficits and a spillover effect in the private sector. The institutionalization of the labor market weakened its disciplinary power. And the social treatment of unemployment imposed serious costs on French business because unemployment compensation came from employee and employer contributions, of which about 80 percent came from the latter.[14]

The story of the period from 1977 onward is that of a slow, hesitant withdrawal of the state from labor regulation and the attempt to throw labor regulation back onto employers and unions.

THE REFORM OF THE FIRM

During the campaign for the presidential elections in May 1974, Giscard d'Estaing promised that, if elected, he would proceed with a far-reaching reform of the firm in France. By advocating reform of the firm Giscard d'Estaing was staking out a claim for the political center. A poll conducted in January 1975 discovered that a slim majority (52 percent) of those questioned favored electing the head of the firm, and large majorities considered the provision of economic and financial information on the firm to the works council, and associating employees with decisions in the firm to be very important.[15] There was also, as Mouriaux has pointed out, another clearly political purpose to Giscard d'Estaing's championing of firm reform.[16] Giscard d'Estaing was attempting to distinguish himself from Chaban-Delmas (who was also running) as the representative of the modernist, large employers as well as of the *cadres*, for whom a reform of the traditional, family-run firm had great appeal.

Once elected, Giscard d'Estaing confirmed his intention to embark on a major reform of the firm with a speech on June 19, 1974: "Another grand transformation of the structures of our society is the evolution of the firm, an evolution that aims to assure for everyone, in the firm . . . a more active participation, more complete information, and a democratization of life in the firm."[17]

Later that month Pierre Sudreau was asked to preside over a commission that would investigate the firm and report on reform possibilities. The commission was comprised of nine people beyond Sudreau: three employers, three unionists, and three lawyers. The unionists represented the CFDT, FO, and CGC. The CGT refused to formally participate, though it submitted a detailed list of proposed reforms.[18]

In February 1975, to much fanfare, the commission presented its report.[19] The report was, as Sudreau admitted, "not a reform, but a collection of proposals" (sixty-nine to be exact). The report took as its point of departure the need to *modernize* the firm. Its language was very similar to that of Chaban-Delmas in his New Society speech. The report argued that in order to modernize the economy it was necessary to modernize the firm, and that in turn required a modernization of social relations within the firm. As Sudreau himself put it: "The fundamental idea that guided us was that we are now living in a society in the process of deep and rapid change. It is necessary that, corresponding to this change, there is just as deep a change in the firm."[20]

Large sections of the report were not concerned directly with the relationships between workers, *cadres*, and employers, but rather focused on providing shareholders with increased information about the firm, separating the functions of ownership and management, making it easier to start up new companies, retiring managers after a certain age, and so on. These sections were explicitly concerned with the creation of modern, dynamic firms on the "American model" in contrast to the stereotypical backward-looking family-owned and managed French firm. Nonetheless, the core of the report, and the part that was most discussed and fought over (comprising chapters one and two as well as twenty-nine specific reform proposals), was concerned with "transforming daily life in the firm" (chapter one) and "establishing the place of man [sic] in firm life" (chapter two).[21] It was these sections that dealt with social relations in the firm and that will be the focus of discussion in this chapter.

The major proposals were as follows: (1) workers should have a right to express themselves on the content of their work in the firm; (2) the works council should be given increased information on the economic and financial situation of the firm, and the report suggested a special "economic delegation" to the works council in larger firms; (3) each firm should establish an annual report on social conditions in the firm (a "*bilan social*"); (4) managers should "recognize the trade union as a partner"; (5) collective bargaining should be encouraged; (6) the works council should be reformed to represent *cadres* better; and (7) a new form of worker representation, "*co-surveillance*" (literally, joint supervision), should be introduced in firms on a trial basis. This last proposal was the most controversial and was designed as a compromise between German-style codetermination and no change at all in worker participation. The idea was to provide one-third of the seats on the *conseil de surveillance* (supervisory council) for workers. These workers would have no managerial function (indeed they would abstain on managerial questions), but they would have the ability to supervise and watch over the running of the firm.

The Sudreau Report was a ragbag of proposals. It really did see its role more as stimulating debate than as proposing a single concrete reform of the firm. Nonetheless, taken as a whole there was a certain coherence. Four aspects of the report should be noted in the context of this study. First, the report was ambivalent on the role of worker representatives inside the firm. The report recognized a critical and legitimate role for trade unions and collective bargaining:

> These activities together constitute the foundation of the legitimacy of the trade union function: the trade union organizations synthesize and express the workers' collective aspirations, placing them in an overall context. . . . Although the role they play is one of challenge, they make for social adjustment by gathering together the centrifugal forces which would otherwise manifest themselves in scattered form.[22]

The goal was not to circumvent and minimize the role of unions, and the report did implicitly at least recognize that conflict was an integral part of life in a capitalist firm and hence needed to be channeled and managed. That said, however, the ultimate authority of management was not challenged and indeed was explicitly and repeatedly affirmed. Worker representatives were to have better access to information but were not to have veto power over decisions. This was true of the *co-surveillance* proposal and the proposals for giving greater power to the works council. As the report put it, the proposals were "designed to bring about a significant updating of the works council without affecting the consultative nature of most of its functions."[23]

Trade unions had always had the so-called union monopoly which prevented nonunion candidates standing in the first round of firm elections. The Sudreau Report argued that the mode of selection of worker representatives for the supervisory councils should be left up to the management's discretion. The management could employ the union monopoly for these positions, but equally it could choose some other form of designating them. Many unionists feared that this was the thin end of the wedge.

Second, and relatedly, the increased powers being suggested for the works councils and for worker representatives on the supervisory council had a strongly economic flavor. The aim was to provide workers with a better sense of the financial situation of the firm in the expectation that this would help workers better understand the constraints under which the firm and its managers operated. This concern was not surprising in light of the rash of strikes in 1973–75 whose purpose was to defend employment in failing firms. The prolonged industrial conflict at the Lip watch factory was only the most dramatic of these. There was therefore a certain *integrative* logic to many of the proposals in the report.

Third, the report showed a great deal of concern for the *cadres*. Along with suggesting more representation for *cadres* on the works council, there were frequent references to decentralizing decision-making to the lowest level possible:

> Most employees wish to be actively involved in the taking of decisions which concern them directly, such as those which have major social consequences. But some employees, *particularly the supervisory grades*, feel that general economic, financial and technical decisions are of direct concern to them. It is essential for their need to participate to be taken into consideration, as much out of respect for the skill with which they serve the company as in the interests of efficiency.[24]

This was aimed at the *cadres* in the sense that the goal was to give *cadres* a better sense of being part of management. While an effort was made to maintain a clear distinction for worker representatives between the role of worker and manager, no such distinction was made for the *cadres*. The *cadres* were the buffer between workers and managers. They were part of a managerial hierarchy and the authority structure of the firm. They thus provided an alternative way of channeling workers' demands to that of trade unions. There was a sense—made explicit by management theorists from the mid-1970s onward—that these two chains of authority were in competition and that the *cadres* were the key to which one prevailed. In this sense the Sudreau Report was simply part of a wider movement. In 1972 the government had instituted a separate college for *cadres* in firm elections, and in July 1974 the CNPF and the CGC (the main union confederation representing *cadres*) had made a joint declaration calling for improved concertation and participation of *cadres* in the firm.[25]

Fourth, the report was very anxious to argue that reform should occur with a minimum of state intervention. The focus was on experimentation and negotiation, in order to take account of differing circumstances in each branch and firm: "This global, pluralist, evolving view breaks with the tradition according to which the state seeks to bring about company reform by legislation and impose change. . . . Law is without significance unless it brings with it a change of attitudes."[26] This is important both for what it tells us about the desire for firm-level, case-by-case action, and for the eventual assessment of the consequences of the Sudreau Report. The minimal amount of legislation that followed the report can be taken to imply that the initiative for firm reform was a failure. But that would not be an entirely fair assessment given the aims of the report. Any assessment would also have to take into account the measures voluntarily taken by employers without legislative prodding.

What did happen? The report was heartily endorsed by Giscard d'Estaing who promised that legislation would soon follow. However, for a long while nothing happened. The report was discussed by the unions and employers' organizations at the July 1975 meeting of the Conseil Économique et Social. While the unions were ambivalent toward the report, it was savaged by the CNPF, which used the forum as an opportunity to attack the principle of the "union monopoly." It was not until April 1976 that the minister of labor presented a report with fifteen proposals on firm reform, some of which involved legislation that was simultaneously presented to parliament.[27] There were four important proposals. First, to establish the *bilan social* on an experimental basis in certain firms and see how it worked. Second, to provide ways for workers to express themselves at their place of work. The Ministry of Labor would examine firms where such practices already existed and make recommendations later. Third, to allow works councils to demand an explanation for the economic problems of a firm and create an economic delegation. This was only to be possible in firms employing two thousand or more workers and was voluntary only. Legislation would simply make it *possible*. Fourth, on the most controversial part of the Sudreau Report, *co-surveillance*, legislation was to be introduced to again make it *possible* for workers in firms employing over two thousand people to be represented on the supervisory council. The shareholders were to decide how those workers would be chosen. The option of whether to respect the union monopoly or not was theirs.

All these proposals were, therefore, voluntary, with the state simply modifying legislation to make changes possible. In addition, the reforms were clearly envisaged only for very large firms. In any case, debate over the proposed legislation in parliament was dominated by the attempts of Gaullist deputies to end the union monopoly for firm elections, *where it had already existed*, and to ensure that the monopoly would not apply to the economic delegations and workers elected to the supervisory councils.

However, while debate was still in progress Chirac was replaced as prime minister by Raymond Barre, and the economic crisis took priority over all other issues. It was not until 1977 and 1978 that the government returned to the subject of firm reform. In April 1977 the Ministry of Labor issued a recommendation on worker expression in the firm. It was a recommendation only, no legislation was envisaged, and it called for negotiations in the firm to put into place some forum for workers to express their views on working conditions. The recommendation stressed that a wide variety of possible models existed, and that the role of the supervisory staff would be critical. Talks on the subject did start in early 1978, as part of the CFDT's new strategy of *recentrage* but were unsuccessful. Not until the Socialists came to power was there to be movement on this issue. In May 1977 the Ministry of Labor issued a list of ninety-six "indicators" which it said should be reported in the *bilan social*, and then legislation was passed that made it obligatory that such a report be given annually to the works council in all firms employing 750 or more people.[28] Then in November 1977 legislation was passed that demanded that discussions take place between management and *cadres* in firms employing five hundred or more people aimed at improving concertation and communication in the firm. Management had to submit a report on the progress made by January 1979.[29]

What is one to make of the meager results of a much-heralded report on firm reform? With the exception of the *bilan social* all the legislation was facultative, voluntary, and aimed at very large firms. It completely ignored the calls for wider recognition of the role of trade unions—indeed it perhaps even undermined the role of unions—and of collective bargaining. Insofar as it envisaged greater involvement for employees, its focus was the supervisory staff rather than blue-collar workers. For the latter the goal seemed to be to provide greater information about the financial and economic situation of the firm, through the *bilan social*, economic delegations, and so on.

The results were limited indeed, and an assessment of the grandiose plans of Giscard d'Estaing and Sudreau would have to say that no wide-ranging reform was attempted, much less implemented. However, this might be to miss the point of the Sudreau Report (which after all did not anticipate a great deal of legislation), and more importantly it would miss the significance of the Sudreau Report for the evolution in thinking about the role of the firm and of the nature of social relations inside the firm. In a sense the report should be seen as the opening shot in the ultimately successful campaign to decentralize the regulation of industrial relations to the firm level, rather than as an isolated and failed episode. What is remarkable is how much of the Sudreau Report did eventually appear either in legislation *after* 1981, or in the day-to-day practices of firms.[30]

The report appeared at precisely the time when the French economy was going into crisis. Thus it is no surprise that the report was so concerned with making workers *aware* of the scale of that crisis, and that it was this aspect of the report that received legislative attention. As *Le Figaro* said of the reform proposals: "In the present period, the dominant preoccupation that guides the choice of [reform] projects seems to be . . . to strengthen French firms. That is why they have a largely economic character. . . . The other aspects of the reform of the firm will only be able to come later."[31]

The trade unions were hostile to the very notion of reform of the firm. They recognized that the issues at stake were those of authority in the firm and of *who* represented workers. FO was hostile to any increase in direct worker participation in decision-making, both because it threatened the mediating role of trade unions, between workers and management, and because (in a somewhat contradictory manner) if trade unions were able to increase their role in the firm the benefit would probably go to the CGT, which was far better implanted in the private sector than FO.

Both the CGT and CFDT were deeply distrustful of the reform of the firm because in practice it appeared to challenge the role of trade unions, despite the relatively high-minded sentiments expressed in the Sudreau Report itself. As the CFDT put it: "For too many deputies the reform of the firm is, more and more, the pretext for reinforcing patronal power and calling into question the rights acquired through long struggle by workers and their union organizations."[32]

The CNPF, and its supporters in parliament, made abolition of the union monopoly a condition for reform. As the CGT pointed out,[33] the creation of economic delegations would amputate from the works council its most important role, and if the union monopoly did not apply to the newly created economic delegations the result, in practice, was to circumvent the institution of the union monopoly without even having to attack it frontally.

In addition, the CGT and CFDT feared the idea of worker expression groups in the workplace. The CFDT supported some form of worker expression and pushed for talks on the subject in 1978.[34] But those talks ultimately failed because the unions demanded that union officials be present at the meetings and that they not be organized by the supervisory staff, and that was unacceptable to employers.[35] Overall there was no constituency among the trade unions for firm reform, at least not if carried out by a right-wing government.

What is, at first glance, paradoxical is that the *patronat* were almost equally hostile to reform, and it was this opposition that proved fatal to the Sudreau reforms. The small employers represented by the Confédération Générale des Petites et Moyennes Entreprises (CGPME) did not like the reforms at all because the entire reform project was an attack on the traditional, family-run firm. And in the context of the close electoral competition of the mid-1970s and the disintegration of de Gaulle's broad cross-class coalition, small employers now had political leverage in a way that they did not when the General himself ruled France.

It was not simply the traditional firms that feared reform. The CNPF, representing large, modern firms also had serious doubts. Initially the CNPF was relieved that the Sudreau Report opted for *co-surveillance* rather than codetermination. But it soon became clear that the government was not even going to force this on employers, and the CNPF's position hardened. The CNPF argued that the guiding principle should be to avoid legislation and instead to allow firms to experiment with schemes that fitted their own particular needs. Indeed from the mid-1970s there was the slow but accelerating development of a wide variety of schemes for worker participation in the firm.

Above all else, employers were concerned that the authority of management not be challenged. This concern crystallized into two related goals. The first was to further integrate the supervisory staff into the managerial hierarchy as an alternative channel of authority to that of the trade unions. The second was to attack the union monopoly or at least bypass it. The CNPF argued that the union monopoly might have been justified until 1968 when unions were excluded from the firm. But since 1968 its presence was no longer justified. It was now necessary, the CNPF argued, to clearly differentiate between the locus of contestation and of concertation in the firm. Thus the CNPF offered an explicit quid pro quo: "If one admits that the works council can be a place of cooperation, and not only an element of counterveiling power, and that it must be more representative of workers, we accept that its power can be extended."[36] In other words, only if the union monopoly was ended would employers allow the works council to be given greater powers. The maintenance of the union monopoly was the fundamental demand of the trade unions, and no government was prepared to consider a frontal attack on the trade unions in the economic and political context of the mid-1970s. Hence a stalemate existed and firm reform was bound to be minimal.

The importance of the employer response to the Sudreau Report was that it marked a clear break with the 1968–74 strategy of cooperation with trade unions. The response to the Sudreau Report showed how short-lived *la grande politique contractuelle* was. As far as employers were concerned (even those in large, modern firms), the New Society either had failed, as strike levels remained high, or had become counterproductive in the new economic context. Both the material conditions and the constituency for a mode of labor regulation based on trade unions and bargaining were evaporating. The Sudreau Report appeared at precisely this turning point, and the consequence (despite the fact that its language in many ways echoed that of the New Society) was that any reform of the firm would take place without the participation of trade unions.

THE BARRE PLAN

The economic crisis brought on by the 1973 oil shock hit France very hard. The French economy had been deeply susceptible to inflation in the postwar period, and indeed French governments had occasion to tolerate higher levels of inflation in order to ease distributional conflicts.[37] The stop-go macroeconomic policies made infamous across the Channel were also practiced in France in the 1950s and 1960s. Periods of high growth engendered high inflation which were treated with deflationary packages of monetary and fiscal policy. Then as the economy went into recession the same instruments were used to expand demand and cheapen credit.

But to this structural bias toward inflation in the French economy, and the exogenous shock of a tripling of energy prices, was added, in the mid-1970s, the results of the New Society wage contracts in the public sector and their spillover effect to the rest of the economy. It will be recalled that in an effort to draw the trade unions into bargaining and signing wage agreements in the public sector, the governments of Chaban-Delmas and his successor, Messmer, had been prepared to offer contracts that inflation-proofed wages and provided a guaranteed 2 to 3 percent a year real wage increase. In 1975 the contracts became even more advantageous to the trade unions because the government agreed to revise wages four times a year (in light of accelerating inflation) and to incorporate the *anticipated* cost-of-living increases at the beginning of each quarter.

By 1975 these wage contracts fulfilled a fundamentally political purpose. They were the price of continued collective bargaining in the public sector, and in a period of very close electoral competition the government did not want to throw away that trump. In this respect FO was the key. The CGT and CFDT had lined up with the Union of the Left so that FO was the only union with a respectable membership and popularity in the firm elections which had not firmly aligned itself with the Left. This made the opinion of FO important to the government, but it also posed a problem for FO itself. The prospect of ending these lucrative contracts was less a problem for the CGT and CFDT than for those union organizations, such as FO, that had made these wage agreements the main foundation of their action.

FO made the continuance of these agreements the condition of its participation in public-sector bargaining. The government was thus trapped between the increasing costs of the contracts and its electoral needs. It held the success or failure of public-sector bargaining in its own hands. The problem lay not only in the public sector. The practice of indexation (which was still technically illegal) was widely copied in the large, modern firms of the private sector. This meant both *high* and *rigid* wage levels. Wage levels were effectively indexed to macroeconomic indicators and bore little relation to the specific financial condition of individual firms. That became a serious concern for employers as they faced a more uncertain and rapidly changing economic environment. The rigidity of wages, which could be considered positively beneficial in the Fordist heyday of the late 1960s and early 1970s, was now increasingly considered an obstacle to economic growth.

The dilemma of the government, and by implication much of the private sector, became acute as inflation accelerated, reaching 9.6 percent in 1975.[38] Between 1974 and 1976, Prime Minister Jacques Chirac steadfastly refused to attack the public-sector wage contracts, despite ever more frequent calls for an incomes policy of some kind. Alternatives were tried. Chirac rehabilitated stop-go policies with a *plan de refroidissement* in June 1974, resulting in a rapid fall in growth and investment, and a rise in unemployment and bankruptcies. This was followed by reflation in January 1975, and then again in September 1975. The one direct instrument of an incomes policy used by Chirac was the *prélèvement conjoncturel*, a tax on excess profits, introduced in December 1974 but suspended within nine months. The government would set a norm for growth in the rate of profit which comprised both an economy-wide component (a 14.3 percent increase in 1975) and a firm-specific component. Profits above that level would be subject to a 33.3 percent tax. The scheme was suspended when profits fell to such low levels as to make a tax unnecessary and counterproductive. It is important to note, however, that Chirac made the same choice that Barre later made, of imposing an incomes policy that operated only *indirectly* on wages; in this case the direct pressure was on profit margins.

This then was the situation when Giscard d'Estaing replaced Chirac as prime minister with Raymond Barre in August 1976. With a deteriorating economic situation and crucial legislative elections less than two years away, Barre's choice was either to break with the policy of collective bargaining, and risk social conflict, or to pursue bargaining at the cost of higher inflation.

In fact, Barre did not interpret the economic problem as purely, or even primarily, one of inflation. Rather, he saw the problem as being one of reduced profitability. When the oil shock hit, the combination of government and employer desires to buy social peace by continuing high real wages and indeed enhancing workers' security by restrictions on layoffs and relatively generous unemployment compensation meant that, almost alone among OECD countries, the costs of the oil shock did not fall first on labor but on capital (through rigid wages and increased social security contributions) and then on the state as, from 1975 onward, the state increasingly took responsibility for the cost of dealing with unemployment.[39] To keep people in work the government strongly encouraged employers to resort to short-time working, rather than layoffs, by offering to pay a proportion of the cost. The goal of the Barre government was, above all, to restore profitability, to reverse the shift in value added going from labor to capital.

In September 1976 Barre launched the so-called Barre Plan, which was in essence an incomes policy that operated through price controls instead of wage controls. Employers were urged to police wages themselves. In the private sector, employers were asked to offer wage increases equivalent to the consumer price index—estimated to rise by 6.5 percent in 1977—but no more, with increases being awarded at the end of each quarter. There was some provision for small real wage increases for the low-paid if the economic situation improved in the course of the year. The CNPF embodied these proposals in a directive sent out to its members in November 1976. The government had two kinds of sanctions to use against employers who did not comply with its directives. The first was a price freeze for the fourth quarter of 1976 to be followed by gradual decontrol in 1977. Thus if employers allowed wages to rise faster than prices, their profits would suffer. The second was a joint CNPF-government committee which was created to monitor the hundred largest companies. The government threatened a variety of sanctions, in the form of denial of government contracts and tax breaks, for those caught ignoring the guidelines.

In the public sector the government had no need for indirect controls on wages. Here the government followed the same guidelines: wages to rise only in line with the consumer price index, some gains for the low-paid, and post-facto adjustments. Barre called for *contrats de stabilité* not *contrats de progrès*. The test case, as in 1969, was EGF where the wage contract for 1977 was being negotiated in the fall of 1976. The government suspended the 1972 codicil to the original 1969 contract which guaranteed a 2 percent real wage increase. All the unions were outraged, but perhaps FO most of all, and as a result none of the trade union confederations signed a wage contract in the public sector in 1977.

However, talks began again in January 1977 and continued intermittently throughout the year. It was a foregone conclusion that the CGT and CFDT would reject any contract given the constraints placed on the negotiators by government directives. But FO and the other reformist unions desperately wanted to be able to sign a contract, and the government also wanted to avoid another year without public-sector contracts as it went into the legislative elections.

The management of EGF (swiftly followed by the other public-sector companies) proposed a formula in which the nominal wage increase would equal the cost of living, but there would be the possibility of a real wage increase if the economic indicators were better than expected. Thus if GDP was 3.5 percent or above and inflation was 8.5 percent or below in 1978, there would be small real wage gains.[40] Neither of these possibilities was likely but the *theoretical possibility* of a real wage increase now existed, and while the CGT and CFDT refused to sign, it was enough for FO, the CGC, and the CFTC to sign contracts at EGF, RATP, and Charbonnages de France.

Two important questions remain. The first is why the government chose the type of incomes policy that it did, and the second is how successful that policy was. Barre chose an incomes policy that was neither statutory nor negotiated and that operated through price controls. One part of Barre's reasoning was no doubt political. If an incomes policy was deemed economically necessary, better that it should maintain the fiction of not interfering with collective bargaining. It is interesting that the Socialist government did suspend the basic 1950 law on collective bargaining in 1982 as part of its incomes policy, while Barre did not feel able to go so far. Barre later admitted that the electoral calendar was "the reason why I avoided, in 1976, measures that would have been perfectly justifiable from a theoretical point of view."[41]

More important is the question of why there was not even an attempt to negotiate a voluntary incomes policy with the unions. It was here that Barre was most criticized. FO and even certain prominent Socialists (for instance Jean-Paul Bachy and Jacques Delors) acknowledged the need for some kind of incomes policy, but they argued that it should be negotiated. However, serious structural obstacles to a negotiated incomes policy existed in France. French trade unions were simply too weak to be able to collaborate in an incomes policy. The structural preconditions for corporatist-style wage-restraint agreements are a high union density and a highly centralized and unified union movement able to control and discipline its members. The Swedish postwar experience and the experience of the 1974–79 British Labour government also suggest that a social democratic party must be in power, to offer full employment and welfare policies as an inducement to wage restraint. French trade unions were weak and divided, and Barre was unprepared (and probably unable) to offer the kinds of inducements that would make wage restraint palatable to workers.[42] For this reason French trade unions could not have participated in an incomes policy without grave risk to their organizations, even had they wanted to, and the CGT and CFDT (in a preelection period) did not. Barre was well aware of this.

France had a situation that was practically the reverse image of corporatism. A high-level wage-restraint agreement was bound to fail. But, perhaps paradoxically, in light of most corporatist theorizing, a policy that *decentralized* wage restraint by operating at the firm level, through the cooperation of employers, had a much better chance of success because the organizational power of unions was weakest at that level. Workers' capacity to resist was therefore reduced.

The choice of operating an incomes policy indirectly was therefore a logical one in the French context. Price control for Barre, control of profits for Chirac were the only ways to limit wages in the private sector short of legislation to suspend collective bargaining altogether. Price control had the additional psychological advantage of making the wage-restraint policy seem more fair. The episode of the Barre Plan provides a good demonstration of the way in which the structure of the labor movement imposes limits on the economic policy options of states.

To what degree was the Barre Plan a success? The answer is not a simple one, but overall the plan must be judged unsuccessful. In comparative perspective, inflation was slightly higher than France's main trading partners, and real wages were significantly higher. For instance, in 1977 real wages rose 2.8 percent in France and 0.3 percent in the European Community as a whole. In 1978 the figures were 3 percent and 2.1 percent respectively.[43] While profitability recovered in 1977–78, it began to deteriorate again after that; and even if real wage increases stabilized, social security costs soared (see table 5.2).

It should also be noted that the Barre Plan did not even *attempt* to deindex wages. Purchasing power was maintained both in the public and

TABLE 5.2
The Distribution of Value Added, 1973–80

	Gross Salaries (in percent)	Employer Social Security Contributions (in percent)	Gross Margin Rate (in percent)
1973	49.8	14.6	27.6
1974	50.9	15.1	27.1
1975	51.7	16.8	24.7
1976	52.0	17.1	24.5
1977	51.5	17.3	24.4
1978	51.4	17.5	24.2
1979	50.4	17.9	24.3
1980	51.4	18.3	23.0

Source: W. Allen Spivey, *Economic Policies in France, 1975–81*, Michigan International Business Studies, no. 18 (Ann Arbor: University of Michigan, 1982), 36, table 14. The gross margin rate is one measure of pretax profits.

private sectors. The Barre Plan was successful in eliminating the built-in 2 to 3 percent annual real wage gains inherited from the New Society (which had in practice been closer to a 5 percent real increase a year), but it did not actually cut real wages. Clearly, a comparison between the Barre government and the Socialist government is impossible because of the very different economic and political conjunctures, but the Socialist government did de-index wages and achieved cuts in real wages (though whether it deserves congratulation for this feat is another question altogether).[44]

Political factors were clearly important. As *L'Express* put it, in explaining the caution shown by the government, and the relatively mild impact of the Barre Plan on real wage levels, "It is useless to hide the fact that the maintenance of purchasing power is a pillar of the country's political equilibrium. Thus it is necessarily part of the electoral strategy of the government."[45] And this was all the more true in the run up to the legislative elections. This helps to explain why Barre did not attempt to impose a more stringent incomes policy. But there was a deeper problem. Wage increases in the private sector were above the government guidelines. And this despite very high levels of unemployment. The CFDT triumphantly published lists of firms that broke the government guidelines.[46]

It is important to recognize that, although the CNPF endorsed the Barre Plan (not least because its success was seen as the only thing likely to prevent a Left electoral victory), many employers had serious misgivings about it. In the Fordist sectors of the economy workers were better organized and reasonably well protected from unemployment, or at least from a sizable drop in their living standards in the event of unemployment. In firms in these sectors of the economy employers were often still prepared to buy industrial peace with real wage increases, regardless of the overall economic strategy of the government of the day.

The "Relaunching" of Collective Bargaining

This next section treats the period after March 1978, when the Right surprisingly retained its majority in the National Assembly. Now, for the first time since 1973, the government did not have to subject all policy to immediate electoral needs. Giscard d'Estaing was anxious to use the defeat of the Left and the ensuing recriminations to build a broader electoral base, and this implied a "logic of opening up" to the center, both to the new middle classes and the reformist unions.

Barre remained prime minister, and he attempted to use this opportunity to change the form of labor regulation in such a way as to be consistent with the new economic realities of the late 1970s, as he understood them. This entailed, above all, an attempt to decentralize labor regulation to the level of the branch, and even the firm, where wages and working conditions could be tailored to the needs of particular sectors and firms and a simultaneous withdrawal or disengagement of the state from labor regulation so as to reimpose the disciplinary power of the labor market.

Barre's program of liberalizing the economy had been severely restricted by the immediate economic crisis that he had faced in 1976, and by the political conjuncture. The situation had, paradoxically, demanded an *increase* in state intervention in labor regulation and the economy more generally. But now he was able to go forward with his goal of liberalization. For Barre this meant restoring profitability, controlling wages, and allowing a restructuring of the economy. The oft-made claim was that "lame ducks" would be allowed to sink, and subsidies would only go to the newer industries, leaving the old core heavy industries to shed labor. The reality was some distance from the neo-liberal rhetoric, but it was certainly true that restructuring now accelerated. Above all, the new stress on nonintervention and restructuring demonstrated that the government recognized that the economic crisis was deep-seated and persistent. It was not possible to simply shore up employment and await an upturn in the business cycle.

For Barre new economic goals required an accompanying modification in labor regulation. Part and parcel of liberalization in the economic sphere was a withdrawal of the state from labor regulation. In the past, so the argument went, the state had made it difficult for firms to adapt. The labor market had lost much of its disciplinary power because of restrictions on layoffs and high levels of unemployment compensation. The minimum wage acted as a floor that was applied, it was argued, indiscriminately, without reference to the particular circumstances of each sector or firm. And the Labor Code was felt to severely restrict the capacity of firms to respond flexibly to changing economic conditions. For instance, the Lucas Report, presented in April 1979, argued that France lagged behind other countries in the number of people in part-time work and proposed modifications in the Labor Code to make such work easier.

The point was that in an economic environment that put a premium on innovation and flexibility, a mode of labor regulation that relied upon rigid and universal rules, wages, and work practices was inappropriate. There was, no doubt, much truth to this economic wisdom. Fordism had made limited and straightforward demands on a mode of labor regulation: steadily increasing wages in line with productivity gains, and industrial peace. The capacity to adapt rapidly, and the focus for that reason upon decision-making inside the firm, had not been important in the heyday of Fordism when rigidity could in fact be considered beneficial. That said, it was not simply an economic logic that drove the reform initiatives of the post-1978 period. The French state and business were anxious to take advantage of the weakness of the political and industrial wings of the Left. The deep recession combined with the disillusionment and recriminations following

March 1978 provided an opportunity to convert conjunctural weakness into structural weakness.

The goal of the Barre government was not just to withdraw the state from labor regulation, but to replace it with collective bargaining. There was to be a kind of devolution of labor regulation from state to social partners. In the advanced sectors of the economy where collective bargaining had existed but had been effectively suspended during the Barre Plan, the assumption was that bargaining would simply resume. But in the traditional sectors of the economy it was recognized that an effort would have to be made to *create* collective bargaining. As Lionel Stoleru, secretary of state in the Ministry of Labor, put it in *Le Monde*, the goal was "le libéralisme contractuel,"[47] which meant a better balance between the state and social partners in the task of labor regulation. However, collective bargaining was now envisioned as something far more decentralized than had been the case in the immediate post-1968 period. The national/confederal level was considered too rigid and inflexible, and even agreement at the branch level limited the flexibility of the firm. Thus firm-level collective bargaining was the goal.

Two other factors made this initiative possible. The first was a resurgent, activist CNPF. As the third section of this chapter described, the CNPF adopted, with much fanfare and media attention, an activist social policy after 1977. At the same time, the CNPF had become actively involved in politics in an effort to keep the Left out of office in 1978, and that politicization continued. There was a new willingness of the CNPF to lobby for and against legislation.[48] In this period it is very difficult to separate out government initiatives in the area of labor regulation from those of the CNPF. In contrast to the episode of the Sudreau Report, there appeared to be little conflict between the two.

The second accommodating factor was the CFDT's adoption of a strategy of *recentrage*. The CFDT reacted to the defeat of the Left with a new strategy.[49] If the problem in the early 1970s had been the absence of a clear link between the transformative goals of the CFDT and its day-to-day activities, with a privileging of the former, *recentrage* involved precisely the opposite. Collective bargaining and a concentration on attainable goals were elevated almost to an end in themselves.[50] Thus the CFDT declared itself ready to negotiate seriously with the CNPF, and bilateral working groups were set up. There is some evidence that the Barre government had hopes for a new reformist axis within the trade union movement centered on the CFDT and FO, and this made the attempt to reinvigorate collective bargaining a more plausible project.[51]

On April 27, 1978, Barre "relaunched" collective bargaining with a letter to the union and employer organizations urging them to begin negotiations on a series of issues including sector-specific minimum wages, the reduction and flexibility of worktime, and unemployment compensation. This was followed in May 1978 with a letter from the CNPF to each trade union confederation calling for negotiations on roughly the same set of issues and laying out the CNPF's position on each of these issues. To the three suggested by Barre was added that of worker expression in the firm because the CNPF and CFDT had set up a working party to discuss its implementation inside the firm.

The first topic for talks was the minimum wage. Barre and the CNPF felt that the role of the SMIC should be reduced. The problem was that it served as a universal floor which applied upward pressure on the entire wage scale (i.e., each category of worker would expect a similar raise to maintain differentials) without respect to the economic circumstances of each industry or sector. The ultimate goal behind the government's and employers' new outlook was to see the function of the national minimum wage progressively replaced by a "minimum family income" and branch-negotiated wage minimums. There was nothing new about branch mini-mums, but they had previously only played a small role because the SMIC had been the motor driving rises in the wages of the low-paid, and because large parts of the labor force were not covered by a collective agreement and hence by branch-negotiated minimums. Barre and the CNPF wanted to reinvigorate the branch minimums and give them the primary role in raising low wages. In addition, employers wanted to change the form of these minimums so that they were computed on an annual basis and thus included the variety of bonuses that were regularly given to workers. The end result would, it was hoped, be that the minimums would become an accurate reflection of the real minimum wage employers could expect to pay. The name given to the new branch minimums was *rémunération annuelle minimale garantie* (RAMG).

The unions agreed to talks on the subject, though the CGT and CFDT were anxious that the CNPF give national direction to its federations and lay down guidelines. Negotiations did take place, and agreements were reached, the most spectacular (because of the number of workers involved) being that signed on July 1978 in the metalworking industry, which all the trade unions signed. The agreement was an *accord-cadre*, meaning that it was an agreement in principle with actual talks being left up to regional organizations. There were a large number of agreements signed on in-dustry minimums. In October 1979 the Ministry of Labor estimated that 280 accords of this type had been signed though they overwhelmingly tended to set monthly minimums.[52] Only about ten branches set annual minimums.[53]

The problem with emphasizing negotiated minimums rather than a leg-islated minimum wage like the SMIC was that many sectors were not cov-ered by collective agreements, and they were precisely the low-paid sectors where minimum wages were most needed. The strength of unions varied so much from one sector to another that the minimums that were negotiated also varied widely, being the result of the local strength of trade unions. The resulting wide variation was due more to the differing strength of labor than the strict economic conditions in each sector. This was inevitable in any strategy that relied on negotiations instead of legislation. In France the result was woefully inadequate protection for the low-paid.[54]

The second important issue was the reduction and "flexibilization" of work time. The two concepts were conceptually distinct. The CFDT and CGT were anxious to reduce the length of the workweek in order to create or at least share jobs. The CNPF, however, was concerned to allow a more flexible use of work time. It suggested, in May 1978, that the social partners move from the notion of a forty-hour workweek to one of a 1,920-hour workyear, which could then be divided up in a variety of ways. These negotiations were particularly important to the CFDT because they were a test case for the new strategy of *recentrage*. They held the promise of compromise: the CFDT would give ground on the issue of flexibility in return for an overall reduction in work time.

In January 1979 the government passed legislation to make the Labor Code less restrictive (and hence facilitate flexibility), should the employers and unions be able to reach agreement. The legislation reduced the maximum workweek from fifty-two to fifty hours, legalized certain kinds of night work for women, and allowed the forty-hour workweek to be divided up not just into six-, five-and-a-half, and five-day periods, but also into four-and-a-half and four-day periods. This was only to be possible if the works council agreed, the Labor Inspectorate was informed, and the agreement did not contradict existing collective agreements.

The negotiations went badly. Some accords were signed at the branch level, but the talks at the confederal level, which were designed to create the framework for lower-level agreements, were repeatedly broken off. They finally collapsed in July 1980. The main problem was that the CNPF wanted any agreements to be signed at the firm level, and even to allow *individual* arrangements between employer and employee.[55] The trade unions were concerned about their weakness at the firm level, and they feared that individual workers, and even union sections, would find it difficult to resist managerial pressure for flexibility that was not in their interests. For the CFDT the failure of these talks was particularly disappointing.

The third issue was that of creating a forum to allow workers to express their views on their work inside the firm. Again, both the trade unions and employers saw potential benefits to such a development. But their conceptions of how such a forum would work were very different. For the unions it was an additional space in the workplace for workers to criticize their work, and for unions to organize. For the CNPF it was a part of the activist social policy in which the existing supervisory hierarchy could wrest control of representing workers from trade unions. For employers worker self-expression had more to do with economic efficiency, as a mechanism for raising productivity, than the humanization of work. In short, unions saw worker self-expression as essentially contestatory while employers saw it as essentially cooperative.

Here, as in the talks on work time, negotiations dragged on with little progress until the CNPF broke off talks in July 1980. The obstacle was remarkably similar.[56] The unions wanted to set the conditions under which worker self-expression took place at the branch level, and they wanted to ensure that the role of unions, works councils, and supervisory staff were clearly specified before firm-level talks settled the final details. The CNPF wanted to leave the details to firm-level bargaining where unions were very often not present or weak. The real conflict was over who controlled the self-expression groups. The trade unions feared that without strict guidelines there was nothing to prevent individual employers setting up opportunities for workers to express themselves under whatever conditions the employer chose. Much of the discussion was in any case moot because employers did not in fact need the agreement of trade unions to set up some kind of firm-based type of worker expression. And though the talks failed, the French Association of Quality Circles (AFCERQ—l'Association Française pour les Cercles de Qualité) was created in May 1981 and by that point quality circles existed in about five hundred firms.[57]

The fourth and final issue was the labor market. In the period 1973–75 French governments had not recognized the severity of the economic crisis or its structural elements. Labor market policy, therefore, was concerned above all with *maintaining* the level of employment and compensating those laid off until the recession passed, as it was expected to. Hence the administrative restrictions on layoffs, the obligatory consultation of the works council, the encouragement of short-time working (as opposed to layoffs), and the special unemployment compensation equal to 90 percent of former income.[58]

However, from 1976–77 onward it became clear that the crisis was deeper than expected and that large-scale industrial restructuring would be necessary. In this context a rigid labor market, which discouraged mobility and failed to exert a disciplinary effect on wages, was less appropriate. Thus after 1977 there was a "rupture" in employment policy,[59] and the goals became to get people *out* of the labor market, improve training, and reduce unemployment compensation. Thus bonuses to persuade immigrants to leave the country, increased family allowances to keep women out of the labor force, and schemes to compensate older workers who took early retirement, all aimed to reduce labor-force participation. A series of three "national youth employment pacts" were negotiated between the government and employers. Employers were absolved of a part of the social security costs of employing young workers in return for providing job-training programs. In both cases the state paid the additional costs.[60] On the issue of unemployment compensation the government abolished the special 90 percent unemployment scheme in 1979.

Thus a series of important issues were raised, negotiations did take place, and in some cases agreements were reached in the period after March 1978 when the Barre government set about self-consciously trying to relaunch collective bargaining in France. The Barre government could, and did, point to an increase in collective bargaining from the second half of 1978 on. The total number of collective agreements, including codicils, rose from a low point of 1,284 in 1978, to 1,487 in 1979, and 2,171 in 1980.[61] There was certainly some success in the central goal of increasing collective bargaining. But the raw figures need to be qualified in a number of ways.

The first thing to say about collective bargaining in this period is that it concerned an agenda that was largely that of the employers. With the possible exception of the issue of worker expression in the workplace, talks focused on issues that the CNPF wanted, that would involve concessions from the trade unions: replacement of the SMIC with industry-specific minimums, greater flexibility of work time, and a reduction in unemployment compensation. This was in keeping with the CNPF's *donnant-donnant* bargaining strategy.

The second characteristic of bargaining in this period was that there were still large gaps in the coverage in collective bargaining. The data on collective bargaining remained poor, but one study conducted in 1980 did show an increase in the proportion of workers who were covered by some form of collective agreement in the period since the last such study in 1972.[62] In 1972, 74.9 percent of workers had some coverage, while in 1980 the figure was 80.1 percent. In 1980, 24.2 percent of workers were covered by a *firm-level* agreement. No figure for firm-level bargaining had been recorded in 1972. However, approximately 1.1 million workers, or 11 percent of those employed in firms with ten or more people, were not covered by a collective agreement of any kind. These workers were concentrated in commerce, services, and the building industry. Since many people worked in firms employing less than ten workers, the real figure was bound to be much higher. It was estimated by the CFDT that in fact approximately one-quarter of the labor force, or three million people, were not covered by any kind of collective agreement.[63] The consequence was that any strategy that sought to shift responsibility for labor regulation from the state to collective bargaining would allow those not covered to fall through the cracks. In a comprehensive study of the use of branch-negotiated wage minimums, Bughin was particularly concerned with this problem.[64] If the

SMIC was allowed to languish in favor of negotiated minimums, then a significant group, precisely those who most needed protection because they were poorly organized, would suffer. The result was to encourage a deepening of the dualism that already existed in the French labor market.

The third characteristic of collective bargaining was that, increasingly, accords were being signed by "minority" unions alone.[65] The CGT published summaries of collective agreements in order to demonstrate that the increase in collective bargaining masked the fact that it was overwhelmingly FO and the CFTC that were signing, rather than the two largest unions, the CGT and CFDT.[66] This development was disturbing when considered in conjunction with a recent piece of government legislation. In January 1978 the government passed a law that aimed to extend monthly status to the remaining 20 percent of the working population who, it was estimated, were not yet covered by the *mensuelisation* accords which had proliferated since 1970. But the legislation also modified the procedure used to "extend" collective agreements by decree. Previous reforms, including the one in 1971, had made this procedure easier. But the earlier reforms had retained the principle that any representative union could veto a proposed extension. The 1978 legislation removed that veto power. In the future, a collective agreement could be extended if two-thirds of the employer and trade union organizations agreed. The two-thirds figure meant that the reformist unions and employers' organizations could prevent a CGT and CFDT veto. The government justified this action by pointing out that there had been increasing use of the veto in the mid-1970s and arguing that the "revolutionary" unions were obstructing the extension of agreements for political purposes.[67]

Be that as it may, the implication of these two developments—one resulting from legislation, the other from conscious choice by employers—was that collective bargaining in France was now increasingly between employers and trade unions that represented only a small minority of workers. What then was the role of trade unions? Whereas in the past employers who were unable to reach agreement with the more radical trade unions had not signed any agreement, now they appeared to be willing to sign with minority unions. This development raised the question of what in substance had changed behind the statistical rise in collective bargaining.

It was probably inevitable that any attempt by the state to withdraw from its dominant role in labor regulation in a period of deep union weakness would result in collective bargaining that took place more on employers' terms than those of workers. As Ginsbourger and Potel's excellent study of collective bargaining shows, when bargaining did take place it was usually a response to pressure from workers, and, as the economic crisis hit, that pressure was less likely to be present. Bargaining sessions in the 1970s "become more and more formal. They limit themselves to reports, and often lively exchanges of fixed positions, they rarely allow a problem to be resolved, however minor."[68] The result was either that negotiation did not take place or that it took place on the agenda and terms of the employers.

CONCLUSION

The mid-1970s were dominated by short-term conjunctural factors: the electoral calendar and closeness of competition between Left and Right, and the oil shock and ensuing deep recession. Only at the beginning of the period, before the scale of the economic crisis was recognized, and at the end, after the defeat of the Left in March 1978, were clear attempts to reform industrial relations made. Giscard d'Estaing did not have a single coherent model of labor regulation in mind, in contrast to Chaban-Delmas. At different points in his seven-year presidency, microcorporatist, collective bargaining, and statist forms of labor regulation all made brief appearances as the inspiration for policy.

However, this period has a coherence independent of the intention of policymakers. It was a transitional period in which the existing mode of labor regulation proved unstable and dysfunctional. Yet it did not fully break down and no alternative mode of labor regulation appeared to replace it. The innovation of the 1968–74 period had been a dualistic form of labor regulation, resting on collective bargaining in the public sector and advanced sectors of the economy, and a state regulation of labor in the rest of the economy. Collective bargaining did not disappear after 1976 but it did change its form. It was increasingly bargaining when employers wanted, on their terrain, and with trade unions chosen for their ideological affinity with management. Bargaining was more about legitimacy than about negotiation between opposing class forces. The tenor of collective bargaining in the public sector was captured well by Delors: "There remains all that is left of a mass celebrated at the eleventh hour without faith: a liturgy empty of sense . . . [they] maintain it as a rite, so as to save face. But the heart is not in it."[69]

As for the second pillar of labor regulation, France remained a nation in which state regulation of labor was important, but from 1978 onward that role was reduced, and the function of state regulation changed. Whereas until the mid-1970s state regulation had substituted for a mode of labor regulation based on collective bargaining and strong trade unions (in order to extend Fordism into the traditional sector), now state regulation was more reactive, designed to "manage" unemployment and as a protector of last resort to those that slipped through the cracks of collective bargaining.

Both collective bargaining and extensive state regulation of labor were perceived by employers and government alike as increasingly inappropriate for the French economy of the late 1970s. However, whether correctly or incorrectly many employers (as evidenced by the CNPF's much-heralded strategic evolution) interpreted the economic crisis as ushering in a new period in which flexibility, adaptability, and "human resource management" would be more important than the Fordist emphasis on predictable wage rises and stable (rigid) labor practices.[70] By the end of the 1970s it was still too early to see what forms of labor regulation, more suited to this new interpretation of economic need, would emerge. But the indications were that flexibility, decentralization, and a focus on firm-based forms of worker organization would play a greater role in any future type of labor regulation.

Yet no new mode of labor regulation did appear in this period. A form of stalemate existed in that, both for electoral reasons and to avoid industrial unrest and social upheaval, collective bargaining had to be maintained and the state could not completely withdraw from labor regulation. The unions still proved capable of mounting impressive national demonstrations of strength; many employers preferred bargaining, however hollow, to no bargaining; and the consequences of labor market regulation (in terms of unemployment and wages) were too great for the state to dismantle its interventionist machinery. Thus the French state could only accommodate the new orthodoxy of flexibility so far.

Two obstacles to the emergence of a new mode of labor regulation existed. The first was the stalemate described above. It was very difficult for a right-wing government to effect major reform of industrial relations even after the defeat of the Left in 1978. Right-wing governments had a problem of legitimacy and could virtually guarantee vociferous working-class opposition to any project that sought to reshape industrial relations. The second obstacle was that no institutional framework appropriate to a new type of labor regulation existed. The collapse of collective bargaining and deregulation by the state was not equivalent to creating a new form of labor regulation. It would simply reintroduce regulation by the labor market. It is a remarkable feature of the 1978–81 period that Barre avoided legislation or any attempt to construct institutions in the sphere of industrial relations. He merely *exhorted* the social partners to bargain.

In May 1981 a Socialist president, François Mitterrand, and shortly after that a Socialist-dominated legislature, were elected on a platform that committed them, rhetorically at least, to a "rupture" with capitalism. The question in 1981 was whether the newly elected Socialist-Communist alliance had an alternative mode of labor regulation in mind for the French labor movement, and whether it would have the legitimacy (in the eyes of labor and capital) to carry out such a project, and the willingness to move beyond exhortation to the construction of a new mode of labor regulation.

PART THREE

Socialist Labor Regulation

PART TWO OF THIS STUDY charted the collapse of the postwar mode of labor regulation, based on the labor market, and the uncertain attempts after 1968 to construct labor regulation around strengthened trade unions and collective-bargaining mechanisms. The New Society reforms, the Sudreau Report, and the attempt to "relaunch" collective bargaining after 1978 were largely failures. Fundamentally, these broad projects ran up against the paradox of the French labor movement: its simultaneous strength and weakness. It was too strong and too prone to industrial unrest to be entirely ignored and regulated by the labor market. Yet it was also too weak, in its organizational structure, to form the keystone of a system of collective bargaining. The degree to which collective bargaining did take place was tied directly to conjunctural factors, and in particular the attitude of the French state and economic conditions. Thus the 1970s were a stalemate, not just in a narrow electoral sense, but in the deeper sense that neither labor nor business and its allies in government could impose a durable form of labor regulation to replace that destroyed by the events of May 1968. The result was an unsteady and patched-together form of labor regulation that was almost entirely dependent on the French state, and that was becoming—or at least was perceived as becoming—increasingly dysfunctional to the French economy as it entered the 1980s.

Part three of this study covers the first period of Socialist government, from 1981 to 1986, and the construction under its aegis of a new mode of labor regulation, one that can be termed microcorporatist. The argument that will be made is that a combination of factors—the economic conjuncture, employer strategy, and the contradictions of the Socialist industrial relations project—contributed to the decentralization of industrial relations to the level of the firm, the withdrawal of the state from labor regulation, the emasculation of trade unions, the flourishing of firm-specific types of worker organization, and a battery of mechanisms designed to foster flexibility in the workplace. Taken together (and acknowledging that this is still something that is in process rather than being already fully formed), this bundle of innovations forms the basis, I believe, for a microcorporatist mode of labor regulation.

The three chapters that make up the third part of this study treat different aspects of the Socialist approach to labor regulation. Chapter 6 looks at the nature and ideology of the Parti Socialiste (PS) in an effort to explain the distinctiveness of its approach, and examines the relationship between the Socialist government and the trade union movement, particularly in light of the government's wage policy. The chapter emphasizes the fact that the PS is not a social democratic party. This had consequences both for its capacity to achieve wage restraint and for the nature of the reform project that was attempted and that is the subject of the next chapter. Chapter 7 is a close analysis of the Auroux Laws, the major industrial relations reforms of the 1981–86 period, and it attempts to explain the structural impact of these reforms on labor regulation and the labor movement. It is argued in chapter 7 that the industrial relations structure put in place by the Auroux Laws was particularly conducive to the introduction of flexibility into the firm. Chapter 8 examines that process in more detail and charts the debates, negotiations, and legislation surrounding the issue of flexibility in France. The chapter also situates the discussion of flexibility within the wider debate over "post-Fordism" and engages in a more theoretical discussion of the forces driving the introduction of flexibility.

These three chapters together make an argument about the relationship between the character and ideology of the Socialist party, the economic and social context within which the Socialists came to power, and the consequences for the project of labor regulation that was subsequently attempted. In short, the argument is that the Socialists did not simply *fail* in their attempt to reform industrial relations. Rather the nature of that project itself played a contributory role in the creation of a new microcorporatist mode of labor regulation. It is true, and important to note, that major aspects of the PS program were deeply anachronistic in the context of the early 1980s. Both the economic and industrial relations policies had been formulated in, and designed for, an earlier period of Fordist growth. They owed much to the period of the early 1970s when sustained growth seemed possible and Delors was still helping Chaban-Delmas to create the New Society. These policies were ill-equipped to deal with the economic situation that the Socialists inherited in 1981.[1]

But Socialist policies in the sphere of industrial relations were not simply anachronisms, obstacles around which more powerful economic and social forces flowed obliviously. Aspects of those Socialist policies marked the emerging form of labor regulation in distinctive ways. Thus the Auroux Laws mattered. Forces beyond the control of the Socialist government imposed irresistible pressures for change in the mode of labor regulation, but the nature of that change and the particular *form* of labor regulation that appeared in France owed a great deal to the nature of the Socialist reform project, and to the character of the PS itself.

One of the major themes of the next three chapters is what might be termed the "plasticity" of ideology and law. It will be argued, for instance, that for all its strident anticapitalist rhetoric, key elements of Socialist party ideology were in fact perfectly compatible with the employers' strategy of "flexibilization." This overlap made the Socialists' embrace of flexibility after 1984 much easier. Similarly, a law or package of laws contains within it a number of different logics. Which one triumphs will depend on the conditions under which that law or laws are applied. This was particularly important in the case of the Auroux Laws, the results of which were in many ways different from the legislators' intent because of the conjuncture of historic union weakness and demobilization. The notion of plasticity and intentionality is important in any attempt to gauge the part that the Socialists played in changing the mode of labor regulation. Some results were certainly deliberate; in other cases they were unintentional consequences of actions, and often the hapless Socialists were forced into actions they did not favor but felt helpless to resist. It is no small irony of history that a Socialist government presided over a fundamental change in the type of labor regulation, one very alien to the European social democratic tradition.

That said, however, discussion of the 1981–86 period is too often overshadowed by the debate over the "defeat" or "failure" of the initial Socialist project, and over the question, in Singer's words, "was the experiment metaphysically doomed, or was it just bungled?"[2] Numerous causes of the Socialists' retreat have been adduced, and increasingly, I think, most political scientists have come to see that retreat as avoidable, whether through different strategic decisions on the part of the PS and the Parti Communiste Français (PCF) in the 1960s and 1970s,[3] or through alternative economic policies once in office.[4] It is not my intention to add one more reason for the abrupt reversal in 1982–83, nor to suggest that alternative modes of labor regulation might have made the reversal unnecessary. My sense is that the failure of the Socialist party's radical project was overdetermined by the international economy, domestic economic constraints, and the class character and ideology of the PS itself. This part of the study is instead concerned with the ways in which the French Socialist government responded to economic change and crisis, and with the long-term structural impact of the Socialist government on labor regulation in France.

CHAPTER SIX

Desperately Seeking Socialism

THIS CHAPTER has two closely related goals. The first is to examine the debate over the nature of the French Socialist party, and more specifically, to ask to what extent the PS can be considered a social democratic party in any recognizable sense of the word.[1] The issue is important for reasons that go beyond the simple affixing of labels. It is necessary to know the ideological and structural underpinnings of the PS in order to understand what the party was trying to achieve in the area of labor regulation—what its "project" was—and also in order to explain how the PS reacted when faced with the need for austerity. It will be argued in this chapter (and the argument further developed in later chapters) that most commentators have been too quick to dismiss one strand of PS thinking, that of *autogestion* (literally, self-management), and that shorn of its radical transformative goal this strand formed the nucleus of the Socialist government's wholesale ideological shift to flexibility. *Autogestion* was less an unwanted obstacle to the "modernization" of Socialist ideology than a means to that end. This helps to explain both the nature of the change in PS ideology after 1982–83, and the remarkable enthusiasm for it and lack of internal party opposition to it.

The second goal is to explore the implications of the weak links that existed between the PS and the labor movement. The PS arrived in power in 1981 as a party that differed markedly from the traditional social democratic parties of Western Europe. Its ties to labor were weak and informal, and its rhetoric was dismissive of social democracy and hostile to capitalism. Whatever its ideological appeal this meant that the Socialist government had no corporatist option. That is to say, the familiar social democratic response to austerity—a negotiated incomes policy—was at least on the face of it unavailable. So the question is, in what alternative ways *did* the PS attempt to regulate wages (particularly from 1982 onward when the need for austerity of some sort was recognized), and more fundamentally, did the anticorporatism of the PS matter?[2]

SOCIAL DEMOCRACY AND THE FRENCH SOCIALIST PARTY

What manner of beast was the PS when it came to power in 1981? The spectrum of opinion ranges widely. Some commentators have taken the rhetorical claims of the PS seriously. Thus Brown, writing in 1982, argued that "the socialist party—through its leaders and intellectuals—has made a virtually complete conversion to *autogestion*."[3] The other end of the spectrum, and the more densely populated one, is occupied by those that dismiss the grandiose claims of "rupture" with capitalism as youthful naïveté, or cynical electioneering, and see the PS as simply another left-of-center party in Western Europe that has made its peace with capitalism. Thus Bell and Criddle have said: "The [Socialist] Party is, in effect, a social democratic party, in the sense of pursuing essentially reformist objectives, and it is only the strategic necessity of living with the Communists that prevents it embracing overtly the reformism of northern-European social democracy."[4] And it should be recognized that, whatever ambiguity may have existed in 1981, a decade later and into the second term of Mitterrand's presidency, this second claim seems more plausible.

There is a danger involved in an obsession with labels, but the issue matters, both if we are to understand the project of the PS and its *capacity* for carrying it out. As Singer has put it, "It is not enough to contribute to the survival of capitalism to be a social democrat."[5] This criterion provides little way of distinguishing between varieties of the European Left, except perhaps between those that have been in office or near office and those that have not. There are two components to the characterization of a political party. One is ideology, and the other is the party's social base and the nature of its links to the major social groups in society.

It is a commonplace that the PS, more than most parties of the Left, has been made up of a shifting balance of "currents," each representing different constituencies and bringing different ideological orientations and programmatic content to the party. This structure in large part reflects the peculiar formation of the PS in 1969–71.[6] The "current" structure has been both a strength and a weakness, and it has been argued that this heterogeneity contributed both to the victory of the PS in 1981 on a radical program and to its internal collapse after the policy reversals of 1982–83.[7]

It is important to recognize the variety of ideological currents within the PS, and most commentators have identified four such currents: statist, *autogestionnaire*, social democratic, and republican/*Mitterrandiste*.[8] In what follows there will be discussion only of those ideological currents that are of importance to the French Socialist project in the social arena, and particularly the sphere of industrial relations. In so doing, greater influence is attributed to the ideological contribution of Jacques Delors than is usual. In the first half of the 1980s there was a marked contrast between the relative isolation of Delors within the PS and the importance of his contribution to PS ideology in the sphere of labor regulation.

Three ideological currents are of importance. The first is statism, or Jacobinism. It has often been argued that the Socialist party retains an unusual attachment to state action over decentralized, autonomous regulation by components of civil society. The main evidence for this position is the PS adoption and implementation of an extensive nationalization program, its frequent refusal to leave certain issues to negotiation, and its weak commitment to the *autogestionnaire* parts of the party's platform.

The statist strand of PS thinking is best represented within the Centre d'Études, de Recherches et d'Éducation Socialiste (CERES) current of the party and is most clearly evident in the party's 1980 campaign document, the *Projet Socialiste*, which was written for the most part by CERES.[9] The *Projet Socialiste* emphasized nationalization and "democratic planning" and at several points argued that *autogestion*, and greater liberty within civil society, were dependent upon greater state control and direction of society as a whole. Thus centralization and decentralization are dialectically (not to say paradoxically) two sides of the same coin. There was a clear refusal to accept an inherent antagonism between the two.[10] So the public and nationalized sector was to be "the first terrain of *autogestionnaire* advances,"[11] and the *Projet Socialiste* stressed that the protection of workers in the workplace would, above all, require an extension of the role of law into social relations inside the firm.[12]

The statism of CERES was very real, and its influence within the party and the first Socialist government went well beyond the numerical strength of the CERES current itself. But the charge has, I think, been exaggerated, not least because a significant and vocal segment of the party disagrees with a statist orientation. Some degree of nationalization has been a part of many social democratic party programs, and in any case the interest of Socialist party leaders in nationalization was at least as much an attempt to first cement an alliance with the PCF, and then avoid being vulnerable on their left. There have also been important instances in which the Socialist government did show its statist colors (the decision of Mitterrand to overrule a series of collective agreements and ensure full wage compensation for the reduction of the workweek to thirty-nine hours being the most notorious).[13] But in a period of severe austerity it would have been very difficult for any government to remain aloof from relations between business and labor (conservative parties had, after all, intervened throughout the 1970s for similar reasons), and for a party of the Left, with a working-class constituency, it would have been suicidal, not to say irresponsible. For the most part, as chapters 7 and 8 illustrate, the Socialist government used legislation in the industrial relations sphere in such a way as to facilitate or create a framework within which negotiations between business and labor could take place, not to substitute for bargaining.

The second ideological current that is important in the area of social relations is social democracy, with its emphasis on trade unions and collective bargaining. The PS did have certain old-style social democrats like Pierre Mauroy, but the ideological impetus behind this strand of PS thinking came from Jacques Delors. As the architect of the New Society in

1969–72, Delors had long been committed to the decentralization of collective bargaining to the firm, the extension and regularization of collective bargaining, and the strengthening of trade unions. This project was above all one of *modernizing* French industrial relations, and minimizing the conflictuality endemic in capital-labor relations in France.

Delors joined the Socialist party after leaving Chaban-Delmas, but to a remarkable extent his ideas about, and vision of, industrial relations remained constant, and he provides a critical continuity between the two periods. Through interviews in the 1970s and his theoretical journal, *Échange et Projets*, the continuity can be clearly seen. For instance, in issues of *Échange et Projets* in 1978 and 1980 (precisely when Barre was attempting with little success to relaunch collective bargaining), a program of industrial relations reform was laid out: extending the coverage of collective bargaining, making collective bargaining obligatory, and preventing minority unions from dominating bargaining.[14] These proposals reappeared as key elements in the Auroux Laws.[15] What is remarkable is how isolated Delors was in the PS, and how little reference to his ideas there was in the PS campaign documents in 1980–81. Collective bargaining was barely mentioned in the *Projet Socialiste* or in Mitterrand's *110 Propositions pour la France*.[16] And yet, despite personal and ideological isolation, Delors' long-standing vision of French labor regulation dominated the most extensive industrial relations reform effort of the postwar era in France.

The third, and final, ideological current is *autogestion*. The very vagueness of *autogestion* allowed it to serve as a useful ideological cement in the 1970s when differing interpretations could be subsumed under a common banner of *autogestion*.[17] In the 1970s *autogestion* captured the PS, and in June 1975 the PS formally declared itself in favor of a *"socialisme autogestionnaire."* In this formulation *autogestion* was clearly linked to the transformative project of moving beyond capitalism to socialism.

Autogestion contained within it a number of uneasy elements which were not in any direct way linked to a socialist society, though their close compatibility was taken for granted. That question, however, whether there was a direct and necessary relationship between *autogestion* and a socialist society and hence an inherent incompatibility between such a project and capitalism, was never satisfactorily answered. *Autogestion* tended to focus on the firm, and power relations within the firm. Its *subject* was workers rather than unions, because of an emphasis on self-transformation through daily struggle in the workplace. It was thus mobilizational and directed toward rank-and-file workers. One concomitant feature was a certain wariness or suspicion, not so much of trade unions per se but of the social democratic model of centralized, highly disciplined, and bureaucratic trade unions.[18] It was here that criticism of social democracy and corporatist-style arrangements was clearest. Corporatism implied deals made above the heads of workers and in which workers were passive participants. In addition, such arrangements tended to concern quantitative wage issues rather than issues of power and control, leaving authority relations in the firm essentially untouched. Above all, social democracy mediated workers' interests and actions through trade unions rather than allowing unmediated, direct expression of workers' demands.

Elements of the *autogestionnaire* project were well represented in the *Projet Socialiste* and the *110 Propositions*. The demand for direct, unmediated worker expression in the firm appeared (Proposition 22); the works councils were to be given important new powers including full financial disclosure, and a veto on firing, hiring, and the reorganization of work (Propositions 60 and 61);[19] worker representation in the public sector was to be decentralized (Proposition 62); and qualitative issues made an appearance through the commitment to reduce work time (Proposition 23).[20]

Too often the *autogestionnaire* aspects of the Socialist government's reforms are dismissed. Certainly, workers' control was not introduced in France, and Yugoslavia was not the model for the Auroux Laws, which in fact explicitly reaffirmed the legitimate right of owners to manage. The radical version of *autogestion* was immediately dropped once the PS took office, and indeed was probably never taken seriously by party leaders. But this misses the essential plasticity of ideology, the multiple directions in which a given ideology can lead. It misses the influence that *autogestion* exercised over policy well after its radical version was dead. What is remarkable is the extent to which an *area of compatibility* existed between *autogestion* and the new managerial emphasis upon flexibility. They shared a focus on, and preference for, the firm as the locus of social regulation, and they shared a distrust of trade unions and preference for firm-specific forms of worker organization and mediation. They also shared a critique of Taylorist and Fordist forms of work organization and work practices, one for reasons of economic efficiency, and the other for reasons related to humanization of the workplace. Above all, they shared an opposition to state intervention in the labor-capital relationship. *Autogestion* had always been, in part, a critique of statism (of the capitalist or actually existing socialist variety), and that central component, plus a myriad of firm-level reforms, remained. To a remarkable degree, as the next two chapters will demonstrate, the PS fulfilled the campaign promises listed in the previous paragraph.

The point is that, shorn of its radical, transformative goal, there was enough of a shared project that *autogestion* and flexibility could find many points at which to converge. This can be seen most clearly in the ideological evolution of Michel Rocard and the CFDT. Both began the 1970s as strong proponents of *autogestion* in its radical form, and both became, by the mid-1980s, the most enthusiastic adherents of flexibility in the PS and the trade union movement respectively. Ideologies are plastic and more adaptive than we often think. Under the conditions of the 1980s the transformation of the *autogestionnaire* project should come as no surprise. This is not the same, however, as saying that ideologies have no effect. On the contrary, it was the Socialist party's attachment to *autogestion* that gave it a way of explaining and justifying its adoption of flexibility, and it meant that in contrast to an orthodox social democratic party this shift could be enthusiastic rather than grudging. Chapters 7 and 8 below will return in more detail to the importance of *autogestionnaire* thinking in the PS for industrial relations reform.

The second element in the characterization of the PS must be its social base, and not simply its electoral composition but also the nature of its links to organized labor. This section will be brief because it is a well-known, and often-told story. While social democratic parties are defined by their more or less formal links to a trade union movement, the PS had no such ties. For reasons of historical development it was the French Communist party which had gained a controlling share of both working-class votes and trade union contacts. In the 1920s and 1930s the Socialist party recruited votes primarily from small-town, rural, semi-industrialized areas, and among the petty bourgeoisie.[21] Its proletarian roots, always weak, progressively shriveled up in the first two decades of the postwar period.[22] But once the new Socialist party was created in 1969–71, out of the shattered SFIO (Section Française de l'Internationale Ouvrière) and left-wing clubs of the 1960s, it consciously targeted the working class. François Mitterrand clearly understood that the dynamic of Fifth Republic electoral politics raised the possibility of the newly created PS attracting working-class votes away from the PCF.[23]

For a variety of reasons related to PCF incompetence and PS prescience and good fortune, by 1978 the PS had taken over from the PCF the largest share of working-class votes. By 1981 the electoral composition of the PS was virtually identical to the socioeconomic structure of the French population, except for a slight overrepresentation of the new middle classes. The PS was, by the time it took office, an almost classic catchall party.[24]

The PS also made a half-hearted effort to replicate the PCF's direct links to workers through the creation of workplace sections. These grew steadily through the 1970s to peak in 1983 at 1,800, before declining.[25] Nonetheless, the number never rivaled the PCF's estimated eight thousand workplace sections, and a 1976 study showed that PS sections were overwhelmingly in very large firms and tended to be dominated by *cadres* rather than blue-collar workers.[26]

More important, though, has been the PS's links, or lack of them, to trade unions. In Britain and Sweden there is an institutional tie between party and trade union movement which strongly colors party policy, and in West Germany the tie is not explicit but nonetheless functions in a similar way. In France the union movement is itself weak and deeply divided. No central, dominant union confederation exists. The PS has a formal requirement that its members belong to trade unions and about 85 percent do.[27] But there are no formal ties. The CGT has close historical, individual, and ideological ties to the PCF, but the CFDT and FO are both strongly antipolitical and neo-syndicalist. Again for historical reasons, and the recent experience of the debacle of the Union of the Left in the mid-1970s, no union has been prepared to openly identify with the Socialist party, much less establish institutional ties. And there has been no great pressure for such a relationship emanating from the PS, whose members are so broadly dispersed among various trade union confederations that an alliance with one would be deeply divisive.

The result has been that the PS's ties to trade unions have been, above all, individual, personal ties through its members and leaders. Individual union officials in fact joined the Socialist government in large numbers, but always on a purely personal basis.[28] Each Socialist leader is known to have some association with a particular union or union leader—Mitterrand with André Bergeron of FO, Pierre Joxe with the CGT, Michel Rocard with the CFDT—but the links go no further than providing a certain degree of access for trade union officials. This kind of access can be very important in the formulation of policy, but personal ties do not permit the imposition of a wage-restraint policy by a union leadership upon the union rank and file. Thus the potential for a corporatist relationship did not exist. This was one among many reasons for the Socialist decision, despite a landslide victory in the legislative elections in June 1981, to invite Communist ministers to join the government. The relationship between the PCF and CGT might, it was hoped, act as a hedge against industrial unrest.

The social base of the PS is not overwhelmingly working class even if workers constitute the largest single electoral bloc. It has often been noted that the PS has a very strong implantation in the new middle classes (and especially teachers). This bloc is overrepresented in the PS electorate, in the workplace sections, and, most strikingly, in the party itself.[29] In a very real sense the PS proved able, in the 1970s, to win the battle for the new middle classes, and this constituency colored the PS project out of all proportion to its numbers. This is perhaps no surprise since it was the swing constituency. Even in the campaign proposals relating to industrial relations, a conscious effort was made to recruit the *cadres* and reassure them that their position would not be challenged, indeed it would be enhanced, by the proposed reforms.[30] In fact, it has been argued more strongly that the Socialist project, and the *autogestionnaire* ideology, were directed far more toward the empowerment of the new middle classes than the working class.

In Garraud's words: "*Autogestion* is susceptible to being a mobilizing theme for the new middle classes, qualified yet excluded from the centers of decision-making."[31] This argument has been made most eloquently and persuasively by Kesselman, for whom the Socialist project "looks toward organizing society under the aegis of the middle strata; what might be termed socialism without the workers."[32]

It should come as no surprise that a correspondence between the Socialist party's ideology and its social base existed. It would have been remarkable if the PS *had* adopted a social democratic ideology in a society in which the type of labor movement necessary for the social democratic project did not exist. Rather, the *autogestionnaire* ideology which dominated the party in the 1970s was a logical and intelligible response to a decentralized and fragmented labor movement whose strength lay in firm-level mobilization and action and the interests of the rapidly expanding and electorally crucial new middle classes.

The rest of this chapter looks more closely at the wage-control policy of the Socialist government and the extent of trade union participation in it. In light of the lack of structural preconditions for a corporatist wage-restraint package, it will be important to ask why a significant degree of success in the government's attempt to hold down wages was achieved. In short, the rest of this chapter seeks to answer the question: did it matter that the French Socialist party lacked institutional, or semi-institutional, ties to a strong, centralized, and disciplined trade union movement?

SOCIALIST WAGE REGULATION

The evolution in economic policy followed by the Socialist government after 1981 has been well documented elsewhere.[33] Evolution is probably too mild a word. After an initial brief attempt to ride a projected world expansion of demand resulted in a spiraling trade deficit, severe pressure on the franc, and a growing budget deficit, the turn to austerity was swift. There were a series of deflationary packages linked to devaluation of the franc in the European Monetary System (EMS) in 1982 and 1983, and in 1984 the change in prime minister from Pierre Mauroy to Laurent Fabius marked a more fundamental change from a reactive economic policy to a more aggressive attempt to steal the "modernizing" clothes of the Right, an attempt that failed in the short run (in that the Right returned to power in 1986) but that may have succeeded in the long run.

From June 1982 a major concern of the Socialist government was the wage level, and the gap between it and that of France's major trading partners.[34] Thus within a year of taking office, wage restraint took center stage in the Socialist government's economic policy. Four elements of that wage policy will be discussed here: the 1982 freeze on incomes and prices; the incomes policy that followed it; the change in the manner in which wages were indexed to prices; and the adoption of a Socialist forced-savings scheme.

One fundamentally important part of the relative success of wage regulation was the decentralization of wage bargaining. In a period of union weakness the obligation to bargain on wages annually in the firm, introduced by the Auroux Laws, both gave employers the upper hand in negotiation and made workers more likely to recognize the link between their wages and the firm's profitability. The effect was to reduce wage increases in the private sector. This was not a direct result of government wage policy, but it was an indirect result of its industrial relations reforms undertaken in a period of high unemployment (as such it will be discussed in more detail in the next chapter). However, it is important in assessing the Socialist wage policy to recognize that the change in the *locus* of wage bargaining was at least partially responsible for the government's success in reducing the rate of wage increases.

In June 1982, as part of a wider deflationary package, the Socialist government introduced a four-and-a-half-month freeze on incomes and prices designed to last until the end of October of that year. The government used Article 49 of the constitution to pass the necessary legislation without amendment or opposition from Socialists and Communists in parliament. Prices, rents, dividends, and wages were all frozen, with only the minimum wage exempted. What was distinctive about this freeze was that it was a statutory incomes policy. The 1950 law on collective bargaining was suspended for the duration of the freeze to prevent wage bargaining from taking place, and fines of 300 to 8,000 francs per violation were introduced to deal with offenders. Thus the Socialists followed Barre in deciding against a voluntary, negotiated incomes policy, but it went one step further in making the policy statutory and suspending collective bargaining. The Socialists, and particularly Jacques Delors as minister of economy and finance, had no illusions about the ability to make an incomes policy stick without legislation. Not only would a voluntary policy require the agreement from six trade union confederations but there was little likelihood that the union leaderships would be able to enforce such a policy on the ground. The government talked frequently about its attachment to collective bargaining, and indeed it tried to sell the end of the wage freeze as a new opportunity to stimulate bargaining on wages,[35] but it believed that it had no choice but to prevent bargaining if it wished to prevent wage increases.

The freeze ended on October 31, 1982, but the government made it clear in a September circular that it wanted a "responsible" return to collective bargaining. This initiated a period of more or less explicit incomes policy, which lasted until the Socialists left office. Each year the government set targets for the level of wage increase that year: 10 percent for 1982, 8 percent for 1983, 5 percent for 1984, and 4.5 percent for 1985. In the public sector these targets were strictly adhered to by management negotiators, even if it meant that no wage contract was signed, as in the civil service in 1984. In the private sector there were no formal wage controls, but prices remained controlled and the Socialist government used the same method that the Barre government had used to control wages. Once again price control and the employers were used, in lieu of union agreement, to ensure wage restraint. As the president of the CNPF's commission on prices put it, the control of prices "implies the control of wages. One does not go without the other. All the evidence suggests that the government is counting on the firms to police wages via the control of prices."[36]

The third element of the Socialists' wage policy, one that was also the brainchild of Delors, involved an attempt to break the rigid wage-price indexation bequeathed France by the New Society. It will be recalled that Barre had relatively successfully attacked the guaranteed real wage increases of 2 to 3 percent annually in public-sector wage contracts, but he had been unable, or unwilling, to seriously challenge wage-price indexation. The guarantee that workers should at least not see their purchasing power reduced had been an article of faith in wage bargaining in the public sector.[37]

This changed with the introduction of the so-called *système Delors* introduced in the fall of 1982. The new system was not in fact de-indexation, at least not at first. Instead it was indexation of wages to inflation *targets* rather than *observed* price levels. Hence it involved setting a series of fixed wage increments at the start of the year based on the government's overall wage target. Then there was either a *clause de sauvegarde* (safeguard clause) guaranteeing that any difference between expected and actual inflation be incorporated in an end-of-year wage increase, or an end-of-year meeting scheduled for the same purpose. The point of the new system was to remove inflationary expectations and give a few months' lead time, instead of the lag that was incorporated in the previous form of indexation. This was adopted throughout the public sector in 1982–83.

It was only a short step from there, however, to eliminating the end-of-year *rattrapage* (catch-up). Thus another government circular in December 1983 announced that there would no longer be safeguard clauses built into wage contracts, and that end-of-year meetings would be consultative only. There was no commitment to make up the difference between wage and price levels. Rather, any *rattrapage* would be dependent upon the "effective situation of the firms."[38] In addition, the notion of maintaining purchasing power was to be applied to the wage bill as a whole, and not to each wage category as before. Thus it would be entirely possible for certain categories of workers to make slight real wage gains while other groups saw their real wages cut.

It is important to emphasize the extent to which this effective de-indexation marked a break with the past, and with the rigidity of French wages, inherited from the early 1970s, which had thus far been immune to France's continuing economic crisis. Just as indexation had been widely copied in the private sector in the early 1970s, so de-indexation was also rapidly adopted in the private sector after 1983. De-indexation was one of the few measures of the Socialist government that was consistently applauded by the CNPF.

The fourth element of Socialist wage policy was of minor importance in terms of its actual effect on wages, but it is nonetheless interesting because it involved the adoption by the Left of a forced-savings scheme, along the lines of the old Gaullist idea of financial *participation*. *Participation*, and the associated schemes to encourage worker shareholding, were by 1981 essentially discredited and ignored, with the exception of some Gaullist rhetorical flourishes around election time. The appeal of such schemes was limited and the sums involved paltry.[39] However, in March 1983 part of the Socialist government's second major austerity package included a compulsory loan to the government of 10 percent of the income of the richest third of the taxpaying population, repayable in three years. This gave birth to discussions, encouraged by the government and with the enthusiastic support of the CFDT,[40] about a new form of worker savings plan to be called the *"fonds salariaux,"* or wage-earner funds, in direct and deliberate reference to Sweden.

The goal was to hold back a portion of wages, which would go into a fund comanaged by workers and management. The fund would be used for productive investment, thus simultaneously reducing consumption and raising investment. This was to be made palatable to workers—and indeed it was sold as a Socialist strategy—by a tax break on the part of wages withheld, some form of comanagement of the fund, and the promise that any investment would be used to create jobs. Thus this was to be a progressive version of *participation*.

A working group of employers and unions issued a report on the *fonds salariaux* in October 1983 which showed that the social partners were deeply divided on the subject. FO was hostile to the whole idea because it saw the plan as an attempt to reduce the purchasing power of workers, pure and simple, and it wanted no part of a disguised incomes policy. The CGT took the more cautious, if ultimately contradictory, position of welcoming the fund so long as it was completely separated from regular wage bargaining and hence could not be part of an attempt to reduce workers' wages. Hence the CGT demanded that any scheme be *voluntary* and *individual*—in other words, individual workers would choose to participate or not. The CNPF supported the idea so long as it did not introduce full comanagement of investment decisions. The CFDT was far and away the most enthusiastic proponent of wage-earner funds. In a stroke of semantic genius the CFDT endorsed a version of the scheme that would be a *"voluntariat collectif,"* meaning that it would be voluntary until the unions in the firm agreed to introduce the scheme, after which it would be compulsory for workers in the firm. The CFDT fully recognized that the scheme had the goal of reducing wage levels.

In July 1984 the government passed legislation that made *possible* the introduction of such schemes and laid down some guidelines. But it left the major issues—the form of comanagement, whether the funds should be individual or collective, voluntary or obligatory—to bargaining between unions and employers.

How successful was the wage policy of the Socialist government? By any measure the reduction in wage growth between 1982 and 1986 was remarkable.[41] Econometric studies of the degree of disinflation estimate that the effect of the freeze on incomes and prices was to reduce inflation by 2.6 percent in 1982, of which only about 0.7 percent was lost in 1983 by attempts to recapture wages foregone in 1982. De-indexation was estimated to have contributed to a decline in inflation of 1.7 percent in 1984 and 1.6 percent in 1985.[42] There was also a clear narrowing of the gap between wage targets and actual wage growth (see table 6.1). As Ginsbourger and Potel put it, after the end of the freeze in 1982 there was "a veritable *indexation* of [wage] increases (negotiated or not) to government targets."[43]

More remarkable still was that, for the first time in twenty years (including the Barre austerity plan), there were significant reductions in the real wages of workers. This was the case in the public sector, where the losses were most severe, but also in the private sector (see tables 6.2 and 6.3). When social security contributions are taken into account, all categories of workers saw their real wages reduced, except those receiving the minimum wage, and casual laborers.[44]

TABLE 6.1
Wage Guidelines (in percent), 1982–85

	1982	1983	1984	1985
Official target	10.0	8.0	5.0	4.5
Gross average salary	12.6	10.1	7.6	5.6
Consumer price index	11.7	9.7	7.5	5.6

Source: Jeffrey Sachs and Charles Wyplosz, "The Economic Consequences of President Mitterrand," *Economic Policy*, no. 2 (April 1986): 299, table 9. The figures for 1985 are official forecasts only.

TABLE 6.2
Purchasing Power (in percent) in the Public Sector, 1981–85

	1982–83	1983–84	1984–85
Civil service	−0.4	−0.6	−1.8
Nationalized firms	−0.9	−0.8	−0.5

Source: Liaisons Sociales: Documents, no. 81 (August 27, 1986): 2–3, 7.

At a qualitative level, the data on collective bargaining in the private sector shows a progressive decline in the number of incremental wage rises in any given year from three or four to less than two, and also a general shift to the government's form of predetermined indexation to targets as well as the disappearance of safeguard clauses from wage contracts.[45]

This success in keeping wages down and eliminating indexation marked a clear break with the past. In 1985 consumer prices in France rose by 4.7 percent, the lowest since 1967.[46] Such success would be noteworthy for any government, but for a government of the Left, one whose natural constituency was the working class, it was remarkable. It is impossible to make a fair comparison between this period and that of the Barre austerity plan. The economic circumstances were different. But it is hard to avoid the conclusion that a Socialist government had been more successful in restraining wage growth than a government of the Right. To, what extent, then, was the government able to succeed *precisely because* it was a government of the Left? Delors certainly believed this to be an important factor, when he said in 1982 that "only the Left can bring about the de-indexation of prices and wages."[47] In the next section the response of the two largest unions to the government's wage policy will be examined.[48] Did the particular and unusual relationship between the Socialist party and the trade union movement in France make a difference?

TABLE 6.3
Purchasing Power (in percent) in the Private and Semi-Private Sectors, 1980–85

Social Category	1980–85
Foreman	−6.09
Employee	−1.24
Skilled worker	−2.67
Unskilled worker	−0.35
Casual laborer	+0.79
Minimum wage	+8.66
Overall	+1.22

Source: Liaisons Sociales: Documents, no. 64 (July 2, 1986): 2.

TRADE UNIONS AND WAGE REGULATION

It is unclear precisely what the PS expected from the trade unions. There was a recognition of the limits imposed on the Socialists by the weak and divided union movement, and no systematic attempt was made to effect a restructuring of the union movement (for instance, in such a way as to favor one union at the expense of another). At certain moments one union's demands, projects, or interests, were favored over those of other unions. The Auroux Laws certainly owed far more to the CFDT for their inspiration than other unions, for example. This was inevitable with a divided union movement. But there was no consistent line, nor any broader project (beyond the hope that "responsible" unions be encouraged) which aimed to "rebalance" forces within the union movement in a manner similar to Mitterrand's highly successful rebalancing of the *political* forces of the Left in the 1970s. The task would have been a large and a long-term one, it would have divided the PS itself, and it would have involved alienating one or more trade unions at a time when an austerity program was already pushing the unions to the limits of their cooperative powers. More realistically, Socialist leaders looked for an Italian-style unionism in which multiple unions did not prevent unity-in-action.[49]

The Socialist government did, however, expect some responsibility from the leftist unions. The CGT and CFDT, it was argued within the PS, shared the same social base as the PS, and a broadly similar set of interests.[50] Their members would benefit more, so the argument went, from a government of the Left than one of the Right and thus should be wary of damaging the electoral viability of the Socialist government. As Claude Estier put it in an editorial in *L'Unité*, the socialist weekly, serious differences could not "persist without bringing harm to the Left as a whole, and so to the unions themselves, and finally to the workers."[51] At various intervals there was some suggestion that the unions and government reach agreement on what would be and would not be permissible action. This was variously called a "code of concertation" (Lionel Jospin), a "code of conduct" (Pierre Joxe), and a "moral contract" (Jacques Delors). Each time such a suggestion was made it was angrily rejected by the unions.[52] The reaction of the Socialist government to these rebuffs was usually low-key, though on one occasion Delors exploded in a newspaper interview that if "the unions prefer the return of the Right, they have only to continue their current actions, the aggravation of their divisions, and their narrowly selfish attacks."[53]

Of all the trade unions the position of the CFDT was the most interesting because it did clearly attempt to exercise restraint, and on occasion Edmond Maire, the CFDT's general secretary, stepped out in *front* of the government in his demand for austerity and his trenchant criticism of the government's economic policy. Maire condemned Mitterrand's announcement that full wage compensation should be paid to workers when the length of the workweek was reduced from forty to thirty-nine hours in terms almost as uncompromising as the CNPF, and he announced the need for a second austerity plan in January 1983, a full month before the Mauroy government accepted the need for such a plan, much to the embarrassment of the government.

The response of the CFDT to the onset of austerity was by no means damning. The CFDT's criticism was reserved more for the manner in which austerity was imposed than its fact. Thus in June 1982 it sharply attacked the decision to suspend collective bargaining while simultaneously calling for "*autodiscipline*" on the part of workers, and a *negotiated* wage freeze.[54] The CFDT backed the *système Delors* for de-indexing wages, supported the wage-earner funds scheme *as a mechanism for wage control* (unlike the CGT which backed it so long as it did not entail wage restraint, and the FO which opposed it), and, in contrast to the other unions, the CFDT accepted the need for real wage cuts in the civil service.[55]

What was interesting about the CFDT leadership position was that calls for wage restraint were coupled with a deep ambivalence toward the Socialist government.[56] There was no correlation between the CFDT's propensity for exercising restraint and its closeness and sympathy to the Left government. Indeed, if anything the relationship was an inverse one. The CFDT became increasingly critical of, and distant to, the PS while its commitment to austerity grew stronger. While the PCF remained in the government the CGT was far less critical of government economic policy than the CFDT, but it was also much less willing to promote or practice wage restraint. Gilbert Declercq made this distinction neatly in a long article critical of the CFDT's line:

> The CFDT appears to the workers of this country more and more, especially since May 1981, as considering itself charged with [defending] the general interest of the nation and of all the French, hence of all social classes. It is much more this policy approach of ours that is criticized by the workers than that of appearing more or less tied or allied to the government or the PS.[57]

The leadership of the CFDT agreed with Declercq's characterization of the union policy, though it disagreed with the implications for the union's declining popularity. Maire argued that the policy of responsibility and restraint was popular, or at least respected, by the rank and file and that the CFDT's poor showing in the elections for the social security administration in October 1983, and in a series of works council elections throughout 1983 and 1984, was a result of the union's being too closely identified with the Socialist government.[58] His response was first to become more critical of the government, and then to reorient the CFDT so that it was no longer a socialist union. In May 1984 the national council of the CFDT recommended opening talks with right-wing political parties, and in 1986 the union made no recommendation to its members as to how to vote in the legislative elections. Yet (and this is the important point) this progressive distancing of itself from the government was not accompanied by a hardening of position against austerity. Quite the contrary. Thus the orthodox social democratic connection of union loyalty to a Left government leading to wage restraint was reversed in the CFDT's case.

However, a willingness to condone austerity and a capacity to impose that austerity on rank-and-file union members are very different things. The organizational costs of taking a high profile on the issue of austerity were high. Maire and the CFDT leadership faced constant and vociferous opposition from within the CFDT, first in 1981–82 on the leadership's opposition to full compensation for the reduction in work time, and second in 1985 over the degree to which the union should favor the negotiation of flexibility over legislation. The Ha-Cui-Tex federation took the unusual step of proposing an entire "counterproject" at the June 1985 CFDT congress instead of the usual procedure of amending the official report, thus demonstrating the depth of its opposition to the confederal position. The Ha-Cui-Tex proposal ultimately failed but 177 unions supported it.[59]

The CFDT thus presents the unexpected picture of a union leadership willing to risk electoral failure and organizational crisis in order to support austerity and a cooperative relationship with employers, *despite* having no formal ties to the party in power and indeed being hostile to that party. It is important here to distinguish between the official neutrality, and even hostility, of the CFDT toward the PS and the continuing influence of informal ties between individual unionists and the party. But this only underlines the point that different types of relationships between party and union have different implications for wage restraint.

There is an autonomy of French union leaderships that is altogether different from that of social democratic union leaderships. The centralized, encompassing trade unions of Scandinavia allow the leadership to exercise a discipline and control over the rank and file that allows them to impose wage restraint. French trade union leaderships have the autonomy to take public positions (favorable toward a government or not) that are not supported by the union membership. But the autonomy is double-edged. The price they pay is that they cannot impose wage restraint upon their members. Union leaders in France are still dependent upon the "social climate" for their ability to bring workers out on strike.

Thus the paradox of Edmond Maire's position as flagbearer for austerity and flexibility is that it had little impact on the way in which rank-and-file union members acted. In a few areas, the civil service being the clearest, the union was responsible for exercising moderation in wage demands. But in most cases the writ of the confederation leadership did not run down to the firm. The overwhelming number of agreements signed by CFDT unions on reduced work time (before Mitterrand made the issue moot) included full wage compensation despite the confederal willingness to trade that for further reduction in hours. If local CFDT union sections exercised restraint after 1982 in wage bargaining, it had far more to do with the state of the labor market and the decentralization of collective bargaining than with Maire's public pronouncements and his annual opinion pieces in *Le Monde* every August, calling for solidarity and restraint on the part of workers.

The CGT was, on the face of it, in a deeper dilemma. Through the union's close links to the PCF it wanted to make the Left experiment in government a success. Thus its initial response to the Left government was more openly supportive than the CFDT's, arguing that it "is in a spirit of concertation that we begin our relationship with the government that we have a right to consider a veritable social partner."[60] And the CGT stressed the need for responsibility more: "The relationship between the CGT and the government of the Union of the Left . . . remains a relationship of total reciprocal independence, leaving room for the freedom of opinion, of criticism, of expression, and of action of each. But there is the necessity for a spirit of exceptional responsibility."[61]

The CGT's criticism of austerity was suitably muted though it sought to distance itself from the austerity program. For the most part the CGT responded to austerity by pressing for the maintenance of real wage levels while avoiding harsh criticism of the government. A quasi-corporatist arrangement did appear at the SNCF where a Communist minister of transport, Charles Fiterman, was able to obtain wage agreements and industrial peace in return for supporting an expansion and reform of the works council structure at the SNCF that strongly favored the CGT.[62] However the CGT's losses in the 1982 Prud'hommes elections, the 1983 social security elections, and works councils elections mounted, and when the PCF pulled out of the government in the summer of 1984 the CGT was only too happy to return to an adversarial stance. Sketchy data on works councils elections before and after the withdrawal of the PCF from government indicated some resurgence of popularity for the CGT from mid-1984 onward.[63]

CONCLUSION

It is difficult to know what to make of the ambiguous relationship between the Socialist government and the two unions most likely to have an interest in supporting its efforts to impose wage restraint on the French working class. Was this a kind of ersatz corporatism? The answer must be no. Both unions, for different reasons, chose to acknowledge the need for some degree of austerity. However, with the exception of small quasi-corporatist enclaves in the public sector (such as the SNCF and civil service) where the unions were strongly implanted, there is very little evidence that the trade unions were complicit in the wage-control policy of the Socialist government. The confederations were anxious to avoid embarrassing the government, but they simply were not in the position to impose wage restraint on their members. The weakness of the unions and their obsession with their popularity as measured in industrial elections (a not unreasonable obsession since these elections were the accepted measure of relative strength and influence of unions) reinforced the tendency of unions to avoid calling for sacrifice. When such calls were made, or even when the unions were wrongly identified with austerity, they suffered. Hence the ritual, which was particularly prevalent during the freeze on incomes and prices in 1982, for French unions to "aller à la base," to consult with the rank and file and see how workers were reacting, before taking a position themselves. Such a practice is quite the opposite of the relationship between leadership and rank and file in corporatist arrangements. The critical factor was not the attitude of the trade unions to the economic dilemma of the Socialist government but the demobilization of workers and the looseness of the labor market.

The autonomy of the PS from the labor movement (like the union leadership from its members) was double-edged.[64] On the one hand it prevented recourse to a negotiated incomes policy. But on the other it made the task of imposing austerity much easier. Both from an ideological and an organizational point of view the PS was able to shift from "Keynesian redistribution"[65] to austerity (and then to flexibility) without the kind of internal party crisis that a genuinely social democratic party could expect to suffer. Indeed the lack of a serious opposition movement within the PS is, in light of the magnitude of the party's policy shift, quite remarkable.[66]

The brutal truth is that in the social and economic circumstances of the 1980s the PS did not need a corporatist relationship with the trade union movement in order to achieve wage restraint; the labor market was quite adequate to that task. The Socialist government could impose austerity with limited cost to itself in a way that social democratic governments elsewhere—and indeed right-wing governments in France in the 1970s—were not able to do. In this sense the PS occupied a privileged terrain.

CHAPTER SEVEN

The Two Logics of the Auroux Laws

IN 1982–83 THE FRENCH SOCIALIST government passed a series of laws known collectively as the Auroux Laws, after the then Minister of Labor Jean Auroux. Their purpose was the wholesale reform of the French system of industrial relations. The Auroux Laws have been the object of much attention, and rightly so because they constituted a deliberate, self-conscious effort to mold labor regulation.[1] Collectively the package of legislation aimed to strengthen trade unions, encourage collective bargaining, give new powers to works councils, allow workers to express themselves in their place of work, and regulate the day-to-day functioning of social relations inside the firm. The reforms were directed at both the public and the private sectors.

This chapter will argue that the Auroux Laws were indeed tremendously important, both in intent and effect. As an attempt to use legislation to bring about a change in the form of labor regulation, the reforms were ambitious as well as courageous. Rarely are such wide-ranging and coherent reforms projects attempted by governments. The vision of industrial relations embodied within the legislative package entailed a fundamental change in the manner of labor regulation practiced in France, and it will be argued that the reforms have indeed had profound consequences for labor regulation.

However, laws rarely carry within them only a single logic. A piece of legislation intended to have one result can have one that is altogether different under different circumstances. There is therefore a certain plasticity of law which goes beyond simple unintended consequences. The problem for the French Socialists and the trade union movement was not that the Auroux Laws had a series of unfortunate and unexpected by-products, but rather that they contained within them two entirely different, indeed contradictory, logics, and two very different models of labor regulation.

One logic led toward a model of generalized collective bargaining between employers and trade unions, in which bargaining was articulated between branch and firm levels, and in which the relationship between the various forms of worker representation in the firm was one of mutual reinforcement. Trade unions had the critical role of privileged representatives of the working class, and workers inside the firm were connected, via national union organizations and articulated bargaining, to workers in other firms and sectors.

The second logic led toward a model of "microcorporatist" bargaining between employers and firm-specific organizations of workers, in which labor regulation was centered on the firm. Trade unions were either banished from the firm or assigned a peripheral role in bargaining, as firm-specific forms of worker representation bargain with management. In this model, workers in the firm are cut off from a wider collectivity of workers, and firm-level bargaining is independent of bargaining at higher levels.

The crucial difference between the two models is that in the first (what might be called a collective-bargaining model) there is an *articulated relationship* between labor regulation in the firm and labor regulation in the wider economy. This is achieved through, first, a hierarchical system of collective bargaining that links firm-level and industry-level bargaining, and second, strong trade unions that link workers in the firm to workers in other firms, industries, or sectors. In the second, microcorporatist model the locus of labor regulation is the firm, as bargaining in the firm is independent of bargaining at higher levels and workers in the firm are isolated from any wider collectivity through firm-specific forms of labor organization.

The line between these two models is easier to draw in theory than practice. The main difficulty is posed by trade unions that exist formally but, through weakness and isolation, come to act more as firm-specific organizations than national ones. As a result there is no neat line that, when crossed, allows one to talk of a change in the mode of labor regulation. Instead some hybrid form of labor regulation is the most likely eventuality. Nevertheless, the distinction between these two models remains important for analytical purposes.

The central question for the fate of the Socialist reform project was whether the Auroux Laws would become *beachheads* for union activity in the firm, or rather create potential *alternatives* to union organization. Under the conditions of the early and mid-1980s it was the latter that prevailed. The conjuncture was not a good one for an attempt to construct a model of labor regulation based on trade unions. The crisis of trade unionism continued and deepened. Membership loss was only briefly halted by the arrival of the Left in power before the slide began again.[2] The *patronat*'s response to the Auroux reforms was negative, and it maintained both its deep hostility to trade unions and its strategy of developing alternative forms of mediation that did not rely on trade unions as the privileged interlocutors of the working class. Both the weakness of the trade unions and the *patronat*'s strategy were structured by the economic crisis. The second oil shock and the Socialist experiment with Keynesianism in one country deepened the structural crisis of the French economy. It further weakened trade unions and it rehabilitated business, which was now able to pose more plausibly as the only group able to produce jobs, wealth, and growth (a claim the Socialist government was unable or unwilling to counter). Increasingly from mid-1982 onward, the demands of the CNPF found a ready ear in government circles.[3] At the same time, the economic situation made the attempt to develop collective bargaining very difficult. As *Le Monde* put it, "How can you negotiate with empty hands?"[4]

The argument of this chapter is that the trajectory of the Auroux Laws was, and still is, open. Hence it is not a question of dubbing the reforms a success or a failure. Rather the laws contained within them a number of elements which can be considered, collectively, as a kind of Trojan horse for an alternative mode of labor regulation. There remained, within the Socialist party, the uneasy coexistence of alternative projects, and the survival, albeit in muted and bastardized form, of *autogestionnaire* elements that formed the nucleus of a microcorporatist mode of labor regulation. But fundamentally, the dominant project of the Auroux Laws was anachronistic. It harked back to the heyday of a booming Fordist economy and a relatively strong labor movement. With both Fordism and trade unionism in crisis, it was the subsidiary, secondary elements of the Auroux Laws that came to the fore.

Two Projects and Two Logics

A number of elements and sources of inspiration competed with each other in the Auroux reforms. It was a major reform effort so it is no surprise that at different times and in different ways a variety of groups in the government, the PS, and the trade unions influenced the form and content of the legislation. The final package was indeed a compromise and a hodgepodge of elements. Nonetheless, two distinct and coherent projects can be discerned within the legislation.

The dominant goal of the first project was, as the Auroux Report put it, that "collective bargaining must become the privileged practice for social progress."[5] It was a goal and a project that had been associated for fifteen years with Jacques Delors, though it clearly had wide support within the PS and trade union movement, particularly the CFDT. As described in the last chapter, in the sphere of industrial relations (as in much else) Delors' position remained remarkably consistent from his period as adviser for social affairs to Chaban-Delmas, through his writings in the mid-1970s in *Échange et Projets*, to his arrival in power as minister of finance in the Socialist government.

The goal of the New Society had been the *modernization* of social relations, understood as the creation of regular collective-bargaining mechanisms and practices, in which labor regulation was devolved onto trade unions and employers. This was a fundamentally antistatist vision of labor regulation. Trade unions and employers would bargain at the branch and firm levels and regulate conflict without the intervention of the state. A key role was given to trade unions. French trade unions had to be simultaneously strengthened, so as to be worth bargaining with, and made *responsible*. Responsibility was understood to mean being responsible for positions taken during negotiations, and for agreements once reached. If unions could be strengthened and made responsible, a virtuous circle of increasing bargaining and increasing union strength would, it was hoped, follow.

Delors hoped that while the New Society had largely failed in the early 1970s the time was now more propitious. This hope was based "upon an apparent convergence between the strategic thinking of the more innovative elements of the patronat and of one of the major trade unions—the CFDT."[6] Thus it seemed plausible that a project that in 1969 was perhaps before its time was now more appropriate. Hence the remarkable similarity in the broad lines of the New Society and the Auroux Laws. The latter deepened and extended the innovations of the former: the New Society provided legal safeguards for trade union sections in firms employing fifty or more people, while the Auroux Laws extended that protection to all firms regardless of size; the New Society reformed collective-bargaining legislation to encourage firm-level bargaining, the Auroux Laws made such bargaining obligatory.

This project was not a radical transformative one. Rather it is "best seen as an attempt to modernize labor-management relations by bringing them more in line with practices elsewhere."[7] The goal was, as in 1969–72, to create a mode of labor regulation that was appropriate for a modern, industrial economy. Collective bargaining would still, it was hoped, channel industrial conflict, though this was a less serious concern in the early 1980s when strike levels were steadily dropping. More important now was the goal of decentralizing collective-bargaining to the firm so that wages and working conditions could reflect the specific needs and conditions of the firm rather than the application of universal legislation, or branch-level agreements.

Delors saw a very clear relationship between industrial relations and economic performance, and he was anxious that "wage bargaining must take place at the level of the firm [so as to] reconcile productivity and wages."[8] For some time Delors had been espousing a "three-part theory of wages" in which he argued that wages should have three elements: a general component, a firm-specific component, and an individual component.[9] Only a decentralized system of collective bargaining would make such a wage structure possible. Delors' goals for wages were in fact very similar to those of Barre in 1976–81, but Delors, more than Barre, recognized the structural preconditions that were necessary for a change in wage bargaining. Unlike Barre, Delors saw a close link between his project for labor regulation and his economic goals. However, for all his sociological acumen,

Delors never satisfactorily answered the question of why, in a period of union weakness, employers *needed* to bargain with unions.

The second project contained within the Auroux Laws was less coherent, and less visible than the first. Yet while it was fed by a diverse set of intellectual traditions—Gaullist *participation*, Sudreau's reform of the firm, *autogestion*—they all shared an essentially microcorporatist focus upon firm-level, firm-specific labor regulation, qualitative rather than quantitative goals, and power relations within the firm. It was the CFDT and *autogestionnaire* currents in the PS that contributed to the microcorporatist elements of the Auroux Laws. These were most visible in the initial Auroux Report with its call for a "New Citizenship" inside the firm, the creation of a "right of direct expression" for workers in their place of work, and increased economic powers to the works council so that it could become an actor inside the firm. This was clearly not a radical, socialist version of *autogestion*. The property structure of the capitalist economy was to be left untouched. Within its confines workers were to be given a larger role in the day-to-day functioning of the firm.

If the dominant project of the Auroux Laws owed much in its inspiration to the project of the New Society, so the second, subsidiary project took much of its inspiration, in terms of concrete proposals, from the Sudreau Report. Commentaries in the mid-1970s on the failure of the Sudreau reforms would have been astonished at the reappearance of many of its elements in the Auroux Laws, such as the extension of the *bilan social* to all firms, the creation of an "economic delegation" to the works council in large firms, and the extensive new rights of consultation and information given to the works councils.

There were both social and economic goals within the overall microcorporatist project. The social goal was the creation of a new relationship between workers and management in the firm, one that was more harmonious and reciprocal.[10] In this sense many aspects of the Auroux Laws did appear to imagine that one could eliminate the conflictual, antagonistic elements of social relations in the capitalist firm. The old *autogestionnaire* project had believed that only the elimination of capitalism itself could create such a work community. When the same project was implemented within the confines of a capitalist economy, it came dangerously close to the belief in the firm as a "community," and an embrace of the *patronat*'s new social strategy of the late 1970s.[11]

There was also a related economic goal. The bulk of the new powers and information given to the works councils were designed to help workers better comprehend the economic and financial situation of the firm in which they worked. Clearly the powers would also enable workers to avoid having to make concessions to management that were not economically necessary. Workers could bargain with management at less of a disadvantage. This goal was part of the dominant project of strengthening trade unions and collective bargaining. But in a situation in which adaptability and flexibility were considered increasingly necessary, it was also important that workers recognize the existence of the basic economic constraints under which the firm operated. A wider economic role for the works council promised both greater understanding and a greater capacity for adaptive, flexible solutions to economic problems.

THE PASSAGE OF THE AUROUX LAWS

Immediately after taking power Jean Auroux announced that a preliminary report, incorporating the advice and recommendations of all concerned groups, would be produced by his ministry as a first step toward legislation to fulfill the Socialist party's promise of industrial relations reform. The consultation process was not a formal one. Bilateral discussions with each union and employers' organization were held, but only the CGT and CFDT produced long, formal lists of recommendations, and it was the CFDT's proposals that found most favor. From the CFDT came the demands for a right of worker expression in the firm and an *obligation* to bargain, which were the main innovations of the reforms and elicited the most controversy. Indeed despite some disagreements with the report (which were for the most part cleared up by the time it was translated into legislation), the CFDT increasingly found itself in the role of the chief defender of the reform project.[12]

The report appeared in September 1981.[13] This was later than expected because of reported disagreements between Auroux and other members of the government.[14] The dominant feature of the report was the enhanced powers of information and consultation given to the works councils. The report rapidly came under fire for not going far enough. The CFDT complained that the new rights (and the old ones for that matter) were not extended to smaller firms, and the CGT called for either a veto power for the works council to prevent layoffs, or at least some greater ability to delay layoffs. Disagreement also came from within the Socialist party. Jean-Paul Bachy, the national secretary of the PS in charge of firms, called for an extension of trade union protection to firms with less than fifty employees and for the legal protection of political sections in the firm.[15]

As the government drafted legislation and prepared to put bills before parliament, it found itself caught between a rock and a hard place. On the one hand it was being attacked by the Right and the CNPF for the radicalism of the reform. In mid-March 1982 the CNPF launched a bitter attack on the reform in the Conseil Économique et Social. It attacked the obligation to bargain and the right of expression, but above all it challenged what it saw as an attempt to institutionalize confrontation and to privilege unions in a reform that "seems to limit the firm to an encounter between the employer and the unions."[16] On the other hand, there was a great deal of opposition to the moderation and limited nature of the legislation from within the PS itself. Of the two thousand amendments to the reform legislation that were submitted, three hundred came from Socialist and Communist deputies.

The calls for a veto power against layoffs and for political sections failed. But the final legislation did provide some increased notice to works councils in the event of layoffs (a "*droit d'alerte*"), and most importantly it removed the fifty-person threshold for the application of legal protection to union sections. It also lowered the firm size for the application of the right of expression from three-hundred- to two-hundred-person firms. Thus the final version went some way toward satisfying the CFDT and PS demands for extension of rights to smaller firms.

The final product was a series of five laws:[17]

> 1. *The Law of August 4, 1982, concerning the liberties of workers.* Written work rules, and the sanctions for their infringement, were made mandatory, and the works council had to be given a copy of those rules and sanctions. The rules were still the unilateral prerogative of employers, but disciplinary acts now became subject to tighter judicial review. A right of worker self-expression was set up on an experimental basis in all firms employing two hundred or more people. The details of the exercise of that right were to be negotiated by unions and employers in each firm. The Ministry of Labor would draw up a balance-sheet of their operation after two years and propose further legislation by the end of 1985.

> 2. *The Law of October 28, 1982, concerning employee representation.* There was a large increase in the number and range of issues on which *consultation* with the works council became mandatory: organization of work, size of labor force, duration of work, layoffs, hiring, working conditions, the introduction of new technologies, and major financial decisions such as mergers and large investments. Management had to provide an annual social and economic report (the *bilan social*) to the works council and allow the creation of an economic delegation to the works council in firms employing one thousand people or more. Management also had to provide training for works council members and to provide outside experts to assist in their work. Trade union sections were given more rights to circulate in the workplace during work time and to collect dues. Unions were also to be provided with some office space. Most important, the fifty-person threshold for union protection was eliminated. Henceforth union delegates in all firms would enjoy legal protection.

> 3. *The Law of November 13, 1982, concerning collective bargaining.* There was now an obligation to bargain annually (though not to *conclude* an agreement), both at the branch and the firm level in all firms with one or more union sections. In the firm, bargaining had to take place on *real* wages and

work time, and firm-level agreements could now "derogate"[18] from legislation and confederal or branch agreements so long as a union or unions gaining at least 50 percent of the votes in the last firm election did not veto such derogatory accords. There was thus a limited right of veto to "majority" unions. On the other hand, the procedure whereby collective agreements could be "extended" by the administration was made easier in that the minister of labor could now override opposition to a proposed extension under certain circumstances.

4. *The Law of December 22, 1982, concerning health and safety*. Health and safety committees in the workplace were merged and their powers strengthened. They could now close down the plant under certain circumstances.

5. *The Law of July 26, 1983, concerning the democratization of the public sector*. The existing form of employee representation (whereby employee representatives have a third of the seats on the boards of directors of public companies) was extended to all firms employing two hundred or more workers in which the French state had at least a 50 percent share of ownership. There was to be a negotiated decentralization of works councils to smaller work units in large public and nationalized firms. A right of worker expression similar to that in the private sector was created in the public sector.

Taken in their entirety these laws were a large and serious attempt at reform. They rewrote one-third of the Labor Code and affected almost every aspect of capital-labor relations. The one obvious area of timidity was the public sector. The Auroux Report promised (in words similar to those of the *Projet Socialiste* before it) that "the public and nationalized firms must play an exemplary role" for the private sector. In fact the reforms in the public sector went no further than those in the private sector. The government was too concerned with the economic role of the public sector to allow a more thorough democratization. This was a pity because had the reform in the public sector been more extensive it might have created a constituency of workers willing to resist privatization when it appeared on the Right's agenda in 1986–88.

The reform effort was impressive. Nevertheless, the twin, competing logics contained within the Auroux reforms made the outcome highly uncertain. It is to the lacunae in the Auroux Laws and the seeds of an alternative mode of labor regulation contained within the legislation that I now turn.

Trapdoors and Trojan Horses

The Auroux Laws contained two kinds of dangers for its primary project of encouraging a mode of labor regulation based on collective bargaining. The first was that such a project depended upon strengthening trade unions, and the Auroux Laws did practically nothing in this direction. The second danger was that in a number of ways the reforms in fact acted to strengthen the microcorporatist features of the French industrial relations system. Taken together, the existing weakness of trade unionism in France, the failure to address that weakness, and the microcorporatist elements of the reforms all tipped the balance from one project to another, from the creation or reinforcement of collective bargaining with trade unions to an essentially microcorporatist form of labor regulation.

The Auroux Report indicated the crucial role that trade unions would have in making the reform package work: "The union organizations are quite obviously the privileged intermediaries of the workers to defend their interests and to create the conditions for change in the firm."[19] The importance of the unions was widely recognized and demanded by proponents of reform. As Murcier of the CFDT put it, unions had to be strengthened "because union rights are the condition of a better balance of forces in the firm, which is itself necessary for the success of negotiations."[20] The argument was that collective bargaining above all resulted from unions that were sufficiently strong so that employers would be forced to bargain with them.[21] With only weak unions, bargaining either would not take place or would be meaningless and tantamount merely to ratifying employer positions. In short, bargaining would have to be imposed on employers; the obligation to bargain was necessary but not sufficient. It was this reasoning that led the CFDT and CGT to press for the extension of union protection and rights to smaller firms.

The Auroux Report envisaged two methods for spreading collective bargaining. The first was greater exercise of the power of "extension" by government (hence the legislation making its use easier), and the second was stronger trade unions. The former was intended to expand the coverage of collective bargaining (in order to close the gaps that still existed), the latter to translate the formal obligation to bargain into *real* bargaining and signed agreements.

However, somewhat surprisingly, and to the anger of the unions and many rank-and-file Socialists, there was very little in the Auroux legislation that actually strengthened trade unions. There were some increases in the capacity of union delegates to operate on the shopfloor—increased hours off work, the right to collect union dues during work time, office facilities in large firms—but these were very limited.[22] Most important, the abolition of the fifty-employee threshold and extension of legal protection to unions in smaller firms was not accompanied by the provision of any of the normal rights given to unions in larger firms. Union delegates received legal protection but not the *capacity* to organize and act. This anomaly was recognized even by opposition politicians like Philippe Séguin who pointed to the empty symbolism of the new legislation during the parliamentary debates: "This union section without attributes (no delegates, no offices, no ethical personality) appears to be a legal fiction."[23]

The reasons for not strengthening unions were varied. First, French trade unions did not, either in 1981–82 or more generally, ask for the kinds of powers often associated with strengthening trade unions (such as the closed shop and dues checkoff). Union pluralism makes these features problematic because they imply that one union will gain at the expense of others, and that one union can gain a stranglehold on particular firms or industries. For the other unions the fear was that the CGT would be the big winner in any attempt to replace genuine pluralism with firm or sectoral monopolies.[24]

Second, there was a cost factor. Allowing union delegates time off from work for union activities and a variety of support services imposed costs on a firm, and small firms operating close to the margins of profitability claimed they could not bear such costs. At a time when the CNPF was making a major issue of the "*charges*" (mainly social security contributions) weighing on firms, the Socialists were loathe to add more of a burden. This, plus the complexity, were the reasons that the Auroux Report gave for not eliminating the fifty-employee threshold. While the final legislation did eliminate that threshold, it compensated by not imposing the additional costs of union sections on the smaller firms.

The third reason why the legislation did not strengthen trade unions directly was that the Auroux Laws intended to strengthen trade unions *indirectly*, through a strengthening of the works councils. The idea was that through their representation on works councils union representatives would benefit from the greatly expanded powers given the works councils. It was a gamble on the symbiotic character of the relationship between unions and works councils, and it ignored both the capacity of employers to use the work councils *against* unions (or in place of unions) and the long-term deterioration of the representation of unions on the works councils. There was in fact no a priori reason why the relationship between union and works council should be cooperative instead of conflictual. The nature of that relationship depended on the wider strength of the trade union movement. All in all, the Auroux Laws failed to strengthen unions and relied instead upon their existing strength. It was a gamble that was poorly timed, and ultimately failed.

The rest of this section will examine a number of microcorporatist features of the reforms which can be considered in some sense as Trojan horses in that they contained within them the potential, under certain circumstances, to weaken collective bargaining with trade unions and encourage microcorporatist firm-level agreements reached without the participation of union sections.

The first such feature was the strengthening of the works council. The second Auroux Law (October 28, 1982) was concerned above all with increasing the number of situations and conditions under which management had to consult with the work council. As Vatinet has pointed out, the line between consultation and negotiation is a fine one.[25] On certain issues the works council was in fact granted a veto over management proposals, and this made it very likely that de facto negotiation would take place to avoid the exercise of a veto. As Vatinet put it, any "reinforcement of the consultative rights of the [works] council would have the result [of] causing the works council to become an instrument of periodic negotiation."[26]

What is important here is that the Auroux Laws encouraged a small but growing trend in collective bargaining, that of agreements "*de fait*" between management and works councils or employee delegates, which were technically illegal (as only union sections had the legal right to conclude agreements) but nonetheless existed and operated unless a legal challenge was made. In any case, the courts were taking an ambivalent position on this kind of agreement, treating them on a case-by-case basis depending on the actual content of the agreement.[27] In 1984, of the firms obligated to bargain with their union sections and *which did not do so*, 36 percent instead signed illegal agreements with their works councils. In 1985 the figure was 50.7 percent.[28] Between 1983 and 1984, 10 percent of all agreements on the application of the right of expression were signed with the works councils rather than the union sections as decreed by law. These agreements were illegal, but they existed nonetheless. An excellent study by Bodin of the application of the Auroux Laws in small and medium-sized firms found that "the frequent accumulation of mandates encourages confusion between different [representative] institutions," and on the issue of negotiations over flexibility "bargaining always takes place with the works council, even if some union representation exists."[29] The reality was that reinforcing the works councils, especially in a period of union weakness and employer hostility to unions, had the effect of encouraging firm-level bargaining in which employers could avoid dealing with trade unions and instead bargain directly with the works council.

The second microcorporatist feature was the right of "derogation." French industrial relations, in its original incarnation in the 1950 Law on Collective Bargaining, envisioned a strict hierarchy in which collective agreements had to at least provide workers with the minimum wages and working conditions set down in legislation. Similarly, lower-level agreements (for instance, firm-level agreements) had to at least provide the minimum wages and working conditions laid down in higher-level (branch or confederal) agreements. So, for instance, branch-level wage minimums had to be at least equivalent to the legislated minimum wage, and real wages negotiated in the firm had to be at least equivalent to the branch-level minimums. This hierarchy acted to protect unorganized workers and to give an important role to trade unions which, while weak on the shopfloor, could exercise influence at higher levels or on the government. This hierarchy was breached in a January 1982 law on work time flexibility and then embodied in the November 13, 1982, law on collective bargaining. Now, on certain issues (though not wages), and so long as no veto was exercised by "majority" unions, a firm-level agreement could derogate, or exempt itself, from a branch-level agreement, or even legislation. So, for instance, the legal protection for workers against excessive flexibility in work time could be overridden to provide greater flexibility than the law allowed.

This provided employers with an incentive to bargain at the firm level where unions were weaker and more vulnerable, and their interests more centered on the firm. This development was dangerous for trade unions which in the past had been able to use their national or sectoral strength to impose a floor under the conditions of workers in the firm.

The data on derogation is poor. One study estimated that 20 percent of all firm-level agreements were derogatory,[30] and of six hundred agreements on flexibility of work time in 1985 eighty were found to have derogatory clauses—that is to say, clauses that were illegal under the Labor Code.[31] Indeed derogation is particularly useful for employers when bargaining over flexibility because it allows them to sign agreements that exempt them from the rigidities imposed by universal legislation or centralized bargaining. A government study said of the effect of the January 1982 law, which permitted derogation on bargaining over flexibility, that "one consequence of the measure was to make negotiation in the firm independent of negotiation at the branch level."[32]

The third microcorporatist feature of the Auroux legislation also had the effect of breaking down the traditional hierarchy of bargaining levels. One of the major criticisms of the reform made by the reformist trade unions was that the obligation to bargain at the firm level every year would have the effect of leading to the decay of branch-level bargaining.[33] The reformist unions, which were even weaker on the shopfloor than the CFDT and CGT, therefore feared anything that would decentralize bargaining. They argued that it made little sense for employers to negotiate minimum wages and conditions at the branch level if they were legally obligated to bargain over *real* wages and conditions in their own firms. One side-effect would be to increase dualism and inequality in wages and conditions between firms because many firms did not have union sections and hence were not obligated to bargain. Workers in these firms would suffer from the deterioration of bargaining at the branch level, which had previously acted as a safety net. In the words of the CFTC, "The strong will gain from negotiation in the firm, the weak will lose from it."[34]

The evidence bears out the fears of the reformist unions. The period since 1982 has seen a simultaneous decline in branch-level bargaining and dramatic increase in firm-level bargaining. The best measure of the *practice* and vitality of branch-level bargaining is the number of annual codicils.

TABLE 7.1
The Evolution of Branch-Level Bargaining, 1982–89

Branch-Level Codicils		Branch-Level Codicils	
1982	1,385	1986	695
1983	1,012	1987	788
1984	939	1988	885
1985	880	1989	840

Source: Bilan de la Négociation Collective 1987 (Paris: La Documentation Française, 1988), 31; Bilan 1988 de la Négociation Collective (Paris: La Documentation Française, 1989), 22; and for the 1989 figures see the summary of the 1989 Bilan Annuel de la Négociation Collective, in Le Monde, June 16, 1990, p. 23.

Here there was deep and rapid decline until 1986 and then stabilization at a lower level than in 1982 (see table 7.1).

More interesting has been the explosion of firm-level agreements because they constitute a new feature in French labor regulation, which has traditionally been underdeveloped at the firm level. While in 1981, 24.2 percent of workers benefited from firm-level agreements, 35.4 percent of workers were covered by such an agreement by 1985.[35] There was a steady rise in the proportion of firms legally obligated to bargain that actually did (from 42 percent in 1983 to 72.2 percent in 1986), and of these about two-thirds concluded agreements.[36] Even if one subtracts agreements implementing the right of expression (which were obligatory and dominated firm-level bargaining in 1983 and 1986), there was a steady rise in bargaining in the firm with the exception of 1988 (see table 7.2).

The fourth and final microcorporatist feature of the reforms was the institution of a "droit d'expression." Its goal was explicitly to create a "non-mediatized"[37] form of worker expression in all firms employing two hundred or more workers. The law set the framework, leaving it up to firm-level bargaining to fill in the details. The right of expression was a "potential two-edged sword"[38] and perhaps best illustrates the twin logics

TABLE 7.2
The Evolution of Firm-Level Bargaining, 1983–89

Firm-Level Agreements		Firm-Level Agreements	
1983	1,955	1987	5,482
1984	3,839	1988	4,891
1985	4,889	1989	5,793 (approx.)
1986	4,890		

Source: Bilan de la Négociation Collective 1987, 12; Bilan 1988 de la Négociation Collective, 11; and Le Monde, June 16, 1990, p. 23. The 1989 figure is approximate because it includes any agreements reached that year on setting up worker (self-)expression groups.

and the potential dangers of the Auroux Laws. Under different circumstances the worker expression groups could operate in very different ways. On the one hand the groups might in practice become dominated by trade unions, and hence become "soviets" in the heart of the firm, a source of strength and organizational capacity for unions and workers alike. This was certainly the CFDT's hope. It was also the great fear of the CNPF and the CGC, representing the *cadres*, for whom the new expression groups implied "a parallel hierarchy, which will weaken the supervisory staff."[39]

On the other hand the groups might come to be dominated by the existing management hierarchy and hence become a form of obligatory quality circle, both increasing productivity and integrating workers into the firm. It was this eventuality that FO feared most, and that constituted its greatest objection to the Auroux Laws. It argued that: "Under cover of democratization, the object [of the reform] remains the elimination of unionism, a process that will take place by an atomization of workers and by an integration of the worker."[40]

The Auroux legislation created a new form of worker organization and opened a new social space in the firm, but it left open whether the expression groups would become instruments for union activity in the firm or rather potential alternatives to union representation. In this sense the *droit d'expression* groups can be viewed as a metaphor for the entire reform project.

The results show clearly that it was the second logic that prevailed. An official study of the application of the new law showed that, by May 1984, 45 percent of the two-hundred-employee firms had signed agreements on worker expression.[41] The great majority of the agreements allowed for one to four meetings a year, each lasting between one and two hours. In 79 percent of cases, the agreements did not allow "outsiders" to participate, and 62 percent of the groups were organized and led by the supervisory staff. A more qualitative investigation of the operation of the expression groups suggested that a "quasi totality" of the groups were in fact led by supervisory staff (even where the actual agreement did not specify this) because workers tended to choose their direct superiors out of deference and fear.[42]

The results defused opposition from the CNPF and the CGC (the latter became positively enthusiastic about the groups once they recognized that the role of *cadres* was enhanced rather than challenged).[43] As foreseen by the original 1982 law, further legislation was passed in January 1986 which extended the obligation to create such groups to all firms employing fifty or more workers and having one or more union sections. A proposal by some Socialist deputies to have workers elect the leaders of the groups was defeated. A study of the application of the January 1986 law showed that the new agreements also gave a predominant role to the *cadres*.[44]

The argument made in this section has been that a number of elements of the Auroux Laws favored firm-level bargaining and firm-specific forms of worker collectivity. There was the hope, in the Auroux Laws, that these elements would in fact rebound to the benefit of trade unions, but it was a hope only. It was not backed up by measures to ensure a role for unions. The combination of already weak unions and a lack of measures to ameliorate that problem created a gaping hole at the heart of the Auroux reform project of strengthening collective bargaining.

TRADE UNION STRENGTH AND COLLECTIVE BARGAINING

The Auroux Laws did have an important impact on collective bargaining. The *coverage* of collective bargaining increased at the branch level as well as at the firm level.[45] Whereas, in 1981, 80.1 percent of workers in firms with ten or more employees were covered by branch agreements, by 1985 that figure was 86.4 percent.[46] The big increase came in the tertiary sector and smaller firms. In 1981, 71.9 percent of workers in the tertiary sector had been covered by a collective agreement while the equivalent figure for 1985 was 85.2 percent, practically the same as the average.[47] There was, as the same study put it, a "saturation effect." The result was that while, in 1981, 2 million workers (about 25 percent of the labor force) had no coverage, that had been reduced to 1.3 million by 1985.[48] A Ministry of Labor study in 1987 estimated that by that date only about half a million workers remained without coverage.[49]

This was success by any measure. But it was achieved by a much-increased use of the "extension" procedure by the government rather than new collective bargaining.[50] Thus it resulted from state intervention rather than spontaneous bargaining, something that should come as no surprise given the weakness of trade unions.

The Auroux Laws did have an important impact. They encouraged the process whereby collective bargaining became the dominant form of labor regulation, thus legitimizing a partial withdrawal of state protection from the large bloc of workers previously not covered by collective agreements. But at the same time, there was a reversal of the usual bargaining pattern and hierarchy with a decline in branch-level bargaining and a rise in firm-level bargaining. The implication of this development depends, of course, on the strength of the trade unions. A rise in firm-level bargaining means one thing if trade unions are strong enough to take advantage of it and quite another if unions are too weak to do so. The character of bargaining is very different in the two cases. In the second case, the result is to encourage microcorporatist bargaining either without trade unions, or with weakened, isolated trade unions. Trade unions that were strong *inside* the firm were, as the Auroux Report and all the trade unions recognized, a fundamental precondition for a collective-bargaining as opposed to a microcorporatist model of labor regulation.

In fact, French trade unionism continued and accelerated its decline in the 1980s. Estimates of union density are always poor in France, but most estimates put the figure at between 7 and 10 percent,[51] and since these are concentrated in the public sector this means the virtual elimination of trade union membership in the rest of the economy. This fact is staggering and makes France unique in the advanced capitalist world.

If trade union membership is very low, there are alternative forms of union "presence." One such form is the existence of union sections or union delegates in the firm. The evolution in the 1980s is difficult to chart because of a change in the form of measurement, as a result of the Auroux Laws, from counting union sections to counting union delegates. Nonetheless, the two measures are roughly equivalent and a pattern does emerge: a rapid rise in union implantation in the firm in the early and mid-1970s, a slowing of the rate of growth after 1977, and then stagnation or decline in the 1980s (see table 7.3). The overall percentages are also heavily skewed toward larger firms (so that, for instance, in 1987 only 34.7 percent of firms employing from fifty to ninety-nine workers had a union delegate).[52]

Many observers, making the best of French trade unionism's obvious weaknesses, argue that the real influence of French unions is not measured in membership or union implantation, but more indirectly through the election of union candidates onto the firm-specific representative institutions, particularly the works councils.[53] The "union monopoly" in the first round of voting combined with the national visibility of unions, it can be

TABLE 7.3
The Evolution of Union Sections, 1970–87

	Percentage of Firms (employing 50 + people) with a Union Section or Delegate
1970	27.5
1977	56.1
1980	60.3
1985	55.1
1987	52.2

Source: Figures for 1970, 1977, and 1980 are adapted from *Liaisons Sociales: Législation Sociale*, no. 5470 (April 4, 1984). The 1985 and 1987 figures come from Jean-Pierre Aujard, "Les Délégués Syndicaux au 31 décembre 1987," *Dossiers statistiques du travail et d'emploi*, no. 50 (July 1989). The 1985 and 1987 figures are for union delegates, not union sections.

The figures used here (percentage of 50 + firms having one or more union sections) constitute the most widely used measure because employing fifty people was the threshold for union protection in the 1968 legislation on union sections (that threshold was eliminated in 1982).

argued, tend to give unions a privileged position in the works councils, which is presumably why there are periodic efforts by the CNPF and some conservative politicians to eliminate the union monopoly. Union influence on works councils does matter because it helps to determine the character and function of works councils, particularly if the practice of illegal bargaining with the works councils is growing.

Again, a pattern emerges. In the 1980s voting for CGT candidates in works council elections has declined significantly while the CFDT vote remained stable. In the first half of the 1980s FO and nonunion candidates gained what the CGT lost, but in recent years the FO vote has also dropped and nonunion candidates have continued to make gains. In the 1989 works council elections, for the first time, nonunion candidates won a higher share of the vote than even the CGT.[54] But these overall figures understate the extent of that tendency in smaller (less than fifty employees) firms. Here the rise of nonunion representation is meteoric. Thus in the period 1978 to 1986 nonunion candidates increased their share of works council votes in small firms by 19 percent. By 1986, in fact, 39 percent of all firms had *only* nonunion candidates standing for election.[55] This puts a different light on the issue of the union monopoly.

Thus by the end of the 1980s trade union membership outside the public sector was negligible, union implantation in the firm was stagnating, and the indirect representation of trade unions on works councils was in serious decline. Indeed in a third of all firms (and a far higher proportion of small firms), even this form of union representation had disappeared.

CONCLUSION

This chapter has argued that a set of largely unexpected and unintended developments flowed from the implementation of the Auroux Laws at a time of profound trade union weakness, employer hostility to unions, and economic crisis. A combination of harsh environmental factors and the ambiguity of the industrial relations legislation led to these results. But the eventual outcome of the Auroux Laws has not been random. Rather, the reform package always carried within it two distinct and coherent projects, or models of labor regulation. The effect of attempting major industrial relations reform at this economic, political, and social conjuncture was to displace the dominant collective-bargaining project and instead bring to the fore the secondary microcorporatist project.

At the same time, as collective bargaining did take hold in the firm, trade unions largely disappeared from private-sector firms. In their place the Auroux Laws encouraged the development, reinforcement, and use of firm-specific forms of worker organization. Clearly this is not yet a completed process and it is too early for a full assessment. Extrapolating from a period of labor market slackness to one closer to full employment (should such a time arrive) would be dangerous. But the developments thus far are important, and they carry with them the possibility, at least, that labor regulation has changed in France to the point where a renewed period of economic growth and tighter labor markets will not be sufficient to revive France's trade union movement. The degree to which labor's conjunctural weakness has been translated into a deeper, structural weakness will be the main subject of the concluding chapter of this study.

A number of consequences flow from the shift in labor regulation, if that is what it indeed is, from a hybrid form of collective bargaining and state regulation, to microcorporatist labor regulation. One consequence is the marginalization of unions, or the integration of the union section into the firm and a loosening of the ties between union section and local union federations and the confederal level. Bodin's detailed study of the application of the Auroux Laws in small firms led him to suggest that the "position of the trade union confederations play little part in negotiation. . . . It is rather a case of firm bargaining in the strict sense of the term."[56] Five years after the Auroux Laws went into effect the CGT believed that there had been such a fundamental shift in the balance of power against trade unions that: "In fact, it is not a case of collective bargaining, that is to say, the negotiation of workers' demands, but the negotiation of employer demands [and] the ratification of employer decisions."[57] It is therefore little wonder that the trade unions have taken branch-level agreements, and their revitalization, more seriously in recent years.[58]

There are also consequences for the substantive issues of bargaining. The evidence of wage bargaining is that wages have come to approximate more and more closely government and employer recommendations.[59] There has also been a growing tendency toward accords that reduce the general part of the wage and replace it with a larger portion tied to individual performance.[60] This area of bargaining—bargaining over flexibility—is the subject of the next chapter, but it is important to note the extent to which the bargaining framework set up by the Auroux Laws, and particularly the microcorporatist elements, aided bargaining over flexibility. Discussions of flexibility made little sense at the branch level, but at the firm level, with firm-specific groups of workers and the capacity to derogate from legislation and higher-level agreements, bargaining over flexibility both made more sense to employers and was more likely to succeed. In this sense a microcorporatist mode of labor regulation can be considered a *precondition* for the introduction of flexibility in France.

Two further points are worth making. The first is that the Auroux Laws were attempted at a time of employer strength and militancy. Employers found their public role rehabilitated in a period of economic crisis and the apparent bankruptcy of Socialist economic policy. The strategy of employers after 1977–78 did not include a role for unions. It was not necessarily overtly hostile to unions, but it saw them as at best an unnecessary interference in the running of the firm. That this strategy was popular with small and medium-sized employers should come as no surprise, and these employers did find themselves with increased influence within the business community as a whole.[61] But it was not a strategy limited to smaller firms. What is interesting in the 1980s is the evolution in the so-called progressive wing of French capital, which represented the very large firms. Thus a whole range of progressive think tanks, very often the same ones that had taken the lead in encouraging *la grande politique contractuelle* in 1968–74, developed explicitly antiunion proposals. Entreprise et Progrès, the Centre des jeunes dirigeants d'entreprises, and others began in 1985 to formulate proposals for new forms of firm-level representation and new forms of bargaining which removed the union monopoly in works council elections, and in bargaining (thus allowing the works councils to conclude collective agreements legally), and which sought to vastly expand the areas where derogation could be applied.[62] The "new look" of employers, large and small alike, made it all but impossible that the Auroux Laws could have worked as intended. It was difficult enough for Chaban-Delmas to create a "New Society." Now a similar project was being proposed at a time when labor was weaker and employers more hostile.

The second point concerns the role played by the Auroux Laws themselves. The extent to which legislation can have results in the face of an adverse economic situation and a hostile business class is questionable. But it would be to trivialize the Auroux Laws to argue that they were simply a failure, mistimed and essentially irrelevant. The double logic contained within the legislative package *facilitated* developments that were already occurring. The Auroux Laws encouraged the shift toward a microcorporatist form of labor regulation and made the transition toward such a model easier.

Some elements of the *patronat* and its intellectuals were quick to recognize the role the Auroux Laws played in this process, and it is important to note that the conservative government of 1986–88 did not seek to dismantle the Auroux reforms.[63] Considering the reaction of the *patronat* to the reforms in 1982–83, this is remarkable in itself. An opinion poll conducted in 1984 found that 66 percent of employers questioned believed that the Auroux Laws had been beneficial, only 6 percent saw the legislation as reinforcing trade unions (70 percent believed it did not), and 47 percent believed that the reforms actually encouraged competition inside the firm with trade unions (26 percent did not, the rest undecided).[64] De Closets, a best-selling author, known for his opposition to the "*toujours plus*" of the unions, and his support for a "partnership" in the firm, saw the Auroux Laws as tremendously important in encouraging his project. As he put it,

"The French have evolved more in the last five years than the previous one hundred."[65] The reforms generalized, by legislation, practices that a few of the most "modernist" employers were already using. Thus the effect of the Socialist reforms was a *forced* evolution of employer practices in the firm. Where before only a few employers had sought to incorporate works councils into the economic running of the firm and create quality circles, now legislation forced most employers to adopt microcorporatist practices. In this sense, the Socialist government had far more influence on employers, and employer practices, than on workers.

CHAPTER EIGHT

The Search for Flexibility

WHEN THE OIL shock and ensuing deep recession hit the advanced capitalist world in the 1970s, the initial responses did not involve, either for the Left or the Right, a fundamental reevaluation of the postwar model of industrial relations. This model, for all its national variants, tended to rest on the identification of trade unions as the privileged representatives of the working class, and collective bargaining as the mechanism by which distributional (and other) conflicts on the shopfloor were resolved. Whatever rigidities were embodied in this system of industrial relations, the overall result was seen as beneficial. Indeed the rigidities themselves could be considered beneficial in that they stabilized demand and minimized industrial conflict.[1]

The initial response to economic crisis in the 1970s did not challenge the basic structure of industrial relations. Rather there were a variety of attempts to reduce labor costs, either through deflation or incomes policies. However, as the economic crisis persisted, it was the industrial relations system itself that came to be seen as the problem, and increasingly attention shifted to social relations within the firm. In an ever more competitive, rapidly changing global economy, adaptability came to be valued above predictability. Thus in the course of the 1980s attention has become focused upon the ways in which industrial relations systems inhibit change and flexibility, and upon alternative ways of organizing social relations. Thus as Boyer has put it: "Since the beginning of the 1980s industrial relations [*les relations sociales du travail*] have constituted, for many, the principal cause of the stagnation of the [economic] crisis, such that firms and governments have notably changed their ideas on this subject and have begun calling them into question."[2]

It is no exaggeration to say, I think, that a consensus is emerging among those who study industrial relations that the shift to more flexible ways of managing industrial relations and organizing production is the wave of the future and is indicative of a profound change in the nature of social relations inside the firm.[3]

While discussion of "post-Fordism," flexible specialization,"[4] and flexibility have come to dominate the industrial relations literature and management journals, the source of the transformation—what is driving it— remains murky. Yet the question is important if one is to understand the particular national face, or character, of that transformation.

It is interesting that the Regulation School, which was highly successful in laying out the economic developments that gave rise to the Fordist regime of accumulation, and the mechanisms that permitted simultaneous increases in production and consumption in a kind of virtuous circle of growth, has been far less successful in understanding and explaining "post-Fordism." Indeed the very term itself indicates that while "it" is not Fordism, it is not clear exactly what "it" actually is. The question of what is causing the current changes can be reformulated, using Regulation School language, in the following way: are we are observing the rise of a new *regime of accumulation*—in which case it is an essentially economic dynamic—to which employers, workers, and governments are being forced to adapt, or in fact is the regime of accumulation only undergoing minor change, and what we are observing is rather a struggle over the *mode of labor regulation*—a dynamic that is much more political and social.

Put in these terms the question may seem arcane, but answering it is central to understanding the changes now taking place in the political economies of advanced capitalist societies. The consensus answer, I think, is that new modes of labor regulation are a response to a new set of economic and technical imperatives; that the dynamic is an essentially economic one. Thus, increasing international competition has put a premium on the capacity of a firm to adapt quickly to new market conditions and to use the work force in more flexible ways. Relative saturation of markets for consumer durables has created a demand for specialized and differentiated goods, which similarly require more flexible work practices and perhaps more skilled employees. Advances in industrial technology and particularly the introduction of computer-aided design and production enables firms to shift product lines rapidly to meet new kinds of demand.

The argument that economic forces are driving changes in industrial relations forms and practices is clearest when coming from employers. A casual glance at the business press confirms the degree to which employers believe that they must adapt, and become more flexible, to survive in a changing, ever more hostile world economy. But the same conclusion is common among social scientists. There is much debate on the extent to which the process can be controlled, on the possible *forms* of flexibility, on the extent to which flexibility can be benign, and on the role of states and trade unions in that process, but rarely is there a challenge to the notion that there is some new economic logic to which firms and workers must adapt. The only question is the form of the response.[5]

It is not my intention to deny that some new dynamic has appeared. There is a mass of scholarly and anecdotal evidence to suggest that firms are facing new economic pressures, that large, safe, domestic markets for mass-produced consumer durables are giving way to import penetration, export competition from low-wage economies, and even a fragmentation of consumer markets in advanced capitalist societies.[6] Every single one of the forms of Fordist labor regulation—collective bargaining, corporatism, state regulation—has come under pressure in the past decade, and some have collapsed.[7] It is the *rigidities* of these forms of labor regulation that have come under attack (such as the creation of a web of rules and regulations hindering flexible use of the work force, rigid demarcation boundaries, and centralized or rigidly indexed wages). Whether the source of the rigidity is high-level corporatist bargaining, de facto trade union control of the shopfloor, or state regulation, the solution—across the advanced capitalist world—has been seen as flexibility. This convergence in the nature of challenges to existing systems of industrial relations gives much credence to the notion that labor regulation is responding to an exogenous economic change.

However, the danger of such a barely concealed economic and technological determinism is that it serves to legitimize indiscriminately and uncritically the demands of employers, and to demobilize opposition to these tendencies in industrial relations. After all, if these economic forces are somehow beyond political control, the choice is between adapting to them (albeit with certain safeguards) and a stubborn, self-destructive refusal to face reality.

It is worth recognizing, at least theoretically, that industrial relations systems are not the product solely of economic need but are also complex structures of social relationships, and as such they rest upon a particular balance of power between two major social actors: employers and workers. Thus struggles between these two groups shape industrial relations at least as much as economic change.[8]

The process of production in the firm, the core of a capitalist economy, is above all a *social* process, which is simultaneously economic and political. As Polanyi recognized, the wage relationship is not simply another economic transaction.[9] This means that the usual division between politics and economics, in which the former stops at the factory gates or the office waiting room, misses the fundamental irreducibility of capitalist production to economics.

The battle over flexibility, in France and elsewhere, is not just about the ability of firms to compete, but also about who controls the labor process and labor itself. Indeed the desire for flexibility on the part of employers is very often indistinguishable from the attempt to reassert control over the labor process and the work force. One goes with the other. Since the mid-1970s employers in France have been attempting, in a more or less self-conscious manner, to regain control of the workplace and to translate the *conjunctural* weakness of labor (resulting from cyclical recession) into a *structural* weakness, so that the ability of workers to inflict damage on employers will be reduced even as the French economy moves out of recession and the labor market tightens.

In truth it makes little sense to separate out the economic from the social and political causes here. There are factors that are making the Fordist mass-production model of the firm less appropriate and opening up opportunities for new "flexible specialization" forms of production. They are not simply exogenous factors however. The Fordist model fostered labor strength by encouraging union organization. Flexible models of industrial relations improve the capacity of firms to respond to economic change precisely because they overcome the virtual veto power afforded labor in the Fordist model. The impact of the individualization of wages is a good example of this issue, as the penultimate section of this chapter will show. Individualization of wages clearly has economic benefits for firms. But it is also a form of labor control as it puts an ever larger part of a worker's income at the discretion of supervisors and can be used to penalize absenteeism and union activity.

Thus it is worth stressing, in any discussion of the causes of flexibility, the *multiple* factors that are encouraging the introduction of greater flexibility, if only because it allows a more critical examination of precisely which employer demands are rooted in economic rationality, and which derive more from the desire to reassert control in the workplace.

A recognition of the multiplicity of factors at work in the conflict over flexibility, and the social nature of that conflict, ought to refocus attention on the institutional context within which flexibility is introduced. This has always been the great strength of the Regulation approach.

Thus an important distinction must be made between the introduction of flexibility into the work process and the organization of the firm—such things as flexible work time, individualized wages, and so on—and flexibility in the industrial relations system itself. Chapter 7 was concerned, in its description of the changes brought to French industrial relations by the Auroux reforms, with the latter. The obligation to bargain in the firm, the encouragement of firm-specific organizations of workers (works councils, worker expression groups), and the capacity to sign derogatory accords, all had the effect of breaking down the rigid, centralized, statist character of French labor regulation. This chapter is concerned with the *results* of the modified system of labor regulation, and particularly the introduction of flexibility into the day-to-day running of the firm. Thus the bulk of this chapter focuses upon three areas of flexibility: flexibility of work time, flexibility in hiring and firing and work contracts, and flexibility in pay practices.

However, it is important to stress the close relationship between the two meanings of flexibility outlined above. The *capacity* to introduce flexibility into the workplace is dependent upon the existence of an "institutional context"[10] within which labor and capital are willing and able to negotiate substantive flexibility issues. The institutional context is logically prior, and in the case of flexibility such an institutional context is a decentralized mode of labor regulation. The argument made in the last chapter, and illustrated in this chapter, is that a *microcorporatist* mode of labor regulation was a necessary precondition for the introduction of flexibility in France. In that sense, the contribution of the Socialist industrial relations reforms, put in place at a time of economic crisis and historic union weakness, was to create an institutional context within which the new management emphasis upon flexibility was possible. The decentralization of bargaining to the firm, the enhancement of the role of works councils, and the other microcorporatist innovations of the early 1980s both placed the locus of labor regulation firmly where it made sense to bargain over flexibility (it made little sense to negotiate flexibility at the branch or national level) and made it more likely that agreement on flexibility would be reached because bargaining now took place where trade unions were weak or absent and hence where their opposition to flexibility was most easily side-stepped.

Thus the Regulation School approach leads one to focus at least as much on the institutional framework—the mode of labor regulation—which made the introduction of flexibility possible, as on the substantive issues of flexibility themselves. Too often discussions of flexibility in France, and indeed elsewhere, narrowly emphasize the flexibility issues and not the context within which the negotiation of these issues is possible. This makes assessment of the success and failure of flexibility initiatives difficult.

The Specificity of Flexibility in France

The French case is striking because the notion of flexibility entered, took hold, and came to dominate French discourse in a very short space of time. In addition, that process occurred under a Socialist government despite the fact that flexibility is usually considered *"une revendication patronale."* The economic problems facing the PS from late 1981 through the second major deflationary package in March 1983 came as a surprise to the Socialists. Their response—deflation to reduce income and consumption and rebuild profit margins—was not markedly different (except perhaps in its scale and rapidity) from that of any other social democratic government coming to terms with the limits imposed on it by a capitalist economy. Thus economic policy in 1982–83 can be seen as reactive and orthodox.

The French Socialists changed, though. In Singer's words, they underwent a "conversion."[11] They came to embrace the firm, entrepreneurialism, and flexibility as virtues in themselves, and as means to emerge from economic crisis.[12] The Socialists came to adopt, as their own, a large part of employers' demands, albeit with some modifications. This shift was symbolized by the replacement of Pierre Mauroy with Laurent Fabius; an old-style social democrat gave way to a modernizer and a technocrat. Fabius, in his first speech to the National Assembly upon becoming prime minister, called for a "modernization of social relations."[13] This language of modernization had been heard before—but in the context of 1984 and a Socialist government chastened by events, its meaning was not that of Chaban-Delmas in 1969 or even Delors in 1981. In 1984 modernizing social relations meant creating a context in which flexibility could be introduced. From 1983–84 onward the Socialists actively encouraged the process of "flexibilization." The period 1981–83 had the effect—a brutal learning experience to be sure—of forcing the Socialists to recognize and come to terms with the exhaustion of Fordism in France and the need for something to replace it with.

The conversion of the PS to flexibility was rapid and thorough, and by no means grudging. As this chapter will demonstrate, the Socialists encouraged flexibility by exhorting the social partners to bargain and by passing legislation that modified or weakened the Labor Code so as to make bargaining possible. The thoroughness of the transformation, and the enthusiasm with which the PS adopted flexibility, have to be understood, in part at least, in the context of the ambiguous ideological heritage of the party, adopted in one form in the 1970s but metamorphosed in the entirely different situation of the mid-1980s. Social democracy was never a strong component of that ideology, and statism seemed to offer no answer for how to deal with the crisis. Indeed statism was seen more as the problem than the solution. Thus *autogestion*, suitably modified, provided an indigenous French and left-wing version of flexibility. It provided a way of explaining the inadequacy of Taylorist and Fordist work practices, and an optimistic prognosis for the effect of introducing flexibility in social relations. The contradictions of Socialist ideology, which had always existed, fractured under the weight of economic crisis and produced an enthusiasm for flexibility unmatched by other European social democratic and left-of-center parties.

Yet flexibility for the Socialists was not quite a blank check for employers, though at times it seemed that way. As Fabius put it, for the Socialists the goal was to find "the equilibrium point between the legitimate protection of the rights of workers and the necessary flexibility for the functioning of the economy and the firms."[14] The PS was acutely aware of the dangers of flexibility and it always faced the dilemma of how to introduce flexibility while simultaneously controlling it; of how to prevent flexibility from simply coming to mean deregulation and precarious employment. The Socialist answer, and what distinguished it from the Right, was to give the trade unions the role of guarantor. If the role of unions in negotiating and implementing flexibility could be institutionalized, it would be relatively safe for the state to withdraw and allow deregulation. It was this difficult balancing act that explains the hesitancy and unsteady progress toward introducing flexibility in France and the constant effort on the part of the Socialist government to get union agreement before legislating. This effort was always akin to keeping a finger in the dike. In the context of weakened trade unions and microcorporatist bargaining, state deregulation was more likely to result in flexibility being unilaterally imposed by employers than negotiated with unions.

The core of this chapter discusses the three main areas in which flexibility was introduced in France. It looks at employers' demands for, and government and union responses to, the introduction of flexible work time, greater flexibility in the ability to hire and fire workers, and flexibility in pay practices. The concluding chapter of the book will address the broader question of what implications the widespread adoption of flexibility is likely to have for French labor, but also for labor movements and labor regulation in other advanced capitalist societies.

FLEXIBLE WORK TIME

The issue of flexible work time dominated discussion of flexibility for eight years—from 1978 until 1986—and it was in many ways a test case for the whole issue of flexibility. It was, for both unions and employers, the main symbol of the battle for flexibility.

It will be recalled from chapter 5 that the issue of flexible work time appeared in 1978, in the wake of the defeat of the Left and the attempt by the Barre government to encourage collective bargaining. The potential for the success of bargaining on this issue was built on a possible convergence of interest between employers and unions. Employers wanted greater flexibility in the length of the workweek so as to be able to use the work force more efficiently in responding to shifting demand. Workers might also be interested in such flexibility if they could have some say in what their schedules were. More important for the trade unions, there was the potential for a trade-off of *flexibility* of work time in return for a *reduction* of the workweek, which had emerged as a major union demand (perhaps *the* main demand of the CFDT) in light of high and enduring unemployment.[15]

The negotiations in 1978–80 failed. There were two obstacles. First, the regulation of work time was unusual in France in the extent to which it was determined by legislation and strictly controlled by the Labor Code rather than being the result of collective bargaining.[16] This was but one part of the more statist form of labor regulation in France. The result was that introducing greater flexibility into work time meant, in France, *deregulation*. It meant that the state would have to loosen the legislative restrictions that governed work time. The Barre government was wary of going too far in this direction for fear of the Left's capitalizing on it.

The second obstacle lay in the difference between the positions of the employers and unions. The unions were only prepared to allow flexibility if it was accompanied by reduction in work time and if union sections in the firm had some control over how that flexibility was implemented. Employers would not give enough in these areas. The result was stalemate. The government was prepared to legislate, but only if the unions and employers could first reach agreement, and this they could not.

The PS arrived in power with a campaign promise to reduce the workweek gradually and through negotiation, from forty hours to thirty-five hours, and to legally institute a fifth week of paid vacation. The Socialists hoped that in bargaining over the reduction of the workweek flexibility would also be discussed. So the newly elected government chose to encourage bargaining first and to promise legislation only later at the conclusion of bargaining. Thus if the negotiations failed, the government could go ahead and legislate instead. If the negotiations were successful then legislation would also be necessary to modify the Labor Code to take account of the agreement and to generalize the agreement to workers and firms not represented in the bargaining.

In July 1981 the CNPF and all the unions except the CGT signed a protocol that agreed to reduce the workweek to thirty-nine hours, generalize the fifth week of vacation, and provide some flexibility by exempting 150 hours of work a year *above the legal limit* from the need for administrative authorization. The protocol set out a schedule of branch-level talks to discuss further reductions, the issue of financial compensation, and greater flexibility. The protocol anticipated that the government would legislate when the branch-level agreements had been concluded. The CNPF and CFDT strongly favored this order of negotiation prior to legislation. As Hubert Lesire-Ozrel, national secretary of the CFDT, put it: "If it is true that legislation will remain necessary to structure and generalize [collective agreements] we wish negotiation to become the rule."[17] The CGT disagreed, preferring legislation first. It argued that bargaining first would present the government with a fait accompli on an issue that was its responsibility.[18]

The branch-level talks in the fall of 1981 went badly. Employers wanted greater flexibility than the unions were comfortable with, and they did not want workers to receive full compensation for the reduction in hours worked.[19] By the end of 1981, after bargaining in seventy branches, only eighteen agreements had been reached.[20] The government decided to step in and legislate. The January 1982 legislation followed the original July 1981 protocol fairly closely in reducing the workweek to thirty-nine hours and generalizing the fifth week of paid vacation. As for flexibility it allowed 130 hours a year above the legal limit to be worked without administrative authorization and provided for "derogatory" firm agreements, which could dispense with certain aspects of the Labor Code that related to flexibility of work time. Nonetheless, the CNPF and the CFDT were angry at the preemptive legislation, and they were made furious by the intervention of Mitterrand in February 1982, under pressure from the CGT and a wave of strikes, demanding that workers receive full compensation for the reduction in the workweek to thirty-nine hours. At a stroke this rendered irrelevant any accords (and there were twenty-seven by February 1982) already signed that had provided for only partial compensation.

The result of this experiment in high-level negotiation and legislative intervention was that the CNPF essentially gave up on the strategy of trying to bargain at the branch level for work time flexibility. Instead employers decentralized their efforts, taking advantage of the newly created obligation to bargain in the firm and the power to derogate legislation and higher-level agreements. There was a sharp decline in the number of industry-level agreements on work time from eighty-two in 1983 to the point where the official report on collective bargaining in 1986 referred to such agreements as *"quasiment inexistante."*[21] There was a simultaneous sharp rise in the number of firm-level agreements concerning work time, as table 8.1 demonstrates. In addition, the overwhelming number of these agreements provided for flexibility rather than reduction of work time. In fact, the proportion of work time agreements concerning work time reduction fell steadily from 24 percent in 1984 to 10 percent in 1987.

A study of agreements on work time in 1985 showed that they only very rarely concerned work time reduction, that they provided very little financial or other compensation for the increased flexibility, and that about one-third of all agreements contained illegal, derogatory clauses (i.e., clauses that allowed greater flexibility than was allowed in the Labor Code).[22] The implication of these developments was that employers were exploiting the decentralization of bargaining and the capacity to override legislative restrictions in order to sign agreements at the firm level that were concluded

TABLE 8.1
Firm-Level Agreements on Work Time, 1984–87

	Concerning Work Time Flexibility	*Concerning Work Time Reduction*	TOTAL
1984	1,200	375	1,575
1985	1,600	310	1,910
1986	1,987	253	2,240
1987	2,272	251	2,523

Source: Compiled from *Bilan Annuel de la Négociation Collective, 1985* (Paris: Ministère des Affaires Sociales et de l'Emploi, 1986); *Bilan Annuel de la Négociation Collective, 1986* (Paris: Ministère des Affaires Sociales et de l'Emploi, 1987); and *Bilan de la Négociation Collective, 1987* (Paris: La Documentation Française, 1988).

on terms more advantageous to employers than workers. This is indicated by the predominance of flexibility agreements rather than reduction of work time agreements, and the lack of compensation of any kind given to workers in return for accepting flexibility. This was precisely the unbalanced type of agreement that the unions and the government had feared. At the firm-level unions were weaker and more likely to agree to employer demands. In this period there was a clear strategic shift on the part of the *patronat*, from privileging branch-level talks to privileging firm-level talks.[23]

The results of bargaining on work time led the Socialist government to legislate once again, just before the 1986 legislative elections. The February 1986 "Loi Delebarre" (named after then Minister of Labor Michel Delebarre) was motivated by two factors which had become clear from bargaining over work time in the previous three years. The first was that if so many illegal agreements were being signed, the legislation had to be loosened so as to remove some of the restrictions on introducing flexibility so that bargaining could take place without the need to step outside the boundaries set by the Labor Code. Thus there was both a recognition that legislation stood in the way of flexibility and a willingness to remove some of the restrictions. The new legislation therefore allowed a greater range of hours to be worked around the weekly legal limit. This responded to one of the employers' main concerns.

The second factor, however, was the desire to protect workers and retain a role for trade unions in bargaining over flexibility. The evidence of bargaining from 1983 to 1985 was that workers were getting little in return for flexibility. As a result the new legislation said that any agreements that sought to take advantage of the increased flexibility had to be accompanied by a reduction of the workweek to thirty-seven and a half or thirty-eight hours, and that such agreements had to be concluded at the branch level, not the firm level. The goal was to control the introduction of flexibility, or rather to allow the unions to control it, which they had a much better chance of doing if bargaining occurred at the branch level. Delebarre explained the pivotal role that he saw for trade unions in the bargaining of flexibility and the dangers of a flexibility introduced without union control:

> This bill is an element that will permit the development of trade unionism. A different evolution could take place instead. It is the development of negotiation on a firm-by-firm basis, putting in place agreements between management and the representatives of workers in the firm who are not necessarily unionized. That is the slope toward . . . a patrimonial conception of relations inside the firm and . . . the development of house unions.[24]

Unfortunately the legislation was too little too late, and it won few friends. Chotard of the CNPF denounced the legislation as "ersatz flexibility,"[25] and Delebarre's successor (after the Right won the March legislative elections), Philippe Séguin, passed new legislation that further weakened the restrictions on flexible work time and eliminated the requirement that such agreements be reached at the branch level or be accompanied by reductions in work time.

The story of the introduction of flexibility into work time illustrates well the dilemma faced by the PS. The Socialist government was attempting to walk a fine line between allowing flexibility but not complete deregulation on the employers' terms. The Socialists hoped that the trade unions could be provided with the means with which to control the process of "flexibilization," but in the context of union weakness this was unrealistic. The reality was that the Socialists had to choose between maintaining strict legislative controls (and hence preventing all but minimal flexibility) and allowing a deregulation that amounted, in effect, to giving unilateral powers to employers.

FLEXIBILITY IN WORK CONTRACTS

This is something of a catchall category. It refers to the attempt to loosen the mass of legislative restrictions that regulated labor contracts in France. As with the length of the workweek, the Labor Code rather than collective agreements regulated the main contours of labor contracts. As a result it was the Labor Code rather than collective bargaining that employers felt to be the source of the rigidities that inhibited their capacity to use the work force flexibly and efficiently. Thus once again employers looked first to the state for flexibility and only later to the trade unions. Flexibility in this area meant, first and foremost, deregulation.

The *patronat* attacked two aspects of the restrictions on hiring and firing in particular.[26] The restriction that for many employers most symbolized the unnecessary and damaging interference of the state was the administrative authorization required before laying off workers. Enacted in 1973 when it was believed that the economic crisis would be short-lived, its goal was to review requests for layoffs to ensure that they were economically justified and thus to act as a disincentive to fire workers unless absolutely necessary. In fact, close to 90 percent of all requests were granted, usually within a month, and studies showed that the delay or refusal to grant a layoff rarely had an adverse impact on the firm's economic health.[27] Nevertheless, the suppression of this requirement became the rallying cry of the *patronat*.

The second set of restrictions made up the tight legislative rules surrounding "atypical" work contracts. The normal type of work contract in France was a contract of unlimited duration, with full-time work, full benefits, and full rights in the firm (for instance, workers covered by such contracts were protected by the administrative authorization on firing, had full social security protection, and could vote in firm elections). Other types of work contract (which will be generically called "atypical" contracts here) could be of numerous types but broadly fell into the categories of fixed-duration contracts, temporary work contracts, and part-time work contracts. These forms of work contract were laid down in the Labor Code, and the conditions under which they could be used were regulated. These forms of atypical work contract had grown rapidly since 1974 in response to the economic crisis.[28] Employers wanted workers who could be hired for a particular job, or a limited period, and then easily fired.

The PS came to power deeply concerned about the growth of "precarious" forms of work. The fear was that the growth of such types of work would not only create a more precarious and vulnerable existence for workers but would also lead to a fragmented, dualistic labor force. Thus both the *Projet Socialiste* and the *110 Propositions pour la France* called for reestablishing typical contracts more firmly by imposing greater restrictions on atypical work. The Bloch-Lainé Report, commissioned by the Socialists on taking office and reporting in December 1981, spent a good deal of time warning against the creation of *"une société duale."*[29] And the Auroux Report, alongside its discussions of collective bargaining, called for measures to "reunify the work group."[30]

Of the three types of work contract generally considered atypical, part-time work was considered less dangerous by the PS. Indeed it was seen as a demand by *workers* for flexibility (and particularly female workers supposedly more concerned with child care) rather than as the employers' demand. Hence, unlike other forms of atypical work, restrictions on part-time work were eased in 1982.[31]

The Socialists moved quickly to carry out their campaign promise, and a series of laws in January and February 1982 served to further regulate atypical work. Thus the conditions under which such forms of work could be used were reduced, the length of atypical work contracts was reduced, and also the number of times that contracts could be renewed was reduced. In addition, workers on this type of contract were entitled to a special bonus for precarious work, and these workers were given full rights in the firm. These benefits, besides compensating workers and more fully integrating them into the firm's life (where they had previously had only a peripheral existence), acted as a disincentive for employers to resort to such contracts. Thus the Socialist government's first moves were to *reduce* flexibility and *increase* the restrictions that employers opposed.

However, it should be stressed that the main goal of the 1982 legislation was not to eliminate atypical work, but rather to prevent its misuse. The fear was that employers whose firms had no particular economic need for atypical work were in fact replacing perfectly good full-contract workers with atypical workers to reduce costs and make such workers easier to fire. Thus the legislation stressed that atypical contracts could be used where they were "economically legitimate" and called not for the abolition of atypical work, but for greater "professionalism" and a more "positive image" of such work.[32] Again the Socialists walked the line between flexibility that responded to some genuine economic need, and that which was simply being used against workers and unions.

The effect of the legislation was mixed in that while there was a sharp decline in the use of temporary work contracts there was a simultaneous rise in the use of fixed-duration contracts.[33] In fact what happened was that, because the legislation was more restrictive for temporary work contracts, employers simply shifted workers on temporary contracts into fixed-duration contracts. In short, the state of the economy and the economic needs of the firms overwhelmed the legislation. There were more loopholes than legislation could plug without outlawing atypical work altogether, and this was not the Socialists' goal.[34]

Despite the continued use of atypical work contracts employers still wanted the legislative restrictions removed. Thus Chotard announced in January 1983 that "1983 will be the year of the struggle against restrictions introduced in legislation during the *trente glorieuses* and which are inappropriate today: the year of the struggle for flexibility."[35] But the CNPF chose not to challenge the government directly. It seemed unlikely that the Socialist government would undo its own legislation so soon after it was enacted. So the strategy chosen by the CNPF was to attempt to reach agreement on flexibility with the trade unions and then present that agreement, as a product of a social consensus, to the government and forcing it to ratify the agreement with the necessary facultative legislation.

In May 1984 the CNPF announced its proposal for "*emplois nouveaux à contraintes allégées*" (ENCAs), which stood for new jobs with reduced legislative constraints attached to them. The idea was that any new hires would be subject to a new regime without many of the normal statutory protections and costs to employers. The ENCA proposal involved the easier use of atypical work contracts, partial exoneration from social security charges, a delayed impact of new hires on the threshold levels of the firm,[36] and the elimination of the requirement for administrative authorization before layoffs.[37] These changes would only apply to new hires (existing ones would continue under the old regime). However, it was not clear what was to prevent existing workers from being fired and new ones hired in their place subject to the new regime. As a sweetner Yvon Gattaz, president of the CNPF since 1981, wielded a survey of employers (conducted by the CNPF) which showed that implementation of the proposal in full would lead to the creation of 471,000 new jobs. With 9.7 percent unemployment in 1984, this was a strong incentive to unions to begin negotiating.[38]

Negotiations followed in the fall of 1984 and culminated, in December 1984, in a proposal from the CNPF for a protocol agreement that was a watered-down version of the original ENCA proposal. The protocol proposed: revising the 1982 legislation on atypical work to loosen the restrictions; annualizing hours;[39] reducing the impact of new hiring on firm thresholds; and while it formally maintained the administrative authorization on layoffs, a number of changes reduced its impact.[40] The protocol found some favor with the leadership of the CFDT, which gave it a "positive recommendation," and the general secretary of FO, Bergeron. But the protocol was widely opposed at lower levels of the CFDT and FO and at all levels of the CGT. Eventually, after consulting with their memberships, all the trade union confederations rejected the plan because it did not provide enough safeguards against misuse.[41] Talks did restart in a half-hearted way in May 1985 but rapidly failed with the unions accusing the CNPF of putting talks on hold until the expected victory of the Right in the March 1986 legislative elections.

Here again the story was similar to that of flexibility in work time. Flexibility required legislative deregulation. But the Socialist government was in a dilemma. It wanted greater flexibility but it feared the misuse of that flexibility by employers. Besides, it could not be seen to countenance flexibility on the employers' terms. Thus, paradoxically, both the government and the CNPF looked to the unions to give legitimacy to an agreement on flexibility, thus getting the government off the hook.[42] The unions were only interested in flexibility that could be supervised by unions in some capacity, not in simply ratifying a plan to give employers carte blanche in the management and organization of the work force. However, the CNPF did not wish simply to replace legislative restrictions with collectively bargained restrictions. It wanted to free the hands of employers in the firm. As Weber has said of CNPF president Yvon Gattaz, he was "in reality more in favor of deregulation than substituting contractual regulation for legislative regulation."[43]

So ultimately the Socialist government could not duck its responsibility. Unions were too weak to act as guardians against deregulation, and they knew it. Employers were not interested in the mild flexibility that the unions did feel able to offer, particularly when they knew that a more sympathetic government lay just around the corner. Indeed, within a year of taking office after the defeat of the Socialists in March 1986, legislation was passed that abolished the requirement for administrative authorization for layoffs and made recourse to various forms of atypical work easier.[44]

Flexibility in Pay Practices

French employers complained a good deal about the rigidity of wages in France, and comparative evidence suggested that wages were indeed more rigid in France than most other advanced capitalist countries.[45] This was in part due to the historical impoverishment of firm-level bargaining so that real wages were not negotiated, rather minimums were set at the branch level. This had been a source of rigidity in the 1950s and 1960s. To this was added the rigidities imposed by the indexation of wages to prices and the activist use of the minimum wage in the early 1970s. This became a greater burden as the decade went on and inflation levels increased. In the 1980s a new, more profound objection appeared from employers: that collective bargaining *itself* prevented a more differentiated, or "individualized," wage structure that could reward individual performance.

Chapters 6 and 7 discussed the partial de-indexation of wages and the decentralization of wage bargaining to the firm level. Both were of tremendous importance. The official survey of collective bargaining in 1986 noted that indexation and safeguard clauses had "practically disappeared"[46] and also that as a result of firm-level bargaining, "the increases in negotiated wages are more and more sensitive to economic developments, both in general and those of the firm."[47]

As for the role of the minimum wage, the Socialists at first intended to use it as a weapon to raise the wages of the low-paid, and it was raised 17 percent in 1981.[48] But this policy did not last. Partly as a result of economic crisis, and partly in response to the growing influence of Delors,[49] the government ceased giving the minimum wage the boosts above inflation that it had intended. Instead Socialist governments were more likely to attempt to trade off restraint in use of the minimum wage for concessions from employers.[50]

The government did formally resist an employer demand for an official subminimum wage for young people, but it created an equivalent, on a smaller scale, by providing for subminimum wages for those hired on a youth unemployment scheme.

It should be noted, though, that despite the government's wish to reduce the role of the minimum wage as a motor for helping the low-paid, it did remain very important for large numbers of people. The government had hoped that collective bargaining would take over from a legislated minimum wage, but a combination of the stagnation of branch-level bargaining and labor market conditions in fact led to an *increase* in the proportion of workers receiving the minimum wage.[51] Thus, after that proportion remaining stable at about 4 percent in the late 1970s, it rose to 8 percent in June 1981, following the sharp increase in the minimum wage when the Socialists took office, and stood at 9.7 percent in July 1985. In fact the figure was much higher for those in small firms employing less than ten people (which are not included in the regular surveys). It was estimated that 45 percent of workers in these firms received the minimum wage.[52]

It was the "individualization of wages" that was the most important development in this period, not just because the practice grew rapidly but also because it has tremendous implications for wage bargaining and indeed for labor regulation itself. Individualization, whether of wages or work hours, or even work contracts, is the logical conclusion of flexibility. It implies an individual relationship between a worker—isolated from any wider collectivity of workers—and the employer.

Individualizing wages meant simply that an ever larger proportion of the wage packet would be made up of an individually assessed component, and hence less and less would come from the general, collectively bargained (or even unilaterally imposed) component. Wages would be tied not to the *job* but to the *individual* performing that job. The logic of individualization, therefore, was the full integration of the worker into the firm—integration in the sense of dependence upon the assessment of his or her work by the established supervisory hierarchy of the firm. This replaces income that is collectively bargained and hence independent of a supervisor's assessment, independent of the individual's performance, and perhaps even independent of the economic situation of the firm itself (for instance, if wages are indexed to prices or other macroeconomic indicators).

It is worth noting an important development here. The New Society wage contracts had attempted to tie wage levels to *macro*economic indicators such as prices and GDP. These contracts embodied a Fordist logic in that they created a link between the level of effective demand and growth in the economy. Individualization of wages, by tying wages to *micro*economic indicators in the firm, embodies an entirely different "post-Fordist" economic logic.

The extent of the individualization of wages is hard to measure because the main source of information is data on collective bargaining, conducted (by definition) with trade unions. Some collective agreements did, in fact, allow for a part of the wage packet to be based on individualized criteria. But this evidence is almost certainly only the tip of the iceberg both because the main union confederations were hostile to this practice, and because where wages are unilaterally set by employers (and hence not negotiated with unions) one might expect individualization to be more widespread. One study quoted a manager as saying that an agreement with unions on individualization is useful only because it "gives a good social facade to the firm."[53]

Individualization, as measured by collective agreements, is more extensive in large firms than small ones, suggesting that smaller firms (either without unions or with weak unions) tend to be able to practice individualization without needing an agreement, while larger ones are forced to negotiate the introduction of individualized wage practices.[54] So it is important to recognize that, for the most part, existing data does not measure the *practice* of individualization but only cases where it is negotiated formally with unions and embedded in a contract.

The official reports on collective bargaining show a significant rise in the practice of individualization. In 1985, 24.5 percent of all firm-level wage agreements had some individualized wage component, while in 1986 the figure was 39.3 percent.[55] At the same time, there was an increase in the use of bonuses to reward individual merit (rather than for seniority, for instance).[56]

The monographic evidence is more interesting than the raw numbers because it provides some explanations for why individualization was used and how it operated.[57] Economic reasons were important. Employers said that individualization acted as an incentive system, it allowed merit and productivity to be rewarded, and it was an indirect way of de-indexing wages from prices.[58] But what is interesting is the extent to which economic factors did not tend to be the most important ones spurring individualization, according to most employers. Individualization was also, and explicitly so, a form of labor control. It reestablished a central role for supervisors while sidestepping the unions as mediators between workers and management. Only a minority of accords on individualization provided for a written, formal evaluation scale; the rest operated in a far more arbitrary manner.[59] As Bodin discovered in his study of small and medium-sized firms, the individualization of wages "rarely takes the form of a formal system. . . . Instead it is a practical demonstration of the discretionary power of the employer."[60] Individualization could be used to punish absenteeism and even, it was claimed, to penalize union membership and activity.[61]

Under these circumstances it is perhaps surprising that unions signed this type of agreement at all. Except for the CGC, which represented the *cadres* and hence supported the practice, all the unions had reservations and the CGT was deeply hostile, as its slogan "Equal pay for equal work" demonstrated.[62] Yet the monographs show very well that many union sections were deeply pessimistic about the impact of individualization and yet signed all the same because employers could proceed without them if they wished. As the study by Grandjean shows, union delegates signed such agreements because "the signature has no particular significance, or rather, the refusal to sign would have no effect."[63] This is a good illustration of the growing isolation of union sections, where they existed, and the way in which such isolation contributed to a de facto enterprise unionism.

In the area of flexibility of wages there was little obstacle posed by legislation. The Socialist government was broadly sympathetic to introducing greater flexibility into wages, and was far less ambivalent or even alert to the possible dangers of flexibility in this area. De-indexation had an important and enduring impact in the private as well as the public sector. But in this area it was the microcorporatist features of the Auroux industrial relations reforms that were most important. The obligation to bargain annually over wages in the firm allowed (in the context of weak unions) employers to set wages at levels that suited the financial situation of the firm.

Conclusion

Between 1981 and 1986 greater flexibility appeared in almost every aspect of the relationship between capital and labor in France. Employers demanded flexibility on a scale, and in areas, which they would not have dreamed of a decade before. The force behind the drive for flexibility was certainly in some sense outside the control of the Socialist government. As in the case of its restrictions on atypical work contracts, its legislative efforts and best intentions could be overwhelmed by the economy, or more accurately, by employers' perceptions of economic imperatives.

However, the fact is that flexibility in the workplace took a qualitative step forward in this period. It is not entirely coincidental that this occurred under a Socialist government, nor were the Socialists (except perhaps for the first two years in office) uniformly hostile to flexibility. On the contrary, when the Right returned to power in March 1986, newly converted to a particularly virulent form of liberalism, and proceeded to sweep away barriers to flexibility, the change nonetheless appeared evolutionary, rather than revolutionary. In a whole series of areas the legislation of the Right merely took a further step in the direction pointed by the Socialists, loosening a restriction here, granting an exemption there.

When the Socialists returned to power after the 1988 legislative elections, there were only very limited attempts to undo the Right's legislation on flexibility. The one area where the Socialists had stood firm—the maintenance of the administrative authorization of layoffs (and whose suppression by the Right in 1986 had provoked lively debate)—was not a campaign issue (at least on the part of the Socialists) in the 1988 elections, nor did the Socialists promise to reestablish it. When the Rocard government did finally introduce legislation on layoffs in May 1989, it went out of its way to stress that the proposed legislation did "not reestablish the administrative authorization for layoffs"[64] but only put in place mechanisms to encourage consultation and training programs for those laid off. Legislation was passed in June 1990 tightening up the regulations surrounding atypical work contracts, but the intent, as in 1982, was to clean up the use of such contracts, not to outlaw them.[65]

One consequence of the greatly increased opportunities for the use of flexible work contracts and flexible pay practices was a polarization and segmentation of the labor force. It is ironic, given the concern shown by the Socialists for dualism when they first arrived in power, that the public and scholarly debate over the growth of "precarious" employment and labor market dualism really took off in the 1980s, under Socialist stewardship. A series of government and other studies, some impressionistic and some statistical, appeared from 1982 onward documenting the impact of flexibility on the labor market.[66] A study by Elbaum looked at the increase in various kinds of *"petits boulots"* (atypical types of work, such as temporary, part-time, and unstable work).[67] Such jobs tended to pay around the minimum wage and to employ a disproportionate number of women, young people, and immigrants. (For instance, 82 percent of part-time workers were women.) In March 1987 there were 1.2 million of these *petits boulots*, an increase of 14.5 percent since 1983.

Piotet has talked not about dualism, in the classic sense, but a deeper fragmentation of the work force,[68] and a study by Linhart and Maruani went further and concluded on a very pessimistic note: "It is the very notion of stability of employment that is at stake, and with it the idea of a secure and stable core [of employment] so what we are now seeing is a renaissance of the market *'pur et dur.'* There are two types of job (precarious jobs and stable jobs), but one looks in vain to find two labor markets."[68]

In addition to the growth in unstable and precarious forms of employment, there was growing evidence that income inequality, having diminished in the course of the 1970s, began to widen again in France from the mid-1980s onward.[69]

The introduction of flexibility in France had two preconditions. The first was that the state be prepared to withdraw from labor regulation. In France, in a way that is less true in other advanced capitalist countries, introducing flexibility involved state deregulation. This followed from the particular history of labor regulation in France, which had led to an especially extensive role for the state and the regulation of many aspects of industrial relations by legislation, where elsewhere they were regulated by collective bargaining. Thus employers had to look first to the state and only later to the trade unions in their quest for flexibility. This gave the French state a pivotal role in the introduction of flexibility.

The Socialists were prepared to accept that some flexibility was necessary. In a variety of areas, particularly work time and wages, it was the state that took the most active part in creating the conditions for greater flexibility. But the Socialists, despite a growing enthusiasm for flexibility, did not want complete deregulation and a *precarious* form of flexibility. Thus they hesitated, and attempted to persuade the unions to negotiate agreements on flexibility which the government could then ratify, bowing, as it were, to the will of the social partners. The problem was that employers were not seriously interested in a negotiated flexibility, except of the kind that would be suicidal for the trade unions.

The second precondition, and the most important given the obstacle posed by the stalemate between state, trade unions, and business, was the creation of an embryonic microcorporatism. If the Socialists were hesitant and the social partners deadlocked, the path to flexibility lay through a decentralized industrial relations system that focused labor regulation where flexibility was most needed, and where there was only a limited capacity of the unions to resist it: the firm. In the firm the trade unions could be ignored, or at least confronted on terrain where they were weak. As the examples of flexibility in work time and individualization of wages demonstrated, the capacity to derogate legislation and the obligation to bargain at the firm level allowed employers to impose flexibility (regardless of the attitude of unions in branch negotiations, and even of the government). It was in their encouragement of a microcorporatist mode of labor regulation that the French Socialists made their greatest contribution to the introduction of flexibility in France. Thus flexibility in France was the product of a partial deregulation on the part of the state and a simultaneous decentralization of labor regulation to the firm.

PART FOUR

Conclusion

CHAPTER NINE

The Future of Labor Regulation

A SUMMARY OF THE ARGUMENT

This study has traced the evolution of labor regulation in France through a series of important industrial relations reform projects in the period since May 1968. In that year a massive wave of strikes brought the French economy to a standstill and threatened the presidency of General de Gaulle thereby setting the agenda for industrial relations reform for the next twenty years. In a number of different political guises—Gaullist, neo-Gaullist, liberal, and Socialist—the French state has sought to respond to the threat posed by the events of 1968.

French industrial relations in the immediate postwar period demonstrated a very poor degree of institutionalization. Collective bargaining was limited in both range and scope. Where it did take place it only rarely involved firm-level bargaining or the negotiation of real wages. Rather, collective agreements, where they existed, tended to be negotiated at the branch or industry-level and concentrated upon setting wage minimums and the broad conditions of work in a particular industry. Only in a small number of modern, technologically advanced, mass-production firms did collective bargaining approach the frequency and form that was the norm in much of the rest of Western Europe. Elsewhere the labor market remained the main instrument of labor regulation.

In large part the weakness of collective bargaining resulted from the weakness of the French labor movement. Trade union confederations with low, fluctuating levels of membership and deep interconfederal rivalries and ideological differences were both too weak to impose bargaining on a *patronat* that was notoriously antiunion and jealous of the prerogatives of property ownership, and too unreliable as bargaining partners. French trade unions exercised only very limited control over their members and were thus rarely able or willing to sign contracts that committed them to maintaining industrial peace. Employers drew the conclusion that French trade unions were of little use in controlling social conflict in the firm, and until after the events of 1968 union activity was not legally protected in the workplace.

This particular form of French exceptionalism might potentially have posed a problem for the political economy. From the perspective of employers in the period immediately after World War II, unions could potentially serve two useful functions. One was to channel and mediate social conflict, to "institutionalize class conflict" in the academic language of the time. In France this was unnecessary in the ten or fifteen years after the Liberation because of the very weakness of labor and the steady increase in the industrial labor force, which resulted from a shrinking agricultural sector. The second function of trade unions was more economic than social.[1] Most European economies, from the 1920s onward, began to make the transition from extensive to intensive accumulation. What this entailed was a change from a form of capitalist growth that relied on the addition of new productive factors (for instance, through an expansion of the labor force or shrinking of the noncapitalist sector) to an intensive form of capitalist growth that relied on the constant expansion of domestic demand. The latter form of growth has, for shorthand purposes, been labeled Fordist because its essence is nicely captured by the image (part true, part mythological) of Henry Ford's mass-production techniques used to produce cars for more than simply a luxury market, while simultaneously paying wages that would enable his workers to buy the goods they produced. Thus Fordism involved a circuit between production and consumption in which wages cease to be merely costs of production but rather increase steadily in line with productivity in order to expand the market for mass-produced goods. The economic role of trade unions and collective bargaining was precisely to close that circuit.

Yet in contrast to the other major industrial powers, France in fact did not develop a properly Fordist economy until the mid-1960s. As a result of the Gaullist modernization program begun in 1958 the French economy was transformed from its dependency upon protected, colonial markets and luxury goods. But until that time the absence of collective-bargaining mechanisms was not an obstacle to growth, and regulation by the labor market remained acceptable for the extensive phase of economic growth.

However, as the modernization program progressed and France came to more closely resemble its Fordist neighbors, the strains of a mode of labor regulation designed for an earlier type of economic growth began to appear. In particular, the costs of economic restructuring—higher unemployment and an incomes policy to build profits and provide state funds for modernization—fell squarely upon the working class, which had the misfortune to be excluded from the broad Gaullist coalition and therefore unprotected. The result, in conjunction with international economic changes, a revival of union organization, and student revolt, was May 1968.

The wave of strikes in 1968 posed such severe problems of social order, economic growth, and political legitimation that it came to dominate any discussion of industrial relations for the next twenty years. All governments, whatever their electoral constituency, social base, or ideological hue, were forced to respond to it. Broadly speaking, the responses were of two kinds, with a third acting as a default whenever the primary responses failed. The first response was to "modernize" French industrial relations along the familiar lines of much of the rest of the advanced capitalist world. This involved strengthening trade unions and encouraging collective bargaining between unions and employers. The second type of response involved bypassing trade unions organizations so as to encourage firm-specific forms of employee representation to emerge, with the intention that they would serve the same channeling and mediating function of trade unions but minimize the influence of the wider, extra-firm interests of workers and emphasize their common interest with the firm that employed them. The third response was expanded state intervention in industrial relations to *substitute* for failure in other forms of labor regulation.

After de Gaulle briefly, and half-heartedly, attempted the second strategy of bypassing trade unions, and failed because he underestimated the renewed influence of unions after the events of May–June 1968, Pompidou's first prime minister, Chaban-Delmas, attempted the first strategy in his New Society program. This self-conscious reform project was a clear and deliberate effort to change the mode of labor regulation in France in the direction of stronger trade unions and regularized collective bargaining. It had some success, particularly in the public sector where the government had the greatest influence and was prepared to buy collective bargaining with lucrative wage contracts, and in the large, modern Fordist sector of the private economy where union recognition and collective bargaining were most clearly appropriate.

Yet, globally, the project was a failure because where it did exist it was heavily contingent upon economic prosperity and government encouragement, and because much of the French economy remained without regularized collective bargaining. French labor remained too weak to impose bargaining on employers, and legislative remedies could have little impact on union strength in the short term. In the remainder of the economy, primarily the traditional sector of the private economy, the third response appeared. The French state used its administrative and legislative powers to create a peculiarly statist form of labor regulation. An activist use of the minimum wage, "extension" of collective agreements, constraints on the labor market, and so on, in a sense substituted for the weakness of trade unions. This despite the fact that the reforms were undertaken by a conservative government that had little time for labor. Thus by 1974 France had a dualistic mode of labor regulation comprising a collective-bargaining regime in the public sector and modern parts of the private sector, and a statist form of labor regulation in the traditional parts of the private sector.

There is some irony in the fact that no sooner had France made the transition to a Fordist economy and begun to grapple with the problems of constructing a form of labor regulation appropriate to this new stage of economic growth, than Fordism itself, throughout the advanced capitalist world, went into crisis. At first this appeared simply as a particularly severe cyclical downturn brought on by the exogenous shock of the oil price rise, but it soon became clear that the oil shock had uncovered more serious structural weaknesses in the industrial economies.

The span of Giscard d'Estaing's presidency closely coincided with this period of economic transition. Thus although Giscard d'Estaing and his prime ministers bubbled with proposals for industrial relations reform, partly in response to the growing intensity of electoral competition, labor regulation was deeply colored by economic uncertainty. The twin pillars of existing labor regulation began to erode as their economic viability declined. The heavily indexed public-sector contracts were too rigid and expensive to maintain in a period of high inflation, while collective bargaining in the modern Fordist sector of the economy became both less necessary as union membership declined and militancy subsided, and less attractive in the context of saturated markets and the need for greater flexibility in production. The heavily statist form of labor regulation also came under pressure because of its costs to the state budget and claims that it imposed too severe costs—both financial and in terms of lost adaptability—on private-sector firms.

Thus the Socialists arrived in power in 1981 at a time when the material supports of the old mode of labor regulation had collapsed, or were in the process of collapsing, and yet no alternative had yet been put in its place. It was clear from the actions and pronouncements of the main organizations representing French employers that any future form of labor regulation would have to be able to respond flexibly to rapidly changing international economic conditions. The rigidity of Fordist forms of labor regulation was now considered an obstacle to economic dynamism, just as that very rigidity had once been an essential bulwark of growth.

Nevertheless, it mattered how the new Socialist government chose to respond to this situation. In the event, the Socialists' first response, embodied in the Auroux Laws, was, on the surface at least, a denial that anything had changed. It was fundamentally anachronistic in the sense that the reform project, in seeking to deepen and extend the New Society reforms, was modeled upon a Fordist economy. It failed to recognize that such an economy was fast disappearing, and hence that any form of labor regulation based upon it could not succeed.

However, alongside the primary reform project was a secondary project which emerged out of the peculiar history and organization of the French Socialist party, and the long-standing suspicion of corporatism and bureaucratic trade unions which marked important segments of the French Left. This *autogestionnaire* current existed in a dormant form within the Auroux Laws. The compatibility that existed between this secondary project and the new managerial emphasis on flexibility ensured that, in the context of the mid-1980s, it was this project that triumphed while trade unions continued to decline. The result was that instead of the Socialist industrial relations project being simply stymied and rendered irrelevant by its anachronism, it instead acted to encourage the development of a new mode of labor regulation that was focused on the firm and on firm-specific collectivities of workers.

The Frailty of State Power

The argument contained within this study operates at a number of different levels. By its very nature the story told here involves a complex interrelationship between broad economic forces, institutional forms, the actions of major social groups, and state policy itself. The central episodes discussed here revolve around the formulation, implementation, and subsequent fate of state policy. The study deliberately focuses on the major industrial relations reform projects undertaken by the French state since 1968. However, no claim is being made here about the primacy of the political or the dominant role of the state. On the contrary, I think that any observer will come away from this study with an enhanced sense of the frailty of state power and the limits to its exercise. This is particularly clear in the period since about 1976 when employers have sought a deregulation of industrial relations and a decentralization of labor regulation to the firm level, and internationalization of the world economy has narrowed the space available for purely "national" solutions to economic problems.

More importantly, I have no wish to enter any debate that insists upon assigning causal primacy to either the economic or the political. It is frankly facile to do so. The use of a mechanical causality of this sort can only ever be a misrepresentation of reality, with few clear benefits for either theory or an understanding of society. In truth, the disciplinary boundaries of the social sciences say far more about the *object* of study than about the direction of causality. The great strength of political economy as a discipline is precisely its capacity for overcoming these boundary disputes. This study emphasizes the French state as an actor, in part because the state has been neglected in discussions of industrial relations, but it recognizes that any state, even one as powerful as the French, operates within a series of overlapping structures which both impose action upon that state and limit the kinds of action available to it.

In the case of this study I assign tremendous importance to the economy. The French economy, like all other industrial economies, underwent a series of major transformations in the forty or so years following World War II. These changes were not entirely outside the control of the French state, but they were sufficiently broad, long term, and international in scope, that in practice governments tended to respond to these transformations rather than to control them. It is here that the Regulation framework seems useful because it suggests that a wide range of institutions are required for a given pattern of economic growth to operate relatively smoothly. In this study I have chosen to focus upon only those institutions that exist in the sphere of industrial relations and that I have termed, collectively, a mode of labor regulation, because it seems self-evident that as a capitalist economy changes so must the institutions that regulate and mediate conflict between capital and labor.

Thus at critical junctures industrial relations institutions proved inadequate to the pattern of economic growth. This "dysfunctionality" was made apparent to governments through crisis, certainly economic and social crisis, and often political crisis as well. The best example is May 1968, but the economic crisis that faced the Socialist government in 1982–83 is another. In these cases governments were *forced* to act; crises tend to accelerate the learning process of governments! But no imperative determined in what way particular governments would respond. More fundamentally, a variety of policy choices existed, of which more than one might be successful. For example, the crisis of May 1968 forced the government of Chaban-Delmas to reform industrial relations, but more than one form of labor regulation was compatible with the Fordist nature of the economy. In fact, when collective bargaining had only limited success the government was able to achieve many of the same ends through a statist mode of labor regulation. Thus what is determined is the boundaries, the *space* for choice, not the choices themselves. This is why state policy matters, even if it is deeply misleading to assert that a state is autonomous or that politics has primacy over economics.

This study suggests that at critical moments the French state was able to act, and that its actions in the area of labor regulation were important. The French state in the postwar period was always fundamentally constrained by two factors: the late and short-lived appearance of a Fordist mass-production economy, and the weakness of the French labor movement. These two factors placed limits on the reform projects of successive governments. But they did not prevent governments from acting.

In chapter 1 a schematic representation of modes of labor regulation was constructed along two axes: the *level* of labor regulation, and the form of labor *collectivity*. This study suggests that the French state found it much easier to alter the locus of labor regulation, particularly by expanding or contracting the role of state involvement in industrial relations, than to change the collectivity of labor. The French state's failure to expand labor collectivity reflects the tremendous weakness of the French labor movement. It also helps to explain why the French state tended to respond to a crisis of labor regulation by expanding its own role in labor regulation.

This study, in focusing upon the state, may also appear to downplay the role of major social actors, in this case the organizations of labor and capital. That would be misleading. Again, no assignment of the importance of social actors relative to the state is being made. It is clear that the actions and strategies of trade unions and employers' organizations were important in the French case, not least because these strategies were often transmitted to the state. For example, the influence of the CFDT on the Auroux reforms has been noted, and before 1981 employers' demands were often incorporated into state actions and employers frequently seemed to have a veto over policy, as in the case of the Sudreau reforms. In any case the boundaries between social actors and states are deeply permeable and the notion of the state as a separate, autonomous actor with distinct interests of its own can be overdrawn.

One final issue that is important here is the role played by partisan difference. When this study was first envisaged it seemed that a useful comparison could probably be made between the responses of different types of government to the crisis posed by May 1968. Thus the industrial relations policies of Gaullist, neo-Gaullist, liberal, and Socialist governments could be compared. In fact, politics, in the narrow sense of partisan difference, was of limited importance. Ideology appears to have played an important role in de Gaulle's short-lived experiment with *participation* in 1968–69, and certainly the Socialists' concern for the democratization of work was motivated by ideology and the party's social and electoral base. Far more remarkable, however, are the continuities and the similarities. Microcorporatist labor regulation appeared under the guise of Gaullist *participation*, Sudreau's reform of the firm, and Socialist *autogestion*, and there were many similarities between Chaban-Delmas's New Society project and the Socialist attempt to develop collective bargaining and strengthen trade unions. At least in the sphere of industrial relations one emerges from this study with a renewed sense of the plasticity and interchangeability of ideology.

Yet political power was important. It mattered that the French Socialists came to power in 1981. The previous government had failed to escape the stalemate imposed by an economy in crisis and a militant labor movement. The mode of labor regulation that emerged after 1982–83 owed a great deal to the particular features of the Socialist reform project. Socialist political power was certainly constrained. The context within which the Socialist government attempted to act operated both to *limit* that government's choices and to *select* and reinforce certain aspects of the reform project at the expense of others. In this way politics and state power are crucial elements of any understanding of the evolution of labor regulation in France, but they are incomprehensible outside a given historical and economic context.

The Future of Trade Unions and Labor Regulation in France

Chapter 7 outlined the decline in the influence of organized labor that has taken place in France since the mid-1970s. By any measure—union membership, union sections, union representation on works councils—trade unions have been weakened to the point that it raises serious questions about the potential of the French labor movement to recover. As a recent OECD country survey for France demonstrates, despite significant disinflation, fair growth, and a marked rebuilding of profits since 1984,[2] the level of unemployment in France is much higher than the OECD average and shows only very slow signs of falling.[3] The OECD argues, in a manner familiar to those who have read the surveys of France in previous years, that the obstacle to lowering the level of unemployment remains wage rigidity and the high level of employer social security contributions. Perhaps. It may be that more of the same—greater flexibility and continued wage restraint—will finally make French firms competitive and lead to increased employment.[4]

The important question, however, is whether the current weakness of French labor is conjunctural and cyclical only, or whether that weakness has been transformed into a structural weakness that will endure even if the labor market improves in the future. It is a question to which no firm answer can be given. But I want to argue that the change in labor regulation is more structural than conjunctural. It seems to me that a new mode of labor regulation is in the process of being created, one in which the role of labor has been fundamentally transformed.

There has been much discussion both in and out of the academy of the "normalizing" or "modernizing" role of Mitterrand since 1981.[5] It is argued that Mitterrand has managed to thaw out the deep ideological divide between Left and Right which has existed since at least the founding of the French Communist party, and perhaps the French Revolution itself. The experience of actually governing has moderated the French Socialist party, while the Communist party has returned to a ghetto that is getting smaller every day. It is in the areas of economic and education policy, and above all in the realm of ideological discourse, that most discussions of normalization are concerned. Most commentators have remarked upon the Socialists' "end of illusions."[6]

However, at least as important is the realm of industrial relations. The scale of the sea change can be gauged by a survey of employers in 1987.[7] While large majorities believed the Right more capable of achieving certain *macroeconomic* ends (encouraging growth, balancing trade, reducing the budget deficit, maintaining the value of the franc), an overwhelming majority (80 percent) believed that a president of the Left would be more capable of avoiding social conflicts, and on the issue of containing wage rises 47 percent believed a president of the Left would be more successful, while only 28 percent believed a president of the Right would be more successful. *Le Monde* commented that "serenity has replaced fear" in the face of a victory of the Left.[8]

More fundamentally, as Rosanvallon has pointed out,[9] the Auroux Laws paradoxically marked the end of a century of debate over, and movement toward, greater democratization of the firm. In a very real sense the French Socialist party's most important contribution to the "modernization" of France has been the creation of a system of industrial relations with a structural bias toward cooperation rather than conflict. Any discussion of future transformation of the firm now concerns greater management-labor cooperation and participation by workers in the life of the firm, not the elimination of private ownership and workers' control. No group within the PS currently contemplates an extension of the rights and powers of workers or trade unions. Socialist governments since 1988 have translated the austerity policies of the early 1980s, which were designed as short-term responses to economic crisis, into a permanent policy bias toward wage restraint, fiscal conservatism, and reduced corporation tax.[10] As Cohen has said, "The arrival of the Left in the context of crisis was necessary to prove to the unions that in an open economy there existed incontrovertible rules of the game."[11] Thus both at the level of discourse and at the level of the political projects of the Left, there has been important change.

At the same time as Socialists and trade unionists have scaled back their expectations, employers have seized the opportunity to demand further marginalization of the role of both trade unions and legislation in the firm. In 1985, Entreprise et Progrès, representing the progressive wing of the French *patronat*, proposed a "*contrat collectif d'entreprise.*" In place of the bargaining monopoly of the trade unions, workers in a given firm would elect representatives to negotiate and sign contracts with management. These contracts would be for a fixed duration (one to three years) and contain an *indivisible* package of wages, conditions of work, flexibility measures, and so on. The right to derogate from existing legislation and collective agreements reached at higher levels would also be greatly expanded because, as the report said, "Legislation is no longer capable of comprehending the reality of our complex and changing society."[12] Thus the Entreprise et Progrès proposal simultaneously attacked the role of trade unions and the role of the state inside the firm.

A proposal from the Centre des jeunes dirigeants d'entreprise in June 1986 was only slightly less radical. It too called for the end of the unions' monopoly on bargaining, to be replaced by a *conseil d'entreprise* which would take the place of all other representative institutions in the firm.[13] This body would then negotiate with management.[14] Such proposals would further accelerate a transformation of labor regulation that is already much advanced. Proposals such as these would not have been considered serious a decade ago. But as the unionized segment of the labor force shrinks, providing unions with a formal monopoly on bargaining seems increasingly anachronistic and adds plausibility to new managerial initiatives.

The defining feature of the newly emerging mode of labor regulation, which I have termed microcorporatist, is that the firm becomes the dominant locus of labor regulation, and the boundaries of the firm become ever more impermeable to outside influence, be it that of the state expressed through legislation and the Labor Code, or a wider collectivity of workers represented by trade unions. The point is that new forms of management that create or reinforce "microcollectivities" of work have a "de-unifying [*désolidarisant*] effect not only at the level of the union organization, but on the workers' movement itself."[15] Amadieu has put forward the hypothesis, one this study shares, that what is taking place now in France is the creation of an *enterprise unionism*, whether it be genuine enterprise unions in the sense of firm-specific unions, or de facto enterprise unions where nominally national union organizations undergo a kind of decapitation so that local unions *act* as enterprise unions.[16]

This leaves the national union organizations as "semipublic" service organizations.[17] Their role becomes that of lobbying governments, legitimizing government initiatives in the realm of social or economic policy,[18] and lending expertise and support to spontaneous strikes. As Furjot and Noel note in a more recent study of strikes in France, in the future unions will appear more "as experts, putting their experience, their infrastructure, and their technical competence at the disposition of strikers who would maintain control [of the strike]."[19] There is thus increasingly a discontinuity between trade unions at the national and industry level, and trade unions at the firm level.

A microcorporatist mode of labor regulation has a structural bias toward cooperation, rather than conflict, because workers in a given firm, isolated from the protection of a wider collectivity of workers or legislation, begin "to identify their interests with those of the firm."[20] It should be quickly stated that this is an enforced cooperation; it does not necessarily imply any change in the attitudes of workers, though that may follow.[21] Rather, if the main "power resource" of labor is its collectivity and hence its capacity for collective action (as this study has argued), microcorporatist labor regulation implies a drastic reduction in the power resources of labor. It is no surprise then that studies of union responses to the individualization of wages in France show very clearly that unions will sign agreements that they basically do not like because their choice is that or irrelevance.

One indirect indication of a change in labor regulation is change in the pattern of French strikes. Since 1977 the number of days lost to industrial action has declined from 3.67 million to 0.90 million in 1989,[22] and strikes have tended to become less frequent, shorter, and involve fewer workers.[23] Overall this suggests a marked decline in the propensity of French workers to strike.

Of course, to some extent, the dramatic reduction in the strike level in France in the past decade is due to adverse labor market conditions and might be expected to revert to form if and when unemployment is reduced. For instance, it could be argued that the recent resurgence of strikes in the public sector, first in the winter of 1986–87, and more recently in the fall of 1988 and 1989, indicates that worker combativity was only temporarily driven underground and has returned as economic conditions improve.[24] And yet these strikes have occurred in only heavily protected and highly unionized parts of the public sector—rail, metro, postal workers, and so on, those with long traditions of militancy. These are precisely the sectors of the economy where microcorporatist labor regulation has made the least inroads. Trade unions remain relatively strong and collective bargaining is both regular and conducted at the industry level. Further, as Furjot and Noel say of the 1986–87 strike, "The fact that a conflict can, on its own, modify the statistics . . . is itself revealing."[25] Public-sector strikes accounted for 87 percent of general conflicts in 1986.[26]

More important than the number of strikes, though, is their form. Conflicts increasingly tend to be very brief, spontaneous stoppages rather than extended strikes. This kind of conflict is logical in the context of microcorporatist labor regulation, because it originates in the firm, requires limited organization and resources, and is intended more to make a point than to threaten the financial viability of the firm itself. But as a form of industrial action these conflicts have the drawback that they prevent wider action and limit the *experience* of collective action. The dangers are nicely captured in Furjot and Noel's formulation that being "without memory, they are also usually without a tomorrow."[27]

The widespread deregulation of the labor market, the decentralization of bargaining, and the decapitation of trade unions fundamentally alters the fragile balance of power between workers and employers in France. In contrast to most West European trade union movements, the golden age of French unions—lasting perhaps a total of only seven or eight years after May 1968—was brief and the gains were limited. But there were gains nonetheless. Real wages rose, the range of income inequality narrowed, and a plethora of social programs were either negotiated with employers or legislated by the state, or both. The reversal since the mid-1980s, as chapters 6 and 8 sought to demonstrate, has been dramatic. Unions now negotiate concessions, not gains, wages have barely kept pace with inflation, unemployment is close to double figures, and income inequality has grown.

In the event that unemployment falls appreciably in France in the future it will be possible to test whether the emerging form of labor regulation has been built upon the shaky foundation of mass unemployment and will collapse once that condition ends, or whether it is a durable form built upon a new organization and integration of workers around the firm. The evidence presented in earlier chapters suggests that the latter scenario is the more plausible. Workers have not simply been *demobilized* by unemployment, they have been *remobilized* and reorganized in new ways that place structural limits upon collective action, and that demand a new, stronger identification with the firm. Thus we are not observing quantitative change only—a decline in union membership, a decline in strike levels—but qualitative change in which the labor movement is *restructured*, and conflicts between labor and capital (which will certainly continue) change in form.

If France is indeed seeing the emergence of a microcorporatist mode of labor regulation, it has profound implications for the role (and even the existence) of trade unions, the capability of the state to intervene in labor regulation, the adaptive capacity of firms, and above all, for workers themselves.

THE COMPARATIVE IMPLICATIONS OF A POST-FORDIST POLITICAL ECONOMY

This has not been a comparative study, rather it has sought to examine and explain important developments in political economy through the lens of a single case. My pessimism about the future of trade unions in France need not have implications for labor movements in other advanced capitalist countries. The French experience is easily assimilated into the notion of a French exceptionalism, in the sense of a notoriously weak labor movement and conflictual industrial relations. In fact, if one were looking for a country where labor might be expected to have lost out disproportionately from the economic changes since the first oil shock, France is where one would probably look first. Organized labor in France lacked the political resources, the numbers, and the network of industrial relations institutions to weather the battering it has taken.

It would be a mistake, however, to write off the French experience as having little by the way of lessons or relevance for other countries. In the context of the emerging post-Fordist political economy, France is a better mirror for the rest of the advanced capitalist world, in the realm of labor regulation at least, than one might think. While divergence and the existence of distinct national patterns of labor regulation marked the Fordist period of economic growth, it can be argued, albeit cautiously and provisionally, that there are good grounds for anticipating convergence in the future.

Social scientists observing the responses of the industrialized nations to the first oil shock noted marked divergences in those responses.[28] This provided compelling evidence against hypotheses of convergence in industrial societies, which had been popular in the 1950s and 1960s.[29] The emphasis on divergence, and the importance of particular national histories and patterns of economic policy-making, have, I think, remained the dominant strains within political economy up to the present.

This is particularly true in the area of industrial relations.[30] What is perhaps surprising is that the Regulation School now exemplifies this tendency. In the mid-1980s, when this study was initiated, the Regulation School was most notable for its focus on the institutional and regulatory requirements of a given pattern of capitalist growth. As I noted in chapter 1, the Regulation School implied that Fordism in one country was little different from Fordism in another, and hence that similar modes of regulation and institutions of industrial relations were necessary in each country with a Fordist economy.

Since that time, like any multifaceted and arresting paradigm the Regulation approach has fragmented and the term "Regulation" has come to refer to a wide range of phenomena. The original approach, for all the disclaimers of many of its adherents, was deeply economistic in that it recognized modes of regulation as, fundamentally, responses to an economic logic imparted by a stage of capitalist growth. That is no longer true. The extent to which the economy is determinant in the Regulation approach is now much reduced. Indeed in its use by some scholars Regulation has come to respond to a fundamentally political, or even ideological/cultural, logic.[31] Among those who focus on industrial relations more narrowly, such as Boyer, there has been an explicit statement of the wide variety of institutional forms compatible with a given pattern of economic growth and a denial that an economic logic is determinant. Thus in Boyer's work the notion of divergence in national forms of labor regulation is reinforced.[32]

The development and elaboration of the Regulation approach in recent years is welcome, and in any case inevitable. Regulation theory now provides a much more nuanced form of analysis, one more sensitive to the range of regulatory mechanisms that are possible at any given time, and to the importance of deeply embedded national social formations. Yet some of the power of the original explanatory framework has been lost in the emphasis on national types and divergence. The loss is particularly unfortunate because the renewed interest in national difference has come at precisely the time when there is mounting evidence of a *narrowing* of national regulatory forms.

If one had been able to take a snapshot of the different national systems of industrial relations in 1973, just before the onset of economic crisis, and then take another today, there would clearly have been much divergence in forms of industrial relations in 1973 and there would also be much divergence today. But what is also true, I think, is that the *contrast* between the two pictures would be more remarkable than the range of variation within each picture.

In 1973 trade unions everywhere played a central role in industrial relations and were *recognized*, by state and employers alike, as the sole legitimate representatives of labor. This was true even where, as in France, the unionized portion of the work force was relatively small. Collective bargaining, whether highly centralized in corporatist arrangements or more decentralized, between unions and employers was the norm, and where it was not, a variety of transfer mechanisms ensured that the gains of collective bargaining were diffused more generally into the poorly unionized sectors of the economy. Above all, social relations in the workplace were highly institutionalized, either by legislation or collective agreement, so as to rigidify every aspect of the capitalist wage relation and work process. Wages, working conditions, and employment all shared this high degree of institutionalization, and this condition was widely considered beneficial.

In the 1990s, albeit to a greater or lesser degree from one country to another, these linchpins of postwar industrial relations are under attack.[33] This process goes well beyond the decomposition of corporatist arrangements alone. Trade union membership has fallen everywhere,[34] and unions' ability and legitimacy to represent workers has been challenged by employers and often the state. Collective bargaining has been decentralized and become more formal: the negotiation of concessions from labor rather than new gains. And, most important, flexibility has come to dominate discourse and to permeate every aspect of workplace social relations. Under the banner of flexibility a whole range of employment protections, wage guarantees, and de facto worker or union controls over the work process have been challenged.

The durability of these changes is arguable but the direction is not, nor is the contrast between this and the earlier pre-1973 period. The danger for a political economy that emphasizes national divergence is that it cannot explain broad transnational change. Above all it cannot explain the transformation in political economy that is taking place in the advanced capitalist world, it can only document its particular national physiognomy.

This is not the place for a comprehensive discussion of the newly emerging political economy, nor do I have the expertise for such a task. Neverthe-

less, some discussion of post-Fordism and, in particular, of its consequences for labor movements will help to explain why my pessimism about
the future of labor movements is not limited to the French case.

Post-Fordism implies, most simply, the eclipse of the nation-state as the
primary locus of economic power. In the heyday of Fordism the nation-
state occupied a strategic position which allowed it to exercise significant
influence over the national economy. This was never equivalent to control,
nor could it be in an economy based on private ownership, but it did mean
that, directly and indirectly, states had sufficient power to alter the environment that individual owners of capital faced and thus influence their decisions. In particular, it was the predominance of the domestic market as a
source of demand that gave the nation-state its power. States had tremendous influence over the level and composition of that demand.

Internationalization, market saturation and fragmentation, new technology, and new economic institutions have eroded the importance of domestic markets and with it the influence of the nation-state. It can be argued, I think, that there has been a simultaneous shift in economic power
"outward" from the state to the international economy and "downward"
from the state to the firm.

The increased mobility of international firms, the greater proportion of
what is produced being traded, and the greater importance and speed of
currency flows have all narrowed the space within which states can pursue
distinct national policy packages. The prison walls of the market, in Lindblom's metaphor, have become more constraining as a result of the increased importance of international markets.[35] This shift in economic
power from the state to the international economy is a long-standing one.
In this context the project to unify a single European market (SEM) by the
end of 1992 is a special, and very important, case. It can be viewed as an
acceleration of the tendencies outlined above.[36]

The SEM project is still under construction and its exact shape is un-
known. But its likely impact, both upon the economic powers of member
states and upon European labor movements, is likely to be devastating. The
project involves a transfer of economic power from the individual states,
not to a new political entity (since no such supranational coordinating
structure is planned for this task), but to ever more mobile capital, now
with enhanced capability and incentive to cross national boundaries. The
form of European integration currently envisaged is unbalanced in the
sense that political integration is much less developed than economic
integration.

The creation of a system of fixed exchange rates and a European central
bank modeled on the independence of the German Bundesbank removes
exchange-rate and monetary policy from the hands of member states; the
greater mobility of people and capital encourages a convergence of tax rates

thus constraining fiscal policy; European competition policy outlaws government subsidies hence limiting the ability to have an industrial policy; and the principle of "mutual recognition" encourages a situation in which firms "shop" around for attractive national regulatory regimes.[37]

The major tools with which national governments traditionally influence the economy—exchange-rate policy, monetary policy, fiscal policy, trade policy, industrial policy, and regulatory policy—are weakened or stripped from states. It is possible that at some point these powers will be recentralized in an invigorated European state, but such a development will lag well behind the process of economic integration. The overall impact is to instill a fundamentally *deregulatory logic* to the process of European integration. Thus, while the SEM project can be seen as an attempt to revitalize Fordism through what Streeck calls a new "Euro-Fordism," based on a larger market for mass-produced consumer goods, it is more likely that 1992 will enhance and reinforce a post-Fordist economic logic, and flexibility in all its forms.[38]

European labor movements (and their social democratic allies) have been largely left out of the planning and construction of the 1992 project.[39] At an organizational level unions are much less able to take advantage of a unified market than business, and all the problems of collective action that workers' organizations traditionally face[40] are only exacerbated at the European level. Trade unions are likely to see national collective-bargaining systems, national wage structures, and national welfare systems eroded by the "regime competition" created by more mobile capital.[41] The attempt to place a floor under wages and conditions through a "Social Charter" has so far been disappointing. Distinct national industrial relations systems are unlikely to survive the SEM, and the hopes of European labor movements must lie in the construction of a European system of industrial relations to take their place. That will be a very slow process indeed.

At the same time as states face greater international constraints on their range of action, so the demands from firms for greater autonomy and flexibility in their ability to respond to market changes imply a shift in the locus of economic power from states to firms. Whereas previously, national regulatory frameworks were put in place by legislation or collective bargaining, now firms are more likely to demand either the removal of certain regulations completely or their renegotiation at the firm level. There is a good deal of debate about the implications for trade unions and industrial relations systems of this much greater emphasis upon flexibility in the firm. Commentators have suggested a number of different possible futures, of different versions of flexibility.

For Piore and Sabel the main "divide" is between a renewal of Fordist mass production on a global scale, and a more or less benign form of "flexible specialization" based on small, community-based flexible craft production, and even a new "yeoman democracy."[42] In the *Second Industrial Divide* there is little discussion of alternative, less cooperative forms of flexibility. This is perhaps because Piore and Sabel believe that flexible specialization will require highly skilled craftsworkers who will thus have the bargaining power to demand a participatory form of workplace flexibility. Thus the economic and technological requirements of flexible specialization would themselves ensure—should this path be chosen—a benign flexibility.

Other commentators (and indeed Sabel himself in other places)[43] have been less concerned with a possible renewal of Fordism and instead see two competing versions of flexibility: a benign version similar to that of Piore and Sabel, in which labor and trade unions are given a role in the organization and running of the firm, and where skills are upgraded and jobs "enriched"; and a "Naples model" in which flexibility means the elimination of trade unions from the workplace, and the predominance of low-skill, low-wage jobs. Davis's chilling descriptions of the labor market in modern-day Los Angeles,[44] and the evidence of a resurgence of sweatshop conditions in New York, should make it clear that there is no automatic link between the rise of post-Fordism and the more benign version of flexibility. After all, one person's flexibility is another's precarious, marginal employment. So the question becomes what determines whether the future of flexibility brings with it the resurgence of the skilled, independent craftsworker, or the sweatshop worker and the emergence of a polarized "split-level economy?"[45]

A consensus is emerging that the future is open, in the sense that no economic or technological dynamic determines which of these possible futures will triumph. As Mahon, in the course of an excellent review of the literature, succinctly puts it, "Technology *per se* has no predetermined socio-economic impact, rather its impact is shaped by the ways it is put to use and that, in turn, is shaped by the broader socio-economic environment."[46] Sorge and Streeck make the same point and are at pains to deny that industrial relations are determined, in some narrow and mechanical way, by technology.[47] Rather, they argue, industrial relations play a role in the choice and utilization of that technology. Mahon makes this point too. It is "the character of a country's industrial relations system that plays a crucial role both because of its direct impact on a firm's choice of a pattern of work organization and because of its indirect impact on product strategy via the effect of collective bargaining on income distribution and thus on effective domestic demand."[48]

For these commentators the attitude of trade unions is crucial. Unions can embrace change and seek to control it, thus minimizing its negative side-effects, or they can bury their heads in the sand, in which case the changes will come anyway, sooner or later, and unions will have lost their chance to determine which version of flexibility emerges. There is, as a result, much discussion of national variants and national contexts.[49] Regulation theorists have developed a number of national "scenarios" of labor regulation to explain why flexibility is accepted earlier in some countries than others, and why its form varies.[50] Thus the long-standing emphasis on difference and divergence in national political economies remains in the current period.

This approach has no difficulty in explaining the experience of flexibility in France, and particularly why its introduction has been accompanied by a weakening and growing irrelevance of trade unions and increased fragmentation and polarization of the work force. Unions have been too weak to participate in the process, and perhaps as a result they have not shown much interest in or inclination to even attempting to control and guide the introduction of flexibility.[51] Thus French employers have preferred to resort to an insecure, unskilled, marginal labor force rather than to encourage retraining and greater security of employment. Thus it is possible to be pessimistic about flexibility and post-Fordism in France without having that pessimism spill over to the opportunities in other countries with very different systems of industrial relations and trade union movements. Other institutional contexts might hold out the promise of a more evenhanded, benign flexibility.

And yet, such a conclusion, based on a case-by-case evaluation of flexibility in all its national variants, is not entirely satisfactory. It depends upon a somewhat simplistic understanding of flexibility, seen very narrowly as a new tool or technique for organizing the work force and the production process so as to improve efficiency. Thus flexibility, in this sense, can be simply tacked onto an existing system of industrial relations, which will determine, or at least color, the way in which it operates: if unions are strong and forward-looking, flexibility can operate in a benign manner; if not, flexibility can have disastrous consequences.

Flexibility must be understood in a much broader sense than this. It must be understood as having a structural impact on the industrial relations system itself, and as a management strategy whose purpose is often precisely to attack the very labor organization on which the industrial relations system is based. The danger is in taking a static view of the relationship between flexibility and labor regulation. It must be recognized that flexibility does not leave the industrial relations system untouched; rather, in a dynamic sense, it *actively undermines the very industrial relations system that is meant to control it.*

Flexibility, beyond its impact on the production process and its narrowly economic goals, undermines and fragments labor organization, and particularly labor organization that stretches beyond the walls of the firm. This study has argued, theoretically and through an examination of the French case, that labor collectivity is a fundamental determinant of the mode of labor regulation. A change in the collective power of labor—in its capacity as a class to impose damage on capital through the control of the supply of labor—implies a change in labor regulation and the institutions of the industrial relations system.

The postwar model of industrial relations in Western Europe revolved, above all, around trade unions. Workers were collectively organized, not just at the firm level, but beyond the firm. Unions expanded the collective power of workers both by linking together workers in entire industries, and by making full employment a political priority so as to enhance the mobility of labor and allow workers to identify with interests beyond the walls of the firm in which they work. The forms of labor regulation that developed in the heyday of Fordism institutionalized this collective power.

Flexibility undermines this model and replaces it with two other kinds of labor organization. In the first place it decentralizes industrial relations and encourages *firm-specific* forms of labor organization. Thus in France worker expression groups, quality circles, and works councils are all forms of collective organization specific to the firm. They encourage microcorporatist bargaining in which workers trade job security, and perhaps increased participation in the running of the firm, for flexibility and an identification with the needs (primarily financial) of the firm. This kind of organization does not itself preclude trade unions, but it is likely to change the *function* of trade unions. It leads to a de facto enterprise unionism in which union sections inside the firm feel cut off from the branch and confederal level and they too come to identify with the firm, or at least have fewer resources with which to resist employers.

As well as encouraging firm-specific forms of labor organization, flexibility threatens to go further and *individualize* the relationship between worker and employer. Employers have greater flexibility and control over the labor process when they can organize the job content, work schedule, and the pay structure of each individual worker. This trend, which is still far less developed than the microcorporatist one, is inevitably destructive of trade unionism, and it is important to note just how huge a transformation in industrial relations it entails. Thus the *practice* of flexibility, both in its encouragement of firm-specific forms of work organization and in its individualizing effect, itself transforms the organizational capacity of labor and the way in which workers come to define their interests.

The strength of European labor in the postwar period has ultimately been rooted in its capacity for collective action and ability to exercise some degree of control over the supply of labor. It has been a collective or class power, rather than a power based on the skills or market position of individual workers. The structural effect of flexibility is to dissolve that collective power. That does not mean that workers cannot benefit from flexibility. What it does mean is that the position of labor as a *class* is in the process of being fundamentally transformed.

That labor movements thrived under Fordism is no coincidence. Fordist growth permitted and even encouraged an expansion of the collective power of labor. Labor was not only able to organize on a national scale, but high and rising wage levels were the engine of economic growth, stimulating increased demand and production. The national focus of Fordism also allowed for a wide range of particular national solutions to the integration and regulation of labor. Common to all was a crucial role for labor, both in the firm and in national economic policy-making. Powerful labor movements, often with institutional or semi-institutional links to social democratic parties, could parlay industrial strength into a wide range of political, social, and economic gains. For all the limitations of this postwar compromise from the perspective of labor, it was a compromise from which labor collectively, and workers individually, benefited.

A post-Fordist political economy challenges this power. Not only does the demand of firms for greater flexibility and autonomy in managing their workforces threaten to decompose national labor movements, but the challenge of economic internationalization is one that labor, as a class, is ill-suited to meet. Labor is not a commodity in the sense of other factors of production and is far less mobile than capital. Labor movements have in the past relied upon nation-states to exercise some political control over the economy, but the capacity of states to do this is now greatly diminished. Post-Fordism, above all, changes the "traditional boundaries of trade union representation."[52] It spells the end of nationally organized labor movements; and if its collective power has indeed been a fundamental element in the advances made by labor, the prognosis for the future is grim indeed.

This suggests, provisionally at least, that we may be witnessing a convergence of national systems of labor regulation. The divergence that marked the bulk of the postwar period rested upon the importance of the nation-state in the political economy. As that importance goes into eclipse, it follows that distinct national types of labor regulation are unlikely to be far behind. Certainly differences will remain, but they will persist as artifacts of an earlier period rather than as the consequence of existing relations of power in the political economy.

Notes

CHAPTER ONE

1. The industrial unrest of 1968 peaked at the end of May, when as many as nine million workers were on strike, but did not subside until well into June. For brevity's sake, however, this study will usually simply refer to the events of May 1968.

2. Alain Faujas, "Des grèves existentielles, *Le Monde*, January 7, 1987, p. 31.

3. See Daniel Furjot and Catherine Noel, "La Conflictualité en 1986," *Travail et Emploi*, no. 34 (December 1987).

4. *Le Monde*, January 23, 1987, p. 1 (my translation).

5. See *Le Monde*, January 13, 1987, p. 42 (my translation).

6. This figure comes from Pierre Rosanvallon, *La Question Syndicale* (Paris: Calmann-Lévy, 1988), 265. It is very difficult to get accurate figures for union membership in France. See chapter 7 below for a more detailed discussion of the current strength of trade unionism in France.

7. Jonathan Zeitlin, "Shopfloor Bargaining and the State: A Contradictory Relationship," in Steven Tolliday and Jonathan Zeitlin, eds., *Shopfloor Bargaining and the State* (New York: Cambridge University Press, 1985), 2.

8. See, for instance, Peter Evans, Theda Skocpol, and Dietrich Rueschemeyer, eds., *Bringing the State Back In* (New York: Cambridge University Press, 1985).

9. In addition, excellent studies of the French employers' organizations and trade unions exist, and I will make extensive use of them in the course of this study.

10. This term is used in France to refer to the trade unions and employers' organizations. It will be used in the same way, as shorthand, in this study. It is not intended to imply the existence of a consensual relationship between unions and employers.

11. Peter Lange, George Ross, and Maurizio Vannicelli, "Unions as Objects of History and Unions as Actors," in Lange, Ross, and Vannicelli, eds., *Unions, Change and Crisis: French and Italian Union Strategy and the Political Economy, 1945–1980* (New York: Allen and Unwin, 1982), 218.

12. Ibid.

13. The best treatment of the differential class power of workers and employers, and of the implications for collective action, is Claus Offe and Helmut Wiesenthal, "Two Logics of Collective Action," in Claus Offe, *Disorganized Capitalism* (Cambridge: MIT Press, 1985).

14. Miriam Golden, Peter Lange, and Jonas Pontusson, "Revised Framework for Workshop on 'Union Politics, Labor Militancy, and Capital Accumulation'" (December 1986), to be published in the book based on this conference: Miriam Golden and Jonas Pontusson, eds., *Union Politics in Comparative Perspective: Economic Change and Intra-Class Conflict* (Ithaca: Cornell University Press, forthcoming).

15. Erik Olin Wright develops a very useful schema of what he calls "modes of determination," which distinguishes between structural limitation and other forms of determination. His discussion of determination is highly pertinent to the discussion in this section. See chapter 1 of his *Class, Crisis and the State* (London: Verso, 1978).

16. There are several different ways of conceptualizing the "weakness" of a labor movement. This issue will be treated in more detail later, but briefly, I will be employing the conventional usage in which "weak" means a low level of unionization, fractured union confederations, and the absence of national-level bargaining between the peak organizations of capital and labor. This does not mean that a "stronger" labor movement, defined in this way, will necessarily be able to extract greater benefits for workers than a "weaker" one. The term refers to the organizational structure of the labor movement alone. It is also important to distinguish between trade unions and workers. The argument that will be made in later chapters (an argument that is of great relevance to France) is that workers can be *conjuncturally* strong as a result of labor market tightness, even though their trade unions are *structurally* weak, in the sense that their organizational structure is weak.

17. Mike Davis, *Prisoners of the American Dream* (London: Verso, 1986), 105.

18. While Davis, *Prisoners of the American Dream*, does not refer explicitly to the corporatist and power resources literatures, his approach is very similar to that used here. Within a broad framework based upon the Regulationist periodization of capitalism, Davis constructs a series of "modes of industrial relations" (pp. 114–15) which bear some resemblance to the "modes of labor regulation" discussed in this chapter. The primary difference is that his models are differentiated on the basis of geography. Thus he talks of a Northern European model, a British/Belgian model, a North American model, and a Japanese model. As a result, the models are descriptive rather than explanatory. I hope to show that the corporatist and power resources approaches can be used to provide an explanation for why different ways of regulating labor appear in different countries.

19. The best summary is provided by Robert Boyer, *La Théorie de la Régulation: Une Analyse Critique* (Paris: Éditions La Découverte, 1986), and, in English, Alain Noël, "Accumulation, Regulation, and Social Change: An Essay on French Political Economy," *International Organizations* 41, no. 2 (Spring 1987).

20. Samuel Bowles, David M. Gordon, and Thomas E. Weisskopf, "Power and Profits: The Social Structure of Accumulation and the Profitability of the Postwar U.S. Economy," *Review of Radical Political Economics* 18, nos. 1 and 2 (Spring–Summer 1986). Bowles, Gordon, Weisskopf, and others have developed a particular American variant of the Regulation approach. For a discussion of the similarities and differences see David M. Kotz, "A Comparative Analysis of the Theory of Regulation and the Social Structure of Accumulation Theory," *Science & Society* 54, no. 1 (Spring 1990).

21. Richard Edwards, Paolo Garonna, and Franz Tödtling, eds., *Unionism in Crisis and Beyond* (Dover, Mass.: Auburn House, 1986), 4–5.

22. Alain Lipietz, "Behind the Crisis: The Exhaustion of a Regime of Accumulation. A 'Regulation School' Perspective on Some French Empirical Works," *Review of Radical Political Economics* 18, nos. 1 and 2 (Spring–Summer 1986):16.

23. Noël, "Accumulation, Regulation, and Social Change," 311–12.

24. For a comparative account of changing patterns of economic growth since the 1930s, within the Regulationist framework, see Andrew Glyn et al., "The Rise and Fall of the Golden Age," in Stephen A. Marglin and Juliet B. Schor, eds., *The Golden Age of Capitalism: Reinterpreting the Postwar Experience* (Oxford: Clarendon Press, 1990).

25. The term "monopolistic" is misleading because wages, and social relations more generally, are not regulated monopolistically—in the usual sense of the word—anywhere in the advanced capitalist world. The Regulationists also use the term "administered," which is probably more appropriate.

26. It is unclear, for instance, whether flexibility and the decentralization of collective bargaining constitute a mode of regulation appropriate to a new post-Fordist regime of accumulation, or rather a new business strategy to circumvent the power of the organized working class and make continued accumulation within the old Fordist regime of accumulation possible. What is required is a way of defining the new post-Fordist regime of accumulation independently of its mode of regulation so that the trap of seeing a new form of regulation and automatically assuming that it corresponds to a new type of accumulation is avoided. As I will argue below, the acceptance that there is more than one mode of regulation possible for a particular regime of accumulation would be a step in the right direction.

27. For a discussion of flexibility, post-Fordism, and the impact of internationalization, see chapters 8 and 9 below. See also Robert Boyer, ed., *La Flexibilité du Travail en Europe* (Paris: Éditions la Découverte, 1986), especially chapter 1, and Michael J. Piore and Charles F. Sabel, *The Second Industrial Divide* (New York: Basic Books, 1984).

28. A good example of this tendency is found in Michel Aglietta and Anton Brender, *Les Métamorphoses de la Société Salariale: La France en Projet* (Paris: Calmann-Lévy, 1984).

29. This mirrors the problem within Marxist theory of linking up the abstract analysis of modes of production, and the more concrete analysis of real social formations. This similarity should come as no surprise because the Regulation approach has been heavily influenced by Marxism. See Boyer, *La Théorie de la Régulation*, 10–35, for a discussion of the intellectual origins and debts of the Regulation School. See also Wright, *Class, Crisis and the State*, chapter 1, for an impressive effort to link up levels of Marxist analysis.

30. See Boyer, ed., *La Flexibilité du Travail en Europe*, for an attempt to provide national specificity within a Regulationist framework. See chapter 9 below for a discussion of the strengths and weaknesses of this effort.

31. Philippe C. Schmitter, "Still the Century of Corporatism?" in Philippe C. Schmitter and Gerhard Lehmbruch, eds., *Trends Towards Corporatist Intermediation* (London: Sage Publications, 1979).

32. Leo Panitch, *Working-Class Politics in Crisis* (London: Verso, 1986). See particularly chapters 5, 6, and 7.

33. This study adopts a particular reading of the corporatist literature and makes no claim that this interpretation would find widespread acceptance among the original proponents of the corporatist paradigm.

34. See David Cameron, "Social Democracy, Corporatism, Labor Quiescence, and the Representation of Economic Interests in Advanced Capitalist Society," in

John H. Goldthorpe, ed., *Order and Conflict in Contemporary Capitalism* (Oxford: Clarendon Press, 1984); Manfred G. Schmidt, "The Role of the Parties in Shaping Macroeconomic Policy," in Francis G. Castles, ed., *The Impact of Parties: Politics and Policies in Democratic Capitalist States* (London: Sage, 1982); and Goran Therborn, *Why Some Peoples Are More Unemployed Than Others* (London: Verso, 1986).

35. See Walter Korpi, *The Democratic Class Struggle* (New York: Routledge, Chapman, and Hall, 1983), especially chapters 3 and 8. I will be using the same measures of labor strength in this study.

36. Panitch, *Working-Class Politics in Crisis*, is the best representative of this position.

37. Cameron, "Social Democracy, Corporatism, Labor Quiescence."

38. See, for instance, Panitch, *Working-Class Politics in Crisis*, chapter 6.

39. Power resources theorists tend to see the present situation as an historical phase on the road to socialism, while corporatist theorists see it more statically as a mode of organizing and enhancing the economic management of a capitalist economy.

40. Some power resources theorists ingeniously sidestep this problem by arguing that the breakdown of corporatist mechanisms reflects the changing balance of class power—in favor of the working class—making corporatism no longer appropriate to labor strength. This assertion has dubious theoretical and empirical foundations.

41. Goran Therborn, "Why Some Classes Are More Successful Than Others," *New Left Review*, no. 138 (March–April 1983): 41.

42. Offe and Wiesenthal, "Two Logics of Collective Action."

43. Charles E. Lindblom, "The Market as Prison," *Journal of Politics* 44, no. 2 (May 1982): 328.

44. The concluding chapter will discuss the importance of European integration for the future of labor regulation in France and elsewhere in Europe.

45. The state can play an active role in this kind of high-level bargaining or it can act in more of a facultative manner, bringing labor and capital together but itself only playing a passive role in the bargaining process. See Gerhard Lehmbruch, "Liberal Corporatism and Party Government," in Schmitter and Lehmbruch, eds., *Trends Towards Corporatist Intermediation*.

46. Robert J. Flanagan, David W. Soskice, and Lloyd Ulman, *Unionism, Economic Stabilization, and Incomes Policies: European Experience* (Washington, D.C.: Brookings Institution, 1983).

47. Stephen McBride, "Corporatism, Public Policy and the Labor Movement: A Comparative Study," *Political Studies* 23, no. 3 (September 1985), argues convincingly that where powerful labor movements engage in corporatist-style bargaining, the ability of the state to intervene is strictly limited. The state can have a more active role only where labor organization is poorly developed. This argument directly contradicts that of Schmitter.

48. See Cameron, "Social Democracy, Corporatism, Labor Quiescence."

49. Peter Katzenstein, *Small States in World Markets: Industrial Policy in Europe* (Ithaca: Cornell University Press, 1985), has suggested that two forms of corporatism exist: liberal and social. The factors outlined above show why there might be

good reason for bourgeois governments to want to find ways of regulating labor which avoid pure labor market regulation. However, corporatism is a particular regulatory mechanism, not an outcome, and as such is not synonymous with state regulation that benefits labor. The position taken here is that corporatism is over-whelmingly a social democratic solution to the problem of labor regulation.

50. See, for instance, Alan Fox, *Industrial Sociology and Industrial Relations* (London: HMSO, 1966).

51. See Leo Panitch, *Social Democracy and Industrial Militancy: The Labour Party, the Trade Unions, and Incomes Policy, 1945–74* (Cambridge: Cambridge University Press, 1976).

52. See Stephen Blank, "Britain: The Politics of Foreign Economic Policy, the Domestic Economy, and the Problem of Pluralistic Stagnation," in Peter Katzenstein, ed., *Between Power and Plenty: Foreign Economic Policies of Advanced Industrial States* (Madison: University of Wisconsin Press, 1979).

53. In the same sense that a wider model of state activism is premised upon a weak working class and state regulation of labor, so the social democratic model is premised upon a strong, highly organized, disciplined working class, and corporatist labor regulation. Indeed, in many ways the social democratic model may be seen as the flip side of the state activist model.

54. Alessandro Pizzorno, "Political Exchange and Collective Identity in Industrial Conflict," in Colin Crouch and Alessandro Pizzorno, eds., *The Resurgence of Class Conflict in Western Europe Since 1968*, vol. 2 (New York: Holmes and Meier, 1978).

55. Whether a high social wage is part of the exchange is in fact far from clear. A high level of transfers that acts to redistribute income from capital to labor would add to capital's costs and neutralize the benefits of wage restraint. It is more likely that transfers redistribute over the life cycle, and within the working class. Indeed social democracy's success has been its ability to unify the working class by a policy of solidarism, rather than the reduction of inequality. As Cameron puts it: "Labor exchanges wage militancy, and more generally militancy in collective bargaining for employment. Important though the other material benefits are that we have described . . . the heart of the exchange involved unemployment. The essential quid for the quo of labor quiescence is full employment over an extended period" ("Social Democracy, Corporatism, Labor Quiescence," 172–73).

56. An additional gain for the Swedes has been that they were able to use centralized wage bargaining as a form of industrial policy, eliminating weaker firms and enhancing the competitiveness of the export sector.

57. Wolfgang Streeck, "Neo-Corporatist Industrial Relations and the Economic Crisis in West Germany," in Goldthorpe, ed., *Order and Conflict in Contemporary Capitalism*.

58. Enterprise unions and works councils have in common the fact that workers in the firm are organized (in contrast to pure labor market regulation), but the form of organization is limited to those employed within the firm.

59. See Streeck, "Neo-Corporatist Industrial Relations," 297.

60. Ibid. It is worth noting that this integration may be partly ideological, in the sense that, unlike corporatism or decentralized collective bargaining, workers

do not derive their interests from a wider collectivity—a class or a trade—but from the firm. This would constitute "integration" into the logic of capitalist production in the fullest sense of the word.

61. The fullest form would be the lifetime employment guarantee, and company-provided welfare benefits found in some Japanese firms. In fact, students of Japanese industrial relations will find many features of microcorporatism familiar.

62. Piore and Sabel, *The Second Industrial Divide.*

63. This is often called, particularly in the Yugoslav context, "enterprise egoism."

64. See Derek C. Jones and Jan Svejnar, eds., *Participatory and Self-managed Firms: Evaluating Economic Performance* (Lexington: Lexington Books, 1982), and Branko Horvat, "The Theory of Worker-Managed Firms Revisited" (unpublished manuscript, 1984).

65. The term is used by George Ross in "The Perils of Politics: French Unions and the Crisis of the 1970s," in Lange, Ross, and Vannicelli, eds., *Unions, Change and Crisis*, 24.

66. Jacques Capdevielle and René Mouriaux, *Mai 68: L'Entre-Deux de la Modernité* (Paris: FNSP, 1982), 12 (my translation).

CHAPTER TWO

1. For the early development of French trade unions see Val R. Lorwin, *The French Labor Movement* (Cambridge: Harvard University Press, 1966).

2. Patrick O'Brien and Gaglar Keyder, *Economic Growth in Britain and France, 1780–1914* (London: Allen and Unwin, 1978), argue that there are numerous forms of transition to an industrial economy and criticize the view that France should be considered a backward version of Britain. Insofar as "backwardness" is used in an evaluative sense this is a fair comment. There is no reason to accept that the British model of industrialization was either the only or the best such model. Nevertheless, the point being made here—one accepted by O'Brien and Keyder—is simply that the manner of industrialization has consequences for class formation and the industrial structure.

3. See Tony Judt, *Marxism and the French Left* (Oxford: Clarendon Press, 1986), and Duncan Gallie, *Social Inequality and Class Radicalism in France and Britain* (Cambridge: Cambridge University Press, 1983).

4. This discussion of the rural bias of early French industrialization owes a great deal to a seminar paper given by Gérard Noiriel, "The Formation and Decline of the French Working Class," at the Harvard Center for European Studies, February 19, 1988. See also Clive Trebilcock, *The Industrialization of the Continental Powers, 1780–1914* (New York: Longman Group, 1981).

5. See Alain Cottereau, "The Distinctiveness of Working-Class Cultures in France, 1848–1900," in Ira Katznelson and Aristide R. Zolberg, eds., *Working-Class Formation* (Princeton: Princeton University Press, 1986).

6. Noiriel, "The Formation and Decline of the French Working Class."

7. Judt, *Marxism and the French Left*, and William Sewell, *Work and Revolution in France* (New York: Cambridge University Press, 1980).

8. These firms were very often those employing no labor, or only family labor. Thus the smallest firms were being squeezed out.

9. This figure comes from François Caron, *An Economic History of Modern France* (New York: Columbia University Press, 1979), 287, table 13.10.

10. Geoffrey K. Ingham, *Strikes and Industrial Conflict* (London: Macmillan, 1974).

11. See Adam Przeworski, Barnett Rubin, and Ernest Underhill, "The Evolution of the Class Structure in France, 1901–1968," *Economic Development and Cultural Change* 28, no. 4 (July 1980).

12. Przeworski and his collaborators have examined the class structures of France and Sweden in parallel studies. The two studies are the article cited in the previous note and an unpublished manuscript by Adam Przeworski, Amy Bridges, Robert Melville, and Ernest Underhill, "The Evolution of Swedish Class Structure, 1900–1960: A Data Report" (1976). The comparison is instructive, not least because Sweden is usually considered to have a "strong" labor movement and France a "weak" labor movement. The study of France highlights two peculiarities of French class structure that are of importance here. The first concerns the process of proletarianization in France. While France experienced the familiar separation of small producers from their property through competition, those former property owners often *did not* enter the working class. Instead they tended to join the "excluded" category, meaning retirees, unemployed, nonworking spouses, etc., which was particularly large in France. Second, employment in the tertiary sector grew particularly rapidly in France after 1936. The rise of a new social group outside the traditional working class had important political implications in the 1970s when the struggle for the "new middle class" became acute.

13. Noiriel, "The Formation and Decline of the French Working Class."

14. Gallie, *Social Inequality and Class Radicalism.*

15. Richard F. Kuisel, *Capitalism and the State in Modern France* (Cambridge: Cambridge University Press, 1981).

16. For a discussion of the early organization of employer interests see Henry Ehrmann, *Organized Business in France* (Princeton: Princeton University Press, 1957). The main employers' peak organization, the Conseil National du Patronat Français (CNPF), was not formed until 1946, and it remained weak and dominated by small and medium-sized firms until after 1968. The national level of the CNPF was given only very limited autonomy by the industrial federations.

17. This pattern persisted into the postwar period as well. In 1955 and 1968 strike waves were followed by an increase in bargaining. This underlines the point that collective bargaining did not really take root even after 1945.

18. Paul Durand, "The Evolution of Industrial Relations Law in France Since the Liberation," *International Labor Review* 74 (1956).

19. For details of these agreements see "Works Agreements of the 'Renault type,'" *International Labor Review* 81 (1960).

20. See Michael Piore, "Convergence in Industrial Relations? The Case of France and the United States," unpublished paper, Massachusetts Institute of Technology, no. 286 (July 1981), 14–15.

21. Gérard Adam and Jean-Daniel Reynaud, *Conflits du Travail et Changement Social* (Paris: Presses Universitaires de France, 1978), 97 (my translation).

22. The best single account for the history, organization, and action of French trade unions is Jean-Daniel Reynaud, *Les Syndicats en France*, 3d ed., 2 vols. (Paris: Éditions du Seuil, 1975).

23. This figure comes from Gérard Adam, *Le Pouvoir Syndical* (Paris: Dunod, 1985), 66. The functions of the works council will be described in greater detail below.

24. See Jean-Pierre Aujard and Serge Volkoff, "Une Analyse chiffrée des audiences syndicales," *Travail et Emploi*, no. 30 (December 1986).

25. For comparative rates of unionization see John D. Stephens, *The Transition from Capitalism to Socialism* (Urbana: University of Illinois, 1986), 115–16.

26. François Sellier's estimates are contained in an unpublished manuscript, "Les problèmes du travail en France 1920–1974" (1976), cited by Adam, *Le Pouvoir Syndical*, 45.

27. Jean-Daniel Reynaud, *Les Syndicats en France* (Paris: Colin, 1963).

28. Piore, "Convergence in Industrial Relations?"

29. Adam, *Le Pouvoir Syndical*, 55–60. The figure for CFDT membership dates from 1972, not 1975.

30. For a discussion of the ideology of FO see Alain Bergounioux, "The Trade Union Strategy of the CGT-FO," in Mark Kesselman, ed., *The French Workers' Movement: Economic Crisis and Political Change* (London: Allen and Unwin, 1984).

31. Adam, *Le Pouvoir Syndical*, 78 (my translation).

32. For an excellent discussion of this dynamic see Martin A. Schain, "Corporatism and Industrial Relations in France," in Philip G. Cerny and Martin A. Schain, eds., *French Politics and Public Policy* (New York: St. Martin's, 1980).

33. See George Ross, *Workers and Communists in France: From Popular Front to Eurocommunism* (Berkeley: University of California Press, 1982).

34. Julio Samuel Valenzuela, "Labor Movement Formation and Politics: The Chilean and French Cases in Comparative Perspective, 1850–1950" (Ph.D diss., Columbia University, 1979), and Giovanni Sartori, *Parties and Party Systems* (New York: Cambridge University Press, 1976).

35. Chapter 6 below discusses the period of Socialist rule when, for a brief time, both major radical unions cooperated with the government, but an incomes policy still had to be of a statutory kind, rather than voluntary or negotiated.

36. Gallie, *Social Inequality and Class Radicalism*, 258.

37. Schain, "Corporatism and Industrial Relations."

38. This description is Schain's (see ibid., 204).

39. The public sector had different structures of worker representation. For details see René Mouriaux, *Les Syndicats dans la Société Française* (Paris: FNSP, 1983), especially pages 169–71.

40. This was the situation until new legislation in 1967 and 1971, which expanded the statutory functions of the works councils. See chapters 3 and 4 below for details.

41. Pizzorno, "Political Exchange and Collective Identity in Industrial Conflict."

42. See chapter 3 below for a discussion of left-wing Gaullist views of class conflict and harmony.

43. Gérard Lyon-Caen, "Critique de la négociation collective," *Après-Demain*, no. 221 (February 1980). He was writing in 1980 after an increase in bargaining

had occurred in the 1970s. His critique is even more accurate for the 1950s and 1960s.

44. Ibid., 8 (my translation).

45. Ibid., 8–9 (my translation).

46. John Keeler, *The Politics of Neo-Corporatism in France* (Oxford: Oxford University Press, 1987).

47. Ross, "The Perils of Politics," 24.

48. Noël, "Accumulation, Regulation, and Social Change," 312.

49. Hugues Bertrand, "France: Modernisations et Piétinements," in Robert Boyer, ed., *Capitalismes fin de siècle* (Paris: Presses Universitaires de France, 1986), 69 (my translation).

50. The original article by Robert Boyer was "Les Salaires en Longue Période," *Économie et Statistique*, no. 103 (September 1978). It was subsequently translated into English and published as "Wage Formation in Historical Perspective: The French Experience" in the *Cambridge Journal of Economics*, no. 2 (June 1979). All future citations will come from the English translation.

51. Alain Doyelle and Marguerite Perrot, "L'Évolution du pouvoir d'achat des salaires depuis trente ans," *Travail et Emploi*, no. 9 (July–September 1981).

52. Boyer, "Wage Formation in Historical Perspective," 103.

53. Robert Boyer, "Wage Labor, Capital Accumulation, and the Crisis, 1968–82," in Kesselman, ed., *The French Workers' Movement*, 20–21.

54. Ibid., 20.

55. Aglietta and Brender, *Les Métamorphoses de la Société Salariale*, 78 (my translation).

56. Sources on planning include Stephen Cohen, *Modern Capitalist Planning: The French Model* (Berkeley: University of California Press, 1977); Peter Hall, *Governing the Economy* (New York: Oxford University Press, 1986); and Andrew Shonfield, *Modern Capitalism* (Oxford: Oxford University Press, 1969).

57. Kuisel, *Capitalism and the State in Modern France*.

58. John Zysman, *Governments, Markets, and Growth* (Ithaca: Cornell University Press, 1983), chapter 3.

59. Zysman, for instance, comes close to this position (ibid.).

60. Eric Nordlinger, *On the Autonomy of the Democratic State* (Cambridge: Harvard University Press, 1981).

61. Kuisel, *Capitalism and the State in Modern France*, 259. The "économie concertée" referred to the planning commissions' consultations with the social partners during the preparatory stages of each new economic plan. As Kuisel suggests, the term was misleading.

62. Zysman, *Governments, Markets, and Growth*, chapter 3.

63. Mikkal Herberg, "Politics, Planning and Capitalism: National Economic Planning in France and Britain," *Political Studies* 29, no. 4 (December 1981): 513.

64. Robert Boyer, "The Influence of Keynes on French Economic Policy: Past and Present," in Harold Wattel, ed., *The Policy Consequences of John Maynard Keynes* (New York: Macmillan, 1985).

65. For a discussion of the varieties of national forms of Keynesianism, see the contributions to Peter Hall, ed., *The Political Power of Economic Ideas* (Princeton: Princeton University Press, 1989).

66. See David Cameron, "Continuity and Change in French Social Policy"

238 · Notes to Chapter Three

(Paper presented at the Annual Meeting of the American Political Science Association, Washington, D.C., September 1988).

67. *Social Expenditure, 1960–90* (Paris: OECD, 1985), 24, table 3.

68. J-J. Carré, P. Dubois, and E. Malinvaud, *French Economic Growth* (Stanford: Stanford University Press, 1975), 383–85.

69. Przeworski, Rubin, and Underhill, "The Evolution of the Class Structure in France," 739.

70. Pierre Dubois, Claude Durand, and Sabine Erbès-Seguin, "The Contradictions of French Trade Unionism," in Crouch and Pizzorno, eds., *The Resurgence of Class Conflict*, vol. 1.

71. This point is made by Dubois, Durand, and Erbès-Seguin, "The Contradictions of French Trade Unionism," 54–58.

72. Stephens, *The Transition from Capitalism to Socialism*, 168.

73. Malcolm Sawyer, "Income Distribution in OECD Countries," *OECD Economic Outlook—Occasional Studies* (Paris: OECD, 1976).

74. Flanagan, Soskice, and Ulman, *Unionism, Economic Stabilization and Incomes Policies*, 578, table 10–2.

75. Maurice Lévy-Leboyer, "The Large Corporation in Modern France," in Alfred Chandler and Herman Daems, eds., *Managerial Hierarchies* (Cambridge: Harvard University Press, 1980).

76. Carré, Dubois, and Malinvaud, *French Economic Growth*, 165.

77. In the mid-1950s one-third of French exports went to the colonies. See Caron, *An Economic History of Modern France*, 217.

78. For details of the use made of the minimum wage see Doyelle and Perrot, "L'Évolution du pouvoir d'achat."

79. Dubois, Durand, and Erbès-Seguin, "The Contradictions of French Trade Unionism," 55.

80. Boyer, "Wage Formation in Historical Perspective," 114.

81. See Jane Marceau, *Class and Status in France* (Oxford: Clarendon Press, 1977), 26.

CHAPTER THREE

1. Hall, *Governing the Economy*, chapter 6.

2. Tony Topham, "New Types of Bargaining," in Robin Blackburn and Alexander Cockburn, eds., *The Incompatibles* (Harmondsworth: Penguin, 1967), 136.

3. Flanagan, Soskice, and Ulman, *Unionism, Economic Stabilization, and Incomes Policies*, 593.

4. Ibid., 578, table 10–2.

5. Emphasis in this section is on the domestic sources of industrial unrest. However, the events of May 1968 did take place within the context of an *international* surge in industrial conflict. There were clearly factors, primarily economic, that were common to most of the industrial economies and account for the synchronicity of strike action. These factors are discussed in David Soskice, "Strike Waves and Wage Explosions, 1968–1970: An Economic Interpretation," in Crouch and Pizzorno, eds., *The Resurgence of Class Conflict*, vol. 2. Nevertheless, the particular form of these strikes was determined by national factors. It should be

noted that the scale of the strikes of May–June 1968 exceeded that of any other strike wave, and that it was also the first such explosion and thus had some impact in stimulating similar action elsewhere. This gives the French strikes a special importance.

6. This was equivalent to 2.1 percent of the total labor force. Figures from *Labour Force Statistics: 1962–1982* (Paris: OECD, 1984).

7. For this point, see Edward Shorter and Charles Tilly, *Strikes in France, 1830–1968* (Cambridge: Cambridge University Press, 1974).

8. Adam and Reynaud, *Conflits du Travail et Changement Social*, 73 (my translation).

9. Capdevielle and Mouriaux, *Mai 68*, 159, reprints a useful chart showing which firms were on strike and for how long.

10. See the report in *Le Monde*, June 18, 1968, p. 11, which discusses the extent to which the Grenelle wage figures were surpassed in actual settlements.

11. Figures from *Liaisons Sociales: Documents*, no. 106 (October 8, 1969), 8.

12. *Le Monde*, June 18, 1968, p. 11.

13. The figure of one hundred and fifty comes from *Liaisons Sociales: Législation Sociale*, no. 3448 (January 2, 1969), 2.

14. For an exhaustive typology of explanations of May 1968 see Philippe Beneton and Jean Touchard, "Les interprétations de la crise de Mai–Juin 1968," *Revue française de science politique*, no. 3 (June 1970); and Capdevielle and Mouriaux, *Mai 68*.

15. The term "detonator" as applied to the student revolt is used by Capdevielle and Mouriaux, *Mai 68*, 138.

16. Michel Crozier, *La Société Bloquée* (Paris: Le Seuil, 1970).

17. See Jean-Daniel Reynaud, Sami Dassa, Josette Dassa, and Pierre Maclouf, "Les événements de mai et juin 1968 et le système français de relations professionnelles," *Sociologie du Travail*, no. 1 (January–March 1971).

18. *Manpower Policy in France* (Paris: OECD, 1973).

19. Ibid. (quotations from 37, 41, 57).

20. See Hall, *Governing the Economy*, 145, 170–71, for details of the Sixth Plan.

21. The account that follows relies heavily on the excellent studies of the CNPF by Henri Weber, *Le Parti des Patrons* (Paris: Seuil, 1986), and of the CGT and CFDT by George Ross. For a general account see Ross, "The Perils of Politics"; see also his more detailed study of the CGT, *Workers and Communists in France*.

22. See Hall, *Governing the Economy*, especially 169–71, for a description of the closer ties between individual industrialists and government.

23. Weber, *Le Parti des Patrons*, 175.

24. Quoted in Weber, *Le Parti des Patrons*, 207 (my translation). Chotard was president of the Social Commission of the CNPF.

25. Quoted in ibid., 172 (my translation).

26. De Gaulle's response during an interview with Michel Droit, as reported in *Le Monde*, June 9–10, 1968, p. 2 (my translation).

27. De Gaulle's response during a press conference, September 9, 1968, as reported in *Le Monde*, September 10, 1968, p. 7 (my translation).

28. See Patrick Guiol, "La Participation, le gaullisme, et le RPR," *Autogestion*, no. 23 (1986): 22.

29. Ibid., 26 (my translation).

30. For details of the 1959 and 1967 legislation and the limited use made of them, see *Liaisons Sociales: Législation Sociale*, no. 4128 (February 28, 1974).

31. This figure comes from "La Participation des travailleurs à l'entreprise à travers les nouveaux textes législatifs," *Revue française des affaires sociales* (January–March 1975): 11.

32. The interview de Gaulle gave to Michel Droit, as reported in *Le Monde*, June 9–10, 1968, provides the most coherent formulation of de Gaulle's interpretation of May 1968 and his approach for dealing with it.

33. The text of de Gaulle's address is reprinted in *Le Monde*, May 26–27, 1968, p. 2.

34. De Gaulle at his September 9, 1968, press conference, as reported in *Le Monde*, September 10, 1968, p. 7 (my translation; emphasis added).

35. *Le Peuple*, no. 819 (April 1–15, 1969). My translation.

36. See the analysis of the referendum by Frédéric Bon, "Le référendum du 27 avril 1969: suicide politique ou nécessité stratégique?" *Revue française de science politique*, no. 2 (April 1970).

37. Capdevielle and Mouriaux, *Mai 68*, 224 (my translation). An article by Alain Lancelot and Pierre Weill, "L'Évolution politique des électeurs français de février à juin 1969," *Revue française de science politique*, no. 2 (April 1970), provides a breakdown of the vote by social group (see especially p. 258). Interestingly, there was stronger opposition to the reform plans from senior executives than from workers. This supports the contention that managers recognized that the reforms would be unworkable.

38. See *Syndicalisme Hebdo*, no. 1397 (June 8, 1972) for details.

CHAPTER FOUR

1. Georges Pompidou, from an interview in *L'Express*, June 9–15, 1969, p. 21 (my translation).

2. Comments as reported in *Le Monde*, September 18, 1969, p. 1 (my translation).

3. Jean Bunel and Paul Meunier, *Chaban-Delmas . . .* (Paris: Stock, 1972), 90.

4. See chapters 6 and 7 below for an elaboration of the similarities between the New Society and the Socialist industrial relations reforms.

5. Jacques Delors, *Changer* (Paris: Stock, 1975), 189 (my translation).

6. Jacques Delors, "La Nouvelle Société," *Preuves*, no. 2 (1970), 105 (my translation).

7. Chaban-Delmas in his speech introducing the New Society program in front of the National Assembly, September 16, 1969. This speech is reprinted in full in "Principales mesures prises en application de la déclaration gouvernementale du 16 septembre: 16 septembre 1969–15 octobre 1970," *Actualités-Documents*, no. 66 (October 1970). The quotation is from page 38 (my translation).

8. Delors, *Changer*, 213 (my translation). This was, in one sense, a precursor of the "overload" theories of the state.

9. From a speech by Chaban-Delmas to the metal industry employers, reprinted in Bunel and Meunier, *Chaban-Delmas . . .*, 285 (my translation).

10. Delors, *Changer*, 98 (my translation).

11. See for instance the interview of Joseph Fontanet, Minister of Labor, by Gérard Adam in "Vers une plus grande clarté des relations syndicales," *Dirigeant* (June–July 1971). See especially the exchange on pp. 11–12.

12. Capdevielle and Mouriaux, *Mai 68*, 233.

13. Quoted in Weber, *Le Parti des Patrons*, 166 (my translation).

14. Joseph Fontanet, "La course-poursuite des salaires et de la croissance économique," *Projet* (May 1971), 535 (my translation).

15. The focus here will be the public-sector services because it was these that occupied the government's attention. Wage bargaining in some of the nationalized industries had always been different from the nationalized services, and the right to strike in the civil service was severely restricted, making it less of a target for government anxieties. The main concern was with the four main public firms: the SNCF, EGF, Charbonnages de France, and the Régie Autonome des Transports Parisiens (RATP). These are the firms that were at the center of the New Society reforms.

16. For the increases given in each nationalized firm see *Liaisons Sociales: Documents*, no. 106 (October 8, 1969), 8.

17. Figures for the level of unionization in particular firms or industries simply do not exist in France because of the highly unstable levels of union membership. The only figures come from the unions themselves and these are generally considered to be overestimates. The counting rules for union membership (how many monthly payments in a year constitutes membership) are not hard and fast. Further, only rarely do unions provide more than the overall raw membership numbers, making any breakdown by firm or sector largely guesswork. The evidence for higher union membership in the public and nationalized sector is largely indirect, through the votes cast for union confederations in professional elections and the greater protection afforded unions in this sector.

18. One crucial difference between 1964 and 1969 was that in 1964 the government was attempting to implement an incomes policy which the unions rejected. The unions were therefore unlikely to accept multiyear contracts that gave them nothing in return. In 1969 the government could afford to be more generous in wage agreements. This is another indication of the conjunctural fragility of the period within which the New Society reforms were attempted.

19. Chaban-Delmas, to the National Assembly, September 16, 1969. Cited in "Principales mesures prises en application de la déclaration gouvernementale du 16 septembre," 44 (my translation).

20. See "L'Audience des syndicats: 10 ans d'élections professionnelles," *Notes et Documents du BRAEC*, no. 17 (1981) for figures. This is another indication of the suggestion made above that the aim of Chaban-Delmas was to tame the CGT rather than circumvent it. The choice of EGF, where the CGT was particularly strong, for the first progress contract would have made little sense otherwise.

21. The best account of the EGF contract is Gérard Lyon-Caen, "La convention sociale d'EGF et le système français des relations professionnelles, *Droit Social*, no. 4 (April 1970).

22. Gilbert Declercq, "Bons et mauvais contrats," *Le Monde*, March 4, 1970, p. 10 (my translation).

23. The bulletin of the FGE-CFDT, *Gaz-Électicité CFDT*, no. 191 (May 1970), reported on the 22nd Congress of the FGE-CFDT and conceded: "We also take note of a whole series of interventions from comrades who consider that the signing [of the EGF contract] was too rapid and the consultation insufficiently broad" (my translation).

24. For details of opposition interventions see *Syndicalisme Hebdo*, no. 1281 (March 1970): 6–7.

25. For details see *Syndicalisme Hebdo*, no. 1291 (May 1970): 9–10.

26. Bunel and Meunier, *Chaban-Delmas . . .* , 111.

27. André Lebon, "Les principaux accords salariaux signés en 1970 et 1971 dans les secteurs public et nationalisé," *Droit Social*, nos. 7–8 (July–August 1971), contains a good summary of the various public-sector wage contracts of the first two and a half years of the New Society.

28. This question cannot be divorced from the wider failure of the New Society project, which will be considered in the conclusion to this chapter. Here the particular flaws of the progress contract approach will be considered.

29. Flanagan, Soskice, Ulman, *Unionism, Economic Stabilization, and Incomes Policies*, 576.

30. Jacques Delors, "La politique contractuelle, naissance d'une autre politique sociale," *Revue française des affaires sociales*, no. 3 (July–September 1978): 121 (my translation).

31. Examples are contracts at Berliet in January 1970, and Merlin & Gerin in April 1970.

32. See *CFDT Nouvelles*, no. 12 (1970), for details.

33. An ordinance of December 30, 1958, had made any automatic indexation to the cost of living illegal.

34. For figures on strike levels in selected firms in the public and nationalized sector see Bunel and Meunier, *Chaban-Delmas. . .* , 114.

35. The French term for such agreements is *interprofessionel*.

36. Note that the accords were still being signed in 1975, well after the end of the New Society.

37. The joint declaration on *la mensuelisation* (literally, payment by month, not hour) is not directly relevant to the discussion here, but it does provide a fascinating example of the new interests and strategies of the French *patronat*. In brief, the accord—which was quickly followed by agreements in almost all branches of industry—provided more security and better pay and benefits to the workers concerned. Yet it was widely supported by the larger employers represented in the CNPF. The reason was that salaried workers had less incentive to leave a firm, which was important when skilled labor was short. It also provided more stable and predictable wage bills than payment based on an hourly wage. Individual firms could have introduced these measures alone, but each faced a collective-action problem in that their wage bill would rise relative to their competitors. A national-level accord solved that problem. Employers were increasingly concerned with nonwage issues and were prepared to pay higher wages in return for a more stable labor force. For further details see Jean Bunel, *La Mensuelisation, une Reforme Tranquille?* (Paris: Éditions Ouvrières, 1973).

38. Lyon-Caen, "Critique de la négociation collective," 7.

39. See *Syndicalisme Hebdo*, no. 1301 (July 23, 1970), for criticism of the agreement along these lines.

40. Delors, "La Nouvelle Société," 103 (my translation).

41. See Michel Despax, "Observations sur la représentativité des organizations syndicales au regard du droit des conventions collective," *Droit Social*, nos. 7–8 (July–August 1979), for details of the way in which the extension procedure was changed. See the conclusion of this chapter for a discussion of the significance of this change.

42. See "Les Périodes d'intense syndicalisation," *Notes et Documents du BRAEC*, no. 18 (October–December 1981): 11.

43. Figures from *Liaisons Sociales: Documents*, no. 98 (November 8, 1974): 1.

44. Ibid., 2.

45. The precise figure is 109.3 percent. See G. Mermillod-Blardet, "Une analyse statistique des élections aux comités d'entreprise depuis 1966," *Revue française des affaires sociale*, no. 3 (1974): 141.

46. Ibid., 145.

47. While official government figures exist for collective agreements at the branch and national levels, no such records exist for firm accords (until 1982). Thus the only data available is from case studies conducted from time to time. The data on firm-level agreements presented here, therefore, is only partial and does not go beyond 1970.

48. Mermillod-Blardet, "Une analyse statistique des élections aux comités d'entreprise."

49. Jean-Paul Bachy, François Dupuy, and Dominique Martin, *Représentation et négociation dans l'entreprise* (Paris: Université "Paris-Sud," 1974).

50. The fullest discussion of the reasons for failure given by Chaban-Delmas and Delors comes from their autobiographies, both published in 1975: Jacques Chaban-Delmas, *L'Ardeur* (Paris: Éditions Stock, 1975), and Delors, *Changer*.

51. "Principales mesures prises en application de la déclaration gouvernementale du 16 septembre."

52. See *Syndicalisme Hebdo*, no. 1337 (April 8, 1971), for an exhaustive list of such tactics, with examples.

53. See interview with Adam, "Vers une plus grande clarté," 10 (my translation).

54. *L'Express* (November 20–26, 1972), 15 (my translation).

55. Michele Salvati, "May 1968 and the Hot Autumn of 1969: The Responses of Two Ruling Classes," in Suzanne Berger, ed., *Organizing Interests in Western Europe* (Cambridge: Cambridge University Press, 1981), 329.

56. Ibid.

57. Boyer, "Wage Formation in Historical Perspective," 115.

58. Flanagan, Soskice, and Ulman, *Unionism, Economic Stabilization, and Incomes Policies*, 623.

59. Bernard Mery, "La Pratique de l'indexation dans les conventions collectives," *Droit Social*, no. 6 (June 1973). Mery lists the beneficiaries of indexation as: civil servants; workers in the large nationalized companies; 0.5 million workers

paid the minimum wage; 2.0 million workers in the private sector; 1.5 million retired people; and indirect indexation for low-paid workers earning close to the minimum wage.

60. Suzanne Berger and Michael Piore, *Dualism and Discontinuity in Industrial Societies* (New York: Cambridge University Press, 1980), especially chapter 4.

61. Note that the proportion of workers affected by the minimum wage varies widely across sectors. Those sectors without collective bargaining—services, for instance—tend to have wage levels very close to the minimum wage.

62. See Doyelle and Perrot, "L'Évolution du pouvoir d'achat," 18.

63. Ibid., 18.

64. For figures on the use of the extension procedure see Claude Jezequel, "Aperçus statistiques sur la vie conventionnelle en France," *Droit Social*, no. 6 (June 1981): 463.

65. For details see *Liaisons Sociales: Législation Sociale*, no. 4238 (February 3, 1975).

66. See *Liaisons Sociales: Législation Sociale*, no. 4302 (August 5, 1975).

CHAPTER FIVE

1. George Ross, "Marxism and the New Middles Classes: French Critiques," *Theory and Society* 5, no. 2 (March 1978).

2. The terminology used to describe social groups is, not surprisingly, different in France from that used in Britain and the United States. This study, because it focuses on the sphere of industrial relations, is only concerned with certain elements of the new middle classes. The French term *cadre* refers to a wide range of supervisory and lower-managerial employees. This was the key social grouping whose political loyalty was seen as *undetermined*, and whose role in labor regulation in the workplace was considered critical. For the most part this term will be used throughout this and later chapters in preference to an English translation.

3. For a survey of strikingly similar perspectives, from both Left and Right, see Claus Offe, *Contradictions of the Welfare State* (Cambridge: MIT Press, 1984), chapter 6.

4. See Zysman, *Governments, Markets, and Growth*, chapter 3.

5. The following section relies heavily on the account given by Weber, *Le Parti des Patrons*, especially chapter 13.

6. Pierre Dubois, "Recherches statistiques et monographiques sur les grèves," *Revue française des affaires sociales*, no. 2 (April–June 1980): 39 (my translation).

7. Quoted in *CNPF Patronat*, no. 386 (December 1977) (my translation).

8. François Ceyrac, quoted in Dominique Pouchin, "Le syndicalisme en crise," *Le Monde*, March 6, 1980, p. 36 (my translation).

9. Ross, "The Perils of Politics." This section relies heavily upon this account.

10. Jacques Moreau to the Conseil National of the CFDT in January 1978. Quoted in Hervé Harmon and Patrick Rotman, *La Deuxième Gauche* (Paris: Éditions Ramsay, 1982), 300 (my translation).

11. For a sampling see René Mouriaux, *Les Syndicats Face à la Crise* (Paris: Éditions la Découverte, 1986); Hubert Landier, *Demain Quels Syndicats?* (Paris:

Librairie Générale Française, 1981); Adam, *Le Pouvoir Syndical*; and Rosanvallon, *La Question Syndicale*.

12. For discussion of the importance of structural change see Aujard and Volkoff, "Une Analyse chiffrée des audiences syndicales."

13. Boyer, "Wage Formation in Historical Perspective," 117.

14. For an excellent summary of the variety of unemployment benefits see *Liaisons Sociales: Législation Sociale*, no. 4321 (October 3, 1975).

15. Reported in *Liaisons Sociales: Documents*, no. 8 (February 5, 1975): 2.

16. René Mouriaux, "Antagonismes sociaux et réforme de l'entreprise: Les silences du Rapport Sudreau," *Etudes* (April 1975).

17. Giscard d'Estaing, as quoted in *Liaisons Sociales: Documents*, no. 8 (February 5, 1975): 1 (my translation).

18. There was some surprise that the CFDT chose to be represented (by Albert Detraz) and the leadership of the CFDT went to some lengths to explain that they had no illusions about reform within the confines of a capitalist economy, but that they felt a voice on the commission would be valuable. They too submitted detailed proposals for reform. For the position of the CFDT see *Syndicalisme Hebdo*, no. 1505 (July 1974).

19. *Rapport Sudreau* (Paris: Documentation Française, 1975).

20. Pierre Sudreau, as quoted in *Quotidien de Paris*, February 20, 1975, p. 3 (my translation).

21. All citations and quotations from the Sudreau Report are taken from the English translation of the report: *The Reform of the Enterprise in France* (Philadelphia: Industrial Research Unit of the Wharton School, University of Pennsylvania, 1975).

22. *The Reform of the Enterprise in France*, 68. Note also the similarity here with the New Society notion of recognizing the role of trade unions in channeling discontent.

23. Ibid., 86.

24. Ibid., 56 (emphasis added).

25. See *Liaisons Sociales: Législation Sociale*, no. 4171 (July 5, 1974): 2, for the text of the declaration.

26. *The Reform of the Enterprise in France*, 206.

27. For details of the proposals see *Liaisons Sociales: Documents*, no. 36 (April 15, 1976).

28. For details see *Liaisons Sociales: Documents*, no. 47 (May 16, 1977).

29. *Liaisons Sociales: Documents*, no. 125 (December 8, 1978), presents a useful summary of what, if anything, was done about each of the sixty-nine proposals in the original Sudreau Report.

30. See chapter 7 below for a discussion of the reappearance of certain key elements of the Sudreau Report in the Socialist industrial relations reforms.

31. *Le Figaro*, April 14, 1977, p. 21 (my translation).

32. *Syndicalisme Hebdo*, no. 1601 (May 20, 1976); my translation.

33. *Le Peuple*, no. 990 (May 15–31, 1976).

34. See Harmon and Rotman, *La Deuxième Gauche*, chapter 10, for a discussion of this episode.

35. The CFDT objections to employer proposals can be found in *Syndicalisme Hebdo*, no. 1785 (November 29, 1979).

36. Quoted in Jacqueline Grapin, "Au Conseil Économique et Social," *Le Monde*, July 1, 1975, p. 30 (my translation).

37. See Zysman, *Governments, Markets, and Growth*, chapter 3.

38. Volkmar Lauber, *The Political Economy of France* (New York: Praeger, 1983), 102. The account of economic policy that follows relies heavily upon Lauber and upon W. Allen Spivey, *Economic Policies in France, 1975–81*, Michigan International Business Studies, no. 18 (Ann Arbor: University of Michigan, 1982).

39. See Lauber, *The Political Economy of France*, 92, for figures on the cost of unemployment to the government.

40. See *Le Monde*, January 16–17, 1977, pp. 1, 19, for details of this proposal and the likely real wage gains based on projected growth and inflation rates.

41. Raymond Barre, *Une Politique pour l'avenir* (Paris: Plon, 1981), 119 (my translation).

42. From 1974 onward Giscard d'Estaing had pursued a campaign to "revalorize work," which in practice meant measures to improve working conditions. This effort continued throughout this period, and frequent references were made to it by those in government to demonstrate the commitment to workers. However, the reforms were piecemeal and of limited scope. They never came close to exciting either the unions or workers, or to being a form of compensation for wage restraint.

43. See Lauber, *The Political Economy of France*, 102, table 7.4.

44. See chapter 6 below for a discussion of the Socialist wage-restraint policy.

45. *L'Express* (December 13–19, 1980), 106 (my translation).

46. *Syndicalisme Hebdo*, no. 1652 (May 12, 1977).

47. *Le Monde*, June 13, 1978, p. 1.

48. See Weber, *Le Parti des Patrons*, chapter 16, especially pp. 288–92.

49. Or rather the expectation of defeat, because the first secret contacts with the CNPF and Barre government took place in January 1978, before the election.

50. Note that the increased interest in collective bargaining went beyond government circles. The year 1978 saw a series of reports and commentaries on the deficiencies of French collective bargaining. See, for example, Jean-Daniel Reynaud's report for the EEC: *Les Syndicats, les patrons et l'état: Tendances de la négociation collective en France* (Paris: Les Éditions ouvrières, 1978).

51. This possibility was suggested by Jean-Claude Casanova, one of Barre's economic advisers, in an interview with the author, Paris, June 30, 1987.

52. *Liaisons Sociales: Législation Sociale*, no. 4813 (October 10, 1979): 3.

53. The main industries concerned were metalworking, chemicals, steel, sugar, and banking. For details see Evelyne Bughin, "L'Évolution des rémunérations minimales garanties et du SMIC depuis le 1er: Janvier 1976," *Travail et Emploi*, no. 4 (April 1980).

54. Bughin, ibid., gives a good summary of the results of the greater reliance on negotiated minimums rather than the SMIC.

55. An additional problem was that employers wanted to tie vacation time to absenteeism so as to create a powerful disincentive to absenteeism. The unions saw this as authoritarian labor control pure and simple.

56. For details of the CFDT's objections see *Syndicalisme Hebdo*, no. 1785 (November 29, 1979).

57. This figure comes from Weber, *Le Parti des Patrons*, 350.

58. It should be noted that this unemployment regime was not available to all workers, nor was it automatically offered for a year. It had to be renewed every three months. It tended to be core workers in normally stable employment that benefited.

59. For accounts of this shift after 1977 see: J-F. Colin, J-C. Cros, E. Verdier, and D. Welcomme, "Politiques d'emploi: La rupture de 1977," *Travail et Emploi*, no. 10 (October–December 1981); and Jean Hervé, "Dix ans de politique de l'emploi (1973–83)," *Etudes* (January 1984).

60. It should be noted that most studies showed that the pacts were in fact used to avoid social security costs and fill temporary demand rather than provide long-term jobs. See Hervé, "Dix ans de politique de l'emploi"; and Marie-Françoise Mouriaux and René Mouriaux, "Unemployment Policy in France, 1976–1982," in Jeremy Richardson and Roger Henning, eds., *Unemployment: Policy Responses in Western Democracies* (London: Sage, 1984).

61. Figures are from René Mouriaux and Françoise Subileau, "Données statistiques concernant le syndicalisme des salariés en France (1945–1986)," Document du Travail (Paris: CEVIPOF, 1986), 39–40. Note also that in October 1979 the Ministry of Labor published a record of bargaining since 1978 which showed that most of the accords had been concerned with establishing wage minimums, and very few with the flexibility of work time. Reported in *Liaisons Sociales: Législation Sociale*, no. 4813 (October 10, 1979).

62. Chantal Baron, "Les conventions collectives," *Bulletin Mensuel des Statistiques du Travail—Supplément*, no. 100 (1982).

63. Jean-Paul Murcier, "Réflexions sur la négociation collective en France," *Droit Social*, nos. 7–8 (July–August 1979).

64. Bughin, "L'Évolution des rémunérations minimales garanties."

65. Of course, all trade unions comprised small minorities of the work force. Minority here refers to scores in firm elections, not membership.

66. See two issues of *Le Peuple*, no. 1069 (September 1979), and no. 1074 (December 1979).

67. Jezequel, "Aperçus statistiques sur la vie conventionnelle en France," 463, gives figures for the use of the extension procedure. There was indeed a decline from a peak of 640 extensions in 1974 to 314 in 1977. The number then rapidly increased to 721 in 1980, possibly as a result of the modified procedure.

68. Francis Ginsbourger and Jean-Yves Potel, "La Pratique de la Négociation Collective," *Travail et Emploi*, no. 20 (June 1984): 13 (my translation).

69. Delors, as quoted in *Le Point*, January 19, 1976, p. 36 (my translation).

70. The shift was much more important for employers in the larger, more modern firms represented by the CNPF. Social relations inside firms in the traditional sector had always stressed flexibility.

INTRODUCTION TO PART III

1. For a good discussion of the "organizational context" that the Socialists faced in 1981 see W. Rand Smith, "The End of Illusions: French Socialism and Industrial Crisis in the 1980s" (manuscript in preparation).

2. Daniel Singer, *Is Socialism Doomed? The Meaning of Mitterrand* (New York: Oxford University Press, 1988), 10.

3. See for instance George Ross and Jane Jenson, "The Tragedy of the French Left," *New Left Review*, no. 171 (September–October 1988).

4. A good example here is the argument made by David Cameron in "The Colors of a Rose: On the Ambiguous Record of French Socialism," Center for European Studies Working Paper, no. 12 (Cambridge, Mass.: Center for European Studies, 1988).

CHAPTER SIX

1. For differing contributions to this debate see: Singer, *Is Socialism Doomed?*; Bernard E. Brown, *Socialism of a Different Kind* (Westport, Conn.: Greenwood Press, 1982); D. S. Bell and Byron Criddle, *The French Socialist Party* (Oxford: Clarendon Press, 1984); and Hughes Portelli, *Le Socialisme français tel qu'il est* (Paris: Presses Universitaires de France, 1980).

2. The term "anti-corporatism" comes from Suzanne Berger, "The Socialists and the Patronat: The Dilemmas of Co-existence in a Mixed Economy," in Howard Machin and Vincent Wright, eds., *Economic Policy and Policy-making Under the Mitterrand Presidency 1981–84* (London: Frances Pinter, 1985), 241.

3. See Brown, *Socialism of a Different Kind*, chapter 4, for the elaboration of this argument.

4. Bell and Criddle, *The French Socialist Party*, 2.

5. Singer, *Is Socialism Doomed?*, 47.

6. Bell and Criddle, *The French Socialist Party*, provides the most accessible account of PS history and organization. This section and the one that follows owe much to this account.

7. On this point see Cameron, "The Colors of a Rose," and George Ross and Jane Jenson, "Pluralism and the Decline of Left Hegemony: The French Left in Power," *Politics and Society* 14, no. 2 (1985).

8. This characterization of PS currents can be found in Bell and Criddle, *The French Socialist Party*, chapter 10; and George Ross and Jane Jenson, "Political Pluralism and Economic Policy," in John S. Ambler, ed., *The French Socialist Experiment* (Philadelphia: Institute for the Study of Human Issues, 1985), 30–31.

9. *Projet Socialiste* (Paris: Club Socialiste de Livre, 1980).

10. See, for instance, *Projet Socialiste*, 196, 234.

11. Ibid., 238.

12. Ibid., 226–27.

13. See chapter 8 below for a more detailed discussion of this episode.

14. See "La Fermeture sociale: Bilan de la négociation sociale depuis mars 1978," *Échange et Projets*, no. 21 (January–March 1980); and the report "Échange et Projets," in *Droit Social*, no. 11 (November 1978).

15. See chapter 7 below for details of the Auroux reforms.

16. For Mitterrand's election manifesto see *Le Monde: Dossiers et Documents*, "L'Élection Presidentielle, 26 avril–10 mai 1981" (May 1981).

17. For this reason I have used the term *autogestion* throughout this study instead of a more value-laden, and misleading, translation. However, some defini-

tion, even if necessarily general, might be useful. Nancy Lieber, in "Ideology and Tactics of the French Socialist Party," *Government and Opposition* 12, no. 4 (Autumn 1977), 459, defines *autogestion* as follows: "*Autogestion*, literally self-management, implies a society in which the democratic process—the consent of the governed—is extended to the social and particularly the economic aspects of life, as well as the political."

18. This suspicion was not unrelated to the fact that the PCF had strong links to the largest trade union confederation.

19. Also *Projet Socialiste*, 241–42, 228.

20. Ibid., 175.

21. See Bell and Criddle, *The French Socialist Party*, chapter 1.

22. See Patrick Hardouin, "Les Caractéristiques sociologiques du Parti Socialiste," *Revue française de science politique* 28, no. 2 (April 1978).

23. Cameron, "The Colors of a Rose," 29–30, and Bell and Criddle, *The French Socialist Party*, chapter 2.

24. See Mark Kesselman, "Socialism Without the Workers: The Case of France," *Kapitalistate*, nos. 10–11 (1983): 20, table 2.

25. For the evolution of PS workplace sections in the 1970s see *Les Socialistes dans L'entreprise* (Paris: Club Socialiste du Livre, 1982), annex 3. The figure for 1983 comes from Jean-Paul Bachy, in an interview with the author, Paris, May 26, 1987.

26. The study conducted by Roland Cayrol and others is reported in Roland Cayrol, "Le Parti Socialiste à L'entreprise," *Revue française de science politique* 28, no. 2 (April 1978).

27. A 1981 study showed that of those PS members who belonged to trade unions, the affiliations were 28 percent CFDT, 26 percent FEN, 10 percent CGT, and 6 percent FO. See Roland Cayrol and C. Ysmal, "Les Militants du PS: Originalité et Diversités," *Projet*, no. 165 (May 1982).

28. Harmon and Rotman give figures for CFDT participation in the first Socialist government in *La Deuxième Gauche*, 341–42.

29. Bell and Criddle vividly demonstrate the declining representation of workers and rising representation of the new middle class as one moves up the PS from membership to leadership positions. See *The French Socialist Party*, 203.

30. See *Projet Socialiste*, 243.

31. Philippe Garraud, "Discours, Pratiques et Ideologie dans L'évolution de Parti Socialiste," *Revue française de science politique* 28, no. 2 (April 1978): 275 (my translation).

32. Kesselman, "Socialism Without the Workers," 23.

33. The literature on this subject is vast. See Alain Fonteneau and Pierre-Alain Muet, *La Gauche Face à la Crise* (Paris: FNSP, 1985); Michel Beaud, *La Politique Économique de la Gauche*, 2 vols. (Paris: Syros, 1983); Lauber, *The Political Economy of France*, part 3; Hall, *Governing the Economy*, chapter 8; and Cameron, "The Colors of a Rose."

34. Information on the wage and inflation differential between France and Germany, and the narrowing of the gap between the two countries during the course of the 1980s, can be found in *OECD Economic Surveys—France, 1988/1989* (Paris: OECD, 1989), 16, table 5.

35. Jean Auroux subtitled his September 1982 "Lettre du Ministre du Travail" (on the prospects for the end of the freeze) "A New Chance for Collective Bargaining."

36. Francis Lepâtre in *CNPF Patronat*, no. 439 (October 1982), 35 (my translation).

37. And also in the private sector, where the indexed accords were widely copied in 1970–74. See chapter 4 above for details.

38. See Jean-Pierre Faugère, *Les Politiques Salariales en France* (Paris: La Documentation Française, 1988), 103.

39. The special issue, "Fonds salariaux," *Échange et Projets*, no. 34 (July 1983), provides information on the extent of participation. In 1981 there were 10,225 *participation* agreements (ibid., 24).

40. For the CFDT's reaction see several issues of *Syndicalisme Hebdo*: no. 1958 (March 31, 1983); no. 1960 (April 14, 1983); and no. 1991 (November 17, 1983).

41. Wage levels rose sharply in 1981 before the application of austerity measures. They subsequently declined.

42. Alain Minczeles and Pierre Sicsic, "La Désinflation 1982–85," *Revue Économique* 37, no. 6 (November 1986): 1139, 1141. See the rest of this issue for other interesting articles on "dis-inflation."

43. Francis Ginsbourger and Jean-Yves Potel, *Les Pratiques de la Négociation de Branche* (Paris: La Documentation Française, 1987), 263 (my translation).

44. Note that there was an increase in the numbers of workers in both these categories after 1981 (indeed most casual laborers were paid at or close to the minimum wage); otherwise, the real wage loss would have been even greater.

45. See the *Bilan de la Négociation Collective en 1985* (Paris: La Documentation Française, 1986), 35, 39.

46. This figure comes from the *OECD Economic Surveys—France, 1988/1989*, 13. The success of wage restraint in France received its ultimate accolade in the highly enthusiastic reports from the economically orthodox OECD in the period after 1985.

47. Delors, as quoted in *Le Monde: Affaires*, September 5, 1987, p. 6 (my translation).

48. This section concentrates on the CGT and CFDT rather than the other, more reformist unions because these were the two unions most likely to have some degree of ideological sympathy for the PS and hence be willing to engage in corporatist wage restraint.

49. See the article by Michel Noblecourt, "Le gouvernement à l'épreuve du pluralisme syndical," *Le Monde*, March 24, 1982, p. 10, on this point. Note Noblecourt's wry comment that "M.Mitterrand n'a pas les syndicats qu'il aurait souhaités" ("Mitterrand does not have the unions that he would have wished for").

50. See the article by Michel Noblecourt, "Le P.S. pour un code de conduite entre gouvernement et syndicats," *Le Monde*, May 22–23, 1983, p. 1.

51. *L'Unité*, April 16, 1982, p. 8 (my translation).

52. See, for instance, comments by Georges Séguy of the CGT in *Le Peuple*, no. 1131 (April 25–30, 1982): 45.

53. My translation. The original interview with Delors was in the newspaper *Le*

Pèlerin and it was reprinted in part in Jean-Pierre Dumont, "La Querelle entre M. Delors et les organisations syndicales," *Le Monde*, April 17, 1982, p. 33.

54. *Syndicalisme Hebdo*, no. 1918 (June 24, 1982).

55. *Syndicalisme Hebdo*, no. 1936 (October 28, 1982).

56. For a discussion of CFDT strategy in this period see Guy Groux and René Mouriaux, *La C.F.D.T.* (Paris: Économica, 1989), chapter 5.

57. See *Resister*, no. 13 (January 1984): 13 (my translation).

58. This case was made in an important interview with Edmond Maire in *Syndicalisme Hebdo*, no. 2013 (April 19, 1984): 5–6.

59. For evidence of rank-and-file discontent within the CFDT see the "Tribunes" section of *Syndicalisme Hebdo* in the run up to the 39th CFDT Congress at Metz, especially no. 1906 (March 25, 1982), and no. 1907 (April 1, 1982). For details of the Ha-Cui-Tex counterproposal see *Syndicalisme Hebdo*, no. 2057 (March 14, 1985).

60. Gérard Gaume in *Le Peuple*, nos. 1107–1108 (May 15–June 15, 1981): 4 (my translation).

61. From the orientation document for the 41st CGT Congress in Lille. Cited in *Le Peuple*, no. 1126 (February 16–28, 1982): 24 (my translation).

62. The story of the reform of worker representation in the SNCF is an interesting one. The issue concerned the number of representative bodies to be created and it was important because the strong CGT implantation among railroad workers was such that the greater the degree of decentralization of worker representation (and hence the more representative bodies) the more influence the CGT would have. Negotiations between unions and management failed and Fiterman stepped in to create 327 "comités d'établissements," a decision that favored the CGT. After Fiterman left the government the Council of State overruled his decision in June 1985, creating thirty-five committees instead. For background on the SNCF see Georges Ribeil, *Les Cheminots* (Paris: Éditions La Découverte, 1984).

63. See *Le Monde*, March 13, 1985, p. 24, for details of CGT gains.

64. Not surprisingly, this autonomy was not universally admired within the PS. The topic arose, interestingly, in the context of the parliamentary debates on the Auroux Laws in the summer of 1982, on the specific issue of "political sections" within the firm. Some members of the PS, and particularly Jean-Paul Bachy, wanted to provide opportunities for political parties to organize and express themselves inside the workplace. Bachy's rationale (interview with author, Paris, May 26, 1987) was that the PS needed its own channel to the working class. The PCF had its own cells in the firm and had the CGT as an ally. The PS could not rely on the other unions, certainly not the CFDT or FO, as a link between the party and the working class. The idea behind giving a certain protection to workplace sections was to give the PS such a link. The defeat of this proposal represented a choice for autonomy and one kind of socialist party over a more organic, firmly rooted kind of working-class party.

65. The term is Hall's, *Governing the Economy*, 193.

66. This is not to say that there has not been a great deal of internal party conflict in the PS. Intraparty conflict is endemic to the PS and has worsened in the period since the 1988 Socialist return to power. However, what is remarkable is the narrow range of debate within the party, the absence of credible alternative policy

proposals, and the narrowly political nature of the conflict. For discussion of recent PS conflict see Julius W. Friend, "The PS Faces the 1990s," *French Politics and Society* 8, no. 1 (Winter 1990); and Chris Howell, "The Fetishism of Small Difference: French Socialism Enters the Nineties," *French Politics and Society* 9, no. 1 (Winter 1991).

CHAPTER SEVEN

1. There is a massive amount of work on the Auroux Laws. For a sampling see: Duncan Gallie, "Les Lois Auroux: The Reform of French Industrial Relations?" in Machin and Wright, eds., *Economic Policy and Policy-Making Under the Mitterrand Presidency*; W. Rand Smith, "Towards *Autogestion* in Socialist France: The Impact of Industrial Relations Reform," *West European Politics* 10, no. 1 (January 1987); Bernard E. Brown, "Worker Democracy in France: Are You Serious?" *French Politics and Society* 8, no. 2 (Spring 1990); François Eyraud and Robert Tchoanian, "The Auroux Reform and Company Level Industrial Relations in France," *British Journal of Industrial Relations* 23, no. 2 (July 1985); Guy Caire, "Recent Trends in Collective Bargaining in France," *International Labour Review* 123 (November–December 1984); and Raymond-Pierre Bodin, *Les Lois Auroux dans les P.M.E.* (Paris: La Documentation Française, 1987).

2. See the penultimate section of this chapter for details of trade union strength.

3. See Weber, *Le Parti des Patrons*, chapter 19. Also issues of the CNPF's journal, *CNPF Patronat*, from the first half of 1982 give a good sense of the CNPF's growing confidence and belligerency.

4. *Le Monde*, December 30, 1983, p. 18 (my translation).

5. Jean Auroux, *Les Droits des Travailleurs* (Paris: La Documentation Française, September 1981), 30.

6. Gallie, "Les Lois Auroux: The Reform of French Industrial Relations?" 218.

7. Rand Smith, "Towards *Autogestion* in Socialist France," 57.

8. Delors, as quoted in *Quotidien de Paris*, November 24, 1983, p. 3 (my translation).

9. One can find Delors putting forward his theory of wages (*"salaire-parité, salaire-spécificité, salaire-promotion"*) as far back as 1976. See the interview with Delors in *L'Expansion* (December 1976). For a more recent version see the interview with Delors in *Le Nouvel Economiste* (December 5, 1983).

10. Employers, in fact, claimed that it was the re-creation of what had been the situation before unions were introduced into the firm.

11. For details of new employer strategies see Pierre Morville, *Les Nouvelles Politiques Sociales du Patronat* (Paris: Éditions la Découverte, 1985), and Weber, *Le Parti des Patrons*, chapter 13.

12. For instance, the research bureau of the CFDT put out a report on the attitudes of employers and the other unions to the Auroux reforms, entitled "Les Autres et les droits nouveaux," *Notes et Documents du BRAEC*, no. 22 (October–December 1982). See also the piece by Jean-Paul Murcier of the CFDT, "La CFDT et les droits nouveaux pour les travailleurs," *Droit Social*, nos. 7–8 (July–August 1982).

13. Auroux, *Les Droits des Travailleurs*.

14. See *Libération*, November 4, 1981, p. 5.

15. For details of opposition within the PS see *Libération*, November 4, 1981, p. 5. Also see chapter 6, note 64, for a brief comment on the issue of political sections.

16. Yvon Chotard of the CNPF in "Le Rapport Auroux," *Droit Social*, no. 4 (April 1982); my translation.

17. Excellent summaries of the Auroux Laws already exist. The most detailed summary and commentary is Mary Ann Glendon, "French Labor Law Reform 1982–83: The Struggle for Collective Bargaining," *American Journal of Comparative Law* 32 (Summer 1984).

18. See the next section of this chapter for a detailed discussion of the meaning and implications of derogation.

19. Auroux, *Les Droits des Travailleurs*, 15 (my translation).

20. Murcier, "La CFDT et les droits nouveaux pour les travailleurs," 503 (my translation).

21. As Ginsbourger and Potel put it in their excellent study of bargaining in the 1970s, "The vitality of negotiation depends in large part on the balance of force between the [social] partners" ("La Pratique de la Négociation Collective," 12; my translation).

22. For a full list of the changes and emphasis on this point about the lack of new powers for unions see Jean-Maurice Verdier, "La Présence syndicale dans l'entreprise et la loi du octobre 1982 relative au développement des institutions representatives du personnel," *Droit Social*, no. 1 (January 1983); and Jean Pelissier, "La Fonction syndicale dans l'entreprise après les lois Auroux," *Droit Social*, no. 1 (January 1984).

23. Séguin, as quoted in *Le Nouveau Journal* (May 27, 1982): 4 (my translation).

24. This point was made by Claire Beauville of the CFDT in an interview with the author, Paris, April 30, 1987.

25. Raymond Vatinet, "La Négociation au sein du comité d'entreprise," *Droit Social*, no. 11 (November 1982).

26. Ibid., 676 (my translation).

27. Ibid., 677.

28. See the *Bilan de la Négociation Collective, 1984* (Paris: Ministère des Affaires Sociales, 1985), and *Bilan de la Négociation Collective en 1985*. One beneficial result of the Auroux Laws from the point of researchers has been much more extensive and systematic collection of data on collective bargaining. Each year the Ministry of Social Affairs publishes a summary of this data in the *Bilan Annuel*. Some are published by La Documentation Française (1985, 1987, 1988), and the rest are made available by the Ministry itself. They are an invaluable source of information.

29. Bodin, *Les Lois Auroux dans les P.M.E.*, 195 (my translation).

30. The study was published in *Liaisons Sociales: Mensuel* (November 1985).

31. *Bilan de la Négociation Collective en 1985*, 36.

32. *Négociation Collective—Quels Enjeux?* (Paris: La Documentation Française, 1988), 56 (my translation).

33. See the BRAEC report "Les Autres et les droits nouveaux," and also Gilles

Bélier, "Le Double niveau de négociation dans les lois Auroux: Un atout pour la politique contractuelle," *Droit Social*, no. 1 (January 1983).

34. "Les Autres et les droits nouveaux," 21 (my translation).

35. See the study by Françoise Dussert, Yves Mouton, and Chantal Salmon, "Évolution et structure du tissu conventionnel," *Dossiers statistiques du travail et emploi*, nos. 27–28 (December 1986): 10. No comparable study has been conducted since 1986.

36. See successive volumes of the *Bilan de la Négociation Collective* (from 1982 to 1988).

37. Auroux, *Les Droits des Travailleurs*, 97.

38. Rand Smith, "Towards *Autogestion* in Socialist France," 53.

39. "Les Autres et les droits nouveaux," 20 (my translation).

40. Ibid., 13 (my translation). Note also that FO signed the smallest proportion of the accords on the *droit d'expression* (62 percent); next lowest was CGT, with 76 percent. For details see Serge Volkoff, "Expression des salariés: Bilan statistique de 3000 accords," *Travail et Emploi*, no. 23 (March 1985): 81.

41. Volkoff, "Expression des salariés," 80.

42. Jean-Jacques Nansot, "Le Droit d'expression des salariés dans les entreprises: Premiers constats," *Travail et Emploi*, no. 24 (June 1985): 15.

43. For a good survey of the way in which the attitudes of the various unions and employers's organizations toward the *droit d'expression* changed, see *Négociation Collective—Quels Enjeux?* The second part of this report consists of commentaries from the social partners and is a useful source for evaluating how attitudes had changed, in light of the experience of collective bargaining, between 1981–82 and 1987.

44. *Bilan de la Négociation Collective, 1986* (Paris: Ministère des Affaires Sociales, 1987), 61; and *Bulletin Social*, no. 2 (1990).

45. It is important to make a distinction between the coverage of collective bargaining, where agreements are extended to new sectors or regions and operate without expiration dates, and the amount of actual bargaining activity. The annual codicils discussed in the last section measure the latter.

46. Dussert, Mouton, and Salmon, "Évolution et structure du tissu conventionnel," 7.

47. Ibid.

48. Ibid., 21. Note that these figures are for firms employing ten or more workers. Estimates for those not covered by any collective agreement *if firms employing less than ten are included* were 3 to 3.5 million in 1981, and 1.9 to 2.75 million in 1985 (ibid.).

49. For details see *Liaisons Sociales: Documents*, no. 41 (May 4, 1988).

50. For this point see the *Bilan de la Négociation Collective, 1982* (Paris: Ministère des Affaires Sociales, 1983), 7.

51. This estimate of the range was provided by Martin Schain in his presentation on the panel "Year Eight of the Mitterrand Experiment" at the Socialist Scholars Conference, New York, April 1, 1989. Rosanvallon gives a figure of 9 percent in *La Question Syndicale*, 265.

52. Aujard, "Les Délégués Syndicaux au 31 décembre 1987," *Dossiers statistiques du travail et d'emploi*, no. 50 (July 1989): 53.

53. This position is most associated with Gérard Adam and his thesis of the "institutionalization" of trade unions. See his book *Le Pouvoir Syndical*. The argument, in brief, is that trade union membership has been replaced as a measure of union strength by union "presence" in workplace representative institutions and in a variety of "semipublic" social institutions such as the social security organizations. As a result, Adam argues, unionism cannot be said to have declined in France, rather it has changed in form and function.

54. For figures for works council elections in the 1980s see *Dossiers statistiques du travail et d'emploi*, nos. 27–28 (December 1986), no. 39 (December 1987), no. 45 (November 1988), and no. 55 (February 1990). The 1989 figures were reported in *Libération*, July 14–15, 1990, p. 27. Nonunion votes mean votes cast for candidates not standing as representatives of a trade union.

55. *Dossiers statistiques du travail et d'emploi*, no. 39 (December 1987).

56. Bodin, *Les Lois Auroux dans les P.M.E.*, 194 (my translation).

57. Quoted in *Négociation Collective—Quels Enjeux?* 221 (my translation).

58. This becomes clear in the union commentaries in part II of *Négociation Collective—Quels Enjeux?* See also the comment that union discourse has been taking branch agreements more seriously recently, in Ginsbourger and Potel, *Les Pratiques de la Négociation de Branche*, 272.

59. See the *Bilan de la Négociation Collective, 1986*, 38–39, and chapter 8 below.

60. For a detailed discussion of this development, see chapter 8 on flexibility.

61. See Weber, *Le Parti des Patrons*, chapter 18, for a discussion of the shift in power within the CNPF toward medium-sized firms.

62. For further details of these proposals see chapter 9 below.

63. For a discussion of the evolution of employer attitudes to the Auroux Laws see Bernard H. Moss, "After the Auroux Laws: Employers, Industrial Relations and the Right in France," *West European Politics* 11, no. 1 (January 1988).

64. Cited in François de Closets, *Tous Ensemble* (Paris: Éditions du Seuil, 1985), 437.

65. Ibid., 8 (my translation).

CHAPTER EIGHT

1. This argument is found in its most developed form in the work of the French Regulation School of political economy. See Boyer, *La Théorie de la Régulation: Une Analyse Critique*, and Boyer, ed., *La Flexibilité du Travail en Europe*, chapter 1.

2. Boyer, ed., *La Flexibilité du Travail en Europe*, 1–2 (my translation).

3. The literature on this subject is vast. See in particular Piore and Sabel, *The Second Industrial Divide*; the special issue, "European Labor in the 1980s," ed. Peter A. Hall, *International Journal of Political Economy* (Fall 1987); and Rianne Mahon, "From Fordism to ?: New Technology, Labour Markets and Unions," *Economic and Industrial Democracy* 8 (1987).

4. These terms are not strictly speaking interchangeable. They are used by different groups of people to mean different things. "Flexible specialization" is the term used by Piore and Sabel in *The Second Industrial Divide*, while "post-Fordism" is a Regulation School term. Nevertheless, there is much overlap in the terms, and

they all refer to the same broad set of socioeconomic developments. My preference is for the term "post-Fordism."

5. There are exceptions. Piore and Sabel's *The Second Industrial Divide*, chapter 10, suggests that global Fordism is one possible future not involving flexibility.

6. See Boyer, ed., *La Flexibilité du Travail en Europe*, chapter 9. The important point is that once domestic mass consumer markets cease to be the main source of demand, the Fordist virtuous circle between increasing domestic consumption and production breaks down, and with it the economic justification for maintaining high and rising wage levels.

7. There are several comparative studies of flexibility. See *Labour Market Flexibility: Trends in Enterprises* (Paris: OECD, 1989); Guido Baglioni and Colin Crouch, eds., *European Industrial Relations: The Challenge of Flexibility* (London: Sage, 1990); and Boyer, ed., *La Flexibilité du Travail en Europe*.

8. It is important to note the extent to which *everyday* conflicts and struggles on the shopfloor have a cumulative effect, and themselves structure and transform broader societal institutions *irrespective* of the intentions of the groups engaged in conflict. For this point see Mike Davis, "Fordism in Crisis," *Review* 2, no. 2 (Fall 1978); 222–26. For the same point made in an entirely different socioeconomic context see James Scott, *Weapons of the Weak* (New Haven: Yale University Press, 1985).

9. Karl Polanyi, *The Great Transformation* (Boston: Beacon, 1944).

10. The term comes from Arndt Sorge and Wolfgang Streeck, "Industrial Relations and Technical Change: The Case for an Extended Perspective," in Richard Hyman and Wolfgang Streeck, eds., *New Technology and Industrial Relations* (Oxford: Basil Blackwell, 1987), 27.

11. Singer, *Is Socialism Doomed?*, chapter 8.

12. See the special issue, "Retour sur l'entreprise," of *Sociologie du Travail*, no. 3 (1986), especially the foreword by Anni Borzeix; see also Denis Segrestin, "L'entrée de l'entreprise en société," *Revue française de science politique* 34, no. 4 (August 1987).

13. Fabius, as quoted by Michel Noblecourt, "Machine de guerre ou nouvelle ambition," in *Le Monde*, October 2, 1984, p. 21. This article is a good introduction to the new thinking within the PS on the issues of flexibility and economic modernization.

14. Fabius, on October 11, 1983, as quoted in *Le Monde*, October 2, 1984, p. 23 (my translation).

15. The notion that flexibility and reduction of work time are, or can be, a specifically worker's demand, has a long intellectual pedigree. The CFDT was not adverse to justifying its bargaining position in terms of an opposition to an authoritarian and rigid Taylorism. It is interesting, in light of the argument made in previous chapters, that a significant area of compatibility exists between *autogestion* and flexibility, that those theorists most concerned with work time as a worker's demand belong, or at one point belonged, to the *autogestionnaire* current of the Left. For the best theoretical discussion of work time as part of a progressive agenda see André Gorz, *Critique of Economic Reason* (New York: Verso, 1989), especially the appendix.

16. See Gérard Lyon-Caen, "La Bataille truquée de la flexibilité," *Droit Social*, no. 12 (December 1985): 805.

17. Lesire-Ozrel, as quoted in *Syndicalisme Hebdo*, no. 1863 (May 28, 1981) (my translation). For the CFDT position see various issues of *Syndicalisme Hebdo*, especially no. 1863 (May 28, 1981) and no. 1865 (June 11, 1981).

18. For the CGT position see *Le Peuple*, no. 1113 (August 16–30, 1981).

19. This was an important and contentious issue. The question was whether workers should receive full compensation for the lost hour (i.e., whether they should continue to be paid for forty hours when they worked thirty-nine hours).

20. See *Syndicalisme Hebdo*, no. 1893 (December 24, 1981): 9, for a summary of the agreements.

21. *Bilan Annuel de la Négociation Collective, 1986*, 50.

22. *Bilan de la Négociation Collective en 1985*, 49.

23. On this point see François Sellier, "Aménagement du temps de travail, articulation entre niveaux de négociation et conflits entre syndicats," *Droit Social*, no. 11 (November 1986).

24. Delebarre, as quoted in François Loubejac, "Aménagement du temps de travail: Un projet a contre-sens?" *Droit Social*, no. 2 (February 1986): 92 (my translation).

25. *CNPF Patronat*, no. 465 (January 1985).

26. A third was the social security contributions paid by employees for new hires. This battle was effectively won in 1982 when, after intensive lobbying by the CNPF, the government agreed to freeze employer contributions until at least July 1983 and to transfer some parts of the cost to the state itself. See Weber, *Le Parti des Patrons*, chapter 19, and *Le Figaro*, April 15, 1982. The issue of the "*charges*" reappeared in 1984 as part of the employer package on flexibility (see later this section).

27. See the study by Mireille Elbaum and Michèle Tonnerre, "La Procédure de licenciement économique," *Dossiers statistiques du travail et d'emploi*, no. 19 (February 1986), 22.

28. See "Bilan de l'ordonnance de 5 février 1982 relative au travail temporaire," *Dossiers statistiques du travail et d'emploi*, no. 11 (April 1985): 5; and François Bloch-Lainé, *La France en Mai 1981: Forces et Faiblesses* (Paris: La Documentation Française, 1981).

29. Bloch-Lainé, *La France en Mai 1981*, 335.

30. Auroux, *Les Droits des Travailleurs*, annex 1.

31. The extent to which the growth of part-time jobs resulted from demand rather than supply factors is controversial. For a forceful statement that the supply of available jobs is a more important factor than the demand for them, see Margaret Maruani and Chantal Nicole-Drancourt, *Au Labeur des Dames: Métiers Masculins, Emplois Féminins* (Paris: Syros, 1989).

32. Quoted in *Liaisons Sociales: Documents*, no. 107 (October 3, 1984): 2.

33. Ibid., and "Bilan de l'ordonnance de 5 février 1982," 9–10.

34. Note that when the Right returned to power in March 1986, many of the restrictions were loosened and the bonus for precarious work was abolished. See "Aménagement du temps de travail," *Regards sur l'Actualité*, no. 131 (May 1987).

35. Yvon Chotard to the General Assembly of the CNPF, cited in Weber, *Le Parti des Patrons*, 344 (my translation). Note that the reference to the *"trente glorieuses"* was to the entire period of the postwar boom. Thus employers were demanding an end to restrictions that were decades old, not simply to those imposed by the Socialists since 1981.

36. French labor law set a series of threshold firm sizes, the most important being the ten-employee and fifty-employee levels, which brought with them increased rights for trade unions, higher costs for firms, and new responsibilities and restrictions for employers. The CNPF argued that this acted as a disincentive for firms to hire that tenth or fiftieth employee. So the ENCA proposal would have allowed for a lag between the hiring of new employees and when the new costs and restrictions took effect. See Henri Gibier, "Seuils: Le PS est-il flexible?" in *Le Nouvel Economiste*, no. 456 (September 17, 1984).

37. See *CNPF Patronat*, no. 457 (May 1984): 50–51, for details of the ENCA proposal.

38. *OECD Economic Surveys—France, 1984/1985* (Paris: OECD, 1986), 34.

39. This part of the protocol was designed to introduce greater flexibility into work time by moving from a weekly legal limit to an annual legal limit.

40. For details of the protocol and reaction from the social partners, see Gilles Bélier, "Après l'échec des négociations sur la flexibilité," and Raymond Soubie, "Après les négociations sur la flexibilité," both in *Droit Social*, no. 2 (February 1985).

41. See Bélier, "Après l'échec des négociations sur la flexibilité."

42. See Raymond Soubie, "Après les négociations sur la flexibilité," *Droit Social*, no. 3 (March 1985): 223, for this point.

43. Weber, *Le Parti des Patrons*, 363 (my translation).

44. See *Regards sur L'Actualité*, no. 29 (March 1987) for details.

45. See *OECD Economic Surveys—France, 1984/1985*, 49–53.

46. *Bilan de la Négociation Collective en 1985*, 39.

47. Ibid., 38 (my translation).

48. Cameron, "The Colors of a Rose," 6–7.

49. See the interview with Delors in *Le Nouvel Economiste* (December 5, 1983) where he argues that the minimum wage should play a smaller role in setting wage levels.

50. In the summer of 1990, for example, the Socialist government of Michel Rocard agreed to limit minimum wage increases in return for an agreement from employers to start talks on raising the negotiated branch minimum wages to the level of the SMIC.

51. See Evelyne Bughin, "Évolution comparée du SMIC et des rémunérations minimales garanties," *Travail et Emploi*, no. 20 (June 1984).

52. *Liaisons Sociales: Documents*, no. 72 (July 29, 1986): 1.

53. G. Duthil, "Les Partenaires sociaux face à l'individualisation des salaires," unpublished working paper for the Commissariat Général du Plan, May 1987, p. 10 (my translation).

54. While 71.4 percent of all firms employing ten or more workers gave *only* general, nonindividualized increases in 1986, the figure was 53.3 percent for firms employing from 200 to 999 workers, and only 15 percent for firms employing from 1,000 to 4,999. Simone Bangoura, "Les Augmentations individualisées en

1985," *Dossiers statistiques du travail et d'emploi*, no. 30 (April 1987): 1. It is worth noting that whereas large firms had been at the cutting edge of the long boom in the 1950s and 1960s, it now appears to be smaller, more flexible, firms that are enjoying a certain comparative advantage, while larger firms are struggling to eliminate the very rigidities that had been sources of strength in the earlier period. For commentary on the differing performance of small and large firms in the 1980s, see Jean-Joel Gurviez, "Une économie qui boite," *L'Expansion* (January 6–19, 1984).

55. *Bilan de la Négociation Collective, 1986*, 38–39.

56. Ibid., 44.

57. See the studies by Dominique Eustache, "Individualisation des salaires et flexibilité," *Travail et Emploi*, no. 29 (September 1986), and Caroline Grandjean, "L'Individualisation des salaires: La Stratégie des entreprises," *Travail et Emploi*, no. 32 (June 1987).

58. See Philippe Eliakim, "Comment individualiser les salaires," *L'Usine Nouvel: Tertiel* (December 1983), for this point.

59. Grandjean, "L'Individualisation des salaires," 19, says that about one-third of agreements had formal written evaluations.

60. Bodin, *Les Lois Auroux dans les P.M.E.*, 201–202 (my translation).

61. Grandjean notes that a major impetus behind the growth of individualization was the "weakening of trade unions" (Grandjean, "L'Individualisation des salaires," 18).

62. For a survey of union attitudes see Duthil, "Les Partenaires sociaux face à l'individualisation des salaires," 10.

63. Grandjean, "L'Individualisation des salaires," 22 (my translation).

64. The quotation is from Jean-Pierre Soisson, minister of labor, as reported in *Liaisons Sociales: Documents*, no. 45 (May 12, 1989): 1 (my translation). This report gives a good summary of the legislation.

65. For details of the legislation see *Liaisons Sociales: Documents*, no. 135 (December 11, 1989).

66. For a useful summary of the growing literature on this subject see Michel Schiray, "La Précarisation du Travail," *Problèmes Politiques et Sociaux*, no. 575 (January 1988).

67. Mireille Elbaum, "Les Petits Boulots," *Économie et Statistique*, no. 205 (December 1987).

68. Françoise Piotet, "Travailler aujourd'hui: Flexibilité et petits boulots," *Études* (March 1987).

69. Danièle Linhart and Margaret Maruani, "Précarisation et déstabilisation des emplois ouvriers," *Travail et Emploi*, no. 11 (January–March 1982): 36 (my translation).

70. The most detailed study of income inequality was the Centre d'Étude des Revenus et des Coûts report *Les Français et Leurs Revenus: Le Tournant des Années 80* (Paris: La Découverte, 1989). For a discussion of income inequality and its consequences for the PS, see Howell, "The Fetishism of Small Difference."

CHAPTER NINE

1. The distinction between social and economic functions is not a clear one. Strike activity had an economic impact as well as a social and political one. This was

particularly true in the public sector where strike action in the transportation and power industries had a damaging impact on the rest of the economy.

2. *OECD Economic Surveys—France, 1988/1989.* The extent of disinflation relative to other OECD countries is shown in table 2, p. 14. Corporate profit ratios are shown in table 8, p. 20.

3. The standardized unemployment rate rose steadily in the 1980s to peak at 10.7 percent in March 1987. It was 9.5 percent in March 1989. This was well above the OECD average. *OECD Economic Surveys—France, 1989/1990* (Paris: OECD, 1990), 21.

4. It should be noted that the share of compensation as a percentage of value added has already fallen seven points, from 72.2 percent in 1981 to 65.5 percent in 1987. *Economic Surveys—France, 1988/1989*, 22, table 9.

5. See, for instance, the contributions to recent conferences on France: "A France of Pluralism and Consensus? Changing Balances in State and Society" at New York University, October 9–11, 1987, and "In Search of the New France" at Brandeis University, May 13–15, 1988. See also Suzanne Berger, "French Politics at a Turning Point?" *French Politics and Society*, no. 15 (November 1986).

6. See Smith, *The End of Illusions.*

7. "Les Patrons face à l'élection présidentielle," *Le Monde: Affaires*, September 5, 1987, pp. 4–6. Note that only large employers, those employing five hundred or more workers, were surveyed.

8. Ibid., 5. It should also be noted that the survey was conducted after the industrial conflict that plagued the Chirac government in late 1986–early 1987. Governments of the Left have since had their share of industrial disputes and the responses might be different.

9. Rosanvallon, *La Question Syndicale*, 139.

10. For a glowing account of the French economy's performance see the *Economist* (May 19, 1990): 77. See also Howell, "The Fetishism of Small Difference," for an evaluation of the economic and social policy of the Rocard government.

11. Elie Cohen, "Le 'moment lois Auroux' ou la désublimation de l'économie," *Sociologie du Travail*, no. 3 (1986) (my translation).

12. Details of this proposal can be found in *Liaisons Sociales: Documents*, no. 27 (March 6, 1985).

13. However, unions would retain their monopoly in the first round of voting for this new body.

14. See *Liaisons Sociales: Documents*, no. 55 (June 18, 1986) for details.

15. Pierre-Eric Tixier, "Management participatif et syndicalisme," *Sociologie du Travail*, no. 3 (1986): 367 (my translation).

16. The work of Jean-Francois Amadieu reaches very similar conclusions to those of this study on the subject of an emerging microcorporatism. See his "Vers un syndicalisme d'entreprise," *Sociologie du Travail*, no. 3 (1986), and "Les Tendances au syndicalisme d'entreprise en France: Quelques hypothèses," *Droit Social*, no. 1 (January 1986).

17. This argument is made by both Rosanvallon, *La Question Syndicale*, and Adam, *Le Pouvoir Syndical.*

18. The issue of legitimation is important. The trade union confederations, whatever their actual degree of representation, are the single most visible

spokespeople for labor and hence have a role in the eyes of government out of all proportion to their membership. It is unclear why else governments of both the Left and the Right would seek to talk to, and be seen to talk to, organizations whose memberships comprise about one-tenth of the work force.

19. Furjot and Noel, "La Conflictualité en 1986," 67 (my translation). The annual summaries and analyses of strike statistics by Furjot and a variety of collaborators are the best source of semidigested strike data available, and the analyses are usually excellent.

20. Amadieu, "Les Tendances au syndicalisme d'entreprise en France," 23 (my translation).

21. For this point see Tixier, "Management participatif et syndicalisme." Tixier argues that participatory management does not end alienation or domination, it merely replaces bureaucratic and Taylorist domination with a "manipulation of the subjectivity and creativity of workers" (ibid., 360; my translation).

22. *Liaisons Sociales: Documents*, no. 64 (May 30, 1990): 1.

23. Information on number and duration of strikes can be found in Furjot and Noel, "La Conflictualité en 1986." They also point out that smaller firms tend to have less strikes than large firms, and there are more and more workers employed in small firms. As they put it: "In a word, there are ever more workers in those categories of firms which produce less and less conflicts" (ibid., 58; my translation).

24. For an account of the industrial conflict in the fall of 1988, and the argument that any emphasis upon consensus and the end of strikes is premature, see George Ross and Jane Jenson, "Quel joli consensus! Strikes and Politics in Autumn 1988," *French Politics and Society* 7, no. 1 (Winter 1989).

25. Furjot and Noel, "La Conflictualité en 1986," 60 (my translation).

26. Ibid.

27. Ibid., 69 (my translation).

28. See Peter Katzenstein, ed., *Between Power and Plenty: Foreign Economic Policies of Advanced Industrial States* (Madison: University of Wisconsin Press, 1978).

29. For a good summary and discussion of theories of industrial society, and "post-capitalist" society, see Richard J. Badham, *Theories of Industrial Society* (Beckenham: Croom Helm, 1986).

30. See the two-volume set of studies of the responses of national union movements to economic crisis, conducted under the aegis of the Harvard Center for European Studies: Lange, Ross, and Vannicelli, eds., *Unions, Change and Crisis*; and Peter Gourevitch, Andrew Martin, George Ross, et al., eds., *Unions and Economic Crisis: Britain, West Germany and Sweden* (London: Allen and Unwin, 1984).

31. See, for instance, the fascinating work of Jane Jenson, who has argued that the "conceptual space for the discussion of collective identity formation is provided by the regulation approach's notion of regularities or norms in the behavior of individuals which allow stabilization of the regime of accumulation," in " 'Different' but not 'Exceptional': Canada's Permeable Fordism" (unpublished manuscript, March 1988), 10.

32. The focus on divergence, national "paths," and politics was particularly emphasized in Robert Boyer's presentation, "The Impact of Industrial Relations Structures in Employment: A Comparative Perspective," at the Harvard Center for

European Studies, Cambridge, March 14, 1989. For five possible scenarios of labor regulation in the future see his "The Capital Labor Relation in OECD Countries: From the 'Golden Age' to the Uncertain Nineties" (unpublished manuscript, March 1989).

33. Very few comparative studies of the development of union organization during the 1980s exist. For individual country studies see Richard M. Locke, "The Resurgence of the Local Union: Industrial Restructuring and Industrial Relations in Italy," *Politics and Society* 18, no. 3 (September 1990); and Kathleen Thelen, *Continuity in Crisis: Labor Politics and Industrial Adjustment in West Germany* (Ithaca: Cornell University Press, 1991). For some broader comparative discussion see Scott Lash and John Urry, *The End of Organized Capitalism* (Madison: University of Wisconsin Press, 1987), chapter 8.

34. The OECD estimates that average trade union density within the OECD fell from 35 percent in 1980 to 28 percent in 1988. See the report in the *Economist* (July 20, 1991): 85.

35. Lindblom, "The Market as Prison."

36. The following discussion of the implications of European integration is heavily influenced by the writings of Wolfgang Streeck on the subject. See Wolfgang Streeck, *The Social Dimension of the European Economy: A Discussion Paper Prepared for the 1989 Meeting of the Andrew Shonfield Association* (London: Andrew Shonfield Association, 1989); Wolfgang Streeck, "More Uncertainties: West German Unions Facing 1992," *Industrial Relations* (forthcoming); and Wolfgang Streeck and Philippe C. Schmitter, "From National Corporatism to Transnational Pluralism: Organized Interests in the Single European Market," *Politics and Society* 19, no. 2 (1991).

37. See Streeck, *The Social Dimension of the European Economy*, for a discussion of the deregulatory impact of the principle of mutual recognition, and for the notion of firms "shopping" for national regulatory regimes.

38. This argument is made by John Grahl and Paul Teague in "The Cost of Neo-Liberal Europe," *New Left Review*, no. 174 (March–April 1989).

39. See Streeck and Schmitter, "From National Corporatism to Transnational Pluralism," for a discussion of the weakness and underdevelopment of labor-interest organizations at the European level.

40. The classic theoretical discussion of this problem is that of Mancur Olson, *The Logic of Collective Action: Public Goods and the Theory of Groups* (Cambridge: Harvard University Press, 1968). See also Offe, *Disorganized Capitalism*, chapter 7. There is also a useful discussion of the practical problems facing European unions in Stephen J. Silvia, "The Prospect of a Unified European Union Movement as a Result of 1992" (Paper presented at the Seventh Conference of Europeanists, Washington, D.C., March 23–25 1990).

41. Streeck, "More Uncertainties: West German Unions Facing 1992," is particularly good on the ways in which the increased mobility of both capital and labor after 1992 will place pressure on the West German industrial relations system.

42. Piore and Sabel, *The Second Industrial Divide*, 303.

43. See Charles Sabel, "A Fighting Chance: Structural Change and New Labor Strategies," *International Journal of Political Economy* (Fall 1987).

44. See both Mike Davis's *Prisoners of the American Dream*, chapter 5, and his excellent book about the political economy of Los Angeles, *City of Quartz* (New York: Verso, 1990).

45. Davis, *Prisoners of the American Dream*, 216.

46. Mahon, "From Fordism to ?" 8.

47. Sorge and Streeck, "Industrial Relations and Technical Change."

48. Mahon, "From Fordism to ?" 51.

49. Mahon, and Sorge and Streeck, all stress the point about the variety and importance of national contexts. See also Hall, "Introduction," *International Journal of Political Economy*.

50. See Boyer, ed., *La Flexibilité du Travail en Europe*, chapter 11, for five scenarios for the future of industrial relations.

51. The exception here is obviously the CFDT.

52. Marino Regini, "Trade Union Responses to the Challenge of Flexibility" (Paper presented at the Sixth International Conference of Europeanists in Washington, D.C., October 30–November 1, 1987).

Selected Bibliography

Adam, Gérard. 1971. "Vers une plus grande clarté des relations syndicales: Interview de Joseph Fontanet." *Dirigeant* (June–July).
———. 1985. *Le Pouvoir Syndical*. Paris: Dunod.
Adam, Gérard, and Jean-Daniel Reynaud. 1978. *Conflits du Travail et Changement Social*. Paris: Presses Universitaires de France.
Aglietta, Michel. 1976. *Régulation et Crises: L'Expérience des États-Unis*. Belgium: Calmann-Lévy.
Aglietta, Michel, and Anton Brender. 1984. *Les Métamorphoses de la Société Salariale: La France en Projet*. Paris: Calmann-Lévy.
Amadieu, Jean-François. 1986. "Les Tendances au syndicalisme d'entreprise en France: Quelques hypothèses." *Droit Social*, no. 1 (January).
———. 1986. "Vers un syndicalisme d'entreprise." *Sociologie du Travail*, no. 3.
"Aménagement du temps de Travail." *Regards sur l'Actualité*, no. 131 (May 1987).
"L'Audience des syndicats: 10 ans d'élections professionnelles." 1981. *Notes et Documents du BRAEC*. no. 17.
Aujard, Jean-Pierre. 1989. "Les Délégués Syndicaux au 31 décembre 1987." *Dossiers statistiques du travail et d'emploi*, no. 50 (July).
Aujard, Jean-Pierre, and Serge Volkoff. 1986. "Une Analyse chiffrée des audiences syndicales." *Travail et Emploi*, no. 30 (December).
Auroux, Jean. 1981. *Les Droits des Travailleurs*. Paris: La Documentation Française, September.
"Les Autres et les droits nouveaux." 1982. *Notes et Documents du BRAEC*, no. 22 (October–December).
Bachy, Jean-Paul, François Dupuy, and Dominique Martin. 1974. *Représentation et négociation dans l'entreprise*. Paris: Université "Paris-Sud."
Badham, Richard J. 1986. *Theories of Industrial Society*. Beckenham: Croom Helm.
Baglioni, Guido, and Colin Crouch, eds. 1990. *European Industrial Relations: The Challenge of Flexibility*. London: Sage.
Bangoura, Simone. "Les Augmentations individualisées en 1985." 1987. *Dossiers statistiques du travail et d'emploi*, no.30 (April).
Baron, Chantal. 1982. "Les conventions collectives." *Bulletin Mensuel des Statistiques du Travail—Supplément*, no. 100.
Barre, Raymond. 1981. *Une Politique pour l'avenir*. Paris: Plon.
Beaud, Michel. 1983. *La Politique Économique de la Gauche*. 2 vols. Paris: Syros.
Bélier, Gilles. 1983. "Le Double niveau de négociation dans les lois Auroux: Un atout pour la politique contractuelle." *Droit Social*, no. 1 (January).
———. 1985. "Après l'échec des négociations sur la flexibilité." *Droit Social*, no. 2 (February).
Bell, D. S., and Byron Criddle. 1984. *The French Socialist Party*. Oxford: Clarendon Press.
Beneton, Philippe, and Jean Touchard. 1970. "Les interprétations de la crise de Mai–Juin 1968." *Revue française de science politique*, no. 3 (June).

Berger, Suzanne. 1985. "The Socialists and the Patronat: The Dilemmas of Co-existence in a Mixed Economy." In Howard Machin and Vincent Wright, eds., *Economic Policy and Policy-making Under the Mitterrand Presidency 1981–84*. London: Frances Pinter.

———. 1986. "French Politics at a Turning Point?" *French Politics and Society*, no. 15 (November).

Berger, Suzanne, and Michael Piore. 1980. *Dualism and Discontinuity in Industrial Societies*. New York: Cambridge University Press.

Bergounioux, Alain. 1984. "The Trade Union Strategy of the CGT-FO." In Mark Kesselman, ed., *The French Workers' Movement: Economic Crisis and Political Change*. London: Allen and Unwin.

Bertrand, Hugues. 1986. "France: Modernisations et Piétinements." In Robert Boyer, ed., *Capitalismes fin de siècle*. Paris: Presses Universitaires de France.

Bilan de la Négociation Collective, 1982. 1983. Paris: Ministère des Affaires Sociales.

Bilan de la Négociation Collective, 1983. 1984. Paris: Ministère des Affaires Sociales.

Bilan de la Négociation Collective, 1984. 1985. Paris: Ministère des Affaires Sociales.

Bilan de la Négociation Collective en 1985. 1986. Paris: La Documentation Française.

Bilan de la Négociation Collective, 1986. 1987. Paris: Ministère des Affaires Sociales.

Bilan de la Négociation Collective 1987. 1988. Paris: La Documentation Française.

Bilan 1988 de la Négociation Collective. 1989. Paris: La Documentation Française.

"Bilan de l'ordonnance de 5 février 1982 relative au travail temporaire." 1985. *Dossiers statistiques du travail et d'emploi*, no. 11 (April).

Blank, Stephen. 1979. "Britain: The Politics of Foreign Economic Policy, the Domestic Economy, and the Problem of Pluralistic Stagnation." In Peter Katzenstein, ed., *Between Power and Plenty: Foreign Economic Policies of Advanced Industrial States*. Madison: University of Wisconsin Press.

Bloch-Lainé, François. 1981. *La France en Mai 1981: Forces et Faiblesses*. Paris: La Documentation Française.

Bodin, Raymond-Pierre. 1987. *Les Lois Auroux dans les P.M.E.* Paris: La Documentation Française.

Bon, Frédéric. 1970. "Le référendum du 27 avril 1969: suicide politique ou nécessité stratégique?" *Revue française de science politique*, no. 2 (April).

Bowles, Samuel, David M. Gordon, and Thomas E. Weisskopf. 1986. "Power and Profits: The Social Structure of Accumulation and the Profitability of the Postwar U.S. Economy." *Review of Radical Political Economics* 18, nos. 1 and 2 (Spring–Summer).

Boyer, Robert. 1978. "Les Salaires en Longue Période" *Économie et Statistique*, no. 103 (September).

———. 1979. "Wage Formation in Historical Perspective: The French Experience" (English translation of "Les Salaires en Longue Période"). *Cambridge Journal of Economics*, no. 2 (June).

———. 1984. "Wage Labor, Capital Accumulation, and the Crisis, 1968–82." In Mark Kesselman, ed., *The French Workers' Movement: Economic Crisis and Political Change*. London: Allen and Unwin.

———. 1985. "The Influence of Keynes on French Economic Policy: Past and Present." In Harold Wattel, ed., *The Policy Consequences of John Maynard Keynes*. New York: Macmillan.

————. 1986. *La Théorie de la Régulation: Une Analyse Critique.* Paris: Éditions la Découverte.

————. 1988. "Comparing Capitalist Economies." Unpublished working paper, May.

————. 1989. "The Impact of Industrial Relations Structures in Employment: A Comparative Perspective." Paper presented at the Harvard Center for European Studies, Cambridge, March 14.

————. 1989. "The Capital Labor Relation in OECD Countries: From the 'Golden Age' to the Uncertain Nineties." Unpublished manuscript, March.

Boyer, Robert, ed. 1986. *La Flexibilité du Travail en Europe.* Paris: Éditions la Découverte.

Brown, Bernard E. 1982. *Socialism of a Different Kind.* Westport, Conn.: Greenwood Press.

————. 1990. "Worker Democracy in France: Are You Serious?" *French Politics and Society* 8, no. 2 (Spring).

Bughin, Evelyne. 1980. "L'Évolution des rémunérations minimales garanties et du SMIC depuis le 1er: Janvier 1976." *Travail et Emploi*, no. 4 (April).

————. 1984. "Évolution comparée du SMIC et des rémunérations minimales garanties." *Travail et Emploi*, no. 20 (June).

Bunel, Jean. 1973. *La Mensuelisation, une Réforme Tranquille?* Paris: Éditions Ouvrières.

Bunel, Jean, and Paul Meunier. 1972. *Chaban-Delmas . . . .* Paris: Stock.

Caire, Guy. 1984. "Recent Trends in Collective Bargaining in France." *International Labour Review* 123 (November–December).

Cameron, David. 1984. "Social Democracy, Corporatism, Labor Quiescence, and the Representation of Economic Interests in Advanced Capitalist Society." In John H. Goldthorpe, ed., *Order and Conflict in Contemporary Capitalism.* Oxford: Clarendon Press.

————. 1988. "The Colors of a Rose: On the Ambiguous Record of French Socialism." Center for European Studies Working Paper, no. 12. Cambridge, Mass.: Center for European Studies.

————. 1988. "Continuity and Change in French Social Policy." Paper presented at the Annual Meeting of the American Political Science Association, Washington, D.C., September.

Capdevielle, 1982. Jacques, and René Mouriaux. *Mai 68: L'Entre-Deux de la Modernité.* Paris: Fondation Nationale des Sciences Politiques.

Caron, François. 1979. *An Economic History of Modern France.* New York: Columbia University Press.

Carré, J-J., P. Dubois, and E. Malinvaud. 1975. *French Economic Growth.* Stanford: Stanford University Press.

Cayrol, Roland. 1978. "Le Parti Socialiste à L'entreprise." *Revue française de science politique* 28, no.2 (April).

Cayrol, Roland, and C. Ysmal. 1982. "Les Militants du PS: Originalité et Diversités." *Projet*, no. 165 (May).

Chaban-Delmas, Jacques. 1975. *L'Ardeur.* Paris: Éditions Stock.

Chotard, Yvon. 1982. "Le Rapport Auroux." *Droit Social*, no. 4 (April).

Cohen, Elie. 1986. "Le 'moment lois Auroux' ou la désublimation de l'économie." *Sociologie du Travail.* no. 3.

Cohen, Stephen. 1977. *Modern Capitalist Planning: The French Model*. Berkeley: University of California Press.

Colin, J-F., J-C. Cros, E. Verdier, and D. Welcomme. 1981. "Politiques d'emploi: La rupture de 1977." *Travail et Emploi*, no. 10 (October–December).

Cottereau, Alain. 1986. "The Distinctiveness of Working-Class Cultures in France, 1848–1900." In Ira Katznelson and Aristide R. Zolberg, eds., *Working-Class Formation*. Princeton: Princeton University Press.

Crouch, Colin, and Alessandro Pizzorno, eds. 1978. *The Resurgence of Class Conflict in Western Europe since 1968*. 2 vols. New York: Holmes and Meier.

Crozier, Michel. 1970. *La Société Bloquée*. Paris: Le Seuil.

Davis, Mike. 1978. "Fordism in Crisis." *Review* 2, no. 2 (Fall).

———. 1986. *Prisoners of the American Dream*. London: Verso.

———. 1990. *City of Quartz*. New York: Verso.

De Closets, François. 1985. *Tous Ensemble*. Paris: Éditions du Seuil.

Delors, Jacques. 1970. "La Nouvelle Société." *Preuves*, no. 2.

———. 1975. *Changer*. Paris: Stock.

———. 1978. "La politique contractuelle, naissance d'une autre politique sociale." *Revue française des affaires sociales*, no. 3 (July–September).

Despax, Michel. 1979. "Observations sur la représentativité des organizations syndicales au regard du droit des conventions collective." *Droit Social*, nos. 7–8 (July–August).

Doyelle, Alain, and Marguerite Perrot. 1981. "L'Évolution du pouvoir d'achat des salaires depuis trente ans." *Travail et Emploi*. no. 9 (July–September).

Dubois, Pierre. 1980. "Recherches statistiques et monographiques sur les grèves." *Revue française des affaires sociales*, no. 2 (April–June).

Dubois, Pierre, Claude Durand, and Sabine Erbès-Seguin. 1978. "The Contradictions of French Trade Unionism." In Colin Crouch and Alessandro Pizzorno, eds., *The Resurgence of Class Conflict in Western Europe Since 1968*. Vol. 1. New York: Holmes and Meier.

Durand, Paul. 1956. "The Evolution of Industrial Relations Law in France Since the Liberation." *International Labor Review* 74.

Dussert, Françoise, Yves Mouton, and Chantal Salmon. 1986. "Évolution et structure du tissu conventionnel." *Dossiers statistiques du travail et emploi*, nos. 27–28 (December).

Duthil, G. 1987. "Les Partenaires sociaux face à l'individualisation des salaires." Unpublished working paper for the Commissariat Général du Plan, May.

"Échange et Projets." *Droit Social*, no. 11 (November 1978).

Edwards, Richard, Paolo Garonna, and Franz Tödtling, eds. 1986. *Unionism in Crisis and Beyond*. Dover, Mass.: Auburn House.

Ehrmann, Henry. *Organized Business in France*. 1957. Princeton: Princeton University Press.

Elbaum, Mireille. 1987. "Les Petits Boulots." *Économie et Statistique*, no. 205 (December).

Elbaum, Mireille, and Michèle Tonnerre. 1986. "La Procédure de licenciement économique." *Dossiers statistiques du travail et d'emploi*, no. 19 (February).

Eliakim, Philippe. 1983. "Comment individualiser les salaires." *L'Usine Nouvel: Tertiel* (December).

Eustache, Dominique. 1986. "Individualisation des salaires et flexibilité." *Travail et Emploi*, no. 29 (September).

Evans, Peter, Theda Skocpol, and Dietrich Rueschemeyer, eds. 1985. *Bringing the State Back In*. New York: Cambridge University Press.

Eyraud, François, and Robert Tchoanian. 1985. "The Auroux Reform and Company Level Industrial Relations in France." *British Journal of Industrial Relations* 23, no. 2 (July).

Faugère, Jean-Pierre. 1988. *Les Politiques Salariales en France*. Paris: La Documentation Française.

"La Fermeture sociale: Bilan de la négociation sociale depuis mars 1978." 1980. *Échange et Projets*, no. 21 (January–March).

Flanagan, Robert J., David W. Soskice, and Lloyd Ulman. 1983. *Unionism, Economic Stabilization, and Incomes Policies: European Experience*. Washington, D.C.: Brookings Institution.

"Fonds salariaux." 1983. *Échange et Projets*. no. 34 (July).

Fontanet, Joseph. 1971. "La course-poursuite des salaires et de la croissance économique." *Projet* (May).

Fonteneau, Alain, and Pierre-Alain Muet. 1985. *La Gauche Face à la Crise*. Paris: Fondation Nationale des Sciences Politiques.

Fox, Alan. *Industrial Sociology and Industrial Relations*. 1966. London: Her Majesty's Stationary Office.

Les Français et Leurs Revenus: Le Tournant des Années 80. 1989. Paris: Éditions la Découverte.

Friend, Julius W. "The PS Faces the 1990s." 1990. *French Politics and Society* 8, no. 1 (Winter).

Furjot, Daniel, and Catherine Noel. 1987. "La Conflictualité en 1986: Bilan statistique et qualitatif." *Travail et Emploi*, no. 34 (December).

Gallie, Duncan. 1983. *Social Inequality and Class Radicalism in France and Britain*. Cambridge: Cambridge University Press.

———. 1985. "Les Lois Auroux: The Reform of French Industrial Relations?" In Howard Machin and Vincent Wright, eds., *Economic Policy and Policy-Making Under the Mitterrand Presidency*. London: Frances Pinter.

Garraud, Philippe. 1978. "Discours, Pratiques et Ideologie dans L'évolution de Parti Socialiste." *Revue française de science politique* 28, no. 2 (April).

Gibier, Henri. 1984. "Seuils: Le PS est-il flexible?" *Le Nouvel Economiste*, no. 456 (September 17).

Ginsbourger, Francis, and Jean-Yves Potel. 1984. "La Pratique de la Négociation Collective." *Travail et Emploi*, no. 20 (June).

———. 1987. *Les Pratiques de la Négociation de Branche*. Paris: La Documentation Française.

Glendon, Mary Ann. 1984. "French Labor Law Reform 1982–83: The Struggle for Collective Bargaining." *American Journal of Comparative Law* 32 (Summer).

Glyn, Andrew, Alan Hughes, Alain Lipietz, and Ajit Singh. 1990. "The Rise and Fall of the Golden Age." In Stephen A. Marglin and Juliet B. Schor, eds., *The Golden Age of Capitalism: Reinterpreting the Postwar Experience*. Oxford: Clarendon Press.

Golden, Miriam, Peter Lange, and Jonas Pontusson. 1986. "Revised Framework for Workshop on 'Union Politics, Labor Militancy, and Capital Accumulation' " (to be published in Golden and Pontusson, eds., *Union Politics in Comparative Perspective*).

Golden, Miriam, and Jonas Pontusson, eds. *Union Politics in Comparative Perspective: Economic Change and Intra-Class Conflict*. Ithaca: Cornell University Press, forthcoming.

Goldthorpe, John H. 1984. "The End of Convergence: Corporatist and Dualist Tendencies in Modern Western Societies." In Goldthorpe, ed., *Order and Conflict in Contemporary Capitalism*. Oxford: Clarendon Press.

Gorz, André. 1989. *Critique of Economic Reason*. New York: Verso.

Gourevitch, Peter, Andrew Martin, George Ross, et al., eds. 1984. *Unions and Economic Crisis: Britain, West Germany and Sweden*. London: Allen and Unwin.

Grahl, John, and Paul Teague. 1989. "The Cost of Neo-Liberal Europe." *New Left Review*, no. 174 (March–April).

Grandjean, Caroline. 1987. "L'Individualisation des salaires: La Stratégie des entreprises." *Travail et Emploi*, no. 32 (June).

Groux, Guy, and René Mouriaux. 1989. *La C.F.D.T.* Paris: Économica.

Guiol, Patrick. 1986. "La Participation, le gaullisme, et le RPR." *Autogestion*, no. 23.

Gurviez, Jean-Joel. 1984. "Une économie qui boite." *L'Expansion* (January 6–19).

Hall, Peter. 1986. *Governing the Economy*. New York: Oxford University Press.

———. 1987. "Introduction" and ed., "European Labor in the 1980s" (special issue), *International Journal of Political Economy* (Fall).

Hall, Peter, ed. 1989. *The Political Power of Economic Ideas*. Princeton: Princeton University Press.

Hardouin, Patrick. 1978. "Les Caractéristiques sociologiques du Parti Socialiste." *Revue française de science politique* 28, no. 2 (April).

Harmon, Hervé, and Patrick Rotman. 1982. *La Deuxième Gauche*. Paris: Éditions Ramsay.

Herberg, Mikkal. 1981. "Politics, Planning and Capitalism: National Economic Planning in France and Britain." *Political Studies* 29, no. 4 (December).

Hervé, Jean. 1984. "Dix ans de politique de l'emploi (1973–83)." *Etudes* (January).

Horvat, Branko. 1984. "The Theory of Worker-Managed Firms Revisited." Unpublished manuscript.

Howell, Chris. 1991. "The Fetishism of Small Difference: French Socialism Enters the Nineties." *French Politics and Society* 9, no. 1 (Winter).

———. 1992. "The Contradictions of French Industrial Relations Reform." *Comparative Politics* 24, no. 2 (January).

Ingham, Geoffrey K. 1974. *Strikes and Industrial Conflict*. London: Macmillan.

Jenson, Jane. 1988. " 'Different' but not 'Exceptional': Canada's Permeable Fordism." Unpublished manuscript, March.

Jezequel, Claude. 1981. "Aperçus statistiques sur la vie conventionnelle en France." *Droit Social*, no. 6 (June).

Jones, Derek C., and Jan Svejnar, eds., 1982. *Participatory and Self-managed Firms: Evaluating Economic Performance*. Lexington: Lexington Books.

Judt, Tony. 1986. *Marxism and the French Left*. Oxford: Clarendon Press.

Katzenstein, Peter. 1985. *Small States in World Markets: Industrial Policy in Europe*. Ithaca: Cornell University Press.

Katzenstein, Peter, ed. 1978. *Between Power and Plenty: Foreign Economic Policies of Advanced Industrial States*. Madison: University of Wisconsin Press.

Keeler, John. 1987. *The Politics of Neo-Corporatism in France*. Oxford: Oxford University Press.

Kesselman, Mark. 1983. "Socialism Without the Workers: The Case of France." *Kapitalistate*, nos. 10–11.

Kesselman, Mark, ed. 1984. *The French Workers' Movement: Economic Crisis and Political Change*. London: Allen and Unwin.

Korpi, Walter. 1983. *The Democratic Class Struggle*. New York: Routledge, Chapman, and Hall.

Kotz, David M. 1990. "A Comparative Analysis of the Theory of Regulation and the Social Structure of Accumulation Theory." *Science & Society* 54, no. 1 (Spring).

Kuisel, Richard F. 1981. *Capitalism and the State in Modern France*. Cambridge: Cambridge University Press.

Labour Force Statistics: 1962–1982. 1984. Paris: OECD.

Labour Market Flexibility: Trends in Enterprises. 1989. Paris: OECD.

Lancelot, Alain, and Pierre Weill. 1970. "L'Évolution politique des électeurs français de février à juin 1969." *Revue française de science politique*, no. 2 (April).

Landier, Hubert. 1981. *Demain Quels Syndicats?* Paris: Librairie Générale Française.

Lange, Peter, George Ross, and Maurizio Vannicelli. 1982. "Unions as Objects of History and Unions as Actors." In Lange, Ross, and Vannicelli, eds., *Unions, Change and Crisis: French and Italian Union Strategy and the Political Economy, 1945–1980*. New York: Allen and Unwin.

Lash, Scott, and John Urry. 1987. *The End of Organized Capitalism*. Madison: University of Wisconsin Press.

Lauber, Volkmar. 1983. *The Political Economy of France*. New York: Praeger.

Lebon, André. 1971. "Les principaux accords salariaux signés en 1970 et 1971 dans les secteurs public et nationalisé." *Droit Social*, nos. 7–8 (July–August).

Lehmbruch, Gerhard. 1979. "Liberal Corporatism and Party Government." In Philippe C. Schmitter and Gerhard Lehmbruch, eds., *Trends Towards Corporatist Intermediation*. London: Sage Publications.

Lévy-Leboyer, Maurice. 1980. "The Large Corporation in Modern France." In Alfred Chandler and Herman Daems, eds., *Managerial Hierarchies*. Cambridge: Harvard University Press.

Lieber, Nancy. 1977. "Ideology and Tactics of the French Socialist Party." *Government and Opposition* 12, no. 4 (Autumn).

Lindblom, Charles E. 1982. "The Market as Prison." *Journal of Politics* 44, no. 2 (May).

Linhart, Danièle, and Margaret Maruani. 1982. "Précarisation et déstabilisation des emplois ouvriers." *Travail et Emploi*, no. 11 (January–March).

Lipietz, Alain. 1986. "Behind the Crisis: The Exhaustion of a Regime of Accumulation. A 'Regulation School' Perspective on Some French Empirical Works."
Review of Radical Political Economics 18, nos. 1 and 2 (Spring–Summer).

Locke, Richard M. 1990. "The Resurgence of the Local Union: Industrial Restructuring and Industrial Relations in Italy." *Politics and Society* 18, no. 3 (September).

Lorwin, Val R. 1966. *The French Labor Movement*. Cambridge: Harvard University
Press.

Loubejac, François. 1986. "Aménagement du temps de travail: Un projet a contre-
sens?" *Droit Social*, no. 2 (February).

Lyon-Caen, Gérard. 1970. "La convention sociale d'EGF et le système français des
relations professionnelles. *Droit Social*, no. 4 (April).

———. 1980. "Critique de la négociation collective." *Après-Demain*, no. 221 (February).

———. 1985. "La Bataille truquée de la flexibilité." *Droit Social*, no. 12 (December).

Machin, Howard, and Vincent Wright, eds. 1985. *Economic Policy and Policy-making Under the Mitterrand Presidency 1981–84*. London: Frances Pinter.

Mahon, Rianne. 1987. "From Fordism to ?: New Technology, Labour Markets
and Unions." *Economic and Industrial Democracy* 8.

Manpower Policy in France. 1973. Paris: OECD.

Marceau, Jane. 1977. *Class and Status in France*. Oxford: Clarendon Press.

Marglin, Stephen A., and Juliet B. Schor, eds. 1990. *The Golden Age of Capitalism:
Reinterpreting the Postwar Experience*. Oxford: Clarendon Press.

Maruani, Margaret, and Chantal Nicole-Drancourt. 1989. *Au Labeur des Dames:
Métiers Masculins, Emplois Féminins*. Paris: Syros.

McBride, Stephen. 1985. "Corporatism, Public Policy and the Labor Movement:
A Comparative Study." *Political Studies* 23, no. 3 (September).

Mermillod-Blardet, G. 1974. "Une analyse statistique des élections aux comités
d'entreprise depuis 1966." *Revue française des affaires sociale*, no. 3.

Mery, Bernard. 1973. "La Pratique de l'indexation dans les conventions collectives." *Droit Social*, no. 6 (June).

Minczeles, Alain, and Pierre Sicsic. 1986. "La Désinflation 1982–85." *Revue Économique* 37, no. 6 (November).

Mitchell, Daniel. 1972. "Incomes Policy and the Labor Market in France." *Industrial and Labor Relations Review* 25, no. 3 (April).

Morville, Pierre. 1985. *Les Nouvelles Politiques Sociales du Patronat*. Paris: Éditions
la Découverte.

Moss, Bernard H. 1988. "After the Auroux Laws: Employers, Industrial Relations
and the Right in France." *West European Politics* 11, no. 1 (January).

Mouriaux, Marie-Françoise, and René Mouriaux. 1984. "Unemployment Policy in
France, 1976–1982." In Jeremy Richardson and Roger Henning, eds., *Unemployment: Policy Responses in Western Democracies*. London: Sage.

Mouriaux, René. 1975. "Antagonismes sociaux et réforme de l'entreprise: Les silences du Rapport Sudreau." *Etudes* (April).

———. 1983. *Les Syndicats dans la Société Française*. Paris: Fondation Nationale des
Sciences Politiques.

———. 1986. *Les Syndicats Face à la Crise*. Paris: Éditions la Découverte.

Mouriaux, René, and Françoise Subileau. 1986. "Données statistiques concernant le syndicalisme des salariés en France (1945–1986)." Document du Travail. Paris: Centre d'Études de la Vie Politique Française.

———. 1987. "Les Effectifs Syndicaux en France, 1895–1986." Document de Travail. Paris: Centre d'Études de la Vie Politique Française.

Murcier, Jean-Paul. 1979. "Réflexions sur la négociation collective en France." *Droit Social*, nos. 7–8 (July–August).

———. 1982. "La CFDT et les droits nouveaux pour les travailleurs." *Droit Social*, nos. 7–8 (July–August).

Nansot, Jean-Jacques. 1985. "Le Droit d'expression des salariés dans les entreprises: Premiers constats." *Travail et Emploi*, no. 24 (June).

Négociation Collective—Quels Enjeux? 1988. Paris: La Documentation Française.

Noël, Alain. 1987. "Accumulation, Regulation, and Social Change: An Essay on French Political Economy." *International Organizations* 41, no. 2 (Spring).

Noiriel, Gérard. 1988. "The Formation and Decline of the French Working Class." Seminar paper given at the Harvard Center for European Studies, February 19.

Nordlinger, Eric. 1981. *On the Autonomy of the Democratic State*. Cambridge: Harvard University Press.

O'Brien, Patrick, and Gaglar Keyder. 1978. *Economic Growth in Britain and France, 1780–1914*. London: Allen and Unwin.

OECD Economic Surveys—France, 1984/1985. 1986. Paris: OECD.

OECD Economic Surveys—France, 1988/1989. 1989. Paris: OECD.

OECD Economic Surveys—France, 1989/1990. 1990. Paris: OECD.

Offe, Claus. 1984. *Contradictions of the Welfare State*. Cambridge: MIT Press.

———. 1985. *Disorganized Capitalism*. Cambridge: MIT Press.

Offe, Claus, and Helmut Wiesenthal. 1985. "Two Logics of Collective Action." In Offe, *Disorganized Capitalism*. Cambridge: MIT Press.

Olson, Mancur. 1968. *The Logic of Collective Action: Public Goods and the Theory of Groups*. Cambridge: Harvard University Press.

Panitch, Leo. 1976. *Social Democracy and Industrial Militancy: The Labour Party, the Trade Unions, and Incomes Policy, 1945–74*. Cambridge: Cambridge University Press.

———. 1986. *Working-Class Politics in Crisis*. London: Verso.

"La Participation des travailleurs à l'entreprise à travers les nouveaux textes législatifs." 1975. *Revue française des affaires sociales* (January–March).

Pelissier, Jean. 1984. "La Fonction syndicale dans l'entreprise après les lois Auroux." *Droit Social*, no. 1 (January).

"Les Périodes d'intense syndicalisation." 1981. *Notes et Documents du BRAEC*, no. 18 (October–December).

Piore, Michael. 1981. "Convergence in Industrial Relations? The Case of France and the United States." Unpublished paper, Massachusetts Institute of Technology, no. 286 (July).

Piore, Michael J., and Charles F. Sabel. 1984. *The Second Industrial Divide*. New York: Basic Books.

Piotet, Françoise. 1987. "Travailler aujourd'hui: Flexibilité et petits boulots." *Études* (March).

Pizzorno, Alessandro. 1978. "Political Exchange and Collective Identity in Industrial Conflict." In Colin Crouch and Alessandro Pizzorno, eds., *The Resurgence of Class Conflict in Western Europe Since 1968*. Vol. 2. New York: Holmes and Meier.

Polanyi, Karl. 1944. *The Great Transformation*. Boston: Beacon.

Portelli, Hughes. 1980. *Le Socialisme français tel qu'il est*. Paris: Presses Universitaires de France.

"Principales mesures prises en application de la déclaration gouvernementale du 16 septembre: 16 septembre 1969–15 octobre 1970." 1970. *Actualités–Documents*, no. 66 (October).

Projet Socialiste. 1980. Paris: Club Socialiste de Livre.

Przeworski, Adam. 1985. *Capitalism and Social Democracy*. Cambridge: Cambridge University Press.

Przeworski, Adam, Amy Bridges, Robert Melville, and Ernest Underhill. 1976. "The Evolution of Swedish Class Structure, 1900–1960: A Data Report." Unpublished manuscript.

Przeworski, Adam, Barnett Rubin, and Ernest Underhill. 1980. "The Evolution of the Class Structure in France, 1901–1968." *Economic Development and Cultural Change* 28, no. 4 (July).

Rapport Sudreau. 1975. Paris: Documentation Française.

The Reform of the Enterprise in France. 1975. Philadelphia: Industrial Research Unit of the Wharton School, University of Pennsylvania.

Regini, Marino. 1987. "Trade Union Responses to the Challenge of Flexibility." Paper presented at the Sixth International Conference of Europeanists in Washington, D.C., October 30–November 1.

"Retour sur l'entreprise," *Sociologie du Travail* (Special Issue), no. 3 (1986).

Reynaud, Jean-Daniel. *Les Syndicats en France*. 1963. Paris: Colin.

———. 1975. *Les Syndicats en France*. 3d ed., 2 vols. Paris: Éditions du Seuil.

———. 1978. *Les Syndicats, les patrons et l'état: Tendances de la négociation collective en France*. Paris: Les Éditions ouvrières.

Reynaud, Jean-Daniel, Sami Dassa, Josette Dassa, and Pierre Maclouf. 1971. "Les événements de mai et juin 1968 et le système français de relations professionnelles." *Sociologie du Travail*, no. 1 (January–March).

Ribeil, Georges. 1984. *Les Cheminots*. Paris: Éditions la Découverte.

Rosanvallon, Pierre. 1988. *La Question Syndicale*. Paris: Calmann-Lévy.

Ross, George. 1978. "Marxism and the New Middles Classes: French Critiques." *Theory and Society* 5, no. 2 (March).

———. 1982. *Workers and Communists in France: From Popular Front to Eurocommunism*. Berkeley: University of California Press.

———. 1982. "The Perils of Politics: French Unions and the Crisis of the 1970s." In Peter Lange, George Ross, and Maurizio Vannicelli, eds., *Unions, Change and Crisis: French and Italian Union Strategy and the Political Economy, 1945–1980*. New York: Allen and Unwin.

Ross, George, and Jane Jenson. 1985. "Pluralism and the Decline of Left Hegemony: The French Left in Power." *Politics and Society* 14, no. 2.

———. 1985. "Political Pluralism and Economic Policy." In John S. Ambler, ed., *The French Socialist Experiment*. Philadelphia: Institute for the Study of Human Issues.

————. 1988. "The Tragedy of the French Left." *New Left Review*, no. 171 (September–October).

————. 1989. "Quel joli consensus! Strikes and Politics in Autumn 1988." *French Politics and Society* 7, no. 1 (Winter).

Sabel, Charles. 1987. "A Fighting Chance: Structural Change and New Labor Strategies." *International Journal of Political Economy* (Fall).

Sachs, Jeffrey, and Charles Wyplosz. 1986. "The Economic Consequences of President Mitterrand." *Economic Policy*, no. 2 (April).

Salvati, Michele. 1981. "May 1968 and the Hot Autumn of 1969: The Responses of Two Ruling Classes." In Suzanne Berger, ed., *Organizing Interests in Western Europe*. Cambridge: Cambridge University Press.

Sartori, Giovanni. 1976. *Parties and Party Systems*. New York: Cambridge University Press.

Sawyer, Malcolm. 1976. "Income Distribution in OECD Countries." *OECD Economic Outlook—Occasional Studies*. Paris: OECD.

Schain, Martin A. 1980. "Corporatism and Industrial Relations in France." In Philip G. Cerny and Martin A. Schain, eds., *French Politics and Public Policy*. New York: St. Martins.

Schiray, Michel. 1988. "La Précarisation du Travail." *Problèmes Politiques et Sociaux*, no. 575 (January).

Schmidt, Manfred G. 1982. "The Role of the Parties in Shaping Macroeconomic Policy." In Francis G. Castles, ed., *The Impact of Parties: Politics and Policies in Democratic Capitalist States*. London: Sage.

Schmitter, Philippe C. 1979. "Still the Century of Corporatism?" In Philippe C. Schmitter and Gerhard Lehmbruch, eds., *Trends Towards Corporatist Intermediation*. London: Sage.

Scott, James. 1985. *Weapons of the Weak*. New Haven: Yale University Press.

Segrestin, Denis. 1987. "L'entrée de l'entreprise en société." *Revue française de science politique* 34, no. 4 (August).

Sellier, François. 1986. "Aménagement du temps de travail, articulation entre niveaux de négociation et conflits entre syndicats." *Droit Social*, no. 11 (November).

Sewell, William. 1980. *Work and Revolution in France*. New York: Cambridge University Press.

Shonfield, Andrew. 1969. *Modern Capitalism*. Oxford: Oxford University Press.

Shorter, Edward, and Charles Tilly. 1974. *Strikes in France, 1830–1968*. Cambridge: Cambridge University Press.

Silvia, Stephen J. 1990. "The Prospect of a Unified European Union Movement as a Result of 1992." Paper presented at the Seventh Conference of Europeanists, Washington, D.C., March 23–25.

Singer, Daniel. 1988. *Is Socialism Doomed? The Meaning of Mitterrand*. New York: Oxford University Press.

Smith, W. Rand. 1987. *Crisis in the French Labour Movement: A Grassroots Perspective*. Basingstoke, Eng.: Macmillan.

————. 1987. "Towards *Autogestion* in Socialist France: The Impact of Industrial Relations Reform." *West European Politics* 10, no. 1 (January).

————. "The End of Illusions: French Socialism and Industrial Crisis in the 1980s" (manuscript in preparation).

276 · Selected Bibliography

Social Expenditure, 1960–90. 1985. Paris: OECD.

Les Socialistes dans L'entreprise. 1982. Paris: Club Socialiste du Livre.

Sorge, Arndt, and Wolfgang Streeck. 1987. "Industrial Relations and Technical Change: The Case for an Extended Perspective." In Richard Hyman and Wolfgang Streeck, eds., *New Technology and Industrial Relations*. Oxford: Basil Blackwell.

Soskice, David. 1978. "Strike Waves and Wage Explosions, 1968–1970: An Economic Interpretation." In Colin Crouch and Alessandro Pizzorno, eds., *The Resurgence of Class Conflict in Western Europe Since 1968*. Vol. 2. New York: Holmes and Meier.

Soubie, Raymond. 1985. "Après les négociations sur la flexibilité." *Droit Social*, no. 2 (February).

———. 1985. "Après les négociations sur la flexibilité." *Droit Social*, no. 3 (March).

Spivey, W. Allen. 1982. *Economic Policies in France, 1975–81*. Michigan International Business Studies, no. 18. Ann Arbor: University of Michigan.

Stephens, John D. 1986. *The Transition from Capitalism to Socialism*. Urbana: University of Illinois.

Streeck, Wolfgang. 1984. "Neo-Corporatist Industrial Relations and the Economic Crisis in West Germany." In John H. Goldthorpe, ed., *Order and Conflict in Contemporary Capitalism*. Oxford: Clarendon Press.

———. 1989. *The Social Dimension of the European Economy: A Discussion Paper Prepared for the 1989 Meeting of the Andrew Shonfield Association*. London: Andrew Shonfield Association.

———. 1991. "More Uncertainties: West German Unions Facing 1992." *Industrial Relations* (forthcoming).

Streeck, Wolfgang, and Philippe C. Schmitter. 1991. "From National Corporatism to Transnational Pluralism: Organized Interests in the Single European Market." *Politics and Society* 19, no. 2.

Thelen, Kathleen. 1991. *Continuity in Crisis: Labor Politics and Industrial Adjustment in West Germany*. Ithaca: Cornell University Press.

Therborn, Goran. 1983. "Why Some Classes Are More Successful Than Others." *New Left Review*, no. 138 (March–April).

———. 1986. *Why Some Peoples Are More Unemployed Than Others*. London: Verso.

Tixier, Pierre-Eric. 1986. "Management participatif et syndicalisme." *Sociologie du Travail*, no. 3.

Topham, Tony. 1967. "New Types of Bargaining." In Robin Blackburn and Alexander Cockburn, eds., *The Incompatibles*. Harmondsworth: Penguin.

Trebilcock, Clive. 1981. *The Industrialization of the Continental Powers, 1780–1914*. New York: Longman Group.

Valenzuela, Julio Samuel. 1979. "Labor Movement Formation and Politics: The Chilean and French Cases in Comparative Perspective, 1850–1950." Ph.D diss., Columbia University.

Vatinet, Raymond. 1982. "La Négociation au sein du comité d'entreprise." *Droit Social*, no. 11 (November).

Verdier, Jean-Maurice. 1983. "La Présence syndicale dans l'entreprise et la loi du octobre 1982 relative au développement des institutions representatives du personnel." *Droit Social*, no. 1 (January).

Volkoff, Serge. 1985. "Expression des salariés: Bilan statistique de 3000 accords." *Travail et Emploi*, no. 23 (March).

Weber, Henri. 1986. *Le Parti des Patrons*. Paris: Seuil.

"Works Agreements of the 'Renault type.' " 1960. *International Labor Review* 81.

Wright, Erik Olin. 1978. *Class, Crisis and the State*. London: Verso.

Zeitlin, Jonathan. 1985. "Shopfloor Bargaining and the State: A Contradictory Relationship." In Steven Tolliday and Jonathan Zeitlin, eds., *Shopfloor Bargaining and the State*. New York: Cambridge University Press.

Zysman, John. 1983. *Governments, Markets, and Growth*. Ithaca: Cornell University Press.

Index

Confédération Générale du Travail (cont.)
Sudreau commission report and, 120;
wage controls, 64, 160, 250n.48
Confédération Générale du Travail Unitaire
(CGTU), 40
Conférence des Revenus, 64–65
Conseil d'entreprise, 217–18
Conseil Économique et Social, 51, 171
Conseil National du Patronat Français
(CNPF), 235n.16; Auroux Laws and,
168, 171, 175, 179, 182; collective bargaining, 134–35; *donnant-donnant* strategy of, 138; economic modernization
and, 71–72; flexible work contracts and,
198–99, 258n.36; flexible work time and,
136–37, 193–96; forced-savings plan
supported by, 158–59; New Society programs and, 107, 125–26; political impact
of, 115–17; power shifts in, 71–72, 83;
role of, in Barre plan, 129–32; suspicion
of Renault agreements, 43; union accords
with, 96, 242n.37; on wage-price controls, 157–58
Conseil de surveillance, 121–22
Consumption, lack of, in postwar French
economy, 34
Contracts: fixed-duration contracts, 198;
flexibility in, 196–99. *See also* specific contracts
Contrat collectif d'entreprise, 217
Contrat de programme, 64, 89–90, 94
Contrats de progrès. See Progress contracts
Corporatism, 9, 13–15; economic planning
and, 54–55; labor regulation and, 22–23;
liberal and social forms of, 232n.49; *participation* program and, 77; role of state in
labor relations in, 232n.47; unions, 48–
51; wage controls and, 131
Cost of living, wage levels and, 42
Couve de Murville, Maurice, 72, 89
Cross-union coordination in strikes, 3–4

De Gaulle, Charles: antiunionism of, 77–78;
cross-class coalition of, 82–83; distrust of
unions, 67–68; economic modernization
program, 34, 52–53, 61–67, 71; failure of
labor regulation under, 211; *participation*
program of, 35, 74–81
Debré, Michel, 64
Declercq, Gilbert, 91, 162
De fait agreements, 176

Deflation, Socialist labor regulation and,
190–91
Deindexation of wages: Barre plan and,
131–32; flexibility and, 200; Socialist
labor reforms and, 157–58
Delebarre, Michel, 195
Délégués de personnel, 49–50
Delors, Jacques, 83–88; Auroux Laws and,
168; belief in unions, 90; on collective
bargaining, 140–41; incomes policies
and, 130, 156–57, 160; membership in
Parti Socialiste (PS), 150–51; minimum
wage policies, 200–203; New Society
programs, 103; private-sector reforms,
98; socialist labor regulation, 149, 161;
three-part wage theory, 169–70
Demand management: economic modernization and, 54–56, 63–67; Fordism and,
256n.6
Depression, accumulation patterns and, 10
Derogation clauses: in Auroux Laws, 176–
77; flexible work time agreements, 194–
95
Descamps, Eugene, 86
Detraz, Albert, 245n.18
Donnant-donnant bargaining strategy, 116,
138
Dues checkoffs, lack of, in French unions,
45, 175

Échange et Projets, 151, 168
Economic growth, 27; British model of, 38,
234n.2; flexibility and, 187–88; frailty of
state and, 213–15; labor market regulation, 37–38, 113–15; productivity and
labor exploitation linked with, 52–53
Economic modernization: development
of, 61–67; Gaullist reforms and, 34–35;
May 1968 strike seen as result of, 68–72;
participation programs and, 79–81; politicization of, 66–67; state role in, 5–6,
54–55
Edwards, Richard, 9
Électricité et Gaz de France (EGF): role of,
in Barre plan, 129–32; *salaire de progrès*,
86, 89–95; wage controls and, 68,
241n.15
Emplois nouveaux à contraintes allégées
(ENCA), 198–99, 258n.36
Employee representation, right of, in Auroux Laws, 172

Income policies (*cont.*)
modernization and, 64; flexibility agreements and, 204; freeze of 1982, 155–56, 159–60; progress contract as, 91; Socialist labor regulation and, 156–57; wage contracts and, 128–32. *See also* Wage controls

Indexation, wage controls and, 127–28 Barre plan and, 131–32; flexibility and, 200; Socialist labor reforms and, 157–58. *See also* Deindexation; Income policies

Industrial relations: collective bargaining and, 21–22 economic growth and, 67, 214–15; flexibility in, 187–90; future trends in, 216–17; impact of 1968 strike on, 66, 69–70, 238n.5; lack of institutionalization, in France, 209–10, 230n.18; political class consciousness and, 48–49; post-Fordism and, 221–22; postwar modernization, 41–42, 57–58; socialist modernization of, 150–51; terminology of, 11; working-class formation and, 38–40

Inflation: corporatist labor regulation and, 23; impact of 1968 strike on, 27; structural bias toward, in French economy, 127; wage controls and, 155–56, 159–60, 249n.34

Interprofessionel agreements, 102–3

Investment resources, economic modernization and, 55–56

Jacobinism, socialist labor regulation and, 149–50

Jospin, Lionel, 161

Joxe, Pierre, 154, 161

Keynesian policy: economic crisis and, 114; fundamentalist vs. effective-demand forms of, 55; lack of, in postwar France, 51–52

Labor Code, 133; derogation and, 177; flexibility regulation and, 136, 191, 193–99

Labor collectivity, modes of labor regulation and, 17–18

Labor market regulation, 18–19; collective bargaining and, 35, 145–47; economic modernization and, 61–62, 63–67, 138–39; Fordism and, 28; impact on strike activity, 219; in postwar France, 59–60;

state regulation and, 37–38, 119; wage controls and, 106–7

Labor movement: corporatist paradigm and, 13–14; European integration and, 16, 232n.44; firm size linked with, 39–40; historical frailty of, in France, 6–7, 34, 230n.16; militancy during 1968 strike, 67–68; political power of, 8–16; repression against, 39; state policy's impact on, 4–8. *See also* Trade unions; Works councils

Labor regulation. *See* Modes of labor regulation

Large firms, Fordism and, 107. *See also* Small firms

Layoffs: Auroux Laws *droit d'alerte* and, 172; flexibility agreements and, 203–4

Lifetime employment guarantees, Japanese model of, 234n.61

Lipietz, Alain, 10

"Loi Delebarre," 195

Lucas Report, 133

Maire, Edmond, 161–64

Management: acceptance of union's legitmacy, 51–52; Auroux Laws and, 183–84; flexible work time proposals and, 192–96; hostility to unions among, 48–49. See also *Patronat*

Martin, René, 89

Martin, Roger, 71

Martin Report, 89–90

Masse salariale, 64–65

Mauroy, Pierre, 150–51, 155, 162, 190–91

May 1968 strikes: economic modernization and, 34–35; comparisons with 1986 strike, 3; impact of, on labor regulation, 67–73; failure of, 27–28, 105–6; postwar labor regulation and, 26–30; social and economic impact of, 210–11, 259n.1

Mensualization accords, 102, 242n.37; collective bargaining agreements, 139

Mergers: increase in, during modernization, 62–63; labor regulation and, 70–71

Messmer, Pierre, 80, 103, 127

Metalworking industry, unionization in, 45–46

Microcorporatism: Auroux Laws and, 167, 174–80; collective bargaining and, 183–85; firm-specific worker representation, 50–51; flexibility agreements and, 190,